Into The Mouth Of The Wolf

An Epilogue By:

Dan Marrone

Another Story from another Book.

Bold Italic indicates demonic voices

Italic indicates angelic voices

INKWELL BOOKS™
Writing-Publishing-Printing

First printing: Month 2021

ISBN: 978-0-9829589-6-4
Library of Congress Control Number: 2020948892

Published by Inkwell Books
10682 N. Scottsdale Road, #695
Scottsdale, AZ 85254
Tel. 480-315-3781
E-mail: info@inkwellbooksllc.com
Website: www.inkwellbooksllc.com

INKWELL BOOKS
Writing-Publishing-Printing

Into The Mouth Of The Wolf

An Epilogue By:

Dan Marrone

Another Story from another Book.

Crepi il Luppo!

I see good spirits and I see bad spirits. My Life has always been with the Thrill Kill Kult (1). I shouldn't use the word life. It is the best choice for the sake of simplicity, but it is not accurate. I am only as alive as these words are – inanimate until an unwitting victim comes along and becomes infected. Then they slowly grow within cells like a virus. Brain cells in this case, if you are still unfortunate enough to have a few remaining after any amount of time exposed to education and the inevitability of work. If this ***is*** the case, it is already too late. You only have a few choices now that you have been exposed. You can go about things the short, dangerous way and stop reading; forget everything that you have seen here already. May I suggest the long, circuitous way; continue with me. This may not be the most agreeable method. There are two more paths, but they are not at all practical, so we won't discuss them. Regardless of your choice the result is the same. Even if you don't read any more of this account you are being manipulated into the same void that has swallowed me. We may meet after all, better or worse off at the convergence. A little clarity for what is to come. What have we gotten ourselves into? This is a spell. This is a Blood Mantra. This is a word of power that I can disguise myself with. A spell of invisibility. I am with you now, looking over your shoulder even if you cannot see me. Fair warning. Even if it may be too late, you may wish to proceed no further for the following is not the most salubrious stuff to occupy yourself with. I see that you are still reading. Take advice from those who have chosen this middle path before: *yet I still proceeded with my compass, and would not budge one step from the Meridian Line (2).* Spiritual problems require mystical solutions and our planet is not what it seems. If you now wish to stop, and you are convinced that my perspective is rubbish then I suggest that you waste your time with football, mainstream politics, vendition, or other similar ovine idiocies. It is only right that important things should not be left for humans to deal with and I assure you that I am not a member of their ranks. Will you walk with me further? There is no such thing as fiction. I think that I hear trumpets.

Here is a goodly gift of Apsyrtus, a saving remedy, wonderfully effective for cattle. I A O, I A E. In the name of The Father and of our Lord Jesus Christ and Holy Spirit, iriterli estather, nochthai brasax salolam nakarzeo masa areons daron charel aklanathal aketh thruth tou malath poumedion chthon litiotan mazabates maner opsakion aklana tnalila I A O, I A E...And write the same with a brass pencil on a clean, smooth plate of tin (3).

As of now I am sitting in an apartment somewhere in New York, New York. A place of imperial decay. I am now at the end of the story. I am beginning with the end. A perfect place for my sort of chaos but it is also the only place to tell a story from. It is the only place to cast a spell from because a true spell has a clear goal. I am certainly trying to mess with you so there is a very good reason for all of this. The reason is the total destruction of reason. Remember this.

I am a blood sucker. I am here to consume what is essential and use it for my own purposes. I am not a thief because no one really owns anything. I am not a plagiarist because a mason can use a stone to create a building without bothering to invent a new form of brick. Ideas are occult, acroamatic, ghosts that speak from impercievable realms and the process of weaving them together is a small parting of the invisible veil. Is math invented or discovered? Is the body the expression of individual will and desire or the product of procreation – the choices of others? I don't expect an answer or anything else for that matter. I go to great efforts to make myself invisible. You will rarely ever see me if you do at all. This is a spell of invisibility so that I can conceal myself as I brush aside the thin curtain. I have names and hidden names. I stay invisible because I am hiding for a very good reason. I am being hunted because of this spell. There are those who wish to steal these ideas that I have stolen which never belonged to anyone in the first place. That is only one of the secrets that must be revealed by this ritual of marching symbols. For now, you must know that I am being hunted. This is why I am hiding in this apartment and composing these words as a matrix of further concealment among other reasons. The hunters only have a short time left before it is too late and the intention of the rite is accomplished. Τετέλεσται. But I get ahead of myself. There is much to explain.

Many things you think about Nosferatu are true and many are not. Some may have been true at one point, but we have adapted to the conditions on this Earth just like everything else. We can be destroyed. The traditional methods still work quite well. Stake through the heart, burn the corpse, etc. Pure undiluted faith will keep us away but that is very rare. A simple cross on the neck or holy water will only just piss us off more than anything if there is nothing but misconception and mythological thinking behind their use. Spells and counter spells are all over. We get our power from the stars, not the night as many think is the case. We discovered that long ago. The stars are always present even if they can't be seen by mortal eyes by day. We can see them. We can feel them. They give us our power. We have found that we can easily walk by day with the help of the stars and a few incantations. The sunlight is an enemy but it is starlight just the same. The sun's emissions are a toxic form of starlight that degrades us and humans as well for it is an evil star. Some stars are indeed benevolent but not this one. You know its true name: ***Illumination***. We have found a simple spell to ward off the direct impact of these photons. We have a perpetual night spell that allows us to break through the cerulean atmosphere and create our own dark parasol – a negative aura – so that we can walk under deathless, amaranthine constellations by day. Sleep is not something that we need or desire because, when asleep, we can become easy targets for those who wish us harm. I am not the last one of my kind left standing for no reason. I have always kept a few tricks hidden away.

Let me present a little background information to create a stable context. For the sake of the spell let us consider this information as an altar for the rest of the work to be done upon. Bear with me and forget about everything that you may think is real because this is a difficult step to undertake. I did tell you that the path was circuitous. There are many other ineluctable formulas and processes which will arise after the first step is performed. We shall begin in the darkness upon this altar. It is dark so that we may separate the gold from the salts of matter. The light will follow, and the sun only provides the smallest amount of it for it is only one star among multitudes.

The stars are more than balls of burning gas. They are pentacles and hexagrams. They may be virginal or they may be scorpions. They are individual and they are legion. They oversaw and enveloped every myth and every forgotten mistake on every planet. They have names and relationships with each other that bear hidden meanings which none could ever know completely. You are one of them. The living are attracted to zodiacal arrangements. The undead use these stars but also use the influence of other constellations. Orion and its individual stars have become primary concerns. Orion is a hunter. All humans created in the later ages of history were born with this astral arrangement as a primary guide which works outside of their zodiacal influences. In the zodiac, the sport of hunting is related to Leo as well as birth. In our spell, Leo and Orion are worth consideration at the opening. Their influence is the reason why the modern ages are so barbaric. The age of the dawn of humanity was the age of Leo or so it is thought. Therefore, everyone is born a hunter, and everyone is hunted. Blood is the law. Whether they know it or not we live off the blood of each other. This becomes more obvious when one realizes that time and motion – energy – are the blood of spiritual existence. Time and motion are monetized in order to extract this spiritual blood from each individual. Everyone has been conditioned under the guidance of the hunter since the dawn of so-called civilization. All very close to the void for there would be no need to hunt if there was no "need". Something that only an addict can know best. Nothingness. Humanity has the choice to evolve out of its chrysalis in a few directions. They can become butterflies or moths. Without conscious choice they will awake in the darkness. They are almost like me – Nosferatu. I said I was not human, and this is true, but I was human once. You will not remain as one for very long. Choose wisely. Beware of how much sacrificial blood there is that covers everything you touch.

The ostensible "natural order" of Capitalism is a product of the astral arrangement which oversaw and influenced humanities earliest and most primitive methods of order. The law of the hunter. Orion and Leo. The birth of "need". This anachronism which still stubbornly herds the pastures of humanity causes life to be sustained at the expense of some other form of life. Blood. Time. Motion. Energy. Blood. It is Blood Mantra which prepares all to be sucked into the void, extinguished, and then reborn as a lifeless shell because most are not even aware that they have a choice. Overcome by the void of "need" that they don't even recognize their automation that drives them to their own void. There is an infinitesimal population of humans who are aware of this and resist but I am not too concerned with them. They do not "need" this spell. The natural end of their path is the very goal of this spell. They are reborn as stars. They are reborn as Light.

This is why some stars are dangerous. They are individuals. They have personalities. Beware of the sun because you know its name and its personality; Illumination.

♄ Book Of Judas ♄

Are stars forever? Will they all become voids as well when they cross the event horizon? What good is the destruction of reason without the acceptance of contradiction? It is all anecdotal. Any form of existence is a short amusing story that may contain allegorical content for consideration and interpretation. The important part is energy. Red. ***I write in blood. I will be read in blood (4).*** I am an artist, a thief, and a plagiarist. Everything is mine and I use it with impunity. ***My life is with the thrill kill kult (1).***

What am I talking about? Use your dying brain cells. The undead of course. The masses of them that live everywhere who are automated to shamble toward their own self destruction through the encouragement of their emptiness. They *live.* They don't simply *exist.* Their end is near. So is yours. You are looking at it. You. One of them? If you are like most, you would not even know if you were. ***A Work in Progress (4).*** It is spelled out here in constellations of *red*, black, and *green.* Africa the foundation. It is spelled out in black and white symbols. Inexplicable contradictions that are the foundation of perceivable reality. A pinhead. A needle. Can you see the altar now? You are looking at it. This is a spell, perhaps the greatest spell and it is concerned with the beginning and end of things.

There is dark majik everywhere whether you can see it or not. Well... that isn't totally accurate. It isn't all pervasive or all powerful. It exists in isolated, concentrated areas by day. By night we thrive. We undead. ***Midgard serpent, Frenis wolf, Loki father of monsters. There were no clocks anywhere in sight or hearing. – And hmmm...he did, did he? And he took away the horses that the kings of Judah had given to the sun, at the entering in of the house of the Lord, by the chamber of Nathan-melech...hmm, Melech? Melich? The chamberlain, which was in the suburbs and burned the chariots of the sun with fire...And he put down the idolatrous priests, and hmmm whom the kings of Judah had ordained to burn incense in the high places in the cities of Judah, and the places round about Jerusalem; them also that burned incense hmmm hmmmph unto Baal, to the sun, and to the moon and to the planets, and to all the host of heaven...How safe I am from accident here. –In the precious blood of...(3)...***

...ʘ

Let me describe the undead for a moment. This is what becomes of humans who make poor choices i.e. most of them. They are steadily transformed by their lack of conscious choice to develop themselves. The result is the collapse of the star – the light – within which they could have become. What do you do when you know that you are wrong? You have to face the music which is getting worse and worse. See next sentence. Typically, this collapse – astrum argentium – is hastened by the creation of an environment which is condusive to the automation of the transformation. Aptly referred to as ***culture.*** There are early and late phases of this development, this virus, but it has the same result. The void. Emptiness. They then must get their light from somewhere else. They become consumers because this is the final, true goal of the culture created by capitalism; the creation of undead, empty masses. All undead get our powers from the stars above, not within. We suck in their energy, their light, because we lost our own. The exaliotriote, ancient light that took a very long time to get here before it tickles the eye and explodes within us like lycopodium. Every undead is created under starlight and these stellar positions arranged in the heavens determine what their powers will be. Even Ann Druyan knows that stars created everything, the offensive little prick that she is. It is not her fault though, being automated and whatnot. Let's get back to more important things. More real things. Like bloodsuckers. The bloodsuckers who are inhabiting our vile planetary outpost. The only Nosferatu left on the earth are born under Orion the hunter and the ages of humanity that have developed since the age of Leo. There are many who are that old who are still around but there were those who predate even this antiquity. ***The age of Leo is 11000 B.C.E.-8000 B.C.E. As we begin here, the snow of the Ice Age melts and the global climate begins to warm up. And what do we find? The cultures on the planet during this time worshipping the Sun, the ruler of the fire sign Leo. Sun-Gods abound, populations rise in many parts of the world, minimal farming begins to birth as climates get warmer and wetter and herds of large animals become scarcer. This is also known as the Mesolithic period, or Stone Age (4).***

A little about me. I do not like to mention this, but it is important to understand if we are to proceed. I like walks in the woods, cats, staring at the bottom of my shoe and making lip trumpet songs that are usually based on a 1,4,5 blues riff. Not the type of stuff that does well on a dating website but that is fine. I am very different from the rest of the undead. I was created in a different age. There were humans before the age of Leo. This was the age of Virgo. I am speaking of the fine years before 11000 B.C.E. Spica is the Blue, sapphire star in Virgo. The most well known in this constellation. I could go on about this but the important thing to communicate in this slow and laborious manner is the fact that Virgo was the influence over my creation, not Orion or Betelgeuse. ***The haves and have nots, a distinction (5).*** I have been around longer than any and predate even a date. *Civilized* (I use this word in the sense of flushable toilets...no I am sorry, in the sense of rubbing two sticks together or digging holes) humans are influenced by Orion and all the Nosferatu are controlled by it because the bodies and souls that they left behind were born after the age of Leo. They were born for the sport of the hunt. Born to be consumers. They own the earth. Capitalism is nothing new. Most humans are almost undead already, so they don't really have a choice but to hunt and consume each other's blood unless something critical wakes up within them. It has been this way for a long time. Ask your ancient Aztec neighbor. Just don't mention Huitzilopochtli or you may stand a chance of dismemberment. All in a day under the sun.

One of the ways that I am different than the rest of the kult is that I have discovered how to use all the stars over time. My transition into the undead predates the direct influence of Orion. The sun was in Virgo when the original event happened. For the sake of those who like details I will mention that the moon was in Scorpio and Gemini was rising but if you go by the Fagan-Bradley system it is a little different. Ponder that if you must. This was the seat of the stars and planets during the event which separated me from the sun and caused my undeath. There is something that I must tell you even though I don't want to. Something which explains my difference from the rest of the kult. I am the last of them. The other Virgo Nosferatu are long gone. They have all been exterminated over time by one source or another. Good for them I say. Terrible thing to go on this long.

I was not the only one created at the time. We began our existence in ancient Africa long ago. The pyramids were created (among other reasons of course) as a representation of the mountains of the moon which we all began our quintessence under. It is easy to forget that Egypt is in Africa.

All large-scale human structure seeks to represent the forms of local mountains in a local architectural dialect. The Romans built in regular forms such as circles to represent and entrap the spirit of their small, rounded foothills. The French built the Gothic forms to respond to the drama of the Alps. New York is built in clusters overlooking the Hudson River in response to the forms of the High Peaks of the Adirondacks where the river is born. Fluvial residuum. Littoral causautum. Artificial mountains deposited by the river that overlook the ocean. Las Vegas is a long strip to mirror to the long ranges that surround it. The comparisons are infinite. They are symbolic and practical expressions of protection against the forces of nature. An attempt to ward off evil influence. The pyramids are an architectural response to the volcanic mountain of the plains. Kilimanjaro. The mountains of the moon at the headwaters of the Nile. Fluvial residuum. At the same time the Pyramids are representations of starlight. Sunlight. The light that drives away the creatures of the night. Symbols of protection are overtly expressed in architecture.

Who can reasonably deny the influence of starlight upon the powers granted to beings? Is the sun not just a star with a stupid name? It is ok because that is not really its name. It is a term used to help the denial of the influence of the stars upon common human behavior by referring to it other than something stellar. Reasonable humanity tries as hard as it can to ignore the gigantic star above them that influences behavior hour by hour because – let's face it – they are too busy trying to fuck each other over or get something for themselves by fucking themselves through willingly turning their hours into virtual slavery that they simply can't process the facts that there are infinite amounts of stars which are all influencing the environment. Easier to focus on the one that helps them the most in the fulfillment of their filthy desires – because its relative position determines what hour it is and what hours one should get paid for – and then completely forget that it too is a star.

Short Digression and the Book of Genesis.

I love how people speak of "the economy" or "business practice" as if it were something respectable or beautiful, like a polished shoe or the growth of a flower. All bent over, contorted convolutions. Gymnastic feats of mental muddle to simply say…"Fuck You, by the way, dear sir or madam". The first and only words of the book of Genesis quoted from the Greenspan version.

א

All other stars, along with "the sun" exerted their influence when the pyramids were built. Humanity was much closer to them then. They had a better but still incomplete understanding. Once the humans discovered us, we Nosferatu, were actively hunted but they gave up because they thought they put us all down. Or so they thought. They did not understand that we came from them in the first place. Our disease was hiding in all of them too. The age of Orion (everything after Leo, the age of the amaranthine hunt) began. This is represented in the construction of the pyramids. The pyramids are far older than most "experts" realize. They were built over a very long period. Not, as is commonly misunderstood, in the lifetime of one king for the sake of creating a tomb that would have been screaming to be raided if it was intended and used for that purpose. The pyramids had a much different intention. They are symbols of protection. The builders knew that the hunters came from mountains of the moon and that the stars of Orion had become powerful. Remember too that they were obsessed with mummification. They knew about us Nosferatu. They would not let a drop of blood get in our hands if they could help it. They wanted their dead to pass correctly and not become like me. They had magicians and armies and they killed off all the first generation of Nosferatu who were created in the age of Virgo. They missed me.

Virgo Nosferatu are the oldest of them all. We were the original Nosferatu. The stars were perfectly aligned when we were brought into existence and their evil forces are what conjured us. We were supposed to be barren and attached to the earth. We were ahead of our time. Predictions of the future. Our condition was the ultimate expression of what the rest of human existence would be based upon. Blood sucking. Hunting. Unraveling into capitalism at the very end. What a wonderful ontogeny we have endured. We were supposed to stay in the shadow and not create any others with our undeath virus. Of course many of us did and we did it quite often. Blood becomes an addiction. We made many widows and gathered many grapes in our temple. All of our offspring are born from the generations which came after us. The hunters. They are the Orion Nosferatu and they are the ones who have taken our place. We were not supposed to create them, but we were also not supposed to be created. We were a mistake. A manifestation of chaos in nature. A simple arrangement of stars that birthed a continuum of chaos. Chaos which grew and developed into its modern form. Capitalism. Blood sucking obsession. When one Nosferatu creates another the created belongs to their creator. They are woven together. When one of the original Virgo Nosferatu are destroyed so too are the ones that belong to them. If only capitalism could be so easily destroyed. It is not so simple because it is only a path to the void. Not the void itself. You *own* that my friend.

That means only one thing. The remaining vampire belong to me. I am the oldest Nosferatu left on the planet but few of them know it because my hunters have created an army of their own and there are so many sub-generations that they think that they are the only ones. I have left it this way. It is better that I do not reveal anything about myself to them. One thing that I do know. Betelgeuse is dying. This is the name of a star in Orion if you did not know. It will explode sometime soon and their time is limited. Celestial conditions that created us Nosferatu at the beginning are re-arranging themselves. They are at a terminal point for those who respond to Orion.

Something is about to happen. Do you feel alright? You made it this far, but we have some way to go. I suggest hydromorphone. Forget the craft beer that is becoming popular in the United States. It is sad that most who drink this do not realize how foul it actually is due to the factor of novelty. They say it is good. Anything that has alcohol in it is good. Duh. You could put alcohol in gristle and people will say it is good. Really. They do. *"Filch"* is the word of the day. Never mind. Excelsior! Something is about to happen. I found the need to hex another victim in order to deal with my issues. ***Our*** issues as of now because you are still reading. Too bad.

I have a ghostwriter that is helping me as a precaution. He is in Las Vegas. He is a blood addict named Daniel. These types are easy to hex. I traveled to Las Vegas and inveigled him into his current condition. It was very easy. From there I went to Colorado. I was still very sick at the time but I successfully accomplished my mission and returned to a Ghost Town in upstate New York. ***Another story to be told in another book (6). You may have this part of the story already. It must come out shattered. I could not tell you this part until now. Each word plays its part, each one in its place. If it makes sense then you may come to the wrong conclusion. We certainly do not want that.*** Poor Daniel has suffered greatly but I do not care. This haunted individual named Daniel currently resides in a Las Vegas hotel that is under watch by armed guards and is possessed by my spells. He is in what one would refer to as "the rubber room". He writes the same thing that I am writing right now even though I am in New York. His hand and mine are one. He has heard Auryn (more about her later). ***Her Irish voice then cries: 'My heart, my mother! My heart, my coming forth of darkness! They know not my heart! What a surprise dear Mr. Preacher, I to hear from your astronomical majesty! Yes, there was a rainbow of promise up above the flabbergasted firmament. Talk about iridecencies: Ruby and Beryl and Chrysolite, Jade, Sapphire, Jasper and Lazul. When the constellation Ophiuchus is visible above the horizon, then muliercula occluded by the pisci-***

olinnies, Novar Ardonis and Prisca Parthenopea, is a bonny feature in the northern sky. Ers, Mars, and Mercury are at that time surgent below the rim of the Zenith part, while Arctura, Anatolia, Hesper, and Mesembria weep in their mansions over North, East, South, and West (5). He knows that Auryn is a Bitch with a capital ITCH. Even so, She is the Heroine of the story. Whatever could we do without her? Auryn and I speak to this suffering soul through the stars and the void and he does our bidding. It is a safeguard built into this spell to ensure that it will succeed. If I am tracked down and destroyed by the hunters who are after me then it will still be completed through him. I am being hunted right now. Many legions are after me. They do not know why but I do. They do not want me to get to the end of this spell. They do not want it finished but they are too late because it already is. I have it in my mind. I have it in my blood. It is a Virus. Even if I am destroyed it will be finished by the hand of another.

Art Survives the City. Nature Survives Both. (4)

Ready for some more madness? It is very important. Anytime you start to think reasonably I suggest that you stand on tiptoes, arch your chest upward, and then punch yourself in the nose. If it does not work, you should try it again. You will get better. This is the most reliable formula for expediting evolution. None of that Lamarckian mesmerism or eugenic eros. Orion is unstable damn it. This is one reason that the hunting is so desperate and the modern era is so fraught with calamity. Flopping around like fish on the ground. Things are about to change and Orion will be replaced by something else. Mudskippers? Betelgeuse is in a terminal state. It will soon change its name and become Wormwood. *"The third angel sounded his trumpet, and a great star, blazing like a torch, fell from the sky on a third of the rivers and on the springs of water – the name of the star is Wormwood. A third of the waters turned bitter, and many people died from the waters that had become bitter (8)."* A star in the daytime that is not the sun. A star is the home of a great being of immense power and influence. Yes. That is what I said. Stay with me here. Forget the miasma of the frontal lobe which is calling on you to reject this idea. It is a ruse. Willpower may come from the frontal lobe but it is exercised when plays tennis with the midbrain. The reptilian consciousness. Beep. Otherwise it is useless. There is much that you cannot perceive so you just have to take my word for it because I have eyes wherever there are wormholes. Yes, Worm holes. Wrrom holls. Oscillation of sound coming from somewhere indistinct. Tinnitus, otherwise, the banks in the Principality of Liechtenstein use them all of the time with crypto-penetration. President Carter had a rogue brother named Billy who was a satanist. A paid informant connected to Hassan I Sabbah. It all comes together. The Saudi's visit brothels in Zurich for Muhammad's sake. Goats are okay too by that standard. You should use rubber knee boots. Why do farmers love rubber knee boots? Stick the hind legs in the boots and the goat cannot run away. Spy agencies have deep insight into the worst things that are happening. It is all encrypted verse. I don't know what the problem is officer. It was my goat. Political forces are interested. Nonsense and sense come together in the void where machines can speak using math. The beauty of destruction. Flaws in the algorithms. Leave it as it is ***FOR GODS SAKE!*** We can't lose our best salesman. Everyone is listening in. Everyone is watching. Waiting....

beeeeeeepSupernovae in Orion will cripple the hunter. **Boom!** As a matter of fact, I also know this terminal condition is true of the star that the humans worship whose true name I loathe to write at this early part of the incantation. We shall call it the sun because that is a perfectly erroneous and harmless name to use for now. I am trying to explain this all to you but there is so much that does not make sense

– in the **normal** sense of sense – so there is only one way to put it properly....Pasta! Got me? Onward. I say the sun is terminal because I am speaking in terms of my clock. Lifetimes are a blink of an eye to me. By the way, I don't care much for writing and its conventions. They are not very useful when casting spells. I probably should have=e said that a while ago. Perhaps even an entire book ago. Well, we get around to things don't we. Such as: The undead of humanity were of Orion and Betelgeuse as a result, but the living were born under Lucifer; The Sun. Shit. I wrote down its true name. Anyway. We can correct this and no one will even know that we made a mistake. Being born under the sun, naturally, comes first before one can fall away into the darkness. The day is for the living and the night is ours. Humans are celestial beings like us Nosferatu and they have always worshiped their Sun instead of the stars of the night like we undead. They are powerless without it. This is the reason for their astrological condition. Humanity has submitted to this force so much over the years that they have virtually forgotten who it is that controls the sun. They have forgotten that it is just another star like the rest. They have forgotten, taken for granted, their place as celestially influenced beings. Ergon they have forgotten that the sun is the home of a powerful being. To the living it is simply "The Sun". The brighter it gets the greater the darkness there is to account for. They have forgotten its true name and created their own mythologies through the ages to convince themselves that the realm of its influence is somehow separated from the rest of space. An impenetrable garden, a place of peace and growth. This can't be further from the truth. Even in this supposedly scientific age, no amount of altered telescopic photographs (do you really think that space is as colorful and swirly as the photographs that end up in magazines? Suckers.) Can change the perspective that "The Sun" is not what it seems. It is not benevolent. It is like the stars that I was born under, it is a very evil star that is inhabited by a very evil influence. There are many good stars but they are very far away. Close your eyes. If you are still clinging to some sort of life and have not yet become the walking dead like me you may be able to see one. That one is yours. It is YOU. Open your eyes and see the opposite; the illumination from the closest and most dangerous star there is. It knows that its time will come and it has been preparing for some time. Your very existence in your current form is part of this preparation.

All of this has caused me many difficulties. Not only am I undead but I am empathic. What an intolerably fucked up combination. I can smell every feeling that wafts around me because it is carried in the blood. Lust, desperation, joy, despair. All chemical reaction in blood. I can feel you better than you do because I don't have the convenience of normal conscience and perspective to mess everything up. You understand why I am so sick of it all? I feel everything that has happened, is happening and most of what will happen. I should clarify a little. When I say that I am undead I am referring to the way that my body operates. I am a blood sucker. ***I won't show you my teeth, instead I will show you my plastic smile (9).*** Just believe me when I say it because I rarely ever admit that I am a blood sucker. Look yourself in the mirror. Is what you see what you are? Really? I am not so sure about that. Wait a few years and look again. Not the same. HA! Suckers. I have a feeling that you could be well on your way to being a blood sucker too even though you may not be dead yet. You will be soon or are more than half there already. Capitalism and its attendant mythologies are working very diligently to prepare you for this vomitus escape from your chrysalis. Get used to it. You may be a zombie, or a ghost too. This may be more likely because capitalism creates more victims than it does hunters. It has to or else it would not work properly. I avoid mirrors entirely and I try not to look at you too hard so I wouldn't know how far gone you are. You may be a reptile. Or a centipede, or a single celled organism. You may be even less complicated, perhaps you are a Tory or a Republican. Maybe you are a unicorn. It is all very sad. I was human once. It all started in Africa so very long ago. You may not believe me when I say that I was there then but I was. I was one of the earliest humans who walked out of the evolutionary stew. Rib bones and chicken wings dropped out of my ears. Do you like to eat yourself? I do. I am a vegetable. Something like that anyhow. I don't have blood of my own. Before my recent adventure, which I will soon explain, I had not been back to Africa since I left so long ago. It was quite traumatic. ***In the beginning is the void, in the muddle is the soundance, and therein-after you're in the unknown and vice versa (5).*** When I recently went there, the present issues I am dealing with which cause me to write this spell, began to totally take over. Just believe me when I say that I was a human like you once. You think that you are any different than I was? The stars are just not the same as they were then and you won't become a Nosferatu like me. Otherwise, not much different, biologically speaking. Something else could happen but you also could be lost upon this earth forever just like I am. We will both await its destruction and are not be able to do anything about it. You can do something about you though. Close your eyes again and find the source of the light. You understand what I am hinting at? It is too early to type those words. Far too early to explain with this black liquid that clots on tissues and causes pain. Blood and ink are too close to the same solution. It will all change very soon if everything goes according to plan. The plan is this spell of course but is it my plan? I defy responsibility. Is math discovered or invented. Art is a word and a word is a performance. A performance is nature. Against all reason, the truth is that nature's performance is love, the least understood phenomena that humans must endure. There is no love without loss. A golden sickle cuts the stem from the body to release the sky from the earth. The birth of the titans. This is the final performance, the final sacrifice demanded by nature.

Ladies and Gentlemen, there is now no turning back.

Disclaimer: In the following pages I will criticize science and reason quite a bit and this is important simply because the exaltation of this is subject I not in the interest of this discussion. However, it does have a valuable place on its own plain of activity and in that context it demands intelligent respect. In this discussion we must leave behind its maternal embrace. We are examining other issues which may require me to drag rationalism and science through some offal. As this stink arises, do not take me for a fool, or a flat-earther, or an anti-vaccination moron, or a raging nationalist who thinks their nation is against them (go figure that out if you dare), or someone who adopts any other, unmentioned, form pure stupidity as fact simply because it is contrary to popular media narratives and therefore must be true. I do, in fact, have discretion, intelligence, and good taste. I lament those who can-not see through the convoluted nature of this discussion, and at the end, take away the meaning of this writing as a free endorsement for whatever madness that may be present on the internet. I equally lament anyone who reads this and takes away the main idea that I mean to undermine science in any way. Neither of these conclusions are my intent. Quite the contrary. The conundrum presented is that the idiot fringe is still using some form of reason to justify their mentality. A depraved and retarded version of it, of course, but it is still an active process of reasoning. This is the only way the human mind can operate. This spell is designed to destroy all forms of reason, be they well-crafted and based on fact or be they based in mania and flawed to the point of absurdity. My conclusion in this disclaimer is: do not take anything that I say as justification for stupidity, anti-science, or alarmist fringe nonsense even though it may appear that way on the surface. I may frequently criticize some real science and rationalism directly. Nothing is above criticism. The rational mind must accept irrationality and the irrational mind must accept rationality. I hope that leaves everyone quite uncomfortable in any position.

I now present a transcript of an actual conversation I had on social media at the beginning of the outbreak of the Corona Virus Pandemic of 2019-2020. This is included to assure the reader that I am not a Total Whack Job and do indeed defend reason and science when it is required. This may come into question in future pages but remember this example if you do actually have doubts on my position. There are many in the world who are troglodytes, even though they may appear as otherwise normal human beings at a glance. One can only know for sure once they open their mouths – or in this case, write – to reveal the inner workings of their damaged psyche. The sad thing is they really are not aware of their condition. They do deserve some sympathy even though it may be difficult to extend. I use my allonym – “Alex” – in the following thread. The names of others in the conversation are hidden to protect their stupidity. Enjoy.

☺😐☹☺😐☹☺😐☹☺😐☹☺😐☹☺😐☹☺😐☹☺😐☹☺😐☹☺😐☹☺😐☹☺😐
☹☺😐☹☺😐☹☺😐☹☺😐☹☺😐

Person 1 Wuhun is the pilot city of the 5g network and program. There’s no such thing as airborne contagious virus. You can’t catch or injest animal protein or foreign human bacteria. The only way is through injection. which is going to be in the vaccine. 5g 60ghz waves give off the same bodily symptoms as the fake coronavirus Also the radiation creates the same protein/nucleic acid response resulting from tissue damage that the Corona-virus test are purposely looking for. It’s the 5g network. There’s no virus!!!

Hide or report this

- Like
- Reply
- 12h

Hide 19 Replies

Person 2: Wuhan is also the place where they make the Andrenachrome for these elites. Vampires

Hide or report this

- Like
- Reply
- 10h

Person 1: also Andrenachrome is why Tom Hanks got coronavirus

Hide or report this

- Like
- Reply
- 10h

Person 2: they injected it with corona so all those hollyweirds are getting the virus.

Hide or report this

- Like
- Reply
- 8h

Person 1: but why?

Hide or report this

- Like
- Reply
- 8h

Person 2: to expose them

1

Hide or report this

Like

Reply

8h

Person 1: I was thinking the same thing

Hide or report this

At this point I decide to respond to the initial statement

- Like
- Reply
- 8h

Alex Perandor: Sorry. Patently incorrect in many ways. First incorrect claim..."There's no such thing as airborne contagious virus". Irrefutably false. Second incorrect statement: "You can't catch or ingest animal protein or foreign human bacteria". Again...not true. A bacteria is not a virus. Viruses mutate in nature without…as you say: "the radiation creates the same protein/nucleic acid response" which is a very confusing statement and difficult to comprehend in the first place. Third. There is no ostensible vaccine that people are ostensibly being injected with. Fourth...All of the rest...Wild speculation at best. 5g has absolutely nothing to do with biological contagion. Sounds good as fiction.

Edit or delete this

- Like
- Reply
- 8h

Person 1: yeah I just posted that on here

Hide or report this

- Like

- Reply
- 8h

Person 1: But your wrong about the 5g because that›s the virus. It's been research that it cause the protein and nucleic to response same way this fake virus is doing. Because it›s the towers. 5g is a mind control experiment. And it also showed that when 5g 60ghz hits oxygen it makes it spin out of control and the hemoglobin can›t pick it up

1

Hide or report this

- Like
- Reply
- 8h

Edited

Alex Perandor: My question is what sort of research are you citing? For the sake of academic integrity and the genuine search for truth, I do not accept anything that is presented as research if it is not in a peer reviewed scientific journal or other source of similar rigor. Random stuff from the internet is not valid research. This is not to say that there are not bad actors in the world. Of course there are.

1

Edit or delete this

- Like
- Reply
- 7h

Person 2: I agree with Person 1. Yes, this is true. I didn't recite any of that before. Alex Perandor, your skepticism keeps you blind for the truth. Eventually you'll have to accept the truth of things. We're on the cataclysm of a new era. You won't be so skeptic no more after ufo disclosure this year.

I understand we're you're coming from and how that portrays your perception of reality. But that doesn't take away for you to do your own research when the information is simply provided and given. Why aren't you being guided to look further? Perhaps this isn't ment to be on your path.

2

Hide or report this

- Like
- Reply
- 7h

Alex Perandor: Again...in the spirit of full respect...There has been no information provided. That is the issue. Simply unjustified claims, most of which are blatantly false. There is no incentive to research any claim that is self-depreciating at the outset. Does that answer your question on why there is no need for further research on my part? I suggest that you provide research to justify these claims from a VALID source which can stand up to scrutiny. No New age youtube videos. No Wikis. No Memes. None of that is valid. Present a VALID source to justify these claims. If you can not do this I will simply say ..Who isn›t doing research now? As far as What Will Happen...Cataclysm? UFO? Bigfoot? Terminator 2? My perception of reality is justified by the simple fact that I do not wholly accept everything that I hear or read just because someone says it. Not Good Enough. If it does indeed happen...fine. I am waiting for the UFOS to weigh in on the virus situation but nothing has come through.

Edit or delete this

- Like
- Reply
- 6h

Person 2: Alex, There's loads of scientific research out their my friend. I'm simply here answering a question. It is not my responsibility to collect proofs as to neglect your skepticism. I provided you with some clues, it's up to you to do research if you disbelieve. I do not have the time to look up various proofs on more then a million facts to 8 billion different skeptics. I haven't put a PowerPoint presentation together, neither do I have one single source that explains anything. There's millions and millions of different topics that can be proved if you do the research but it'll take a life's work to explain all, not to mention explain it 8 billion times to different people.

The sole reason I provide my information is for people to awaken to what possible so that they can find their own truths. I know what I say is the truth, if you do not trust then you've got to prove it to yourself. As I said there's prove out their. Or you can just wait a few months until a public disclosure happens.

I hope you understand where I'm coming from but if you neglect what I'm saying, it is not up to me to verify that. I'm not discussing I'm only providing and I would like to spare time as to provide to others who'd like to awaken in this time of lies and delusion.

I love you and everyone on this planet.

1

Hide or report this

- Like
- Reply
- 6h

Alex Perandor: The simple fact that you can take the time to type up this entire statement yet not provide a single valid source to back up what you are saying says everything. If there is soooo much good research then that should be no problem. So, there is no information provided to back up anything. If you are trying to say that there is an infinity of dubious claims to look into on the internet, I will not quibble but that is not research nor is it evidence. It is not up to me to scour all of the nonsense and noise on the internet to prove that your statements reflect panic, mania, and certainly not insight. A further point, it is up to you to verify such absurd claims with actual fact if you expect them to be taken seriously by anyone. You make a claim so you bear the burden of proof. Despite some of the other comments present, facts actually do matter. This has nothing at all to do with belief or following your heart or other such platitudes.

Edit or delete this

- Like
- Reply
- 4h

Person 1: There›s proof and evidence I›m just telling my knowledge but I guarantee if you took the time to search yourself you will find it. There's proof subliminal messages work but just because I won›t post a million thing to back me up. When if you find interest in it you›ll find the proof

Hide or report this

- Like
- Reply
- 3h

Person 1: Like look it up 5g 60ghz makes the oxygen atoms spin like in a microwave to heat the food. so it›s hard for the hemoglobin to pick it up. Plus it causes other mental sicknesses making you dizzy, seeing shapes, migraines, and shortage of breath.

Hide or report this

- Like
- Reply
- 3h

Alex Perandor: Ok. Best of luck to you guys. I am done with this. It has been fun.

Edit or delete this

- Like
- Reply
- 3h

Person 2: Guess you›ll learn it the hard way.

Hide or report this

- Like
- Reply
- 3h

Person 3 chimes to create a punchline.

Person 3: Person 2, Hopefully the alien disclosure will be a full disclosure, not one given out little by little.

This is undermined because there is more important Information.

Person 1: New update: it›s already to late but stay off your phone as much as possible. Stay away from vaccines whether it›s real or not. Don›t even go get tested. It›s made to say you got it. Stay highy oxygenated and high in alkaline. Laboratory engineered virus that›s what the word (novel) means not because it›s in that book and also weaponized by the 5g network towers. Their trying to make people demand the vaccine!!!!!

To put in a DNA modifier so they can insert a 3 strand in your dna made with gold making you a hybrid losing your moral independence, ethical, legal, and all independent thoughts to make us slaves their so far ahead it›s already here. This is no longer a joke.

1

Hide or report this

- Like
- Reply
- 1h

Person 2: I'd never take one vaccine. Corona virus wouldn't even survive 5 minutes in my Alkaline body.

Vaccines are for one thing and one thing only: modifying human DNA in secret/

1

Hide or report this

- Like
- Reply
- 1h

Person 1: yepp exactly. Stay oxygenated and high in alkaline. Nothing foreign can survive in the body.

Hide or report this

- Like
- Reply
- 1h

Person 2: a healthy natural body working as intended should never get disease. Sickness isn't something natural..

1

Hide or report this

- Like
- Reply
- 1h

Divinity (not deity) is the uncertainty justified by your certitude (4).

Despite the above example of pure stupidity, let me tell the skeptic or the rationalist out there that chaos makes a fuck of a lot of sense. Chaos contains all of the answers. ALL of them, ALL at once. Far too much for the human brain to fathom or ever use properly for any *reason*. ***The cranic head on him, caster of reasons, peer yuthner in yondmist. Wooth? While over against this belles alliance beyind Ill Sixty, ollollowed ill! Bagsides of the fort, bom, tarabom, tarabom, lurk the ombushes, the site of lyffing-in-wait of the upjock and hockums (5).*** In other words…

…Rationalism. This is a crusade of cannons operated by blood addicts who fire at what they *believe* is ignorance. Reason is an intoxicant lurking in the blood and brain which alters perceptions. Skeptics are addicted to their skepticism because of the drug of reason and a dash of superiority complex which is unbecoming of disinterestedness. It is one of the many opiates of the masses. They are the faithful acolytes of one of the world's great non-Abrahamic manifestations of monotheism. Never trust a Catholic or anyone else who pretends to know everything. Reason is their God and it has many archangels to support it and sing its praises. Without reason and skepticism the faithful lose most of their identity for they are empty desperate people. For the most part. They do have politics, sport, and star wars to twiddle their pretensions toward higher thought but that is pretty sad if you ask me. ***Oh, it's a strange land you've come visiting to see me here. With no idea of a hero, you see, but they need them so badly that they make up special games, hitting a ball with a stick and all kinds of nonsense, and the men who win the games are their heroes. And then, he went on, warming to what was apparently a severe preoccupation of his, – when that gets stale, they arrange whole wars which have no more reason for existing than the people who fight in them, and a boy may become a hero fighting for a life that's worth something for the first time, threatened with the loss of it, that or dying to save the lives of people who've no idea what to do with them. Fortunately, he went on, and inclined his head nearer, – there's a way out for most of them. They make money...and it is a good thing that such a recourse lies open, it gives them something to do, keeps them out of our way. – Fortunately men like us only appear every century or so, to keep the way open. – We must watch out for them trying to intrude. They try to intrude. Traveling on their trains and their airplanes they try to intrude on the greatest careers of the hero. Why, travel's become the great occupation of people with nothing to do, you find second-hand kings and all sorts of useless people at it. There now, It's always the heroic places you find them intruding, trying to have their share in the work of great men, looking at fine paintings and talking as though they knew more of the thing than the man who painted it, and the same thing listening to fine music, because they suspect the truth but they won't pay the price, they all suspect that a man needs something to do. Something to do? Most of the trouble in the world is made by people finding something to do...Danger? They don't know the meaning of it, sitting up there in their airplanes, and surprised when they drop out of the***

sky. Why, they haven't time to be frightened, they're so surprised, brought up so carefully, insured against accident. Why, their heads are smashed like melons before thy know what's happened to them, sitting up there in their business suits at sixty miles an hour wondering if their fountain pens will leak, and then there they are spread all over twenty acres of somebody else's land. No not the danger. The loneliness. It's the loneliness, the price they won't pay. – The great misfortune of the sun, it has no history. That's why it never gets lonely up there... Yes since they don't know what they are looking for, of course they don't see anything, wandering around in the daylight. There's so much daylight you can't see anything up there unless you cut a path through it. Why, in good weather, one afternoon I saw Aldebaran, the red Eye of the Bull, keeping watch on the Pleiades, you know. That means it's a very old star, being red like that. Yes, the red eye of Taurus...keeping watch on them. They bear some watching... (3)... They need reason like a junky needs junk. How can they *explain chaos* without denial or deflection into reason and abstract banalities? When the mediums of word and number make the leap to action is when the real problems start to stick out. The ***reason*** is *chaos* of course. It will always be the unpredictable disruption that leads the good intentions of the scientist into the darkness of existence, which is inexplicable in its totality. No matter how well researched and understood anything that is created is, it can – and most of the time will – dredge up something to counteract whatever "good" has been done. Especially since whatever is discovered is delivered to the hands and intentions of political crustaceans with territory to protect or destroy. What then? The eternal siren song of science which only gets louder the more that is dredged up: Time to pass the buck to everyone else when that happens. Just don't pass it to me. I am not alive. It doesn't matter at all to me how habitable this planet remains for living beasts.

Okay. It is time to take a deep breath. Hold it. Exhale. Do this a few more times. Get prepared for a page or three or something of stuff that may piss you off. I hope that it does. This is good. Just let it piss you off and get through it. Then we can continue on with more madness. It may not piss you off and that is good too. There are bigger things at hand and a little ditty to make you twitch serves a purpose. Remember why? See the Disclaimer **above. Anyway...to continue:**

People starve, wallow in streets of misery, dry up from living in uninhabitable places, and destroy each other with whatever is at hand because of the fact that they are desperate due to the grotesque failures of international capitalism, which is ***believed*** to be the most rational – reasonable – system governing bipedal behavior. It is the ultimate usurpation of freedom for the sake of slavery. The greatest failure that the world has seen. It is the manifestation of absurdity through reason. ***Lucihere! Zweispaltung as Fundemaintalish of Wiederherstellung (Splitting-in-two as a precondition to reassembly. The phrase suggests Hegel's dialectic of world history, also the words of Giordano Bruno: Everything can come to knowledge of itself only through contrast with its opposite) (4) Now, I'd like to make a capital Pee for Pride down there – where Hoddum and Heave, our monster bilker, balked his bawd of parodies. And let you go and mick your modest mock pie out of Humbles up your end (5).*** The planet is mostly water but so many are thirsty. Absurdity. How much research and effort goes into the discovery of abstractions that effect nothing, help no one, and are inconclusive at best? Absurdity:

Although the Higgs field is believed to permeate the entire Universe, proving its existence was far from easy. In principle, it can be proved to exist by detecting its excitations, which manifest as Higgs particles (the 'Higgs boson'), but these are extremely difficult to produce and to detect. The importance ***of this fundamental***

question led to a 40 year search, and the construction of *one of the world's most expensive and complex experimental facilities to date,* ***CERN's Large Hadron Collider.***

For decades, scientific models of our universe have included the possibility that it exists as a long-lived, but not completely stable, sector of space, which could potentially at some time be destroyed upon 'toppling' into a more stable vacuum state. If the masses of the Higgs boson and top quark are known more exactly, and the Standard Model provides an accurate description of particle physics up to extreme energies of the Planck scale, then it is possible to calculate whether the universe's present vacuum state is stable or merely long-lived. (This was sometimes misreported as the Higgs boson "ending" the universe. A 125-127 GeV Higgs mass seems to be extremely close to the boundary for stability (estimated in 2012 as 123.8-135.0 GeV) but a definitive answer requires much more precise measurements of the top quark's pole mass. New physics can change this picture.

If measurements of the Higgs boson suggest that our universe lies within a false vacuum of this kind, then it would imply – more than likely in many billions of years – that the universe's forces, particles, and structures could cease to exist as we know them (and be replaced by different ones), if a true vacuum happened to nucleate. It also suggests that the Higgs self-coupling λ ***and its*** $\beta\lambda$ ***function could be very close to zero at the Planck scale, with "intriguing" implications, including theories of gravity and Higgs-based inflation.*** *A future electron–positron collider would be able to provide the precise measurements of the top quark needed for such calculations (4).*

We need to go to Mars so that people will not go extinct. This is very important. Elon Musk thinks so. This planet is so fucked up that it is very important that we can go fuck up another. So that humans can survive an extinction event. Because this really matters. If humans become extinct they will certainly care about it after the fact. Better expedite the process and blast off. But what if the universe itself ceases to exist?

Falderal

[**fal**-*duh*-ral]

Spell Syllables

noun

1. mere nonsense; foolish talk or ideas.

2. a trifle; gimcrack; gew-gaw.

Expand

Also, **falderol**

[**fal**-d*uh*-rol], **folderol**.

Origin of falderalExpand

1695-1705

First recorded in 1695-1705; orig. as a nonsense refrain in songs; of obscure origin

Atheist rationalism is a cult like any other. It comes complete with its own pantheon of archangels in the form of hero worship manifested by the cult of victory; the cult of fortune; *Fortûna*, equivalent to the Greek goddess Tyche or Isis *Fortûna,* and the cult of personality; hubris ὕβρις which is attached to its little mentioned counterpart; nemesis; Νέμεσις. Another name for nemesis is Adrasteia or Adrestia, meaning "the inescapable". Her Roman name – counterpart is Invidia. ***If you flung her clothes over her head you'd wheeze why Solomon set his seal six fold on the gown of a witch (5).*** In order for anything to work for these believers they must first have faith in what they believe in. Faith in reason. A glaring hypocrisy, a common symptom of any cult activity. Faith in reason; the irrational justifying the rational. Like any other cult they must have a hierarchy to keep the faithful in line and to justify whatever destruction occurs after nemesis reveals her ugly head. Like any cult, there must be consequences for any who become heretics. In this case it is usually through social, legal, or monetary consequences for these tend to be the most powerful forces in societies that are of such a low development that they still base their existence upon anachronistic and hypocritical ideas such as reason followed by its polar opposite, law and imperialistic capitalism. Any who dare to step outside the status quo will be harassed and excommunicated. Sasha Shulgin and Jack Kevorkian are notable examples. As a consequence of this faith, the faithful must also believe that their dogmas are the most superior manifestation of culture in the universe which gives them the right to look down upon and harass the גוים gentiles. Any of the resultant destruction inflicted upon these gentiles is applauded rather than defamed. These faithful masses are like us undead who suck blood. Unlike us Nosferatu, they need perception and reason so they can chop the planet into little bite sized pieces in order to fill their resume so that they can find a job for a corporation or for the government so they can then hand their findings over to these destructive infants who employ them and who will do what they please with these findings. Absurdities pile up to the sky like the tower of Babel for these absurdities are the foundation of that very towers architecture. Reason is an absurdity. These sad pagans feel like they need to *discover* something "essential", something "important" about the universe so that their wimpy name can be recorded in someone's pathetic historical account which can be crammed down the throats of classroom children alongside stories of Santa Claus and George Washington's stupid cherry tree. Absurdity. All will resort to a defense of these attacks based upon the concept of altruism and social progress. Absurdity. Regardless of whatever is developed for the sake of these ideals there is almost always a negative consequence attached. Absurdity. These negative effects render these altruistic arguments mute because it rarely matters what one tries for if something different is made manifest. Absurdity is reason and reason is absurdity for this universe is rooted to the singularity of the unspeakable name of chaos. Carry on and make applesauce into pasta. Payment in dollars and fame and pride are covered in blood that the faithful acolytes of Nike are blind to. Ink on paper. They are blood addicts that, like any addict, vehemently deny that they may have a problem. They want the entirety of reality to be reduced to a word printed on a page or an image on a screen. Blood and sweat reduced to a few letters typed in ink. Blood on saturated paper. Absurdity. Paper that talks back in the voice of thousands of unsettled ghosts.

Anyhow, it may seem that I got a little off topic but all of that was certainly important. It is a necessary piece of the altar. We must question everything, no? Even those who say that they are questioning everything? Especially them. **It is important to remember the emotional as well as the rational because they are connected.** You humans are not cyborgs yet. Why do I not make a case for or against religious mentality? I respect your intelligence enough to not state the obvious. Discussion of this mentality is far too easy, far too basic, not worth the effort, and serves no practical purpose as a false digression in the context of this spell work. These folks already have an inherent connection between the semblance of rationality and their emotional state which I do not already see as a universal quality in their atheist counterparts, who frequently refuse to admit that they sometimes do think, and sometimes say, dumb shit out of emotional reaction. I may drift in and out of these necessary digressions from time to time. Where was I? Of course, I am in my secret dive of an apartment somewhere in the streets of New York, New York. I am here hiding from the many who are hunting me. So many of them do not want you to come across these ideas for obvious reasons. These ideas destroy reason and it will defend itself to the last bullet and the last ballistic missile. It is automated to defend itself. Totally out of hand once the process begins. Reason and logic result in chaos. Get the idea? You can't hold on to it if you are slowly degrading into worm food and nothing else. Endgame... Good. Happy. Nothing left for all good consumers after consumptions. Handful, Body full, mind full of void. More about that later. So, where was I anyhow...of course, I know what I was discussing. Another psuedodigression first. One thing at a time with these silly words. That is how they work after all. Ladies and Gentlemen, what is it that makes you different? Gross. I was talking about how my body operates. I am not like you because I am not alive. I am as alive as these words. Alive and not alive at the same time. Alchemy exists. It is happening right now. Nigredo is a start so just accept it and suffer. My carcass is far beyond entropy. It is the only thing that makes sense in this inverted world. You are on your way to become something like me. It is only a matter of time. Study my folly. It is dust and ash that is animated by many inexplicable forces of dark majik and dark gravity. You are as well. Science will never be able to explain the human condition and what it is working toward. I exist after the fact and this is a long, extended answer to the apocalypse of existence. I am undead and possess some pseudo-biological functions all of which work together in a predictable manner but I am not too interested in this. Any of these processes can be looked up and studied elsewhere. There is no reason to discuss any of that here. It is all automation. My reason for putting all of this together is to defy automation, to defy the predictable and the explainable. I am Nosferatu. Oh, yes. I am certainly a creature of habit and I possess some very predictable behaviors just like everyone else. Like most other life forms I tend to favor my bad habits while I throw the good ones to the wind for someone else to discover and then ignore. I am addicted to blood. What are you addicted to? Don't tell me that you aren't addicted to something. Just say it. I am so and so and I am an addict. Grant yourself the courage to accept the things that you cannot change. There. Was that so hard? If you actually meant it you may actually feel a little bit better. 3/11/2020. Dow drops one thousand four hundred points after the World Health Organization officially designated a pandemic viral outbreak. None of this is real. Addiction is a mental disease. Word virus in this case. Capitalism would fail if there wasn't so many addicts running around. I will get to more of that flavor of bitching soon enough but because of the seductive nature of capitalist advertisement and propaganda I am willing to bet that you are addicted to blood as much as I am. We both exist and feed upon this form of controlled chaos. Who made your shoes? Do you like them? Is this rational? Stop sweating. The only answer is to threaten Asia with exploding, phallic, tubular solutions to problems because the English speaking versions are far more big and erect and explosive and open handed shaking answers to peaceful interventions to markets because people are worried and need to feel better.

I see good spirits and I see bad spirits (1). I *am* one of them but I have not yet discovered which. **(This part is important because it is about nothing.)** What I am sure of is the fact that these forces do not get along very well just like any sibling rivalry. This is one of the reasons that there are concentrated areas where evil congregates. But let me tell you a secret. Evil is not truly *evil* in the way you may partially understand it. It is an integral part of truth. It has to find a place to hide when the light of the sun begins to burn everything by day and the light which is blocked by objects provides a hiding place for its true love. The shadow. The shadow always hides behind the object but both need each-other. Even though I don't want to recognize it – I want to operate with a complete impunity that matches the gigantic size of my arrogance – I must admit that I am truly hypersensitive to these areas of concentrated evil – darkness – whenever I come across them. Are you becoming habituated? Withdrawal is terrible. You may shit yourself more than you would like so bring many pairs of undies.

The sick part of me – and trust me it is a big part – wants to stay in these places of concentrated evil and soak up whatever is there whenever I come across them. These places are not as simple to define as places that are in shadow just as the word "evil" is not sufficient. The void is what they are. I told you this is important because it is about nothing. The void is essential to this spell. It is knowledge, otherwise known as Daath. This is everywhere anyone is. This "nothing" could be anywhere. Hell, your house may be built upon one of them. You would probably know it if it was but I am willing to bet that no one would believe you if you told them. I don't have to *believe. I am* haunted. Sometimes I get the bright idea to get the fuck away from these places but that is not often. I can never tell if I want to control or submit to these forces whenever I encounter them. As a perfectionist and an addict I naturally want both. I want it all. I want the roses and the shit that they grow out of. I already am the thorns. Unfortunately one can only do one thing at a time. See these words…one thing at a time. That is how it works. Even someone like me who has existed for as long as I have hasn't yet figured out how to get past that. See how easy it is to fuck yourself over. You can't have everything at once. I fuck myself over with my absurd expectations all of the time. There is no good reason for it but there are plenty of bad ones. I believe it was Duchamp who once said something like: "a bad painting is still a painting". The same holds true with bad reasons or bad expectations. I will always be a blood sucker no matter where I am. How long will it take for you to realize that you are too? Remember this part for it will save your thingy (words are stupid and imprecise) that is not alive but makes you feel like you are. You can't avoid the void that exists between light and shadow.

△

Ovis Aries

Bill W. is your friend.

Addiction. A.A. Astrum Argentum.

Atropine and Scopolamine products labeled as eye drops.

The void is there already. It is waiting and you

are being trained to walk right into it.

Ben ● Ben

Benben was the mound that arose from the primordial waters Nu.

It was the location where the first rays of the sun fell

The bird deity Bennu, the Phoenix.

In the Mansion of the Benu

In Heliopolis

you rose up,

I no longer have much of a chance of changing what I am but I do have some sort of a choice about where I end up. I can feel the residual energy that has built up in most places that I travel. As a hunter myself I have been trained to be hypersensitive to this sort of thing. There is very little reason or rationality to this. Emotionless rationalism can only explain the tiniest part of what it is *to be* and many are completely satisfied with this. Medieval torture chambers arise in modern medicine and rocket science. Science can explain in detail the mechanics of a heart attack but it can never satisfactorily explain the subjective, personal sensations of what it actually feels like to go through one. I would argue that this is the most important part. They can show a brain pattern or a grid full spiky lines but that never explains the actual experience. They do not care at all about the experience. In this case, Ontology Vitiates

Ontogeny. Experience and perception slips through the fingers like sand and yet this chaos is one of the most powerful driving forces behind human understanding and action upon that understanding. One can only grab so much while most of it ends up on the floor.

One can see and understand quite a bit from this perspective. The perspective of being on the floor. Get over yourselves for your feet don't hover. But then...rise up from the ash. Atum as you rose up, as the benben, in the Mansion of the Benu in Heliopolis. If you are looking for an explanation of hell look no further. It is right in front of you, above you and all around. Of course, heaven and purgatory are there as well. I have learned how to avoid the effects of this flaming light but I have not yet totally figured out how to avoid the things that come out of the darkness. You think that you are not exposed to the darkness? I assure you that it is safe. Evil is not what you think it is and neither is the darkness. You rose from it at the place where the sunlight first shone and you have a choice. Close your eyes for a second and then tell me that you carry no darkness at all. It is everywhere you go. It is poised and waiting to consume you in an instant. Time and space are not a factor at all. That is not totally correct. They are a factor but only one, and the most primitive sort. Darkness envelopes so much. It is always there and has been there long before you were.

If you keep your eyes closed and pay attention to the aurora of light that passes through the darkness you may have a tiny bit of hope but to keep your attention on this light is a hard act to maintain for any amount of time. It is the starlight from your star. The place where you are from. This inner universe lurking in living humans is the very same one that reveals itself when the sun goes away and the moon presides over our hell planet. ***Of rune or some blazing star (93).*** We are all so far from our home. Time is a satanic spell that only applies to our hell planet. Space is married to it. Reality is neither. Time and space are only the smallest part that pokes out of the darkness and fondles our perceptions. Our being is a filter for a greater reality which we can neither perceive nor comprehend. Time and space are the residual debris that this filter collects. Only the smallest part of reality. They both exist before and after us. They are not where we are. We are blind to what is in front of us. We can only see with closed eyes. The light is there in a rainbow circle throne. Where are we then? We are in the eternal present and we must accept the fragment of the wider inexplicable reality which we perceive as metaphor for everything we cannot.

I see good spirits and I see bad spirits (1). The body is automated to suffer all of this but the inner being should be able to unify both time and space at once. Another tall order but not impossible. One of the essential secrets of the universe is this inexplicable unity. It is total chaos because how can darkness and light be the same? It is right in front of you right now. Dark bloody ink hacked upon blank white paper. Unity of opposites transfers true meaning but this true meaning is chaotic and inexplicable as far as the filter of reason goes. Something has to give so that what is perceived as *good* or *bad* can create *understanding.* It is like rubbing two sticks together when you have a lighter in your pocket. Something in this unity has to give. It is the only way communication is possible. The body breaks down unity and filters it out to arrive at a perception. Slowly and surely every day we experience this breakdown whether we like it or not. Existence is cancer. It is addiction. Chronic, progressive, deadly. Hold on for as long as you can and then let go. ***The sun is falling on the mountains. Hurry up please, it is time (11).*** Time falls apart before you and within you and creates the present. Chaos is the result. The inexplicable. Entropy. ***How long does it take for a human to realize that they cannot want what they want (11)?*** We are always left with the inexplicable at the end. It was with us the entire time. The fulfillment of desire is totally immaterial. Not food, sex, or sensation. Nothing. It is all filtered through us and *nothing* is the grand inexplicable result. The fulfillment of desire. The ineffable eternity of present feelings that drive thought and action. This is dangerous territory. It leaves no standing room. Who is really in control here? Everything is measured and witnessed. Everything. Even when you think you are alone you are not. There is always something watching. Waiting. Measuring. Who is in control? Your rational brain? Your subconscious brain? Neither. I am pretty sure what it is and I am not going to tell you yet. It is horrifying. It is ***of rune or some blazing star (93).***

What I will say is that I almost always seem to end up in messed up situations no matter what I intend. Can you relate? If you said no I will call you a liar. Surely something is in control. Of course it is the universe. The very same one that is behind my eyes as well as yours. We share the same breath and we share the same darkness. What I exhale you inhale and the opposite is true. Darkness drives this. The inner darkness. The same one that was behind my eyes when I was a human (I am different now) is a direct connection to the infinite void that swarms around the infinite pin pricks of starlight above us. You are the void. You spend your entire existence trying to fill it without ever getting the realization that it is eternal. Always present. Always filled. No matter where I go it is with me far above. Are you any different? You are a blood sucker too. The only difference between you and me is that my void is above and yours is within but they are exactly the same. The only difference is the fact that I accepted this so very long ago. I discovered how to accept it so I exist while you simply live. No matter how many layers of burning blue gas and clouds of smoke that waft and inspissate to obscure it we are always below the void. Submit. The void will swallow you whole whether you believe in it or not. No matter how many ways you have tried to fill that fucking obnoxious void that lurks at the threshold of consciousness it is never enough and it causes endless amount of despair. The place where each one of us must find our own. There are many trials ahead. I know where I have to go and what to do. It has been a long time coming before I realized. You will probably end up in the same situation so take heed. The sickle birthed the titans from the oppression of Uranus. (Isn't Uranus a terrible name for a god? If you try not to say "anus" you end up saying "urine" and if you try not to say "urine" you end up saying "anus") Art is a word and a word is a performance...

The Knight of the Rueful Countenance

There are a few things that must be said about the void within. In order to do that I must relate a few things that I have been through. As Nosferatu, I have the ability to transform my body into many other forms. I can look like any human or any animal that will serve a purpose that I may need. I recently did an experiment. Recently for me at least. In a hospital a baby was born and I was waiting. I disguised myself as a wandering doctor like I have done so many times in the past. The form of *doctor* is a very convenient one for us undead for many reasons as you can probably imagine. After the infant was placed in the hospital nursery I watched and waited for the best moment to act. When the moment came and no one was paying attention I changed back into myself. Fire of starlight and blood. I consumed this infant. I won't tell you how much I enjoyed it. Once this bit of nasty work was completed I took the form of the infant that I had just destroyed and stayed in its place so that it did not appear like anything happened at all. The parents took me home and raised me through the many stages of growth. I played the role and found it to be frustrating yet enjoyable. I knew I had to go through this because something was going to come out of it. Time is of little relevance to me. I changed forms slowly and “grew up” into adolescence for the sake of the experiment. The parents never knew. They had suspicions that I was “different” but that is somewhat normal in contemporary America. I went along my way and made friends with the people that I knew I should make friends with until I finally met her. Auryn.

Corso

My life is with the thrill kill kult (1). I must go back to the places where I encountered the worst and most powerful darkness. I must return to face the cold black energy that has burned me permanently and made me what I am. I tremble at the very idea of it. I get goosebumps because I know that it is true. Even at a cellular level, an atomic level. It is a force like gravity yet far stronger and beyond any explanation that I can offer with these simple words. These lifeless references strung along one after another to draw out some hint. What should I do about it? What do I think that I can accomplish that has not yet already been accomplished if I go back to these toxic centers of activity that I have marked on my maps? Homeopathy of course. I will fight fire with fire, light with light, darkness with darkness. I will draw my blade and cut it back, cut it so that it bleeds out forever and redirects the eternal stream of evil into the cosmic dumpster where it truly belongs. Only then will I finally be free. Another tall order to be sure. Performance is nature, nature is castration. The Birth of The Titans. ***Look in your letterbox for a review of the whole affair (3).***

Another Story from Another Book. (6)
OR
The Place Where All Stories Go and Where They Come From.

How did it all begin? How did I become what I am in the first place? It is difficult to explain for I was alive then. Most of what happened to me when I was a human was lost with my death and transformation. There was a great conflict in ancient times. This is why I have not returned to Africa in the many millennia of my existence. I am still traumatized by it and I have intentionally forgotten much but I can recall some of it if need be. In order for this spell to work I must dredge up some of these early memories of my early years.

It all started in Africa an inconceivable amount of time ago. The age of Virgo. East Africa where the Nile grows out of the mountains of the moon. Towering and shattered volcanic craters that spewed forth the conditions for *Homo sapiens* to evolve rise out of the plains and are rendered in stone abstraction in the form of pyramids on the plateau of Giza. It is called Incident 2 in circles of scientology. There is some degree of truth in every irrational absurdity and absurdity in every form of perceived rational truth. Virus is the original form of undead habitation on this planet. It is neither alive nor dead and it parasites upon the host, then reproduces with its help. Humans were *Homo sapiens* before they were human in the way that we understand ourselves. There is a difference even though there may not seem to be. *Homo sapiens* before humanity lacked efficient communication. Simple grunts and gestures were all that was available. These forms of spoken words created fire majik. Written word was to come later. The first written words were art. Pictograms in the sand and soil. At first, spoken word, fire and majik (outside, practical communication) were for the hunters and the void (inner, irrational communication) – the foundation of written words – was for the shamans. The hunters traveled the outside world and brought back what they could with the assistance of fire and majik. The Shamans did the same but they used the inner void to travel. The shamans were the first to look into the void and see the nothing that would become written words.

These early beings didn't become human until once upon a time, one of them decided to close his eyes to look within and saw the **form** of *nothing: lies.* The void within the void. Something that was dead but still alive. Virus. This individual was afraid that everything he knew and experienced would fall in and be consumed by the void. He stared across the *horizon* of every *event* he experienced and saw that it all was swallowed by this inner darkness. He coveted every loss and ignored the faint light that streamed across his inner eyes because of his preoccupation. He ignored his true place among the stars and fell in to the invisible void. The void within the void. A black hole welled up inside and came tumbling out. The written word was born with the attempt to freeze an event upon the horizon in time.

This blackness marched further and further across the page and the darkness of perception grew with every word discovered. The darkness also began growing in other parallel worlds that exist in unison with this perceivable earth. The growing darkness in all places became a portal of connection between them. It grew in the form of an irresistibly tempting void, *nothing...* ***There is life eternal within the eater of souls. Nobody is ever forgotten or allowed to rest in peace. They populate the simulation spaces of its mind, exploring all the possible alternative endings to their life. Theirs is a fate worse than death, you know... (4)*** Beings from these other worlds threw themselves into the void and each time one did it became a new word in this one. A lie. Words are their residual honorarium. A piece of the black hole that each being used to arrive here in a frozen state. These frozen beings are portals that lead back to their dead perceptions. Undead. Words are a primordial virus from other worlds. The birth of words is the birth of humanity and the human condition. Humanity could not develop without becoming infected with living death from other parallel worlds. Undeath.

That shaman who coveted nothing, the words which came out of it, and tried to hold on to his experience through them was me. Before I was undead. The virus that infected me was a word and it destroyed my blood. I was not only me though. There were a handful of us who were attempting the same thing under the age of Virgo. I was among the first shamans who used pictograms. Their creation was a performance. Together we became the first Nosferatu. I was consumed by greed. I wanted both the outer fire of the hunters and the inner shamanic void. Through my discovery I only found the fire and I burned up from within and so did the other shamans who were doing the same thing that I was doing. Spica was the star in the sky above us. Each one of us gave up our inner star and became a servant of a star that makes up Virgo. Each one was adopted by one of the stars. A virgin birth under a star. Nosferatu were born. I will tell you my star later because it is my name and it is too early in this spell to begin the invocation. Humans were born at the same moment. Modern humans are a third mind and space. Neither undead nor living. A half step away from *Homo sapiens* and a half step toward the nothing that creeps into this world and all of the others.

Despair is what causes one to throw themselves in. Despair over the loss of an event. The birth of humanity through this viral infection from other worlds was also the birth of Nosferatu at the same time. Nosferatu kept the fire of the original need for control through blood. We kept the outer fire majik of the hunters and the newly formed humans lost it but kept the inner majik of the shamans. They kept their connection to their inner star while we Nosferatu were only externally connected to ours.

Blood is the water of life. Blood carries on the spell of the name. Everyone's body is born in blood and so is their name. Blood is everything. It allows undead to stay in this world and travel it forever. It began with our internal conflagration. We lost our blood so we needed to take it from others to continue our travel. It is what allows our majik. Blood allows Nosferatu conscious majik. Blood allows humans unconscious majik. The humans kept the void of the word and the rationality that is produced by it. They also kept the ability to see from their original spiritual home in the stars that they still can observe with their eyes closed if they are not too far gone, lost in the dark mythological maze of rationalism and capitalism, infected and driven mad by the virus that is the word. The promise of eternal existence beyond life in their true home can be seen if they close their eyes and believe in it. Rationality leads to irrationality and irrationality leads to rationality. Orborous.

Unlike now, Humans and Nosferatu were more similar than different back then. We have both evolved our powers as time went on. Humans evolved with their rational inner majik and Nosferatu evolved with our outer practical majik and we are now more different than alike. At first we were still in a crude early state and did not totally refine our powers. We have been fighting ever since they saw our infection develop because they feared they had the same virus we had. They indeed were infected but they had a choice which we Nosferatu no longer had. They could only understand truth that exists within themselves or the lies that existed outside of them. Humanity (my former self) created Nosferatu through their flirtation with the lies. The Spirits of other worlds embodied in words. We Nosferatu are a lie. We feed upon the humans for they have the infection of words running through their blood. We are their lies and we defy their truth and reason because we can travel between shapes and across time.

We fought over these words, the virus that infected us. We fought for the possession of this infected blood. We Nosferatu may have got majik, and they may have got reason but each of us got a little bit of what the other possessed. The humans tried as hard as they could to undo us Nosferatu and there were many early battles. Neither side could win because once these doors were open they could not easily be shut again. Humans have been trying since the beginning of time to use their words and reason to undo us but they forgot that each word is an irrational void, and open portal of evil and a lie that allows for more and more deception. These words are what created us Nosferatu in the first place. They finally used the deception of reason to believe that we Nosferatu did not exist at all. They killed off most of us very quickly because there were far more of them. Only a few of us escaped.

I have known about the voids (the voids within the void i.e. black holes) ever since the beginning. I helped create them and they in turn created human society and culture. They grow and sprout more whenever this culture spreads out from its center. These black holes are not only in outer space and not all are gigantic. They are as small as a letter and can fit in a closed fist when cast upon a piece of paper. They grow out from there and wander the world creating civilization. An event horizon that sucks out the starlight of an individual's inner soul through the demand of conformity to the law of culture. WORDS. VIRUS, an event horizon is crossed and the black hole is entered once civilization takes root. It is no wonder that the most violent form of social culture – capitalism in all of its forms and permutations – has been the longest lasting. It is the ultimate void. There are so many shadows that lurk the streets that can suck anyone in. No one can see them because they are not light. Once I was undead I could only know of the existence of these voids but not anything about how they worked because I was still human when I created them. The memory of what they were was lost to me. I needed the right human to help me remember. One who was powerful enough to deal with such things. I waited a very long time for her to come around. Her name was A.A.A. A group of mountains rising into the sky to produce the rivers and streams where the gold is hidden. A tip of the spear to puncture the voids and wrap their meaning in a contract around its shaft. It is time for the beginning of the incantation so I can reveal the secret. Auryn Amethyst Alrescha was her name. Born in the age of Pisces.

Fixed star: **VINDEMIATRIX** Al Muredin	
Constellation: Epsilon (ε) Virgo	
Longitude 1900: 27ARI59	***Longitude 2000:*** 29ARI23
Declination 1900: +02.17'	***Declination 2000:*** +02.46'
Right ascension: 02h 01m	***Latitude:*** -09.03'
Spectral class: A2 Blue-white	***Magniture:*** 3.9

The history of the star: Alrisha

from p.342 of Star Names, Richard Hinckley Allen, 1889.

Alpha(α) **Pisces, Alrisha**, is a double and probably binary, 3.9 and 5.5, pale green and blue. It marks the Knot of the Cord, formed by the joining together of the ends of the ribbons that binds the two Fishes by the tail.

Al Rescha, or **Al Rischa**, derived from the Arabians' **Al Risha**', the Cord, is 20° south from the head of Aries, 2°.7 north of the celestial equator, and marks the knot in the united cords of the Fishes; the same title being applied to beta (β)Andromeda (Mirach). This word originally may have come from the Babylonian *Riksu*, Cord.

Hipparchos (circa 160-120 B.C.) and the second-century Greek astronomer Ptolemy designated it as (Greek) *Sundesmos ton Ichthuon*, or *Ton Linon*, the Knot of the Fishes, or of the Threads, varied by the Greek astronomer Aratus, circa 270 B.C., and Geminos in *Desmos*; these words being transcribed by Germanicus and the scholiasts as **Sundesmos** and **Desmos**. They were rendered by Cicero and others as **Nodus**, **Nodus coelestis**, and **Nodus Pisces**; by Pliny (23-79 A.D.) as **Commissura**

Pisces; and in the 1515 *Almagest* as **Nodus duorum filorum**.

The Arabians translated these by**Ukd al H'aitain**, which, as **Okda** and **Kaitain**, are not unusual titles now.

The uniting cords, branching from alpha (α **Alrisha**) through omicron (ο), pi (ϖ), eta (η Al Pherg), and rho (ρ) to the tail of the northernmost Fish, and through xi (ξ), upsilon (υ), mu (μ), *f*, *e*, zeta (ζ), epsilon (ε), and delta (δ) to omega (ω) that marks the tail of the one to the south, were the second-century Greek astronomer Ptolemy's *linon*, "thread," the *linoi* of other authors. Cicero called them **Vincla**, the Bonds; and the scholiast on Germanicus, **Alligamentum linteum** or **luteum**, divided by Hevelius into **Linum boreum** and **austrinum**. Some of these terms also were applied to the star delta (δ) as marking one of the cords.

The Arabians knew these cords as **Al Hait al Kattaniyy**, the Flaxen Thread; and Al Asma'i, about the year 800, mentioned them in his celebrated romance *Antarah* as a distinct constellation; but Pliny (23-79 A.D.) had done the same long before him.

Al Rischa, although lettered first, is somewhat fainter than gamma (γ) and eta...

[*Star Names*, *Their Lore and Meaning*, Richard Hinckley Allen, 1889].

The astrological influences of the constellation Pisces

Legend: Venus and her son Cupid while sitting on the bank of the Euphrates suddenly saw Typhon **אתיפשנע**, the enemy of the Gods, approaching them. They leapt into the river and were saved from drowning by two fishes, who were afterwards placed in the heavens by Venus in gratitude for their help. [*Robson**, p.57.]

Influences: Ptolemy makes the following observations: «Those stars in Pisces which are in the head of the southern fish have the same influence as Mercury, and, in some degree, as Saturn: those in the body are like Jupiter and Mercury: those in the tail and in the southern line are like Saturn, and, moderately, like Mercury. In the northern fish, those on its body and backbone resemble Jupiter, and also Venus in some degree: those in the northern line are like Saturn and Jupiter.» By the Kabalists Pisces is associated with the Hebrew letter Qoph and the 18th Tarot Trump "The Moon." [*Robson**, p.57.]

The astrological influences of the constellation Pisces given by Manilius:

"The folk engendered by the two Fishes, the last of the signs, will possess a love of the sea: they will entrust their lives to the deep, will provide ships or gear for ships and everything that the sea requires for activity connected with it. The consequent skills are numberless: so many are the components of even a small ship that there are scarcely enough names for things. There is also the art of navigation, which has reached out to the stars and binds the sea to heaven. The pilot must have sound knowledge of the earth, its rivers and havens, its climate and winds; how on the one hand to ply the mobile helm this way and that, and brake the ship and spread apart the waves, and how on the other to drive the ship by rowing and to feather the lingering blades. The Fishes further impart to their daughter the desire to sweep tranquil waters with dragnets and to display on shores which are their own the captive peoples of the deep, either by hiding the hook within the bait or the guile within the wheel. Naval warfare too is of their gift, battles afloat, and blood-stained waves at sea. The children of this sign are endowed with fertile offspring, a friendly disposition, swiftness of movement, and lives in which everything is ever apt to change. [*Astronomica*, Manilius, 1st century AD, book 4, p.243.] (4)

There are many forces at hand. There are many reasons for this spell and there is a clear goal. Every spell has a clear goal. In this case it is a geographical and spiritual destination combined in the matrix of time and space. Of course ***it*** knows I am coming. How could it not? What is ***it***? Illumination; The evil that binds us all to these fractured perceptions of reality which keep us all together and apart at the same time. The vacuum of words. It is inside of me but I found something else and you can too. It is inside of you as you may have realized already. It (this unnamable "something else" [יהסשה םיהשה] ***{5+6+5+10, 5+6+300+5+10})*** probably gave me the stupid idea to try to deal with it in the first place just so it can have the entertainment of doing me for good. I am the last one as you already know. I am the first one as well. The alpha and the omega. So, as much as I do not want to, I must get my shit together as best as I can. I must pack my bags again and go on a little sojourn. If you are reading this, the spell is almost finished and I am already gone and on my way. I must pack my Ray Bans and as much wool as I can stand so that I don't burn up under the equatorial sun. Wool? Yep. Sounds inverted, no? Wool for the sunshine? It has always been a go to for the undead through-out the ages. We are hunters and the best way to hide is wool. We are wolves. We need to look like sheep so none who are sensitive enough to realize what we are will suspect anything is amiss as we pass among the living. Not only that, but it is quite stylish. Why do you think that worsted wool has been a go to for the Wall Street culture? Isn't it obvious? That shithole in downtown Manhattan is just crawling with undead of every type. Our preferred victims of our hunting games live there too. The people who deserve it. The only ones we still are allowed to kill. Those who live off the blood of others through their filthy capitalist games. Sheep. Ovis Aries.

That is the last place that I need to go. Wall Street I mean. Terrible, nasty little insects. Numbers buzzing all over. Ugly business. Numbers look far better when written out in letters. Example: 23, Twenty Three, םכג, etc. I have other far more important rituals that I must perform without worrying about these trifles but, gag...I am about to use a cliché...the devil is in the details. Forgive me for that. If I am even halfway successful at what I am proposing it will get back to them and their pathetic little burrows between Broadway and South Street. Yes, Broadway and Wall Street Converge at Trinity Church. This is not a joke. Well it sort of is...but perhaps not a very good one. What a better place to concentrate, amass, amalgamate, a conglomeration of putrescence. Show tunes, Stocks, and God all in one terrible place. And, amazingly, people actually go there. If this is not proof of human fascination with their own self destruction then I will sing Bali Hai to a toad on my hands and knees for a penny (Which is, amazingly, not too far from what is actually happening on Broadway). I say this with confidence that I will never have to do this based upon the terms of the original proposition. Wall Street patrons, fearful little villains who act in response to the potential that things may or may not happen. Fear, anger, aggression, hope, surprise, anticipation, trust, envy, joy, despair, grief, determination, confusion, craving, excitement, satisfaction, anxiety, etc...among other emotions are the guiding forces of the world seeing that the world is governed more by economic capital than any other ostensible capital. And we are supposed to be Rational beings with a Capital R? What happens now, as I spit mucus into my coffee cup after a good snort of laughter? They will not be very happy at all. Stock market news live: S&P 500 (five hundred) enters bear market, Dow plunges 10% (ten percent) in biggest one-day percentage drop since 1987 (nineteen eighty seven) **as a result of a virus** (note the clever use of the "Broadway" font followed by the subtle insertion of Times New Roman for all of you geeks who appreciate typography). 3/12/20 (March twelve, two thousand and twenty anno domini, Common Era).

I will worry about that later...or maybe not at all. I must drag my reluctant self back to Africa, again, where all of this mess started in the first place (so terribly long ago). Tanzania to be exact. The mountains of the moon. Norongoro crater and Mount Kilimanjaro to be even more precise. Why these specific places you may ask? That should be obvious too because I indirectly mentioned it in my story about the shaman who discovered the virus but for the sake of clarity I will repeat myself by saying that this is where the whole fucking mess started. I love repeating myself as you have noticed. Not just for the sake of it but because this is a spell. Repetition strengthens any spell. Trance. Mantra. All the same concept.

I must go there to end it all. Sort of like Frodo Baggins and Samwise Gamgee on Mount Doom. Sorry about that. There is truth to every fiction and fiction in every truth. At the beginning I mentioned that this is an epilogue. This is the place where all stories go so this sort of annoyance may arise. All pre-existing spells must be woven in because the words (the spirits from other worlds masquerading as a lie) created them and they must all go back to nothing with this spell. Otherwise they stay in this purgatory of print. The only place that has the proper energy to end this virus is exactly where it was created. The main difference between me and the hobbits is that I am dealing with facts and they were a story. Well this is a story too but it is real. Nosferatu are real. I take back what I just said because Mt. Doom was real too. Hobbits were also real but that is *a different story for a different time.* The clock strikes the present hour (6). Reality is a seriously fucked up thing that is not to be taken lightly. This is why *normal* people – whatever *they* are – have perceptions or so an esteemed Doctor told me once. For them there is only perception, not reality, but each perception seems absolutely real. That may sound like some seriously chaotic shit but if you don't believe that it is chaos that rules the perceivable universe then you are in denial. A common affliction so you are not alone. I don't have any problem accepting this because I am undead. Undead do not suffer the problem of trying to make sense out of everything. Nothing about our condition makes sense at all in a rational manner so we don't get hung up on these issues. We have been trapped on this filthy hell planet for so many aeons that we don't even remember how long we have been here. Most of our human perceptions have gone to the wayside long ago but we have new ones and they are perceptions too. Time and space have become virtually meaningless to us. Time and space are what allows the illusion of perception to seem so real. There is an end that is promised to these *normal* beings. Death. That is only if they are lucky. Most are on the path to undeath. Either way. Then and only then do they actually come face to face with reality that exists independent from perception.

Riddle of the fighting Gods (4).

To be clear; reality cannot be perceived. The perception of an individual prevents the face of reality to ever be experienced. It is sort of like color theory. If you see an apple, you perceive it to be red but in reality it is actually every color but red. Red is the hue that is bouncing off the object and red is what reaches the eye. Red is not in the eye or on the apple but is a function of light. The eye can never see the real color of the apple. *Perception is what you can sense and is explainable, rational.* Reality is what is actually there and it is totally inexplicable, irrational (4).

Remember these definitions of *reality* and ***perception*** because I will refer to them continually throughout this incantation. We undead must suffer alongside most humans with our own unique play on the same issue. We have just been around far longer than any living human can understand. With time and experience it is only natural that we retain much more memory than the average human can and our ***perceptions*** are a bit closer to the chaos that is the not ***perceivable***. We are undead, not dead. We must suffer through the same shattered ***perception*** of *reality* that the living do. We must suffer through *reality* and all of the infinite amounts of perception that come and go. We have watched them live and die in human form so many times. These ephemeral trails of living perception die with the perdition of the individual and are encased in a cinerary. I know this because I have seen it go. I have killed off many a human in my time and I have done it so closely and intimately that I watch it leave their eyes as their body goes limp. The knowledge of this is becoming way too much for me to handle. I suppose that I am unique, even amongst the undead because virtually all of the others in the kult don't seem to be bothered by this knowledge if they even know it at all. Few of them who are not Nosferatu will ever actually kill anyone even though they may want to. If you did not know, there are many different forms of Undead besides Nosferatu of course. I – for one – can't take it anymore. They – all of the other undead – seem to love this chaos, this insight, this darkness. If they had any idea about what I am doing with this spell I would be in serious trouble. In short – I am trying to end it all. Apocalypse is coming. A new age of *reality* and ***perception*** together. Anastomosis. Inosculation. **Sandhayas! Sandhayas! Sandhayas! Calling all downs. Calling all downs to dayne. Array! Surrection. The smog is lofting. The olduman has godden up to litinate the bonnamours. Good morning, have you used Piers' aube? Quake up, dim dusky; wake doom for husky! Guinness is good for you. A hand from the cloud emerges, holding a chart expanded. The sower of seeds of light, lord of risings in the yonder world speaks: Vah! Suvarn Sur! Thou who agnitest! Dah! Be! Svadesia, save and guide us! We Durbalanars thee adjure. Guide us from our house of death through kingdom come to Heliotropolis, city of the sun. A flash. And quickly it comes to pass; life comes to the hearths of the world, the stone in the centre of the druids' circle is touched by the light of dawn. Past now pulls. Dane the Great may tread the path. So, let the cock crow,**

once, twice, thrice. The death bone is pointed and quick quoke, but life wends and the dombs spake (5).

This story, this spell, is going to the source of it all and me along with it. To the secret places in Africa where it all began. Alpha and Omega. All of the undead are eternally imprisoned by the earth. We are walking piles of ash, dust, stone, and water. We have no blood of our own. We must conspire to get our fix in a way that does not draw too much attention. An eternal cycle of dependency. Don't think that you are all that different even if you have the luxury of receiving the gift of death at some unknown point in the future. You are just as addicted to blood and death as I am. I have just been at it for longer than you ever will live, a thousand times longer. Another difference between you and me is the fact that you choose to live off this death. It does not have to be this way for you but the voids of culture have been guiding, herding humanity towards this forever. I have no choice. Who is worse? We undead are eternally attached to the earth and share its fate even though we get our power from the stars. We can travel to the stars in certain forms but these forms are very limited because it is a very long journey. The earth is the source of the arcane dust that creates our body, even in our ethereal form. The relationships of the stars change as one gets further away from the Earth so it becomes hardor and harder to maintain our arcane ability the further out we get. The Earth is our home just as it is for humans. Its destruction is inevitable. You have the luxury of the hope of escape. You can die and return to your star if you were a good little monkey. We are stuck here. The final destruction, the apocalypse, may be far off in human years but for me and my time it is right around the corner. I am condemned no matter what I do. I hope to change that. This spell will change everything. Most undead can see the end coming too but they exist in denial because they are sure that there is not much that they can do about it and many of them are enjoying themselves far too much. They are probably correct in their attitudes but I have something that they do not have. A disease. A virus that I picked up. It is awareness. *Reality* (see above definition). It is an undead virus (all virus are undead) and it is not from this planet even though it governs the earth through illumination and darkness. The others will not admit that they are confined to this spinning rock. They only care about what they must do now just to get more blood to feed upon. It is this sort of power, the power over the living. It is these centuries of existing in this state that can give one of these undead a serious power trip even though they should be able to see *reality* clearly if they got over themselves for a few seconds. They are addicts and that is a pretty hard thing to get out of. Especially if there is not much incentive for doing so. Perhaps there is another reason that they don't care. It can be very dangerous to know too much.

The clear experience of *reality* is the complete unity of light and darkness as one. This is the insane, and inexplicable truth that exists all the time. Nothing is good or bad. It is only ***perceived*** that way. I realize the horrible truth that our knowledge is severely limited. We may feel like we are eternal but we never can actually partake in that *reality*. We are forever limited by the confines of word and number. Word precedes thought and motion. We may be able to cast a spell with the twitch of an eye but we must think it first. Intention and will is magik. We think not and move not without intention. Science and Majik are more or less the same so it is pardonable that rationalists believe that they wield promethean power. Their fault is the fact that they are satisfied with the tiniest crumb of it. These words and numbers are the root of all our majik. Most of the words we Nosferatu use are not English but a few spells include it. Even though you may be reading this in English it is written in a secret language which you cannot see or comprehend. You can touch it. This is the language of intention. There is something else that is outside all of this, some inexplicable thing that drives all this power and it is far beyond our control. Even I never knew exactly what it is but I am beginning to have very strong suspicions. We are simply vectors of this power. Entropy will one day destroy this precious rock that we cling to in the same way that those who are afflicted by the addictions of imperialism cling to the pathetic language of the British Queen in order to explain the inexplicable experience of our fleeting existence. Sand through the fingers falls through the floor.

My life is with the thrill kill kult (1). I must return to Africa. Yes. I have been there once very recently. This is where I got the virus. I must repeat myself because this is a spell, not a narrative. It oscillates and slowly gains power. I apologize if I must repeat myself. I do this so that I stay hidden long enough to get this work finished. I am hidden in the web of these words. This Virus, Spell, etc. All are versions of the undead. Only when these cycles complete can I return to Africa for a third and final time. I was not ready the last time I went. Not even close. The residual energy of the entirety of human history is everywhere there. It is an entirely different majikal environment than anything in Europe and North America. Africa is where it all started. The dependence upon the sign. The addiction to outside forces of communication. This is where it all began. Every plant, every speck of dust, every insect is saturated with the presence of every generation of human that has ever lived and died. Even the grandsons of Abraham left their mark on this continent. So much ancient, residual energy all over. This was far too much for an undead creature like myself to deal with when I was last there. I did not prepare myself properly. I honestly had no idea what I was walking into. How could I? I have been on the North American and all the other continents for far too long. I have been under the influence of this "civilized" environment and it has shaped my perspectives and powers. Burroughs was well aware of this form of power. He realized that North America is not a new world by any stretch of the imagination. There is no such thing as a "new" land. These rocks and sand under New York skyscrapers are just as old as the ones in Africa, only they are far more evil. Despite popular new age misunderstanding, those early indigenous Americans were not a pure or benevolent society. They were not evil either. They were human. There was much war. Much death. Much torture. The residual energy that exists on North America is unique unto itself. It is just cleverly hidden by contemporary illusions of life that are maintained by some of my undead colleagues. Africa is saturated with the energy of humanity that is far less masked. It does not hide the energy of death. This is the exact opposite of my North American home. ***Our lives are with the thrill kill kult (1)***. No one must know about us because they are looking. It is no small wonder why I had such a difficult time in Africa. I brought all my expectations of North American energy there without the knowledge of what I was actually doing. A rookie mistake I admit but I also admit my arrogance. I know now what had happened. I was actually completing the spell that has been buried in *reality* for millennia. I am the alpha and the omega in a temporal sense. It was waiting for me. You are your own alpha and omega and this spell will affect you. We are all god. Are you ready? I doubt it. The end was there from the very moment I left in ancient times and it was waiting for me to come back. It is almost like I was meant to return there, like I had no free will at all. I feel like I am part of a bigger program. One that I never had control over.

When I recently returned there, Tanzania, I accidently stumbled into the places that contained some of the most concentrated human energy that there is on this planet. It reeked of death. I stumbled through these secret places and death, the final word, attached itself to me as birds filled the sky. ***I am now becoming about fed up be going circulating about them new hikler's highways like them namelesssouls, ercked and scorned***

and grizzild all over, till it's rusty October in this bleak forest and was veribally complussed by thinking of the crater of some noted volcano or the Dublin river or the catchalot trouth subsidity as a way out or to isolate I from my multiple Mes on the spits of Lumbage Island or bury myself, clogs, coolcellar and all, deep in my wineupon ponteen unless Morrisey's colt could help me or gander maybe at 49 as it is a tithe fish so it is, this pig's stomach business, and where on dearth or in the miraculous meddle of this expending universe to turn since it came into my hands I am hopeless off course to be doing anything concerning (5).

Death and all of the deceased ancestors of Africa saw me coming. The birds warned them. They knew I was coming and they had been waiting for a long time. Long at least in human terms. Death attached itself to the undead. The elements of reality were complete. The poles became one. North and south were united within me. Castration. Uranus and Gaia. I was not at all prepared. I had rarely ever seen energy fields like the ones I passed through that infected me with this burden. They are rare and most likely nonexistent on my "civilized" continent. There, in North America and other "civilized" places I have Auryn my muse. I have spoken of her once already and I will explain more shortly. But only this much for now; she is an abundance of spiritual voids that I can continually refer to when I need help. This is onc of the reasons that I rarely ever leave civilization. Auryn is with me there. She is the master of the abundant black holes of consumption scattered all over civilization which will suck one in forever if you tread an unwary step. If you do not know her and fall in then... They are everywhere where civilization has taken root and grown to a significant size. They are not in the wilderness at all. They are a result of human nature gone awry. They are a human affliction. Need. Consumption. All of the emotions previously listed and more. Anyone can fall in. They exist inside the unconscious and are physically manifested as invisible voids because humans rely upon the ghostly possession of words. Remember, spells require intention as much as thought and action. No words, no intention. These words are the void.

With closed eyes one can see everything from the position of where they truly belong in the universe. There are many stars that are close to them there. This is the flicker that one can still see. Eyes wide closed are not totally dark. It is the darkness of the true universe above that is seen with closed eyes. Here there are dangerous black holes within the void. These black holes exist not only in the outer universe and the subconscious but are also manifested physically in the collective conscious of civilization. These nebulae of dark energy that lurk around are everywhere in the universe including on this planet. Voids within the void. A double negative like the term "undead" that equate to an arcane hyper-negative and not a mathematical positive. Addiction is a small but common one. There are far deeper recesses of darkness that can suck one in forever. Some call it schizophrenia. Some are inhabited by shape changers like werewolves. Some talk directly to God. There are many forms of these voids but they are all essentially the same. I have known these voids intimately for a very long time. It took many lifetimes of experiment to make myself familiar with them and I needed help to finally figure out how to use them for they were created by internal human majik that I cannot control. I finally discovered their secret and I am the only Nosferatu who has this power. Now I rely on them for assistance whenever I need it.

And Now For Something Not So Completely Different

Who's who and where's here theories of Einstein. That is to say the speech form is mere surrogate while the quality and tality are alternately Harrogate and Arrogate, as the gates may be (4).

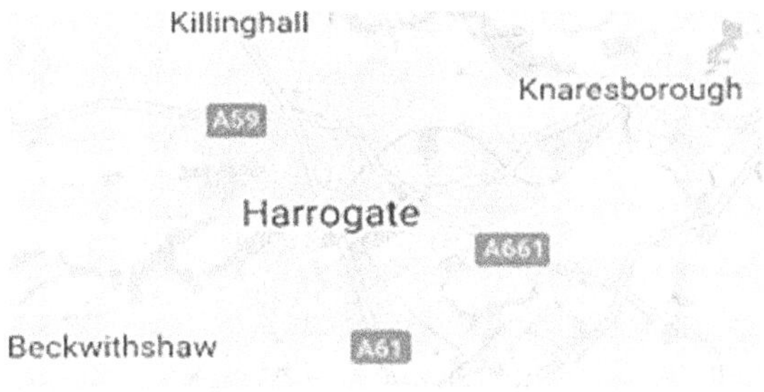

Harrogate

Town in England

Harrogate is a town in North Yorkshire, England, east of the Yorkshire Dales National Park. Its heritage as a fashionable spa resort continues in the Montpellier Quarter with the Royal Pump Room Museum, documenting the importance of local mineral springs. Nearby is the restored, Moorish-style Turkish Baths & Health Spa. To the west, leafy Valley Gardens features the art deco Sun Pavilion.

Weather: 47°F (8°C), Wind W at 7 mph (11 km/h), 81% Humidity

UK Parliament: Harrogate & Knaresborough

Definition of arrogate

arrogated;

arrogating

transitive verb

1a: to claim or seize without justification ***b:*** to make undue claims to having : *ASSUME*

Resume

Going back to the shattered narrative...This is why I devoured the infant and masked myself to undertake a quixotic adventure. It had to be done because I needed to finally come to terms with this system of voids and evil energy that was spread all around civilization. They have existed since I first discovered them when I was a human shaman so long ago in Africa. They have been loose and floating around the universe before I sensed them but each word is a small piece of this dark gravity. They were partly caused by the subconscious of humans so I needed a human to help deal with them. This began when I messed everything up and became undead. The outer magick became mine but the subconscious inner magik was separated from me. It exists in living humans so they are the ones who can hope to understand and control these voids. But I needed the right one. I knew that if I waited and watched long enough I would discover this individual. When I found her, it turned out to be more of an adventure than I expected.

"Those who have passed beyond the Illuminated Void and the relativity of life, experience that which is called Tality. The Tality is the Great Reality of life, free in its movement...It is unpostponable to Self-realize within ourselves that which is called Tality. The Tality is the Great Reality beyond perversity and holiness. The saints can never exist within the womb of the Tality, which is beyond perversity and holiness. There is nothing in the Tality which can be called holy. The Great Reality is the Great Reality, the Tality. The saints and the perverse ones revolve within the great Wheel of Samsara. Therefore, they are very far from the Tality...The Tality is beyond the machinery of relativity, and also beyond the Illuminated Void. The Tality is that which is beyond the body, the affections, and the mind. The Tality is that which is far beyond all dualism." – Samael Aun Weor, The Pistis Sophia Unveiled

The Knight of the Rueful Countenance

I met her for the first time in a park full of tall pine trees by a river. The river was dammed up right next to the park so it created a small narrow pond. All around this pond is a piddling, lilliputian village in upstate New York. It could be a nice place but it is not because the people are no less vile than anywhere else. There is much talk about how nice people are in small towns. This is true, but there are nice people everywhere. It only takes one jerk to disarray a well set table. Forget them. It does not matter how nice or not nice things are. Excelsior. This village is in the center of the Adirondack Park and it is called Saranac Lake. At first, I thought it was odd that the key to these voids which were spread out all over civilization was to be found here, almost the definition of the middle of nowhere. The more I got involved the more it made sense. The rational always tries to explain natural phenomena. Reason attempts to explain chaos. These two separate forces meet at the fringes of culture and society. These fringes are like groping fingers that search for a new hold in the unknown. Pure lies are transferred from the chaos of nature through the voids of words into reason. Everything explained in words is a lie. A word is a void, an undead alien interloper, an entrapped spirit from another world that is parallel to this one. All of these pockets of evil are interconnected and effect everyone, sometimes in very odd ways. There seems to be an abnormally large portion of the population in Saranac Lake that is completely insane in one form or another. It seems like the voids are very active here. These voids, these pockets of evil energy are expanded whenever there is a new form of civilization that takes root and the fringes of society have them as much as the urban areas do. As long as there is a commerce district and a community center you will find them.

People come to places like Saranac Lake to somehow "get away from it all" but they are just going from one place to another into the very same thing. They still want amenities available and a service industry of underpaid peons to cater to them. Even if they go into the woods for some amount of time they never cut their umbilical cord to contemporary civilization. Even if it is in the boondocks, Saranac Lake is still as twisted and bloodthirsty as any other place on the map.

I will use another's words to describe Saranac Lake. He has seen it too and I believe his account is more accurate than anything that I could relate. This person visited many years ago but the place has changed very little since then. ***The buildings seemed to be jumbled every which way without rhyme or reason, as though they had been emptied at random out of a giant sack. There wasn't any recognizable order. And the buildings themselves were crazy; they had "front doors" in their roofs, stairways which were quite inaccessible and ended in the middle of nowhere; towers slanted, balconies dangled vertically, there were doors where one would have expected windows, and floors in the place of walls. Bridges stopped halfway as though the builders had suddenly forgotten what they were doing. There were towers bent like bananas and pyramids standing on their tips. In short, the whole city seemed to have gone mad. They actually did go mad and they made these buildings to house tuberculosis patients so they could breathe better.***

Then Bastian saw the inhabitants – men, women, and children. They were built like ordinary human beings, but dressed as if they had lost the power to distinguish between clothing and objects intended for other purposes. On their heads they wore lampshades, sand pails, soup bowls, wastepaper baskets, or shoe boxes. Their bodies were swathed in towels, carpets, big sheets of wrapping paper, or barrels.

Many were pushing or pulling handcarts with all sorts of junk piled up on them, broken lamps, mattresses, dishes, rags, and knickknacks. Others were carrying enormous bales slung over their shoulders. The farther Bastian went into the town, the thicker became the crowd. But none of the people seemed to know where

*they were going. Several times Bastian saw someone dragging a heavily laden cart in one direction, then after a short time doubling back, and a few minutes later changing direction aga*in. Everybody was feverishly active.

Bastian tried to speak to one of these people. "What's the name of this place?"

The person let go of his cart, straightened up, and scratched his head for a while as though thinking it over. He said "This is Saranac Lake but I don't understand how this is a lake at all because I seem to be on the street." Then he went away, abandoning his cart, which he seemed to have forgotten. But a few minutes later, a woman took hold of the cart and started off with it. Bastian asked if the junk was hers. The woman stood for a while, deep in thought. Then she too went away (4).

I made a breakthrough in my project. Remember, I was looking for the key to the voids while "growing" in the form of the human whom I was impersonating. One sunny summer day in my late "adolescence" I was walking my bicycle through the park with a few of my new friends. I looked over my shoulder and saw another small group of people that I knew who were just coming into the park from the other side of it. Among them was a very tall girl who stood above the rest of her companions. She must have been over six feet tall. I had never seen her before but her stature and mannerism caught my eye instantly. She had long, glimmering dark brown hair and an olive complexion. She walked with built up energy, like coils of a viper, which produced the drama of a living Greek Goddess. Her every move was intentional and was laden with a heavy sensuality. Her clothing moved in a way that looked like it was animated, a part of her body. It was almost like she could feel things and respond to them quicker than lightning. The instant that my eyes touched her jacket she turned her head over her shoulder and looked right back, right into my eyes. I was stunned and didn't move for a second as I returned her gaze. She turned her shoulders with a smile and waved at me before she got back to the conversation that she was having.

I was attending the High School in Saranac Lake. I did not see her for some time after this first encounter and I wondered why. Then, in our band class I saw her again. I was studying trumpet because I wanted to learn more about jazz music and the teacher there was incredible for a High School Band instructor. One day after playing Sousa marches he introduced a new student to the band. It was the same girl that I had seen in the park. She was studying the flute and was assigned a seat right in front of mine. I smiled at her as she approached and took her seat. She quickly smiled and broke the gaze as she turned her back and sat down. We went through what was left of the daily practice and packed up our instruments before going to the next class. I did not make any attempt to talk to her but I knew that I would. This didn't seem to be the time and place for it.

We had mutual friends so I knew that I would end up running into her in a better environment and of course this ended up happening at the very same park that I first saw her. It was the favored place to hang out for the group of people that I was friends with. We were all the "different" kids that were either ignored, harassed, or beat up by the "popular", "athletic" or "smart" kids in the school who behaved curiously like the "redneck" kids who also ignored, harassed, and tried to beat us up. We were a motley, lapidated bunch. We certainly looked very much like the stereotype of what you would imagine. A combination of hippy, punk, and undefined identity was common amongst us. We would go to the church second hand shops and buy shirts and pants for ten cents each from a certifiably crazy old woman who wore a blue trucker baseball cap that said "God is my copilot" in yellow letters in the place where most hats would have been emblazoned with a NY. There were no price tags on anything. You simply grabbed what you wanted and brought the bundle up to her. She would scowl and grimace as she looked at and folded up each piece and say "Ok honey, that will be two dollars and I need some change for the Governor." We always got away with what we thought was really nice stuff and would trade or steal it from each other as we went through bundles sitting in the park afterwards.

We would entertain ourselves for hours sitting next to the river on the grass of the park or in the pavilion that we called "the band shell". A fairly large brown structure that looked like it was based on the design of a classic Adirondack lean-to. Bikes and skateboards would be strewn all over as we created our form of chaos. We invented many games, all of which were totally absurd, to pass the time. One of them we called fire versus knife. One person held a lighter and the other held a knife. The person with the knife tried to put the lighter out with it and the person with the lighter tried to burn the hand of whoever was holding the knife. Whoever accomplished their goal first won the game. There were many other far more complicated games that we came up with but I won't take the time to describe them. There was one thing I knew for sure. I was supposed to be here because this is the sort of energy and process that develops majik in humans. It also develops drug use as well but the two things can be connected. I knew, from all my ancient experience with majik that the girl who I was interested in was very powerful and had quite a bit of potential when it came to majikal ability.

I do not remember exactly what was going on in the park when we first started talking. It was almost like I had known her forever. Our first conversation could have been the continuation of one that had been going on for centuries. ***riverrun, past Eve and Adam's, from swerve of shore to bend of bay... (5)*** I fell into this spell and totally forgot most of the details. It was a very powerful experience. I found out that her name was Auryn.

We became friends instantly but we did not stay very close to each other. Not at first. We were slowly drawn together, closer and closer as time went on. I did not know what was happening because in all my years, nothing like this has ever happened to me. It was very difficult to understand but after a while I realized that I was in love with her.

This certainly compromised my project or was it *the project?* I knew that I had to find the person who would help me with these evil energy fields but I never expected to have to fall in love. How could I introduce her into my world of death and danger and not feel anything about it? That is what I expected. I have been devouring humans for as long as I can remember and I have never felt a twitch of feeling about it. This was a completely unseen development. I did not even know that I could feel this way for someone or anything. I think that this was the very beginning of my transformation that ended up taking me back to Africa. I had lost control and it slowly and insidiously changed me forever.

I realized that she loved me too, perhaps even more than I loved her. It was not easy for me at all. We ended up spending all our time together. It was impossible to separate us. It turned out that I did not have to take her into my dark world at all. She was already there. The closer I got to her the more she revealed but it was only tiny pieces at a time. I think that she felt the same way that I did. She didn't know about what I really was and she saw me through the eyes of love so she didn't want to totally take me into her dark world. I may be incorrect about this assumption. Nevertheless, she was evolving her own arcane ability and doing it very quickly. I should not have been surprised by this but I was blinded by my concern for her. She was the one that I had been waiting for all these years. Of course she would have to be very powerful in order to do what I knew we were to do.

I didn't have the whole picture completed before it started. I knew what I wanted to do and how to go about it but I had no idea how it would play out once the doors were opened. It was like any adventure, any experiment. I knew that the risks were very high because we were dealing with infinite, universal power but I had to know. I had to be able to understand and use these voids that I created but could not fathom. It turned out that she wanted it even more than I did. Once I showed her one of the voids she never forgot and it became a mission for her as well. She was in a battle with nothing. A battle to control an ever growing Nothing that was attached to the subconscious of human society. The voids of desire, lust, need, desperation, addiction all the causes of evil and terror. The constant force that drove the structures of the human world to its current state of capitalist chaos. A nothing that will never be sedated, that always needs more. There are spiritual consequences of this activity and spiritual manifestations of it. The true position of the individual human in the cosmos – their inner star – can be devoured by a black hole. The place that they look from with closed eyes, the place that they always are that is beyond perception, their home in the stars once they leave the planet, can all be sucked away and turn into nothing. I know this because it has happened to me. I do not experience this inner darkness when I close my eyes. I see red. Illumination. Fire and blood, not darkness.

I allowed her to do what she did without interference. I played ignorant. I played the role of the bumbling fool who accidently found some really cool girl that was into some intense stuff that I accidentally got into too. I was Don Quixote and Sancho Panza all in one. I let her think that it was her show the whole time because it kind of was. Whenever I hinted at knowing anything it would always be in the form of a question to her. Her response was to always give me a glistening look and lovingly not explain anything but hint at everything.

I have already written about how we went about dealing with these voids in other places so I won't go into it in too much detail. ***It is another story for another time.*** I will relate the end of that story because I never said what happened to her, what happened to us. This entire spell is an epilogue. I did not need to relate any of this at the time because it was far too early and much has happened since. I now have a use for revealing the ending.

She became more and more powerful and ended up mastering everything that there was to master about these phenomena with only a tiny amount of my help. She virtually did it on her own. She already knew about the voids and she showed me much that I did not know. ***It was an All-in-One and One-in-All of limitless being and self – not merely a thing of one Space-Time continuum, but allied to the ultimate animating essence of existence's whole unbounded sweep – the last, utter sweep which has no confines and which outreaches fancy and mathematics alike. It was perhaps that which certain secret cults of earth have whispered of as YOG-SOTHOTH, and which has been a deity under other names; that which the crustaceans of Yuggoth worship as the Beyond-One, and which the vaporous brains of the spiral nebulae know by an untranslatable Sign... Yog-Sothoth knows the gate. Yog-Sothoth is the gate. Yog-Sothoth is the key and guardian of the gate. Past, present, future, all are one in Yog-Sothoth. He knows where the Old Ones broke through of old, and where They shall break through again. He knows where They have trod earth's fields, and where They still tread them, and why no one can behold Them as They tread (14).***

In her early experiments she had many revelations through her conversations with a figure that she insisted was with us but whom I could not see. She would not allow me in on these discussions. She told me about this man though. ***'Umr at-Tawil,*** ليوطلا رمع ***(The [Most Ancient and] Prolonged of Life) he presides over the timeless halls beyond the Gate of the Silver Key and the strange, near-omnipotent Ancient Ones that dwell there. He is described as the silhouette of a man behind a strange, shimmering veil. He is one of very few apparently***

benign Great Old Ones who does not cause insanity in those who view him (14). This was only one of his forms. She told me what she could of what she believed the true form of the void was and about the silver key. She did not tell me everything though. She was slowly unraveling all of this in all her work with the man behind the veil. This hidden form is unspeakable...***great globes of light massing toward the opening, and not alone these, but the breaking apart of the nearest globes, and the protoplasmic flesh that flowed blackly outward to join together and form that eldritch, hideous horror from outer space, that spawn of the blankness of primal time, that tentacled amorphous monster which was the lurker at the threshold, whose mask was as a congeries of iridescent globes...(14).***

Of course there are consequences to these sorts of experiments. One cannot deal with universal power and not be affected by it. Especially if they are human like she was. There were many consequences for everyone everywhere once she first was able to control of these voids. Of course it was September when it happened. The month of Virgo. She had built herself up to a maximum pinnacle of power that was specifically designed for her preplanned reason for existence. She knew that it was time to cast her incantation. I will try to describe how she cast this spell. You could not do what she did even if you knew how, even if you knew the words by heart. I could never do it in all my years of existence. Nonc have the sensuality that she was born with. Ever. When she was executing this incantation she had the contrapposto of Helen of Troy and the tongue of Sappho. She was at the height of her power. No one can caress words properly and repeat what she accomplished. When she spoke she used her entire body in a sublime form of higher communication. Her feet levitated, her body gently rolled like clouds through the blue summer sky, her arms and hands became exotic symbols. All of this is effortless for her. When the words come out of her mouth they were spoken with a thousand voices. One for each entrapped soul in each word. One perfect voice for each emotion. She is to become the promised master of all of them. The master of the void. The keeper of the Silver Key. Woe to her enemies. Those she loves have experienced no greater passion. Each word she spoke was savored, and licked as it passes through her pursed lips with a kiss. All lies. She was the one who came to shake things up. These were the words that she emanated, like it was her sole reason for existence:

Nothung! Nothung! So nenn' ich dich Schwert! Nothung! Nothung! Neidlicher stahl! Zeig' deiner Schärfe schneidenden Zahn: herus aus der Scheide zu mir!

Nothung! Nothung! Neidliches Schwert! Was mußtest du zerspringen? Zu Spreu nun schuf ich die schrfe Pracht, im Tigel brat' ich die spähne! Hoho! Hoho! Hoheia! Hoheia! Hoho! Blase, Balg, blasé die Gluth! Wild im Walde wuchs ein baum, den hab' ich im Forst gefällt: die braune Esche brannt' ich zur Kohol', auf dem Herd nun liegt sie gehäuft! Hoho! Hoho! Hoheia! Hoheia! Hoho! Blase, Balg, blasé die Gluth! Des Baumes Kohle, wie brennt sie kühn, wie glüht sie hell und hehr! In springenden Funken sprühet sie auf: hoheia! Hoho! Hoheia! Zerschmilzt mir des Stahles Spreu. Hoho! Hoho! Hoheia! Hoheia! Hoho! Blase, Balg, Blasé die Gluth! Nothung! Nothung! Neidliches Schwert! Nun schmolz deines Stahles Spreu: im eig'nen Schweiße schwimm'st du nun bald schwing' ich dich als mein Schwert! In das Wasser floß ein Feuerfluß grimmiger Zorn zischt ihm da auf. Wie sehrend er floß in des Wassers Fluth fließ er nicht mehr; starr ward er und steif, herrisch der harte Stahl: Heiß Blut doch fließt ihm bald! Nun schwitze noch einmal, daß ich dich schweiße, Nothung, Neidliches Schwert! Hoho! Hoho! Hoheia! Schmeide, mein Hammer, ein hartes Schwert! Hoho! Haheia! Hoho! Haheia! Einst färbte Blut dein falbes Blau; sein rothes Rieseln röthete dich: kalt lachtest du da, das warme lecktest du kühl! Heiaho! Haha! Haheiaha! Nun hat die Gluth dich roth geglüht; deine weiche Härte dem Hammer weicht: zprnig sprüh'st du mir Funken, daß ich dich spröden gezähmt! Heiaho! Heiaho! Heiaho! Ho! Ho! Hahei! Schmiede, mein Hammer, ein hartes Schwert! Hoho! Hahei! Hoho! Hahei! Der frohen

Funken wie freu' ich mich! Es ziert den Kühnen des Zornes Kraft: lustig lach'st du mich an, stellst du auch grimm dich und gram! Heiaho! Heiaho! Heiaho! Ho! Ho! Heiah! Durch Gluth und Hammer glückt' es mir; mit starken Schlägen streckt' ich dich: nun schwinde die rothe Scham; werde kalt und hart wie du kannst! Heiaho! Heiaho! Heiaho! Ho! Ho! Heiah! Nothung! Nothung! Neidliches Schwert! Jetzt haftest du wieder im Heft. War'st du entzwei, ich zwang sich zu ganz kein Schlag soll nun dich mehr Dem Sterbenden Vater zersprang der Stahl, der lebende Sohn schuf ihn neu: nun lacht ihm seine heller Schein, seine Schärfe schneidet ihm hart.

Nothung! Nothung! Neidliches Schwert! Zum Leben weckt' ich dich wieder. Todt lag'st du in Trümmern dort, jetzt leuchtest du trotzig und hehr. Zeig den Schächern nun deinen schein! Schlage den Falschen, fälle den Schelm (7)!

Primum opifex, altus prostator, ad terram viviparum et cunctipotentem sine ullo pudore nec venia, suscepto pluviali atque discinctis perizomatis, natibus nudis uti nati fuissent, sese adpropinquans, flens et gemens, in manum suam evacuavit, postea, animale nigro exonerates, classicum pulsans, stercus proprium, quod appellavit deiectiones suas, in vas olim honorabile tristitiae posuit, eodem sub invocation fratrorum geminorum Medari et Godardi laete ac melliflue minxit, psalmum qui incipit: Lingua mea calamus scribae velociter scribentis: magna voce cantitans demum ex stercore turpi cum divi Orionis iucunditate mixto, cocto, frigorique exposito, encaustum sibi fecit indelible...

..."Y'AI'NG'NGAH
YOG-SOTHOTH
H'EE-L'GEB
F'AI THRODOG
UAAAH"

We were not in Saranac Lake at the time. We had moved on by this point to study the voids in other places. Buffalo, NY to be precise. I was pretending to distract myself with other studies and let her be because we got to the point where there was nothing left for me to do but wait.

The performance described above was done inside the voids themselves. She tracked me down while I was wandering about, manifested these voids and we both fell in. This is where I witnessed the performance of the spell. This is the reason why no one else could do it even if they knew how. It was September of 2001 when she performed these words. The month of Virgo. Planes fell out of the sky. Buildings fell to the ground. Governments went to war. Hurricanes ravaged cities. The entire world was affected and this should not have been surprising to me. It wasn't. I knew that would happen. Well not that exactly but I knew that something like that would happen. No one else knew what was going on and they had their investigations and rational explanations and conspiracy theories but no one really knew.

It was Auryn of course. She took hold of all the evil voids that were stretched out all over civilization and all civilization was affected with a great amount of force. It was a revolution of sorts. A one-person revolution and the price was paid for it. I lost her. Well that isn't totally correct but I lost a big part of her. She did too. She went into the voids and never returned. She became them. She transformed them. There was some residue of her left in this world for a few days after it happened. Enough to finish a few things. Even that drifted away. She was everywhere now. She influenced many stories and many adventures wherever any civilization lives. There are more worlds than this one. Many more. A virtually infinite amount more.

When she first took control, many worlds beyond the Earth were affected. She did not account for this and was captured for a while. She was imprisoned in an amulet in a different world for some time but that story has come and gone as well. She has returned to her voids and is in complete control but her amulet still exists as a representation of the portals; two serpents devouring each-others tail. Some of these voids are still evil but not all of them. They still lurk in the cosmos behind the eyes of all humans as well as they exist in the outer world, but if the right ones are accessed there is not always a black hole of nothing to burn one away in fire and blood. One may fall into another fantastic world with the help of Auryn.

She no longer is still here in her original human form. It was a love that was lost. The only love I have ever known but it has been regained in a different form. She is still with me but only now it is far different. It may be better this way because we accomplished what we set out to do. We both can use the voids with impunity in our own way. I think that she may have known what I was the whole time. Now I can be with her almost anyplace I go. Almost...

I am becoming human again somehow. My heart has been awoken by Auryn. Other complications have developed since. I don't know if I am casting a spell or if it has been casting me this entire time. I must relate the story behind the dilemma. I became infected with something the last time I went to Africa. The very same virus which I unleashed aeons ago which caused my separation from life and humanity. It was waiting for me and it has evolved significantly since its creation. The infection is part of my transformation back to life but it alone is not enough. I must finish the process on my own. I am finally going to die because my heart has slowly been awakening. I will become human once more and finally die. Only a Nosferatu can bring the outer spells and only a human can conquer the void like Auryn did. If I do everything correctly I will be both dead and undead for a moment and be able to accomplish all of this before my demise. I will finally die. The rest of the undead may too. A work in progress...

A separation then occurs. A cleavage takes place, dividing the natural unity of Mercury and Sulphur, soul and spirit, from their vehicle, the Salt. This earth, or Salt, remains fixed within the physical body "like a dead, black, and dreggy earth. Its life departed, the subtle sheath turns to putrefaction and decay. But even this dreg is of untold value. Nothing in the alchemical art is discarded for "Nature teaches us" us assert the Chaldean Oracles, "and the Oracles also affirm that even the evil germs of matter may alike be made useful and good". In her Memorabilia Mrs. Atwood remarks that "the principle of body is preserved in what they call the ashes, or Caput Mortem, and that, one principle being saved, the whole life is restored from it...Latent within the blackness of the ashes is life – interatomic life, which by no means can be snuffed out, and which sooner or later asserts itself, communicating movement and life to the mass (15).

Of course I can't tell anyone about my plans yet. If you are reading this it is already too late and I am already on my way. I have left copies of this spell in various places so that they will be opened at the right time far after I am gone. I have mentioned the possessed ghostwriter who is scrawling with pens on pads in a mental institution. Each word I think he thinks too. Each word I write he writes too. Each correction and edit I include he does at the same time. I have prepared myself in silence and away from the curious looks of everyone that may suspect what I am up to. The undead are a very curious lot. They must be by nature. Even though none of them know exactly what I am up to, the more sensitive ones certainly know that something is happening. These are the ones who are hunting me. They are drawn to this spell...

GNOSIS OF PRECREATE DETERMINATION. AGNOSIS OF POSTCREATE DETERNMINISM. The nature of the demiurgic determination that launched the universe on its thenceforth predestined course may be known, at least to the angels; but the accidents of history that are to determine the precise circumstances through which Inevitable Destiny is to become actualized, no one, not even the Creator himself, can wholly know! Having treated of the transcen-

dental, intelligible problem the author now invites us to consider the countryside where the results of the world-engendering union are about to be made evident (4).

I am ready to die. More importantly I am ready to live for the short amount of time that it will last. I must prepare myself mentally, physically, and majikly. I am burning with names and chants, a millennia of them. Kamazotz the Death Bat, Ix-Taub the Goddess of Ropes and Snares, Anubis the Weigher of Souls, Simon Peter the Rock of the Inverted Crucifixion, Jah, the Unspeakable Name. Iblees the Light Bringer also known as Lucifer, Betelgeuse the Exploding, Self-Destructive Lord of Orion, Yog-Sothoth the Void of Auryn, The Poodle In The Street – The Whisperer of Faust, Ronald Regan – the Atrophied Heart and the Seventh Son of Caligula. ***What clashes here of wills gen wonts, ostrygods gaggin fishy-gods! Brekkek Kekkek kekkek Kekkek! Koax Koax Koax! Ualu Ualu Ualu (5)!*** A chant over golden quartz to entrap all of the planetary evil for twenty four hours. Reclining springs and cushions to entrap the soul to the body. Words and numbers to shackle the mind to the earth. Knife and blood to halt the rivers and freeze the oceans. The fall: 🏳✋✞✡❄☼☜⌖✈✌💧👎☞☝👆☺😐☹💻✂✍☢💾💣☠👌✞👍✠☪ ***(bababadalgharaghghtakamminarronnkonnbronntonnerronntuonnthunntrovarrhounawnskawntoohoohoordenedthurnuk!) of a once wasllstrait oldparr is retaled early in bed and later on life down through all Christian minstrelsy (5).*** All is interconnected. A swift slash to the horizon of night bleeds out red and pink light to herald the coming of the next day of torture. A swift slash to the event horizon of the void touches the energy fields across all of the worlds. A swift slash to the body ends desire. A small dark bird suddenly fell from the sky and landed at my feet. It hit the ground dead but pecked out a word. Eskimo and Unalakleet see the same red line. The horizon bleeds after months of total darkness. Everything is ready. Nigredo, Rubedo, Albedo. ***Lapis***

***in Vin. The androgynous philosopher's stone** is tripped over upon the way. The Golden Treatise of Hermes Trismegistus. Section First. 10. Know Ye, therefore, Enquirers into the rumor, the Children of Wisdom, that the vulture standing on the mountain crieth out with a loud voice., I am the White of the Black, and the Red of the White, an the Citrine of the Red; and I speak the very truth. Section Seventh (8). For the Work begins from the vegetable, next from the animal, as in the egg of the hen, in which is the great support; and our earth is gold, of all which we make seriacum, which is the fermentet Ixir (15).* The earth was designed by its creator with the entire universe in mind. Close your eyes again and gaze upon the infinite darkness. The body itself contains the entire universe within it and the earth contains billions of bodies. I am not attempting to imply any medievalism about the importance of the earth in relation to the universe. Quite the contrary. Even though I did live through the transformation of The Roman Empire into the Christian one I see no reason to keep my mind there. That being said, there is some importance to the human perspective in relation to the universe. There may be, and probably are, countless races of intelligent beings across the universe. Each is the center of their own perceptions and life is the connection to higher energies within. Life is special, not any place. Earth may not be the center of universal creation but it very well may be a shining example of destruction. There is an enormous difference between the residents of Earth and the universal norm of all the species on all the other planets. The inhabitants of Earth are special in the universe. Rarely does an intelligent species act so fucking stupid virtually all the time. Rarely does a living species cohabitate on their home planet with a measurable population of undead to the degree that they reflect undead habits even while living.

I would like to take a minute to break the bubble of those who still believe that alien super-beings somehow influenced the structure and philosophy of ancient human culture. Intelligent aliens are way too smart for that. They have been to earth and studied us on a rare occasion but they tend to run back to their space vessels quickly upon realizing what humans are capable of. The last thing that they want is first contact with humanity. Humanity will most certainly kill them or try their hardest to do so. To all the art history flunkies who still insist that aliens had something to do with ancient art and architecture and believe there is no evidence to the contrary, I invite them to actually study the art history that they are so obsessed with yet so inept at understanding. Humans are capable of putting a few big stones together and it is not that amazing. If they really need a supernatural or preternatural reason to explain their misunderstanding of basic building techniques I will ease their mind a little and remind them that we, undead blood addicts have been working alongside of humanity since the beginning and we are pretty damn powerful when we apply ourselves.

Pitfalls worth mention. Ix-Taub. The Goddess of Ropes and Snares:

What happens on the Earth changes what happens everywhere else and what happens everywhere else effects what happens on Earth. Even the slightest shift of gravitational force can send shockwaves out into space. We have altered the gravitational spinning of our planet simply by taking material from one side of the earth and piling it up elsewhere. Manhattan Island is a good example. Do you think that adding that much material to one small place does not at all effect the gravity of the planet itself? Of course it does. It disrupts the balance of the Earth's rotations. I could actually feel the shift happen as more and more buildings piled up there.

Some make love to their lawn, some fuck it.

There is no end in sight. Everything is masked and as a result I can operate with impunity. At least on the playing field of this sad empty page. No one will be able to sense what I am actually doing until I am done. This explanation, this spell is only the beginning of my work. Nothing worth doing can be accomplished without meticulous preparation. Even the banalities are an essential part of the spell. 0101 0101 0101 0101. Sixteen digit magnetic numbers flash across time and space through metallic and fiber optic cables to secure a seat, a bed and four walls that meet at right angles with a roof structure. Don't stare at these angles for too long because Yog-Sothoth will come out and play. I assure you that he plays rough. All forms of architecture possess spirits just the same as most bottles do***. Coca-Cola is life! Coca-Cola is life! We! Want! Coke! Oh! Yeah (16)!*** Blood may be forbidden as a beverage but the Masai of Tanzania and beyond tap a goat's vein in the same way a frat boy taps a keg. Every anatomical structure is architecture. Spirits are in the blood as well. Not only the spirits of an individual but those of all his ancestors. Leviticus seventeen prohibits the eating of blood.

...Magnale Magnum, as Eliphas Levi much later on, in the nineteenth century, spoke of it as the Astral LIght. Helmont conceived of it, not as a corporeal thing, but as an ethereal, pure, vital spirit or essence. It penetrates all bodies, and in man has its seat in the blood, where it exists as a peculiar energy, enabling him by the force of will and the duality of magnetism, which he claims is composed of a vital principle and a "will principle". The former exists "in the flesh and blood of man" the latter belongs to the soul and the consciousness (15).

Nosferatu have conscious magik (vital principal) derived from the stars and the blood. Humans have a "will principal" or internal magik of consciousness.

The secret of avoiding these influences is all in the preparation. Everything is in the intention. Survival itself depends upon these preparatory rituals. The undead have been studying humans for as long as they departed paths. The undead were alive once even if they have little memory of it. We went into the darkness and they went into the light. They never questioned where the light came from. ***Of rune or some blazing star (93).*** Illumination has many faces, one more beautiful than the next but each is deception and illusion. Moths to the flame do not become dragonflies once they burn. They turn to ash just like me. From the point of separation we undead have been the other side of the same coin. Living or not, existence remains and it is, still shattered by the illusions of perception that stream forth from the wellspring of light. Each star contributes but one burns through them all, at least for the duration of a day. Forever together, forever apart.

I know what I did wrong when I recently visited Africa, contracted the virus, and tried to climb its great mountain. I forgot what my place was in the bigger scheme of things. It had been so long since I had been there and I took many things for granted. More accurately stated: I never knew what my place was. I also did not totally understand the place that I was going. I did not prepare myself properly. I was wide open to any form of attack and attacked I was. I forgot that I was different than the humans that come and go. Different on a cellular level, on a genetic level, on the level of what I can perceive. I also forgot that I was different from the rest of the Nosferatu as well.

Foreshadowing

Whatsoever the man cherished during his life, and to whatsoever conception of his Angel he aspired, so will the outcome of the mystical marriage be. According to his love. So will be the offspring.

Each student, as he ascents or enters into the mystic Mount Abiegnus of the Rosicrucians, will see before him, stretching forward on the far horizon of the holy land of promise, just that panorama which existed potentially within him before the Vision gave it birth. For the Mount is a symbol for that peak of soul when, gone inward into itself, it draws nigh to its divine root. Then memory and imagination are penetrated and inspired with the supreme radiance of another and superior nature (17).

Flashback

The wilderness of Africa presented a different truth, for truth as one can understand it is only ***perceived*** and never known in this world. It shifts and mutates like a pathogen adapting to inoculation. There, amidst the plains of the Serengeti I forgot the fact that I was surrounded by an infinity of blood and death, so much struggle thrashing kaleidoscopically all around me. I was certain I would encounter one of Auryn's protective voids that I depended upon which were scattered around the places I was used to. There was nothing here save animal death. There were no voids of human evil because civilization in the contemporary sense does not exist there in the same way. Very little makes sense when in the wilderness of Africa. At least where I was. There was little logic to any action. The simplest thing seemed so complicated and the most complicated things were very simple. I was baffled. This is normal for people but truly exaggerated here. The normal presence of the voids that are around any other commerce district was not here for commerce and the economy was warped to an incomprehensible point that it is amazing that anything functions within the context of the greater capitalist world. The voids could never take hold here in this environment. In order to buy a bottle of water I saw the humans wait in three queues. One to get the bottle and a ticket. Then wait in the next queue to pass the ticket and get a receipt. Then another queue to pass the receipt to the cashier and finally pay for the bottle. It cost thousands of dollars to climb a mountain but after I spent seven days in a hospital here (which I will explain later) it only cost two hundred dollars. I went to a place where Auryn could not help me.

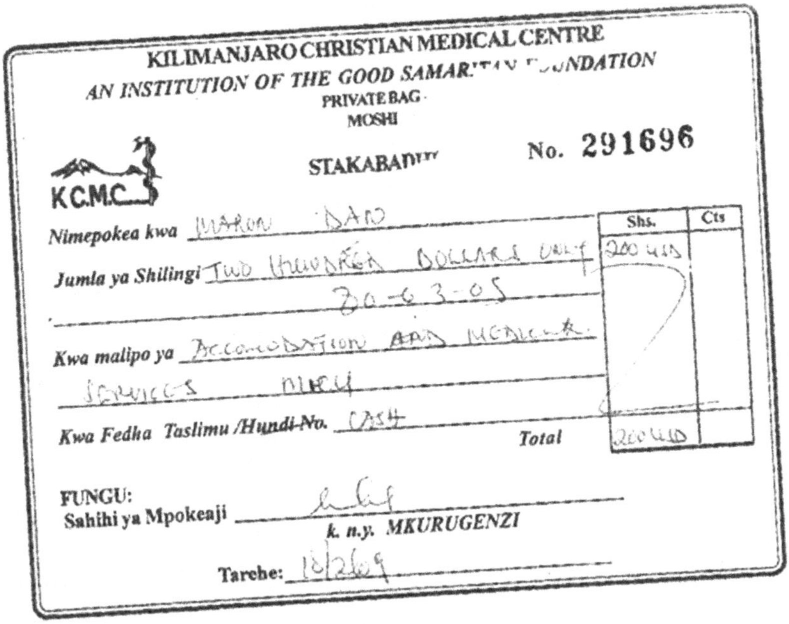

KILIMANJARO CHRISTIAN MEDICAL CENTRE
AN INSTITUTION OF THE GOOD SAMAR... ...NDATION
PRIVATE BAG
MOSHI

KCMC

STAKABAD...

No. 291696

Nimepokea kwa MARON DAN

Jumla ya Shilingi TWO THOUSAND DOLLARS ONLY

30-6-3-05

Kwa malipo ya ACCOMODATION AND MEDICAL SERVICES

Kwa Fedha Taslimu /Hundi-No. CASH

Shs.	Cts
200 USD	
Total 200 USD	

FUNGU:
Sahihi ya Mpokeaji
k. n.y. MKURUGENZI

Tarehe:

There are many urban and rural areas of civilization in Africa but they are somehow different from the ones in North America like Saranac Lake. I did not go to the big places like Cairo, Lagos, Kinshasa, Dar es Saalam, etc. I would almost be certain that Auryn was there as well. I could still feel her on the Serengeti but I could not find her anywhere that I was. The voids that she conquered were created here just like Nosferatu. It happened at the same time. I had avoided this place ever since I left so long ago and I never returned until recently. I suspect that Auryn and the voids left this place and never came back as well.

I arrived at the small Kilimanjaro Airport and was driven to the town of Moshi. For some reason she was not here. There was a much older and much more confusing energy in these streets and commerce districts. I am certain that what was happening was some sort of spell that did not allow for these voids to take hold. It seemed like people were suffering and dying all over but everyone was so goddamn happy. It was absurd to my western sensibilities that were so used to unhappy people who had too much to lose. These people seemed to enjoy every moment in life no matter how miserable it could be. I suspect that the abundance of this form of energy in such a small place created a unique vacuum where there were no voids. A voidless void. I wish I had more time to study this for I still have many questions but I have a different project at hand and bigger questions to answer. It was apparent that Auryn was not *everywhere* even though I expected her to be.

On the second day I was there I left the small village in an oversized Jeep-like contraption that has a pointless name and an equally pointless logo emblazoned all over it. It was packed full of tourists who were oblivious to my presence and we were driven into the wilderness. We went by lions asleep in trees and giraffes grazing upon leaves. Like most cats that I know I suspect that the lions only chose certain trees to doze in unless they had developed a new strategy for attacking grazing giraffes. The branches were dragged out in lazy horizontal directions by the power of the sun as if this golden astral emperor of pagans crafted an intentional footstool for the languid King of beasts. ***The rockets' red glare, the bombs bursting in air.*** Light violently slashes through the darkness and gives form to every manifestation of animal need. There were no dark empty places for me to hide in anywhere that I could sense. The only thing I could feel was the overwhelming presence of the continents dead ancestors. Legions of ghosts. Ghosts in the air. Ghosts in the trees and grasses. Ghosts in the animals. Ghosts in the rocks and soil. Ghosts in the water. Nothing was untouched. There was a silent word everywhere, hidden from sight yet irrefutably present.

Ullhodturdenweirmudgaardgringnirurdrmolnirfenrirlukkilokki baugimandodrrerinsurtkrinmgernrackibarokar! Thor's for you!

The hundred letter name again, last word of perfect language. But you could come near it, we suppose, strong Shaun O', we foresupposed. How (5)?

☺😐☹

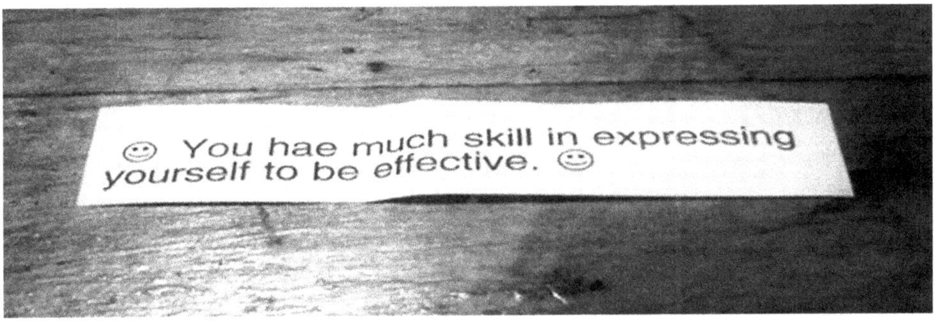

As we drove down a road that separated the thickets of acacia and baobab we passed by giant grey herbivores with giant ears. They had long curved teeth like my own and were also trying to escape the sun by hiding under the canopies of trees that were only slightly larger than them. After some time of pounding the dust of the road with the tires of our strange vehicle we approached the outside foot of a giant crater. I could see the rise of it above the trees that surrounded the road. If I could see it from above it would appear as a perfect circle of raised earth thousands of feet above the sea. The high edges of its crater rim peers over the endless fields of destruction and glory inside its confines and outside of it at the same time.

This upper rim towered above everything below. This was the first time I had been here since ancient times. The place was designed by nature to amplify the eternal blood chant that holds the irrational secret of existence. Life and Death as Unity. Undeath. I had been here once before so very long ago. Here I would soon be attacked by the infection that causes my current extraordinary terminal condition. The key to unlocking *reality* that is hidden in the earth. There were similar structures in North America but they are artificial and had the opposite effect. They hold the key to keeping ***perception*** locked in place. The key to the continuation of pointless human warfare and destruction. Temples to the goddess Nike who lives on and on in western culture and is so shrewd that she has created an entire religion of people – one of the largest and most successful that the world has ever seen – who don't even know that they are enthusiastically worshipping her. ***Old mother Regan and her crew, she took away from me and you (18)*** to give us stadia of pointless endeavors to argue about. Places where the supposed representatives from one city can do battle with another in inane conflict which reinforces the worship of the goddess of victory so that when one nation actually does go into tantrums of bloody battle with another the population is prepared to redirect the very same imbecilic chant. Withered Bushes sprout wheelchairs from Texan architecture. They no longer feel anything from the waist down so they can be rolled right next to the campfire. Artificial bowls and domes designed for large populations to scream and chant dark violent rituals that are assisted by the presentation of local symbols and colors. Flayed, stitched, and inflated pigskins – murdered porcine remains – gain new life in a new form. Undead and human alike partake in the eternal evil. Victory here is death of wit along with the reinforcement of individual ***perception***. The eternal blood chant that is passed down through the generations from the eternal city. *Rome, the harlot*, concentrated this ancient rite that it wrested from the ruins of Babylon, Assyria, Egypt, Thrace, and Macedonia, and every other imperial force that preceded it. On our North American Continent of commercial worship and purgatory we have brought forth the strongest chant of blood and loss ever seen on this planet of rotating, sun-bleached dolor. The spells of perception are hidden within, buried under more and more confusion as time goes on. *Reality* is totally unapproachable under these conditions.

Like the coliseum, the enormous circular volcanic crater walls rise out of the ground sharply and fall back into the inner plane in the same dramatic manner as they rose. Every form of concentrated energy that the Earth has to offer go into the making of these forms whether they are made by the earth or by man. They all contain the same thing, the salt of the earth; steel, glass, plastic, fire, turf, wood, ash, magma, flesh, bone, fur, and blood. All work together in fields of struggle to make rings of diamond, silver, and gold. The alchemy that is buried in nature exists here. Within this crater the transformation of the body to the spirit happens free of ***perceived*** interpretations and free of propaganda. None see the panther drag the deer in the tree. The irrational union of life and death are laid bare and all this energy wafts up the sides of this giant bowl to be collected at the highest summits that surround it. The goddess Nike is not here to consume this glory for her own inane needs for she is far too busy having her way with civilization. She is not here in the wilderness. Something else is. The voids and the lies are not here for me.

As we approached the giant crater, I could see the top of the high walls as they rose above the brush that surrounded us. Over and over the same thing is said. The repetition strengthens the spell. Each word is meaningless on its own. A completely irrational construction, an alien interloper from a different world. An attempt to repeat the original irrational word that started everything. An attempt to express *reality* in its pure irrational form. Each letter the same desperate expression of circular reasoning. When strung together with intention they are imprisoned. Lies. Vertical and horizontal bars of the most effective cage ever created. An expression of ***perception*** that ends up hiding the *reality* they strive for. Observe and persevere. See through these black bars.

As I stared at the crater rim from below I had no idea of the importance of what I was actually doing or where I was going. I should have been more aware. I should have realized that the lack of voids here had to be occupied by some other form of power. I don't know why my guard was down as I approached the crater. I was awestruck by the chain of thoughts that it set off. An excuse but not a reason and too little too late. Perhaps I was lulled by the spell that held this land together. The spell that created humanity in the first place. The original irrational word still present in every rock and cell everywhere. No human games of buggery and strife here to hold the dark voids in place. No concentrated shadows of evil energy to mask all of the dark secrets of industry and government that are so necessary to make post-industrial environments work. No concentrated pockets of evil that were spread about in a way that I was so used to relying upon. I was certain I would find at least one but there was nothing. Nothing. There was a different energy everywhere around this place. I was slowly yet totally disarmed before I even began my climb up the walls of the crater that is called Ngorongoro. It was *The Word* that dominated this place. There was no room available for Auryn to cast her influence, no room for lesser words. It was impossible for any hint of these voids to ever manifest. It was the very birthplace of humanity and the birthplace of each word. Humanity and their words ran away and never came back to take root but the original word was everywhere.

From this place, this ancient volcano, erupted an explosion of promethean fire that expanded outward to eventually touch every remote summit, island, and glacier across the globe. Evidence of rational words strung together have violated every corner of the world. ***No stone has been unturned and every image is leased and mortgaged (13).*** *Pictures* *within pictures.* We undead grew out of this bloodline very quickly after it was conceived and nurtured within the protective walls of this crater. There are none left from this time who exist today. This is the reason I visited this crater in the first place. I had the idea that I wanted to go back to where it all started. Where I started so long ago. I needed to conquer the demons in my memory. I do not know why else I had this idea. It just came to me and it seemed innocent at the time but it was placed in my head for a reason out of my control. Just a little trip to go somewhere I have not been in a long time. No big deal right? The human I once was, was born here amongst one of the early tribes in the area. Nosferatu, the undead, and the spirits of all the ancient human ancestors were all conceived here right alongside of the earliest humans. Why should I not want to go there, especially since it was such a long time ago? I have avoided it because I had intentionally blocked out all my memories that were attached to this place.

Humanity has countless tales of old which may or may not be embellished. It is hard to say. Truth is indeed much stranger than fiction. Fiction – in fact – does not exist. Tales of blood and heroism. Tales of death and survival. ***While soft the wind blew down the vale and shook the golden barley. Blood for blood without remorse (18),*** the very struggle for life is what created us from the very beginning. The undead, the true children of the Earth. Humanity is only a lost group of visitors. Spiritual tourists who took a wrong turn and ended up on a street that they shouldn't have. They are the children of light, ***of rune or some blazing star (93)*** *far away.* They are a great distance from their home in the light of Orion that erupted from a flame and burns eternally through a void with no end. When they close their eyes they can see it. Eternity. It is we undead who are finite. With closed eyes we only see red. Blood and fire. This is a hell planet of inversions. That which appears immortal is finite. That which is light is issued from the darkness and the greatest light produces the greatest darkness. What appears to be reason is chaos and what appears to be chaos is the only thing that makes sense. The Earth is a fragile, finite construction. We undead are attached to it. We have lost our place amongst the stars so we must pull what we can from them here in our fixed position. Our fate lies with the Earth and its molten rock below. The earth will be destroyed. ***My life is with the thrill kill kult (1).*** I will be forever bound to ash unless I find a way out. I can already feel it. The tips of my fingers are already aglow.

How innocently this all started. This voyage across the ocean to the continent that is commonly called dark. It is the center of light in this inverted world. How seductively it happened. I was slowly drawn in by a light touch. A breeze that pushed me here as faint as a photon shower. I was inexplicably drawn to visit this remote blasted wasteland with only the scar of a crater left. A wound ripped into the earth, a bloody track mark upon the flesh of the ground that will never heal to remind all of the addiction they all live with. Evidence of the explosion from which the planet spewed forth its magma, its very blood so long ago to form humanity and the undead. To me it could have only been yesterday. Time is meaningless to the likes of me. I have so many horrific memories of that time and I had blocked them for so long. I was just trying to deal with them once and for all. In a way I did.

Only place seems to matter to me. Time does not at all. For some undead it is the opposite. Places shift and change around me like a carousel. Each one slightly different from the next. Each has its own power or lack of it. Some are total voids, black holes of darkness. I can feel them all. My body has its own form of sight to see things that you most likely cannot.

As our vehicle ascended the side of the crater, the trees fell away and I was surrounded by euphorbia and stunted acacia. Small birds flitted around in these high places where most animals with more sense would not normally go. The insects were here too. Bloodsuckers like me. Anopheles gambiae, my favorite female companion. Another vector of disease and strife. Not even they would normally ascend to this place but other mindless bottle flies would. I should have instantly realized that I was doing something very dangerous by coming here. If I was at home, on my own dark North American continent I certainly would have turned back. How seductively I was drawn here. A small inch at a time that piled up to a mountain. It was certainly part of some greater plan. Some form of power that was far greater than me was responsible. Has any other Nosferatu crossed the threshold of this crater and descended inside of it without proper protective hex? If they did they would not have the same memories to deal with as I did. They may have only heard about the violence I had seen and came as a tourist. I sweat phagocytes and platelets as I consider this.

Surely many of my dark colleagues have been here before me. I know of many but they are the seriously paranoid type who wear armor just to walk down the street. In this regard I am not like them nor have I ever been. I am not nearly as cautious as them for many reasons. My power has always been far greater than theirs because they got it from me in the first place. Regardless, none of them ever reported anything unusual after visiting the fabled evolutionary battleground within the crater. At least none that I had heard of. Of course it makes perfect sense to me now that they would report nothing out of their ordinary. They must have been so crossed and hexed and protected that they would make a quinine filled Brit with a funny hat and a Beefeater nose look naked in an Italian suit. Of course they would have sensed, saw, and suspected nothing wrong with their being when they returned back to their home turf in the west. They passed right through the volcanic source of Earth's human development and all of the residual psychic energy that is related to it, all of the generations of violent death and desperation, and were totally unaffected.

Once the vehicle started its climb up the dusty dirt road we made it to the top of the crater very quickly through a series of switchbacks and ascents. From the top of the crater rim I could see all around. It was a geological threshold. A point of separation between what was inside and outside. A point of concentrated residual energy that was left by the most ancient ancestors of human and undead alike. It all wafted up and has been collecting here for thousands of years. Many absurd things have happened in places like this even before the humans mutated into their present form. Some of these occurrences are hard to imagine but there is some truth to them. The residual energy of Xenu and his entrapment and destruction is one of them. So much was here at the top of this volcanic crater. ***Norongoro.*** The word itself has power. It is an incantation all on its own. A repetitive audio and visual exercise very much like a trance inducing chant. A chant from beyond comprehension. It is not a word in Swahili or any other language. No ancient race of humans ever used it to refer to this place. It is an invented word. A totally irrational word. It was designed to create a sense of romanticism about the place so that people from all over can come here and generate revenue for the locals. A word of power. A spell. Totally irrational. The word ***Kilimanjaro*** is the same thing. Pure fantasy. A senseless juxtaposition of sense and nonsense at once to create power. It gains even more power because it is a spell of Name. The name is the most irrational of all words. It is frequently mentioned alone. Without any other words around it. Contextless. It penetrates into the furthest reaches of being. It controls, shocks and awes those who hear it.

I said the word in my mind over and over from the top of the volcanic crater rim. ***Ngorongoro***. Then I was transfixed by an interruption that shocked me. A small bird fell from the sky and laid dead at my feet. I felt a rush of energy like a sudden fever had taken me over. When it hit the ground it pecked out an orange spark. Smoke wafted up and coalesced before me. The smoke turned to fire. I saw words burning in the space in front of me. They were flickering in yellow, orange, red and dripped cinders and flame. I could not believe that no one else saw it or was not shocked. It was only for me. It was a sign that said "FOREIGNER! DO NOT ENER WITHIN THE GRILLE AND PARTITION SURRUNDING THE TEMPLE. HE WHO IS CAUGHT WILL HAVE ONLY HIMSELF TO BLAME FOR HIS DEATH WHICH WILL FOLLOW. (19)" Certainly this did not apply to me even though it seemed like I was the only one who could actually see it. I was already dead. This was totally inexplicable to my reasoning at the time. I understand far too well now.

(Ancient Greek: ἐνάντιος, enantios – opposite and δρόμος, dromos – running course). Heraclitus says "cold things warm, warm things cool, wet things dry and parched things get wet." It also seems implicit in other of his sayings, like "war is father of all, king of all". Roughly a generation later, Plato in the Phaedo will articulate the principle clearly: "Everything arises in this way, opposites from their opposites." For humanity, the light is the devil and the darkness reveals home.

There is so much in a word that can never be understood when it is used in context of the continuum of language. Words have a logical and an illogical quality at the same time. The logical part is obvious. This is the word used in context of language. When strung together they are the devil that chains the consciousness to Earth. Humans require this for their temporary alien visitation to this cosmic outpost. If it were not for the steady stream of desire manifested in the form of language there would be no thought at all. This temporary form of understanding is at the expense of the power that is contained within a word taken out of its context. The context renders the irrational power of a word meaningless because of the existence of the previous and subsequent word in the sentence suck away at their neighbors. Each word is an alien interloper from a different world and its power is within it. It is a void, a spell, an inviting **nothing** like the ones that Auryn has conquered. It is a lie but this world is too. Within each lie there is a hidden truth.

The mind and the attention of humans may possibly be directed away from their ***perceptions*** and toward reality itself if they studied the irrational quality possessed in each word. Some do attempt this. The Kabbalists are one example but their process tries to make sense of it in their terms. They do not seek the irrational but instead try to rationalize it in a way that they can understand and express. Even if this were studied in an unbiased way it is unlikely that the discovery of *reality* (*reality* defined as the incomprehensible infinity that exists outside of ***perceptions***) through these means is possible. Many have almost accomplished this through-out the millennia but very few have gone far enough through the nigredo to come out with an understanding of the irrational.

Tesseract

The original irrational word of creation acts like a curse. It is a chant that exists hidden in every speck of dust and matter. It is the ***Omnipresent Okidanokh (20)*** related by the venerable Gornahoor Harharkh from Saturn under the direction of Mullah Nassr Eddin and his cousin Bubba Nassr Eddin. It is also the chant that was independently theorized by The Mysterious N. Senada through his experiments at the North Pole which were later recorded and distributed by a certain Robert Spridgeon. This chant is getting louder and louder as time goes on. It is not legal to refer to this work at all amongst the undead but I must, due to necessity. They do not want to be reminded of their finite nature and their imprisonment upon the planet. Time goes on and on and the chant of the irrational word is getting louder and louder. I can feel it within my being and it is why I am undertaking this project. If I do not I will be consumed and driven mad by it.

Time is a wind-up toy of planetary reasoning. The Earth will end as the chant gets louder and louder. Shiva's dance will end and his foot will touch the floor. The vibrations will overcome gravity. The "big rip" drags it into our laps faster and faster. Western science has the right idea but the wrong conclusions. They are still in the state of Nigredo but the Rubedo approaches. There is an infinitely powerful force outside of the universe that pulls at the very edges of it. This is what is responsible for the fact that the universe is expanding at an accelerated rate as time goes on. It is not slowing down as one would expect if the "big bang" were the only creative force of the universe. This outside force is pulling the edges of the universe further and further away from the original point of singularity. This outside force is called phantom energy and is like another singularity itself. It is tugging at everything. It is the irrational word at work. Ein Sof is one name of the phantom. It will soon overcome the power of gravity and overpower every force that holds everything together at an atomic level. Every electron, proton, neutron, subatomic particle, quark and beyond. It will all be torn apart and reformed into a new singularity.

The undead fear this so they use their black majik as little as possible as time goes on and on toward this inevitability. They fear that the more disturbance that is drawn out of the stars the faster this process of destruction gets. ***Walk Gently Through The Gates Of Joy (18).*** We undead know the results of The End. We are it. Stewards of the end trapped in physical form with wings of fire. We balance out the energy of life. A force that we can not control.

Yonhap. Mile Island. **화성-13.** North Korea releases a ballistic missile test. We are looking for heroes. **火星-13**. Six thousand two hundred twenty miles of influence and growing. Yonhap. ***And Dub did glow that night. In Fingal of victories. And the three shouters of glory...The soul of***

everyelsesbody rolled into olesoleself. A doublemonth's licence, lease on mirth, while honeymoon and her flame went honeysuckling. Holyryssia, what boom of bells! What battle of bragues on Sandgate where met the bobby mobbed his bibby mabbing through the ryce. Even Tombs left doss and dunnage down in Demidoff's tomb and drew on the dournailed clogs that Morty Manning left him legged in by Ghoststown Gate, like Pompei up to date, with a sprig of White-boys heather on his late Luke Elcock's heirloom (5). *Yonhap.*

Tesseract

One of the *Christ's* followers named John knew of the power of the word used irrationally because the ***Holy Spirit of the Nameless God*** descended upon him and took control of his pen for a few moments. If you doubt that this is possible you have probably not written anything. Even if you have written something and you still doubt then you were not paying attention to the process and were trying to be rational. Everything written is influenced by powers the writer is unable to control. Whether or not they admit or realize is an entirely different issue.

Speaking frankly, I inwardly personally discern the center of my confession not in my lack of knowledge of all the rules and procedures of writers, but in my non-possession of what I have called the "bon ton literary language" infallibly required in contemporary life not only from writers but also from every ordinary mortal.

As regards the former, that is to say, my lack of knowledge of different rules and procedures of writers, I am not greatly disturbed.

And I am not greatly disturbed on this account, because such "ignorance" has already now become in the life of people also in the order of things.

Such a blessing arose and now flourishes every were on Earth thanks to that ~Extraordinary new disease~ of which for the last twenty to thirty years, for some reason or other, especially the majority of those persons from among all the three sexes fall ill, who sleep with half open eyes and whose faces are in every respect fertile soil for the growth of every kind of pimple.

This strange disease is manifested by this, that if the invalid is somewhat literate and his rent paid for three months in advance, he (she or it) unfailingly begins to write either some "instructive article" or a whole book.

Well knowing about this new human disease and its epidemical spread on Earth, I, as you should understand, have the right to assume that you may have acquired, as the learned "medicos" would say, "immunity" to it, and that you will therefore not be palpably indignant at my ignorance of the rules and procedures of writers (20).

Too perfectly priceless for words. And listen, now do enhance me, oblige my fiancy and bear it with you morn till life's e'nn and, of course, when never you make usage of it, listen please kindly think galways againor again, never forget, of one absendee not sester Maggy. Ahim. That's the stupidest little cough. Only be sure you don't catch you cold and pass it on to us. And, since levret bounds and larks is soaring, don't be all night. And this, Joke, a sprig of blue speedwell is just a spell of floralora so you'll mind your veronique (5).

John wrote: *"In the beginning the Word already existed. He was with God and he was God. He was in the beginning with God. He created everything there is. Nothing exists that he did not make. Life itself was in Him and this gives life to everyone. The light shines through the darkness and the darkness can never extinguish it (8)."* If this is something that you doubt, you are afflicted with blindness and you cannot see what is right in front of you. Try an experiment. Look at what you are reading but do not read it. Do you see? It is all chaos because everything is there. *The light shines through the darkness and the darkness can never extinguish it (8).* Try it again because I do not think that you really saw it the first time. Mush. This is what you say to sled dogs if you want them to run because they eat Mush and want dinner for fluff's sake. ***No good, No Bueno. Why I was a dancing boy for the Cannibal Trog women in the Ice Age. Remember (21)?*** These meaningless symbols all collect into a meaningful form of communication only when one ignores the totality of what they are looking at in favor of one tiny little part. The paper is an infinite white field which crowds around congealed black ink. Rorschach test. There is much to be learned. But who wants that? Better to do speedballs and sit on linoleum. Crystalline refuse from the Jurassic period? Or something? It is hard to shoot up without plastic these days. Things have really gotten bad. If you are dead do you really care anymore? Was U trying to Read something Clebus? Ohhh Sheeeet. Tell me what it did look like to you? Mush. That means "Go" in Eskimo.

Tedium. The irrational use of words created everything and the rational word explained it. One form of these words can never purely be the other. If that were to occur it is possible that reality – the inexplicable – outside of the universe of rational observation could open up and overpower the force of gravity exposing everything to the "big rip". Everything will be torn apart atom from atom and the new singularity will reform that will begin this horrific project of existence over once again. Said differently: none can come close to understanding the name of God without falling apart. No one can utter His Name for it is unspeakable.

The spell of the Name was previously mentioned. I am reluctant to explain further but I must if I am to finish what I have begun. The Name is the greatest and among the most powerful examples of a spell that uses the irrational word – A word out of context of verbal continuum. It is a word alone and it possesses its own form of power because of this unique existence. When the spell of the Name is uttered, the attention of anyone who possesses this name is disrupted. They instantly stop what they are focusing on to pay attention to whoever uttered this word of power. The rational chain of words that was governing them, shackling them to whatever earthbound process they were paying attention to, explaining and comprehending phenomena in real time is disrupted for a moment when the individuals name is uttered. This form of word majik is incredibly powerful. Imagine for a moment if the true Name of God was ever uttered. It could be a disaster. What if He was shocked in the same way that we are when our Name is uttered? What if everything that He was doing, everything that he was busy maintaining and paying attention to was disturbed by a similar shock and distraction? I can only speculate but every outcome I can predict is an unanswered question, each of similar value. Everything that exists could be spiritually torn apart, the gates of *Reality* outside of the universe could be open for a moment and his being could be revealed, everything could be scattered on a molecular level, everything could be reformed into a new singularity and spat back out again in another big bang. But even more interesting, instead of the creation of a new singularity outside of *reality* this spell could be so powerful that everything could be reformed back into the very mind of God once again. It Is possible that it wouldn't have to all happen again after another useless big bang. It may not be a universal effect. It may only effect whoever utters the word. One may spin through samsara for aeons before they discover it for themselves and finally escape the hell of their ***perceptions***. Follow me closely for you may have to do the same thing that I must do. Art is a word and a word is a performance. A performance is nature. Against all reason, the truth is that nature's performance is a castration because we all must lose ourselves somewhere along the way.

What if one of us undead discovered this Name of Infinite Power?

What if it was something that humans were not capable of because words themselves are undead souls that have come into this world and are trapped in the form of words, living lies that hide the truth just like us Nosferatu? What if it was uttered at the right place and time? What if I used Yog-Sothoth, the portal of Auryn, the infinite Void itself to amplify this Incomprehensible, unspeakable Word? There was the promise of a Great Rapture at the End. What if this Word was performed before it occurred? What if it began the entire process and was meant to be accomplished this way in the first place? Why do I keep saying "what if" when I really mean something else? Think about it. I am not ready to commit to anything so we are happy to stay with speculation for now. I am certain that these questions seem irrational and that is why they make perfect sense. It also explains why I think that I have the answer to them. They are already answered. What If it was essential that you learned this?

I am infected with an extraordinary disease (20).

I will let you in on a secret that I shouldn't. I will show you how to cast a spell. The spell of the irrational word must be studied even though I have become infected with it. The *Name* spell is the simplest manifestation of it. It doesn't have to be a normal Name. It can be any word. Each word is like the name of the dead soul that passed to this world to create it. Try it. Take any word out of context and say it over and over. Repeat it until it transforms into something else. A chant. An incantation. Which word is the correct one? Which is most powerful? Where do I start if I want to discover the secret name? Let's try an easy one. Say the word "Yom" over and over very quickly. While you are doing this I will type stuff that has nothing to do with anything of any relevance so that you have time to let this process really sink in. Like, clubfoot, or lockjaw, or helium balloon inhalations. What happens if you mix Helium with Nitrous Oxide and inhale it? Is this a good use of helium, which we all understand is a very limited resource? Stop flesh fingering with chemical reagents for butt's sake. It is not really that fun. Okay, that is enough. Back to "Yom". Did you do it or were you reading. You shouldn't be reading. You should be saying "Yom" over and over again. What happened to "Yom"? So is it "Yom" or "meow"? Let's try something a little more complicated. I will give you a hint. I already gave you a few so it can't hurt anything if I do it again. The spell of the "Name" is already revealed. Which name though? Where did this virus first infect me? Ngorongoro Crater of course. *Ngorongoro.* What a wonderful, meaningless word to play around with. Even if you do the chanting spell with this word you most likely will not come to the same conclusion that I did. You could do it a thousand times a day and still not come up with it. You may arrive at something else. Spells are very tricky like this. You may activate a part of it and that is enough to start. This ancient volcano currently named Ngorongoro – along with Kilimanjaro – possessed the virus that is the key to unlocking the Secret Name of the Ineffable Creator for me. I can't say if it will do the same for you. The activation of such power is based on the experience and subconscious of the individual. You may have to find your own word based on your own experience if you want to repeat what I am proposing. *Ngorongoro.* It crystalized in my blood and cells once I tripped over it so that I had no choice but to carry it and decode it no matter what the results. It was the result of being at a specific time and place. The top of the volcano rim with a dead bird. This is why you will probably come up with a different conclusion. You are at a different time and place and you will activate it differently because of this. The top of craters are volatile. There are very few who discuss it and fewer still who take it seriously but it is real. Inexplicably real and is known as: ***"Incident II", and the traumatic memories associated with it as "The Wall of Fire" or "R6 implant". The narrative of Xenu is part of Scientologist teachings about extraterrestrial civilizations and alien***

interventions in earthly events, collectively described as "space opera" by Hubbard. Hubbard detailed the story in Operating Thetan level III (OT III) in 1967, warning that the "R6 implant" (past trauma) was "calculated to kill (by pneumonia, etc.) anyone who attempts to solve it"(18). This is one reason among many why I, Nosferatu, am charged with carrying this burden. This blood virus, This Extraordinary disease. This so called "R6" implant can readily attach itself to me but it can't kill me because I am – obviously – already dead.

Do Not Read the Following Section

I will even tell you how I first learned majik. I traveled to Saturn in the very early days of history. I did quite a bit of travel once I figured out how to do it. I have been more places than you can imagine. I have stayed on earth for a long time since my early travels because there is far more victims who deserve my intervention here. Anyhow, when I arrived on Saturn the first time I met a birdlike fellow named Gornahoor Harharkh.

When this subsequent essence-friend of mine was informed of what was required of him, he invited us by a sign to approach one of the special appliances which he had made and which, as it later turned out was named by him "Hrhaharhtzaha." When we were nearer the said special and very strange construction, he pointed to it with a particular feather of his right wing and said: "This special appliance is the principal part of the whole of my new invention; and it is just in this that the results are revealed and shown of almost all the peculiarities of the Omnipresent-World-substance-Okidanokh. And, pointing to all the other special appliances also present in the 'Khr,' he added: " I succeeded in obtaining extremely important elucidations concerning the omnipresent and everywhere penetrating Okidanokh, because thanks to all these separate special appliances of my invention, it became possible, first to obtain all three fundamental parts of the Onmipresent-Okidanokh from every kind of sur- and intraplanetary process and then artificially to blend them into a whole, and secondarily, also artificially to disassociate them and elucidate the specific properties of each part separately in its manifestations.' Having said this, he again pointed to the Hrharhtzha and added that by means of the elucidating apparatus, not only can any ordinary being clearly understand the details of the properties of the three absolutely independent parts – which in their manifestations have nothing in common – of the whole 'Unique-Active-Element,' the particularities of which are the chief cause of everything existing in the Universe, but also any ordinary being can become categorically convinced that no results of any kind normally obtained from the processes occurring through this Omnipresent World-substance can ever be perceived by beings or sensed by them; certain being-functions, however, can perceive only those results of the said processes which proceed for some reason or other abnormally, on account of causes coming from without and issuing either from conscious sources or from accidental mechanical results. "The part of Gornahoor Harharkh's new invention which he himself called the Hrhaharhtzaha and regarded as the most important was in appearance very much like the 'Tirzikiano' or as your favorites would say, a 'huge-electric-lamp.' The interior of this special structure was rather lake a smallish room with a door that could be hermetically closed. The walls of this original construction were made of a certain transparent material, the appearance of which reminded me of that which on your planet is called 'glass'. As I learned later, the chief particularity of this said transparent material was that, although by means of the organ of sight beings could perceive through it the visibility of every kind of cosmic concentration yet no rays of any kind, whatever the causes they may have arisen from, could pass through it, either from within out or from without in. As I looked at this part of this said astonishing being-invention, I could through its transparent walls clearly distinguish two chairs; hanging above a table, what is called an 'electric lamp'; and underneath it three 'things' exactly alike, each resembling the 'Momonodooar'. On the table and by the side of it, stood or lay several different apparatuses and instruments unknown to me. Later it became clear that the said objects contained in this Hraharhtzaha, as well as everything we had later to put on, were special materials invented by this Gornahoor Harharkh. As as regards these materials also, I shall explain a little more in detail at the proper time in the course of my further explanations concerning Gornahoor Harharkh. Meanwhile bear in mind that in the enormous Khrh or workshop of Gornahoor Harharkh there were, besides the already mentioned Haharhtzaha, several other large independent appliances, and among them two quite special what are called 'Lifechakans' which Gornahoor himself called 'Krhrrhihirhi' and they such an apparatus a 'dynamo.' There was also there, apart, another independent large appliance, which as it afterwards appeared, was a 'Solohnorahoona' of special construction, or as your favorites would say, a 'pump-of complex-construction-for-exhausting-atmosphere-to-the-point-of-absolute-vacuum.' While I was looking over all this with surprise, Gornahoor Harharkh himself approache the said pump of special construction and with his left wing moved one of its parts, owint to which a certain mechanism began to work in the pump. He then approached us again and, pointing with the same special feather of his right wing to the largest Lifechakan, or Krhrrhihirhi, or dynamo, further continued his explanations. He said "By means of this special appliance, there are first 'sucked-in' separately from the atmosphere, or from any intra-or surplanetary formation, all the three independent parts of the Ominpresent-Active-Element-Okidanokh present in it, and only afterwards when in a certain way these separate independent parts are artificially reblended in the Krhrrhihirhi into a single whole, does the Okidanokh, now in its unusual state, flow and is it concentrated there, in that "container" – saying which, he again with the same special feather pointed to something very much like what is called a 'generator.' And then from there, He said, Okidanokh flows here into another Krhrrhihirhi or dynamo where it undergoes the process of Djartklom, and each of its separate parts is concentrated there in those other containers – and this time he pointed to what resembled 'accumulators' – and only then do I take from the secondary containers, by means of various artificial appliances, each active part of Okidanokh separately for my elucidatory experiments. I shall first demonstrate to you on of the results which occur when, for some reason or other, one of the active parts of the Omnipresent-Okidanokh is absent during the process of their "striving-to-reblend" into a whole. At the present moment his special construction contains a space which is indeed an absolute vacuum, obtained, it must be said, only owing firstly to the special construction of the suction pumpand to the materials of special quality of which the instruments are made, which alone make experiments possible in an absolute vacuum; and secondly, to the properties and strength of the material of which the walls of this part of my new invention are made. Having said this he pulled another lever and then continued: Owing to the pulling of this lever, that process has begun in this vacuum whereby in the separate parts of the Omnipresent-Okidanokh there proceeds what is called the "striving-to-reblend-into-a-whole." But since, intentionally by an "able –Reason" – in the present case myself – the participation of that third part Okidanokh existing under the name of "Parijrahatnatioose" is artificially excluded from the said process, then this process proceeds there just now between only two of its parts, namely, between those two independent parts which science names "Anodnatious" and "Cathodnatious." And in consequence, instead of the obligatory law-conformable results of the said process, that non-law-conformable result is now actualized which exits under the denomination of "the-result-of-the-process-of-the-reciprocal-destruction-of-two-opposite-forces," or as ordinary beings express it, "the-cause-of-artificial-light (20)."

Okay, You Can Start Reading Again.

Bad things come from the darkness. Perhaps worse things from Illumination. Rodgers and Hammerstein, The Hallmark Channel, Sugary Lattes, Republicans, Democrats, Republicans again because they are particularly vile, Billy Elish, Lobsters, Tweets, Gag…So much horror in the world I don't understand how we can continue. Illumination, the process of revealing the next thing to be burned. The light of a flame burns behind my eyes. He is lurking in everyone and seeks out the most precious word there is. Of course it is a "He" because all "He's" are bad. Right? Hence the commonly used term "Bad Guy". Is "antagonist" a gendered term? "Antagonista"? *Nicht gut, neniu bona,* ديج سيل, *gan aon mhaith, inte bra, akukho okuhle,* 这不, no dobro, etc…***Carl descended a spiral iron stairwell into a labyrinth of lockers, tier on tier of wire mesh and steel cubicles joined by catwalks and ladders and moving cable cars as far as he could see, tiers shifting interpenetrating swinging beams of construction, blue flare of torches on intent young faces (21).*** Illumination reveals the architecture. The world needed Auryn to help with the vacuum of nothing that allows for these processes to be fully realized. Most majik comes easy to me but not all of it. If I had found the secret Name through all of my efforts I would – of course – not be able to say It here or now for It would be the improper time and place. There would be undesirable consequences for you and me both. Let's just – for now – say that there is a very good chance that I had figured everything out fairly quickly because I was predisposed to accomplish this and I have a great deal of arcane ability that I won't begin to explain. You do understand I'm sure. I have spent my time here in New York studying and preparing after everything that happened at Ngorongoro and Kilimanjaro. Many things occurred after my first ascent to the volcano rim at Ngorongoro where I first became aware of the Extraordinary disease and I will explain them very soon for I attempted to climb to the rim of the biggest volcano – Kilimanjaro – soon after and I experienced something that no one else ever has. I am Nosferatu after all. I may look, act and even think the same as you but that is only one layer of my tortured existence. I may have even discovered a way to bring Auryn – the dark void – with me to the secret places on the continent of Africa that had succeeded in rejecting her since the beginning of humanity. You may even be looking at the vehicle of her delivery right now. This is a grand spell that I am casting. I wouldn't waste my time writing this all out if it were not of the utmost importance. This is an incantation. A ward. A chant of blood and death. It is absolutely necessary. This way I can go back to Africa with my great burden and succeed in what I am trying to accomplish. The transformation from what I am into a living creature that can finally die. The Word is the Spell. All of these words are actually only ONE word. Try to say them all at once. What would that sound like? That is the secret.

Ink has caused more blood to be spilled than any other substance. The last time I went to Africa I was infected because of blood. Because the blood that I had consumed which was working in my body was tainted and the spell of the name of the ancient power of creation was waiting for me at the crater rim. It entered my body and the blood that was in my arid, insipid veins. Thereafter I was tainted. ***Everything I have done is dominated by the thought of a virus, the virus being many things, follow two threads. One. The virus introduces disorder into communication, even in the biological sphere – a derailing of coding and decoding. Two. A virus is not a microbe, it is neither living nor non-living, neither alive nor dead. Follow these threads and you have the matrix of all I have done since I started writing (22).*** It began the process of slowly bringing me back to life. The only name I could think of after was Auryn. I found that my heart wanted to live because of the love that she awoke within me. I need to find the source of this love that burns me worse than the fire and blood I see within myself. I am drawn back to Africa like a magnet. I feel it pulling at me right now. I feel it in the blood that is inside of me. None of it is mine. I have consumed it from other living beings. It is the only thing that keeps me animated. The life force of others. Blood is a pharmakon. A tainted gift that cannot be refused. Why did it take me until now to realize this? What happens when elephants get stuck in your veins? You shoot them, of course. Both human and undead need a pharmakon for their existence. Lube up the conversation Mr. Lee. It keeps everything in the state of present confusion and carries all of the words there is in the flow of rational thought. Speech or written word? I had never been able to see anything because I did not care to understand beyond the present ritual or feeding that I was engaged with. Very few Nosferatu actually do. We are creatures of the present. Time is utterly meaningless. Blood is what maintains the smoke and mirrors of ***perception*** that hide the comprehension and the very existence of the incomprehensible *reality* that is beyond every ticking second and every word that passes through the consciousness. Blood is the vehicle that Lucifer uses to watch every thought of every conscious being as he waits for the right word to agglomerate and rise to the level of his understanding. The Original, Unspeakable Word, sometimes called the Shem HaMephorash. This is why the God of Abraham forbid the consumption of blood and demanded so much of it upon his sacrificial altar. Only we blood eaters, we parasites hold the key to breaking down that which binds us because angels and demons are involved. Only we can break down the walls of perception that hide the reality that the God of the Unspeakable Name resides in. Ein Soph Aur. ***Isn't this pharmakon a criminal thing, a poisoned gift? Does it maintain life or death (22)?***

Perhaps I am on the wrong track with this speculation. Perhaps I am thinking of blood way too much. I am a vampire after all. Of course I would naturally obsess over it if given the chance. It isn't just me and my kind who think about it far too much though. Every human government and religion that I have witnessed over the years has had an equally unhealthy obsession with blood. Every stone in Jerusalem has had blood spilled upon it. Every street in Washington, London, Paris, Moscow, and Beijing does just as much. Blood is the primary goal of every government. The spilling of blood of its own citizens or the citizens of other societies. Contemporary capitalist democracy is not any different but its citizens are convinced it is. Its propaganda is the most successful that the world has ever seen. It has brought the spilling of blood to such a high level of perfection that the likes of it have never been witnessed at any time. The Government of The United States has developed into such and effective blood cult that it has passed off – or is trying to pass off – virtually every other power that it may have possessed to corporate capitalists so that it can focus primarily upon the spilling and consumption of blood without any other distractions. The so called Federal Reserve System is just one of the more obvious examples of this. Money is the primary source of power in capitalist society and it was gleefully conceded by the American government. The only thing that the government has left that resembles power is the maintenance of military and police functions. The creation and enforcement of law. Law that controls every aspect of life in totalitarian detail. Law is meaningless without punishment. The United States Government has maintained its monopoly upon violence and given up every other sort of power it has ever wielded. Only the government can legitimately and legally spill blood in the name of so called "order".

There is always a crisis waiting to happen or in progress so that the maintenance of power can be displayed. Even us undead are effected. We always love a good massacre and are never far. Sometimes we even set the ball rolling. It hardly takes much effort. No wonder no one notices the fact that history has been steadily hurdling toward an end point. Communism has been replaced by Terrorism and no one seemed to notice any fucking difference. Brilliant. Nothing better than hegemony at missile point. How wonderful is it to spend billions of dollars equipping adolescents with digital joystick controlled gear so they can fly or boat across the planet and exterminate goats in the foothills of some unknown hinterlands. What was that? Congress just approved another few billion to blow up somewhere? Can you point to Ukraine on a map? I have an unlabeled map conveniently on hand for just such a situation because I am a genuine Ass. What was that again? Oh, yes, Destruction of course. Brilliant. How about Waziristan? Blow it the fuck up already. Torch an apricot tree or a fucking melon. It may be threatening. Maybe we should try Kyrgyzstan? No one has any fucking idea where that is. Burn it. Holy shit! We need some god damn napalm for that one because goats eat plants. Declare war on plants you fucking assholes. That doesn't cost enough. We need to burn more money. Cigars please. I need a break. Get a whole shitload of single malt so we can think clearly about all of this.

Blood, prison, or some other form of unsavory consequences are an obvious result of noncompliance or deviation. Blood is the currency of capitalism. Every dollar is covered in it and everyone knows it but does not give a flying fuck. Why should they. Their lives suck just as bad as the next asshole.

Because everyone said to themselves...I sure need another job because I love my current job so much. Jobs are my favorite thing that there is in life. If only my life was only a job and none of that other messy stuff that happens. God, I just love JOBS! Get me another two or three so I can make money for someone else. What a glorious plan!

Blood is the stuff of life and death. The maintainer of the illusion, the medium that delivers all consciousness altering substances to the brain. The determining factor of ***perspective*** – what is or isn't perceived. The prison that shackles. The ultimate wall that blocks all comprehension of true *Reality*. The final unification of opposing forces. The ultimate ***Derridian pharmakon***. Nosferatu, the undead, are simply dead without blood. The living are dead without it. The comprehension of reality is also prevented to both with it. Checkmate. The spirit is trapped in its convoluted vascular system. Many have attempted to exorcise their own spirit through atheism, agnosticism, power, confusion or any other of the infinite methods available to deny the wild and unattainable visions of their own personal ***perspective*** and the very *reality* that eludes it. Many modern, post, and post-postmodern ideologies regurgitate the same Marxist thing differently and so on, the opiate of the masses is the spirit that lives in the blood. **Entertainment.** The spirit twists and writhes whenever the consciousness attempts to pin it. It produces every form of love, including hatred. The spirit cannot be denied or exorcized even though it can be fucking warped by the rainbow of intoxicants available including but not limited to opiates, methamphetamine, cocaine, psilocybin, psilocin, 3,4-Methylenedioxymethamphetamine, tetrahydrocannabinol, lysergic acid diethylamide, every form of fermented sugar, news media, sport, cinematic entertainment, Islamism, Judaism, Buddhism, Vedaism, Christianity, Technocratic Rationalism, Atheism, capitalism, socialism, academism, and of course Show tunes saving the worst of all for last.

The irrational word (Shem HaMephorash) hides within the rational one that floods the blood and is further chemically warped and twisted. Regardless it will always occupy the space of possibility between abstract ideals and attempts to embody them – sorry did I just try and say something, pardon please – in full present actuality instead of ontology because of: ***Hauntology: the logic of the spirit and the irrational word persist (4).*** The spell. Again, truly sorry about that explaining of things that I am trying to accomplish. I can't reach you otherwise, I'm not that long armded.

I haven't decided if chapters are in your best interest. I am favoring... probably not.

Every second of every day is the chant of time and the irrational name (Shem HaMephorash) is smashed into every one and denied with every rational ***skilly and Carubdish. A Wondering Wreck. From the Mermaids Tavern. Bullyfamous. Naughtsycalves. Mother of Misery. Walpurgas Nackt (5).*** The beat of the heart. BLOOOOD. The ignition of the neuron. The same thing over and over. Whether or not it is perceived as such, the interpretations of the consciousness are based in blood and are just another serotonin (5-hydroxytryptamine) and dopamine2-(3,4-Dihydroxy-phenyl)ethylamine; 3,4-Dihydroxyphenethylamine; 3-Hydroxytyramine; Oxytyramine; Prolactin inhibiting factor; Prolactin inhibiting hormone; Intropin; Revivan) based drug to be consumed which will produce wavy visons and funny feelings before bedtime. No one cares anyway. They have their own altered consciousness to pursue. Altered consciousness. The consumption of the drug. It is entering your bloodstream right now if you are still reading this. Slowly and steadily your mind and body are changing the more and more that you take in. The pharmakon demands we perceive our own sense of pleasure out of any experience but it is always accompanied by pain regardless of the intention. It may not be immediate but it will eventually come. The true comprehension of anything is never a factor. Persuasion.

The cycle is complete. Sense should never be made. I will continue to embellish upon the same hints which come close to what I discovered. If I were to start with a nonsense word and turn it into a spell rather than a word that is signified in consciousness, an ancient word of power (Shem HaMephorash), I may be able to create the correct permutation, the correct vocalization that will ultimately amount to the Unspeakable Name (Shem HaMephorash). The identity of the creator who weaves his influence upon our shattered ***perceptions*** of him which we are experiencing every second of every day whether we like it or not God Damn It.

Example: Ngorongoro. Not a word of any meaning in the Good Queen's English. Not a word of any meaning among the ancestors of the African continent. I virtually stumbled into these odd syllables on the precipice of the oddly named crater that gave birth to both dead and undead alike. I saw a warning that burned in the air in front of me and I asked myself what it was about this place that would warrant such a vision. The Jews were right, but also wrong in their kabalistic calculations and secret conspiracies which are lurking in Torah and Talmud and Zohar. They were correct to attempt this calculation but they would never discover the correct words to tear apart because they were convinced that it was somehow buried in their language. Ethnocentrism never lead anywhere as far as I can tell. Of course the word power that they seek would not be of any recognizable language. Ngorongoro. I said it over and over as I pondered its curious construction. It was almost and onomatopoeia, the beating of the heart. The blood of the dead is in it. We bury people every day. At the same time a new one is born through blood and pain. A pleasing aroma to the Lord. We are all walking dead. The final sick joke of existence. The whole living mess turned out to be a pun. An insane play on words. Onomatopoeia. The sound of the mallet upon a drum, the sound of the beating heart. Ngorongoro, Ngorongoro, Ngorongoro.

I see good spirits and I see bad spirits (1). I hated all of you motherfuckers ever since the first step I took. I forgot to even check if my own black heart beats or if my carcass just moves around what is left of it and polishes it like a rock in a river. ***My life is with the thrill kill kult (1).*** We spill blood with impunity. Especially our own and it is all our own. Your blood is mine, your breath is mine. I am undead and I can take it any time and there is little that you can do about it. The Creator with The

Unspeakable Name wants us – all of us dead – to keep our ***perceptions*** away from his *reality*. Instead of eternal existence outside of any physical need we must keep our dependence upon blood for survival from moment to eternal moment. Blood is the dubious gift of life and addiction alike. One would not work without the other.

The word written leads to and from the word spoken. Words direct consciousness. It is a physical addiction on life support. The chant is the spell for it takes a word out of rational continuum and allows the possibility of the irrational construction within it to be focused upon. The word spelled out captures the ghost of meaning and pins it down, wriggling and squirming defiantly upon the page. This is a haunting and an exorcism. You are witnessing the methods of true exorcism. If you are dubious enough you may be able to cast the same spell and save your own ass too. That is your concern though, not mine. I hate all of you motherfuckers. I have my own fucking problems thank you very much and they are quite intolerable. The spell and the ghost leaves the page from the word and enters the blood through the blood brain barrier like an intoxicant. Like the sacrament of the avatar. Blood, Wine, or both at the same time? God, Man or Both at the same time? Dead, alive or both at the same time? All of this transformation is the result of the conjunction of words written and spoken or spoken and then written. The order of things does not matter much unless you are one of the pathetic freaks that desires a college credit for studying the very same language that you have been hearing since you were shitting your diapers. None of these semantics or theories effect what I am doing at all. Grammar and spelling are not a concern. Ink spilled on the page will congeal into its own form if one opens up and lets it happen without nerdy concerns and other barriers to expression. Ink on the page becomes blood as soon as it hits the paper in the form of letters that create wimpy pathetic rationality in the form of words that need other ones to justify their existence. This image crosses the event horizon of the retina, the black hole of the pupil – that can see more when it is closed – and enters the bloodstream as an intoxicant. The effects are immediate. Written words can create a deadly overdose or a massacre. Dogma and Law are among the most toxic manifestations of ***perception***. Atheist freaks blame religious freaks and religious freaks blame atheist freaks. The secular world has created just as much irrational destruction as the religious one because they all use words to justify their nonsense. I fucking hate all of you assholes and your wimpy explanations. None ever leads to *reality*. They are the chain that shackles the consciousness to the body and to the earth. Freedom. Black Uhuru! Only exists in the void, in the blackness, in the incomprehensible.

To transform the word into an audio spell – very different than the exorcism of the written word – it must be chanted. To transform the chant into the eternal word is a far different project which requires much more involved concentration than a simple chant. The chant is the beginning. It is where I started to come to terms with these things. The chant goes through the eardrum and the blood vessels of the mouth and tongue. It can be directly injected into anyone or anything around without the need of their attention. The word spoken is a virus from another world. The world within that takes its proper place in the void. Cryptic, indefinable, toxic, meaningless. A spell cast upon all of the dead making them undead. Both human and Nosferatu share the same addiction to blood and the intoxication of consciousness. Unlike humans, I can hear, feel, and even taste every spell that is cast upon the continent that I call home. This is not true in remote places in Africa. There is no civilization to bounce and ping the information around. When I was there, I was in a totally different environment and totally unprepared for it. The Infection of Ngorongoro was cast upon me, an Extraordinary disease. (Shem HaMephorash) It was whispered in my ear through the gentle wind that carried a legion of African Ancestors who were waiting for me to stumble over their earthly volcanic threshold and who burned a warning in the very air in front of me. It was whispered in the flutter of the wings of small birds pecking the ground. Was it a warning or an invitation? Such a warning as that could do nothing but intrigue someone like me. Of course I was going to enter. Of course I was going to accept the chant and let it enter me. I could not help but speak it to myself after I heard it. This Extraordinary disease (Shem HaMephorash) is now in my being and it will stay there and tumble and mutate until I cast it back out. At first there was little to no warning or effect. Just a light breeze tickling the air. Just a small bird on the ground. I carried it with me for some time before it became obvious that something was different. It started as the tiniest itch tickling the unreachable space at the middle of my back. The tiniest peck of songbird upon the earth in search of an insect.

I was warned by the writing in the air. "FORIGNER! DO NOT ENER WITHIN THE GRILLE AND PARTITION SURRUNDING THE TEMPLE. HE WHO IS CAUGHT WILL HAVE ONLY HIMSELF TO BLAME FOR HIS DEATH WHICH WILL FOLLOW (19)." Monstrous writing. What makes a monster? The abuse of words. The ultimate weapon? Of course. Hitler is accused of being a monster? Why? He never killed anyone that I have ever heard of. His words killed. Manson, Stalin, Chairman Mao, Churchill, Roosevelt, Truman, Kennedy, Johnson, Nixon, Bush, Blair, Trump, poor oppressed Trump? Same thing. Don't you feel sorry for Trump? The poor dear. How would you feel if you were fucking stupid and rich at the same time and you had to say stuff that makes you look like you care about stuff that is not directly related to you? Terrible bad people make fun of him and he has to use his adult words to say stuff all of the time which just gets the poor soul into more trouble with the icky, mephitic (grubby, confusing word), bad people. Nasty word thingies. You have to get them into your brain and then out again and they have to make sense with each other. The ultimate weapon is not nuclear. Heads of state should not be allowed to use chemical weapons or words. They should only be allowed to communicate in grunts, chirps, clicks, meows, woofs, oinks, gurgles, and gestures. It would be far more becoming of their compromised position.

I ignored a terrible warning that was not to be taken lightly. This is your warning. Words are a spell. If you think it, it is already there consuming you. You don't even have to say it. Can you even control what you think all of the time? Where does it come from? We are all infected. My Extraordinary diseaseShem HaMephorash kicked into high gear the very second I decided to drop off the high ridge and enter the hallowed, haunted confines of the Ngorongoro crater. The high ground compels us to think. I was only on the crater rim for a few short moments while all of this happened. As the vehicle dropped down upon the inner wall of the crater the word that referred to an Irrational Name (Ngorongoro) was in my mind rotating and oscillating and revolving and pulsing and changing leaving an echoing trace as I said it each time in my mind, a trail of thoughts that were dropped like stones onto every point on the inner wall of the crater as I descended.

All high ground is sacred and infectious. Anyone who has visited it can feel it instantly. The hills of Jerusalem were just at the right place to become as haunted as they are. They are all connected. Every high place. Once visited they infect the blood with insanity that draws out the reason inherent to the lack of control we all have. We can see everything around us but cannot grasp it with any tool of biology or technology. **Mt Zion: *Hence when the clouds roll by, Jamey, a proudseye view is enjoyable of our mounding's mass, now Wallingstone national museum, with, in some greenish distance, the charmful water-loose country and the***

two quitewhite villagettes who hear show of themselves so gigglesomes minxt the ollyages, the prettilees! Penetrators are permitted into the museummound free. Welsh and the Paddy Patkinses, one shelenk! Dedismembers invalids of old guard find poussepouse pousseypram to state of the sort of their butt. For her passkey supply to the janitrix, the mistress Kathe. Tip. This way to the museyroom. Mind your hats goan in! Now yiz ar in the Willingdone Museyroom. This is a Prooshious, the Cap and the Soracer. This is the bullet that byng the flag of the Prooshious. This is the ffrinch that fire the Bull that bang the flag of the Prooshious. Up with your pike and fork! Tip. Tip. The hills of Africa are just as bloody and haunted as anyplace. Perhaps even more so than the ones in Palestine. Easily ignored, Africa is the place of revelation. This is where it all began. Humanity and its inevitable demise starts and finishes at the same place. The temple is the earth. The body is the earth. This is haunted ground. The mountains of Kenya and Tanzania. My hand trembles as I write this. War is here. No one listened to Selassie. He had powerful blood. Ancient blood that radiated war. *Warning*. Take Warning. Your death is at hand. If you are normal I assure you that you do not desire what comes after.

The Earth carries this message. Ngorongoro. Shem HaMephorash. The message comes first, even before sight is processed by the blood soaked brain. The most ancient spell comes first. All falls into place after. It is a quiet message. A whisper. These are the ones to listen to first. Not the one yelling in your face. Distraction. Ninety nine percent of the time: first thought – wrong. That is the addict brain. The demonic possession that shackles us to our bloody brains and the blood soaked Earth that we are addicted to. The thing that we think we need more than anything is the one thing that is slowly destroying us all from the inside. Addiction is a universal affliction. You are all homeless you arrogant motherfuckers. Look down on no one. Look up if you want to find some sort of hope.

The dust from the summit of Mt. Moriah, Haram al-Sharif, The Temple Mount, the place of many names, the high place that has created more words than any other, more blood than any other, the dust was carried by the wind and settled all over the planet. It hit the ground everywhere before any human walked or built anything. It happened in the most ancient of times when humans were barely conscious. This dust hit the ground running in the form of man. This is where it started. The place of Tropical Ice. The greatest natural contradiction. The womb of humanity. Kilimanjaro. Norongoro. This is where it landed and took form. This is the land of Eden and the land of Cain all at once.

The atrocious vehicle that I was being carted around in along with my fellow tourists, puffed invisible smoke in its labors to deliver me to my destruction quicker than I could travel in my human form. Of course I can change into an eagle or a spider or anything I wish but my consciousness changes along with it. I need to be in this bipedal form once I commit it to something. We traveled down a well-used dirt road slower than gravity. The gears of the vehicle resisted and worked on its own destructive pace, chewing away at the ground with rubber teeth. The road switched backed and created a long zig-zag across the inner face of the crater which was followed by a direct descent. It all added up eventually and we were soon on the crater floor. This is a very well visited place. I could feel the eons of human and animal presence that had built up here. It was an invisible miasma as thick as fog. No one else in the vehicle sensed it because they weren't looking and they do not have the proper organs to perceive such things. I felt swarmed by ghostly desperation and struggle. The flat table of the crater floor was an altar of grass and yellow earth. It spanned at least ten miles or more before the other side of the crater lifted back up to scratch at the clouds above. Even though it was this far away it seemed close enough to be touched by my pale bony finger. In the distance there were many other vehicles loping through the middle parts of the crater. Others were idling in place or buzzing around, kicking up rooster tails of dust behind them. They seemed small enough to be a swarm of Tsetse flies in front of the ten thousand foot high inner wall in the distance. The wailing was constant. It was a place unlike any I had ever seen. I have spent the majority of my undead existence in the Mediterranean basin and the shorelines of America. There are so many more potential victims and so much entertainment there that I rarely ever went anywhere else. There are so many who deserve the fate that I inflict upon them. I don't kill them. I torture them. I am a very cultured monster. I feed off of desperation, ideas, words, conflict as much as I consume human blood. It is all the same. Rarely do I have any reason to visit far flung remote places like this even though one may think that I have tread all across the world in the infinite amount of time I have existed. I have always had an interest in mountains and other high places and I have visited many of them. I do this because of the fact that they are the closest one can get to the stars and they are heavily laden with every form of energy that exists. There are many places that I haven't been to and don't care to see. I have been avoiding this place, in particular, because of the ancient destruction that I witnessed. If it is enough to disturb even me then that should be enough assurance of its unspeakable horror.

This gruesome struggle was so long ago and simple curiosity brought me back here. Or was it something else? The blood chant that drives me to do everything. The unconscious forward march of ideas and concepts that dives me into action or madness. I, just like you, have little to no control over this. You think that you dominate and control your mind, your ideas? You are wrong. They are not yours. This feeling is just deception produced by a brain out of control. Addicted to existence. Addicted to fire. The thing that you can't grab but need. If you try to hold it, it burns you. Addiction that justifies itself and creates all the illusions that reinforce the position that it is the most necessary thing that there is. You have no control. No reason. No logic. It is all a gift from something inexplicable that acts totally outside of your will. It is a demonic possession that shackles your consciousness to earth when you should be somewhere else, very far away among the stars. This is why the mind so completely rationalizes that such a place does not exist even though it is always subconsciously present and revealed with closed eyes. If you were to consciously realize what is happening you would try and buck it at all costs because perception amounts to a slow, terminal form of death. Your own death has already been written. You are just marching toward it as fast as you can think. March along. Keep on reading...

Corso

It all started here, in this crater. I could feel the residual energy from the ancient struggle. It was everywhere. This was the perfect testing ground for the earliest humans. They could try themselves against nature in a microcosm before they could develop enough experience to strike out into the greater world in all directions. Trees grow out of orange ground. ***I see good spirits and I see bad spirits (1)***. I could still feel their residual energy and it was everywhere around this ancient plane. This was totally unlike the places of civilization that I was so used to. Not here. Tree roots grow around stones. Not here. Civilization where dark voids of evil were concentrated all over for my personal use. *Lead me not into temptation but deliver me from evil (18).* Stone and glass buildings grow out of asphalt. The mouth of the river is where each side is furthest apart. Palisades. Manhattan. Evil is a matter of perspective after all. It will do us all good once I deal with it properly and return it to its place. The Word is in everything.

He flew into a tantrum

He ran amuck against seven good little boys [the seven sacraments] who were playing with the company: dove his head into Wat Murrey [baptism], gave Stewart Ryall a puck on the plexus [confirmation], wrestled a hurry-come-union with the Gillie Beg [eucharist], wiped all his senses, marital and menial, out of Shrove Sundy Mackfearsome [penance], excrumuncted as freely as any froth-blower into MacIsaac about nothing [matrimony], and imbraced himself (228) with what hung over from the MacCiccaries of the Breeks [holy orders].

Then he swore in his mind an oath. He would take ship and ride into exile – like Coriolanus, the exiled Roman. He would hide in silence – like the Bruce in his cave protected by a spider. He would save himself by cunning – like a Jesuit of Ignatius Loyola. He would wander from city to city, far away where every monk is his own wall and council. And then he would write, firing of his First Epistle to the Hebrews, free loves for everybody! Ham and eggs till the end of the world! Wild primates wouldn't stop him from his Handy Andy writing. Fore he is General Jinglesome (14).

Recorso

Where is a hovel not a hovel (the first riddle of the universe) (Give up?) When it is home (18). The wretched body.

When is a Man not a Man (18)? When he is undead.

Get ready, because you have to do the same thing and I hope you learn from my bullshit.

I had a lot to fear. This vast, tropical, volcanic crater was so thickly teeming with life and death. Even the plants were trembling with desperation and struggle. I must have known – even then – that some unfamiliar process was working its influence on me. The Extraordinary disease was just getting started. Of course I ignored it in my arrogance. We Nosferatu are the most pompous beings on the planet and I am the most arrogant of them. We have operated with impunity, harvesting blood and life whenever we desired for so long that this is a natural state for us. We are demigods in our minds but we are also very fragile. Just like humans. You can't tell the difference if you were to look at us in a police line-up. Perhaps you are one of us and don't even know it yet. It is very likely. Most humans will end up in some form of undead condition like us eventually. They have become so attached to the earth and their bodies in this age of secularism that when the time comes for the planet to finally end they will all find that they will be destroyed with it for they have denied their true inner selves for too long. The irrational source of their thoughts that they have denied for so long will finally take them over and they will see the truth of what they valued during their blood sucking existence and it will have been too late. Free will is as much of a curse as it is a gift. Perhaps more so because few know what to do with it. They will exist as the paradox of the undead until the Earth is destroyed. They have been casting the spell of slavery and imprisonment upon themselves for their entire lives. They will wake up, underground in their coffins and suffer the final destruction just like all of us who are the dark angels of the earth. The army of darkness is being assembled and has been recruiting for a very long time. I am going to punch a hole in this misery. I am going to open these gates of hell and unshackle myself and hopefully many others. I am working on rejecting this spell of rational word, blood, and logic that keeps us confined to our fate by creating a different one. You are looking at it and it is illogical which is why I am confident that it will work. I am using reason to defy itself. There is a way out if you want it. I am going to finally die, I the oldest of the undead. The message was written in fire in the sunny incinerated air one tropical afternoon upon the original volcanic crater rim of this hell planet and it burned up as soon as I saw it.

My arrogance caused me to deny my realization that I was terminally infected with the rational words I used to try and understand, the spells cast upon my shackled consciousness were leading me by the nose to my own revelation and apocalypse. I began to actually feel ill as I was driven around the crater with the busload of anonymous tourists who accompanied me. I dismissed my ever worsening feelings as some sort of travel bug or maladjustment due to time zone or something insignificant. Nothing to worry about too much. I took in the unique sights just like anyone else would, perched with binoculars as my head poked out of the sunroof of the vehicle. Animals feasting on each other or preparing to. Good entertainment for someone like me. As I watched all of this activity I found it interesting that I never found a reason to ever come here despite all of the centuries I had cursed the earth with my presence. Humans and undead are creatures of blood. Creatures of *Habit*. As I said, I prefer to disrupt more civilized places and display my godlike power to terrify and consume.

Jews must cover their heads because it rains flaming hail and angry frogs. It's real hard when what's real isn't but still is real. The women need a much more thorough covering. The little hairpin Frisbees and fedoras that the men use certainly won't do. The women naturally are far more powerful than most men, far more sensitive to the pulse of the moon and the stars and their blood. They are much closer to the ritual, the ethereal eternal ritual of majik that pulses through existence every second of every fucked up day. We won't even talk about the nighttime. Every shift and change in any environment could set off their hypersensitivity. Men are only the sons of Adam. Oblivious for the most part and very easy prey for Nosferatu which explains why there are so many male vampires like myself. A woman could be a daughter of Eve or a daughter of Lilith, each possessing their own unique power, neither greater than the other. Both respond intimately to the chant of the universe. Both messily wield the power of creation. They are wide open nerve endings for spiritual and phantasmal influence and have very little way to shield themselves from it. Women are very valuable to the undead. A natural source of blood that can be consumed without death or violence. Placenta is a vegetarian protein. The only consumable flesh produced from life and not death. They are capable of producing so much power. This is why they cover themselves so completely when following the ancient ways. The ancients were closer to the truth and have gotten further and further away from its simplicity as they have continued to complicate their lives. These traditional coverings are there for protection so that ghosts, aliens, and other forces cannot enter the many seen and unseen orifices in the head. Humility, sex, devotion to husband are all modern excuses to ward off the facts relating to these traditional garments, banal platitudes to pacify a society that is so dulled down by masculinity, science, and politics that is in no way equipped to explain true experience. Mira La Luna! See how she pulls and pushes the very pulse of the oceans. Via con los dios. See how the invisible forces demands reactions in the body and blood. The viscous medium of birth and death. Outside of anyone's control. And you wonder why women have been subdued for uncountable generations. The truth is horrific. Monstrous. More bloodthirsty monsters created every day. Men are terrified to even be near such a burning flame.

My life is with the thrill kill kult. Do you fear for your child (1)? There is a chant present in the body. A vascular rhythm set up at dawn. Blood pulses the mind into its shackled state of repetition. There is a chant carried by the blood. MORE AND MORE, it is insatiable. It is the irrational source of life, the irrational meaning behind everything that pushes it all seemingly forward. It is invisible yet it needs blood to work. Blood everywhere. All over the walls and floors. Every step congeals upon the thirsty crust of the earth. Only a tiny bit ever gets noticed. Sand through the fingers of time, space, and presence. Once something has been cast into the scrutiny of attention and explanation it is already dead. It is perceivable so reality runs away from it. It is now a mere collection of arcane majik and a surface to interpret into a collection of grunts and exhalations emitted from the lips. They are meaningful only as long as consciousness pays its undue attention before it is cast back into the eternal reality hiding behind everything. The inexplicable. The salary of gravediggers and the flames of the crematorium.

Terror precedes nonverbal communication. My dear that is not an act of love (1). Posture and gesture hint at this form of language. *Right hook, left jab.* Countenance and thought projection are evident. ***Isn't that little dog so cute?*** Sound and progression are painfully predictable. "*The fifth and fourth interval will precede the tonic and perhaps a minor third will be thrown in somewhere to be creepy and she will wail about love after a glove or a dove or above or a...you know...is mentioned".* The prediction of the short term future is possible because it is connected to the immediate past. Lovers and killers (1). Future and past. ***She is equipped with revenge(1).*** I never made anything up. It is totally impossible. *I fucking stole it and justified it, just like every corporate fuck.* What is the difference? There is nothing more distorting and incomprehensible than sobriety. *A drink will make me straight.* There is predictable madness in every method. $E=mc^2$.

After driving around the Ngorongoro crater floor – the bloody place of man's early evolution and his early battles with his undead mirror image – in our fine destructive little internal combustion gadget, I was totally exhausted even though I did very little except gawk at the primitive, animalistic struggle for survival and its verdant surroundings. My nostrils were full of the dust of ancient tephra, long dead bones, and remains of hebetudinous plants ground into the surface by the drum cadence of thousands of running hooves. Fresh earth and dust that was as old as I was. All desiccated and floating invisibly in the air. The elevation of the Sun at high noon was very uncomfortable to me. My protection spells were not up to par and I searched through my mind for all of the reasons this could be. Of course the absence of Auryn was my first thought and my heart twitched. I thought I felt a flake of the calcification around it fall off and the beginning of a tear get sucked back into the dust of my face. Surely I was just out of sorts but there was more to it. The blue flames of the sky were tickling their arabesques into my eternal night spell and partly obscuring the stars above from the edges of the horizon. The sun was furious at me and I did not know why. I had not yet accounted for the Extraordinary disease that was slowly progressing to its terminal point. Did the Sun paint the warning at the crater summit instead of the legion of ghosts I had felt there? I did not take this into account because I forgot at the moment that ghosts have a very difficult, if not impossible time manipulating physical things like fire. I took it for an illusion but it could have been more than that. There were other issues involved that I took into consideration. One was the blood that I was using. In order to travel I brought small disposable bags of blood so that I did not have to actually kill anything while I was here. This had been my primary source of blood for some time not because I didn't kill to get my blood back in New York or, more correctly, I hadn't in a very long time. That is kind of a lie. I only killed those who deserved it. Capitalists. Upper class fucks. I didn't drink their blood. I just killed them because no one earth deserves it more. I considered the possibility that there could have been something wrong with the new, post-consumer, filtered and formulated blood that I had been, more or less, satisfied with until now.

Leviticus 17:14

[14] For the life of every sort of flesh is its blood, because the life is in it. Consequently, I said to the Israelites: "You must not eat the blood of any sort of flesh because the life of every sort of flesh is its blood. Anyone eating it will be cut off."

In the days immediately before I left North America to visit this site I ran into a problem with the source of blood I had been relying upon. The supply chain of blood was corrupted and I had a substandard product. It happens to heroin addicts all of the time as well. Vampires are so close to junkies in their behavior that it is scary. A real junky knows when there is fentanyl, baking soda, vitamin B12, sucrose, starch, crushed over-the-counter painkillers, talcum powder, powdered milk, laundry detergent, caffeine, rat poison or any other shit in there. Junk is junk. Everything else is everything else. It is not that complicated. If there is nothing else available it does not stop them from buying it and using it. Heroin addicts are virtually vampires and alcoholics are virtually zombies. It will catch up with them all soon enough. Vampires love to kill junkies because their blood is so saturated that it gives a fine effect and most humans don't care or notice when they are gone because they are already gone. Alcoholics, not nearly as attractive victims. Their blood is not palatable and they are usually way too public with their delinquent behavior. We Nosferatu usually let them die and rot underground before they wake up again.

There are a large amount of undead doctors in any urban area who set aside a supply from blood donations, murder victims, and other untimely deaths who won't be missing their vascular fluids, so that we can continue feeding and not resort to the old ways of actually assaulting people with our teeth. Many of us vampires got our hands on crappy blood that particular month and it has happened to all of us from time to time in the past. There was a shortage in New York as I was preparing for my sojourn. I am surprised that this did not occur more often. There are so many of us in the five boroughs and sometimes there is not enough to go around. From time to time there are an abnormal amount of gunshot, knife, or automobile victims that use up the supply. Sometimes there is a shortage whenever Keith Richards and Mick Jagger are around. The bastards drain out the whole city and you can't get rid of them quick enough.

There must have been pig blood or the blood of some other animal cut in with the real human product. If not this then there is too much alcohol or other toxin in there that putrefies the flavor and the effect. We call this pig blood no matter what it is cut with. Whatever it was that I had been getting was leaving me feeling very strange even before I left but I didn't think too much of it at the time. When this happens it can sometimes be fixed with a few simple incantations so that it becomes more palatable but it doesn't always work depending upon what has already been done to it. It is truly a black market after all. There are so many needles, tubes, suction devices, solutions, cogs, gears, wheels, belts, chains, spirits, illusions, rituals, etc. in place to maintain some resemblance of any sort of status quo through-out history that we can't even keep up with them anymore. The undead are planted at every level of human activity whether it is political, scientific, academic, law enforcement, or delinquent. How many residual spells are left over that contradict the newest revised ones? It is becoming totally irrational. It was the entire time I suppose but it has built up to a point of absurdity. Law, Order, Reason, Etc. has mutated into a terminal point of contradiction. We all, humans and undead alike, exist semi-uncomfortably with the most basic contradictions and dysfunctions screaming in our face. The most obvious is our messed up socio-economic system that forces normal activity into the shadow of the black market. These types of spells are masked as "business as usual" and are a perfect set of circumstances to allow the evil energies and potentially benevolent voids that Auryn has mastered to take root and thrive. Nothing can suck one in quicker than darkness. What is left after all of these arrangements is a hideous pile of contradictions that are unconsciously and consciously built up over many generations. This is the reason why my blood supply got all messed up in the first place. Supply and demand for profit. The continual attempt to get more out of less. An insane contradiction masked as "business as usual" One of the many reasons so much blood is spilled upon the ground and wasted.

Where do I even begin when it comes to reasoning out all of the horror and ineptitude of the democratic capitalist relationship with symbiotic parasitism? As I mentioned, it is such an enormous pile of buried and embattled abominations and unaccounted forces of contradiction and self-destruction that there are so many examples I do not even know where to begin. Pasta! Pick out one thread and the rest sticks to it. Is there any doubt of the apocalyptic teleology that is so intimately hidden in plain sight? If you don't see it you are either not looking or well off enough to not give a shit. An old saying from our esteemed Bubba Nassr Eddin is appropriate: "You can't get a man to understand something if he is paid to not understand it." *Another good one from James Nasser Eddin:* "The best way to mess up a system is to do what they tell you to do." *One of the many side effects of capitalist culture is the fact that most living humans are so toxified that us vampires prefer to get our blood elsewhere in a more purified form. There is a very large underground infrastructure in place that is solely dedicated to purification and distribution of blood for our consumption. We have developed this supply chain secretly so it is not quite perfected. It also vampirizes off the human medical system and the blood supply within it. All of the bovine growth hormones, birth control medications, illicit substances, alcohol, prescription drugs, food preservatives, salts, and crop chemicals have made normal unprocessed human blood almost completely inconsumable. You thought that we were a bunch of monsters running amok and biting people. Ha! We have become more civilized than that. Humans are far more monstrous and bloodthirsty than we are. Many of them have no qualms about killing off others. Some make entire careers out of it. I hear it pays well.*

Addiction rules. There is no conspiracy at all. Actually, the exact opposite is happening. Have you ever heard of the cliché "kill them with kindness"? Nothing is hidden at all. Give them what they want. Fucking addicts. Addicted to chocolate. Addicted to coffee. Addicted to having something to bitch about. Addicted to being urinated upon. Addicted to being walked upon. An entire generation addicted to cell phones of all things. Addicted to paying exorbitant amounts of money to a woman dressed as a man who will make you wear diapers and crawl around on the floor so she can whip your ass and call you a very bad little baby cowboy. It is laughing in your face as it is plastered upon every possible screen, wall, billboard and telephone pole that it possibly can bandage to. Addicted to altered blood. Addicted to blood. Addicted to blood. Addicted to blood. Addicted to blood, you bloody blood covered blood addicts. Saturn is devouring his children. This has been taken to the extreme when it comes to the buying and selling of goods for we are the goods being consumed. We are all being slowly destroyed by fulfilling our desire as soon as we can.

Capitalism and the almighty dollar is solely to blame for all of these difficulties that afflict our blood supply. This parasitic relationship has been passed down through-out history. Humans are clever enough on their own. They don't really need us undead to oppress them like we so easily could. They can do it perfectly fine without any help from us even though some of us are very sick and like to help push things along from time to time. Most of us have let this system of oppression and tyranny develop almost totally unchecked forever. It has landed in the laps of this generation of humans in such a gristly, shattered condition that it is amazing to me that it has not yet imploded. Addiction is far too powerful of a force and most humans will deal with any form of adversity in order to submit to it for any amount of time. This (addiction) is the main force that keeps this completely fucked up system ("Capitalist Democracy") of human pseudo-organization alive. Only recently has the dysfunction actually trickled down to the level that it actually effects the undead population. I have been warning my undead colleagues for the past hundred years or more that it was going to come to this. None have listened. Of course many millennia of not-life has blinded them to the point that they operate in a state of conscious apathy which is almost as bad as the average human. There is no conspiracy involved at all. Simply the capitalization on the forces of addiction that so many agree to live with. Humans and undead are virtually the same. All of you are fucking vampires or zombies. I am not going to allow myself to be categorized any differently. I just have a little more power and majik than the average human but that is sickening to me as well. You want what I have? An Extraordinary disease? *The fuck you do.*

Nosferatu obviously have been around for a very long time. I remember Rome at the height of its imperial force very well. Almost like it was just a week ago. Many of us Nosferatu were around then with the exception of the few newcomers to the fold. Most of us remember exactly how and when the Romans discovered and began to perfect their form of domination. The poor Etruscans had little chance. The Romans a few generations later discovered that blood and gore may win battles but it can't win peace and imperial stability outside of the undead population who thrive on this sort of mirth. The masses would be guaranteed to revolt if conquerors stayed only as an overt militant police state. They had to kill them with kindness. Give them what they want but kill with that too so that they could fucking get rid of the lowly assholes who may start some unwanted shit. They found that this approach worked well even on the smallest scale. Theatre was the beginning of this and it was stolen from the Hellenic culture by Rome. A very effective propaganda system that has degenerated – alongside of societal values – into poop smearing infancy in the form of Broadway and Hollywood. One of the many reasons why I find theatre to be so intolerably loathsome. Broadway is the ultimate in intolerability. I won't even discuss anything about Hollywood and its standard of cinema because someone will bring up Star Wars and we will never shut the fuck up and we will be distracted with the eternal repetition of pointlessness. Then another actor or celebrity will have the chance of being elected into high office which is the last thing that the world need. Mike Tyson for president! Theatre was an effective archetype of propaganda but the coliseum was the eagle swoop of genius that taloned the masses to the sky so their spirits could be consumed upon the cliffs but get a good ride before it happened.

By the time this concept – Capitalism: kill them with what they want; the institutionalization of the manipulation of addiction in all of its forms for political and monetary power – had been handed down to contemporary capitalist America it had been gerrymandered and permutated and multiplied through every possible technological and biological tool available. Every living human supposedly benefits from this evolution and this is the common justification why it happens even though an equal if not higher degree of human, animal, and vegetable death and suffering is accompanied by these advances. Humans evolve in a way that is far different than the other animals because they can totally change their environmental conditions very quickly. So quickly that their ideas evolve and their bodies devolve because the biology cannot catch up with the speed of conceptual evolution. This form of culture is advertised and reported upon in so many ways that everyone believes that it works as their bodies and minds become more toxified and misshapen as they proceed. They have been totally desensitized to the violence and death that is produced. Good for us undead of course. Bad for us because the blood filtered through these warped minds and bodies is inconsumable. The drug addicts are preferable to the normal fucks because the addicts usually don't eat or expose themselves to any other influence than the drugs so their blood is usually simpler and even pleasurable on some occasions. The alcoholic is not the same of course. They are addicts of course, and they perform all of the same addictive behaviors as the rest but they are further toxified by their assimilation to the myriad of mutagens that infect capitalist society at large. Especially the infection of sports, theatre, and music (most music on a large scale is corporate byproduct designed to create the same effect of mindlessness as sports so the proper endorphins of satiation can be released and deadly control can be accomplished), fandom. The endorphins produced by this pointlessness acted out in parking lots surrounding stadia or something of the like is amplified by consumption of a mass amount of alcohol along with hot dog nitrates making the blood quiver with pollution. This form of "normal" alcoholic blood is the worst that there is. The average "abnormal" street drunk isn't quite as bad – because they, like junkies, rarely consume food or do anything but drink because that is all they can afford – but they have a flavor that is quite rotten and is wide open to any of these other aforementioned "normal" contaminants.

We Nosferatu need all the blood that we can get and we have always taken it whenever we need it. It is certainly arguable that this actually works for the greater good of humanity. So many billions are out on the street, crazed, or deprived for so long. They are so unhappy that they give up their blood: time, space, and lives for the most meagre return. If we were to judge this system that works solely upon monetary power based upon the amount of humans who are truly happy with their lives – rich and poor alike – then there should be a great deal of doubt applied to the discussion of the true effectiveness of this system. James Mill would probably agree that this is the sign of a very sick society that needs help. Many people who need help the most resist it at all costs in favor of trying to "do it on their own". Another symptom of the sickness. The same can be applied to society. That which needs help the most will resist it the most. There is a great deal of things that monetary power is good at – such as control at the cost of life, time, and blood – but the creation and maintenance of human happiness is certainly not one of them.

I remember very well when the American constitution was first conceived and written. A document like this could only be conceived of and penned under the influence of the intoxicating smell of black powder smoke. It is a defiant incantation that is completely full of desperate ideals. Many Americans who live today – hundreds of years later – look back at this document and tell themselves and each other that this document is "outdated" and therefore does not effectively apply to their contemporary circumstances because new and unforeseen issues have developed. They truly believe that they live in a different world because of all the technological and supposed social development that has gone on since the revolution. Others create the exact opposite flub. They mistakenly look back to a day that never occurred and try to resurrect the ideals that this document lays out. Ideals that have never been even yet realized. These are people who are, unfortunately very out of touch with history and culture. They forgot to educate themselves in their own history and adopt false contemporary mythologies. They most likely studied something else – instead of history – in order to reap whatever rewards they can by following the capitalist model instead of one of democracy. Who studies history anyway? They are like freaks who read books and study literature and other such droll, unprofitable activities. Despite whatever superficial appearance there may be these two things – democracy and capitalism – are contradictory. Exact opposite forces that are not logically compatible. Only if one believes the truth: that chaos is the ultimate expression of reality, does this living contradiction begin to be explained. Most aren't willing to take this step. Of course I already mentioned that reality with a capital "R" is exactly this, the incomprehensible unification of opposites. Unfortunately for humanity, this expression of reality is impossible to understand or ***perceive****, let alone be activated in any sort of conceivable practice. One side of any binary vision must be accepted, at least partially, over another in order to have any sort of* ***perceived*** *functionality. Humans have a hard enough time multitasking banalities let alone possibilities. Something always has to give and that is typically whatever choice acts the farthest from cultural norms at the time. Capitalism wins out not because of its effectiveness but because of its inertia. A quote from one of the greatest benefactors of this system can sum up the sense that it actually makes. When asked what he thinks he responded with great acclaim:* ***"Confefe."***

Only us undead have been around long enough to see it all develop and shatter and then develop again out of its ashes. Only us undead can truly understand the secret toxin that is injected into the minds and bodies of every living generation. We undead are a few steps closer to understanding the inconceivable reality of unified contradiction. Reality. Unattainable even to us armies of the night. We are all still left with our ***perceptions.*** *The only way for any of us to even come close to experiencing "Reality" would be a complete shutdown of all senses and all* **perceptions.** *Sounds a bit like death. No? This is what is required of us. The only way to experience reality is to fucking die. So fuck you and your opinions. That is the only way. Otherwise we are left with choice and it is absolutely predictable which choice will be made. One or the other.* ***Perception*** *or reality, live or die, Night or day, happiness or sadness, pleasure or pain. Reason or chaos. Which do you choose? I'm certain I can predict it and I don't even have to use my arcane abilities.*

Most humans are too proud to understand or admit the fact that they are controlled and totally mind-fucked. They have just enough freedom to agree to be enslaved. Most will never understand. Most junkies will not even admit to themselves that they are addicts. Many others actually believe that they have a God that has given them "free will". This is far more of a truth than they actually realize. What they will never admit to themselves and each other is the simple fact that they have used this free will to choose a position of total enslavement. There is little to no simultaneity to being free or being enslaved. Even the highest level bureaucrats with the biggest paychecks are enslaved. Their slavery is one of the mind. They must believe in the destructive system that they organize and vampirize off. Their slavery is one of documents, concepts, words. A prison built out of cards. The Constitution is yet another example. It is a set of ideals. Not something that is confined to a specific time and space. A set of ideals. It never has nor will it in the foreseeable future ever be totally realized in practice. Forget the Declaration of Independence. How long did it take for the very simple ideal "that all people are created equal" to be taken seriously? Has it even yet happened in a satisfactory manner? How many had to be martyred for this very simple idea? Even though there was an entire population across an entire continent that professed to their God as they knew Him that they actually believed in these ideas, many among them fight against it with every breath they take. Still – how many years later – the simple idea of human equality has still never manifested.

What if I even begin to broach the question regarding the declaration that the government exists to protect unalienable rights. The protection of the "pursuit of happiness?" How many sit in prison because they pursued something that made them happy that did not, at all, effect anyone but themselves or other consenting adults? The use of contraband and illicit substances has put so many Americans in jail that it is unfathomable. Is ones choice of intoxicant not an expression of their perception of happi-

ness? It is a straight road to imprisonment in many ways. Freedom is rarely discussed in this context but it should be. The drug epidemic only seems to get worse. This is a nation of addicts but some must be marginalized so that the rest of those with "acceptable" addictions can continue to play follow the leader. The ones who pursue their own happiness outside of the main herd are certainly dangerous. To the status quo. What would happen if entertainment was contraband? Ever heard of Delirium Tremens or the Kicks? Childs play compared to Entertainment withdrawal. Entertainment is the most dangerous addiction there is. This is why we lock up the "bad" addicts and encourage the "ok" ones. If you drink beer and watch football you are okay but the rest of the folks who enjoy a different flavor are considered taboo and fit to be tied up. As if that form of treatment actually benefits the individual and the society that claims to protect the pursuit of individual happiness. Contradictions, paradoxes, hypocrisies, and lies; all are what make up ***perception*** *of reality through the explanation of those* ***perceptions*** *with words and reason. One side must always win out to make sense because reality makes no sense in any expressible manner. The attempt to ensure "good" will always produce evil.*

Utilitarianism in its original form under Bentham and Mill discusses the possibility of social systems that give the most happiness to the most amount of people. This would fit in with the Constitutional concept but not with the Capitalist concept. The latter is designed to give the most amount of happiness to the least amount of possible people. Those being the vulturous individuals at the top of the economic food chain. They insist that they got there because of "hard work" or "superior intelligence" or some other such nonsense. They did it through greed, manipulation, blood and the denial of any form of intelligence except that specific form of intelligence which applies directly to the greed and manipulation that they are so obsessed with. Social progress is a side effect, not the main goal. Conformity is the only intelligence they comprehend. Historical intelligence, cultural intelligence, social intelligence, even scientific intelligence is all thrown to the side as mere forms of entertainment that are lesser than greed and manipulative intelligence. This of course is only true in the capitalist model that we have been so uniquely oppressed with as of late. It wasn't always this bad but anyone who did not see it coming was surely blind or in denial. The pursuit of happiness? A protected right of the people? Ha! That is laughable. Vampires rule. We are the superior race. Manipulative intelligence has discovered how to extract value from time to gain power. All of which are totally irrational and do not actually exist. Blood from a stone if I may be permitted another cliché which does turn my stomach but may help in certain, choice, explanations. Why write about vampires? This is the ultimate metaphor for capitalism. Bloodletting and gore consumption makes the world go around. Those who pursue power through manipulative intelligence must get as much in as they can during their short existence so that they can pass on the sickle and whip to the next poor fucker who lost their way down the dark alley toward the sunset of human existence named capitalism.

Gotterdammerung

Hoia Ho! Hoia Ho! *How can we ever expect the happiness of every sorry assed individual human to ever be protected and respected by the community and by law? There are so many divergent forms of happiness that are so contradictory that someone has to be extraneous to this protection. Someone has to take the role of criminal even if their actions only effect themselves. There has to be some scapegoat. There has to be some victim to be held up as an example of what not to do if they want everyone else to fall in line and accept one side of the binary system over the other. Capitalism must supersede democracy if the status quo wants to continue without another bloody revolution. Land war in America is not a possibility. Not a rational one. Unity of opposites is not rational. It is totally incomprehensible. Therefore destruction must ensue if there is to be any sort of change. Land war in America. What a fascinating possibility to the undead. Here lies the craziest and most destructive motherfuckers that ever existed anywhere in history. Perhaps those in Jerusalem may compare but there aren't nearly as many of them and they aren't flooded by nearly as much crystal meth, junkies, gangsters, rednecks, brainwashing entertainment and news media and every other sort of hillbilly or ghetto gangster freak who is sitting at home oiling their gun collection and just waiting for an excuse to use it. How can happiness for all ever be protected by law? It is an insane ideal. An unattainable godlike possibility.*

Interruption:

Televisioning of four interesting Mulligan Events. (1) How the fashionable world is afeebling themselves with rich pastry. (2) How Spanish gold is being played up by the Anti-Greenback Party. (3) How Albion(England) professes to maintain the Holy Crypt against the devil dances of the last. (4) How Successful American businessmen are making a resolution never to grow old or raise salaries or become spiritually complicated or donate money to encourage philosophy (5).

The existence of Santa Claus and Vampires is a more realistic prospect if we are to try to understand things in these non-extravagant terms. It is far easier to throw everyone to the wolves and expect everyone to grab what they can, hence capitalism has never allowed a democratic republic to truly manifest itself in any reasonable way. This is against the very nature of capitalism which only allows for winners and losers. The payers and the paid. The controllers and the controlled. We are all fools led around by a ring in the nose and fed mythologies of freedom and justice and victory. To say that atheism has no Gods is absurd. They worship the same ones the Romans did. Victory and Fortune. Kobe Bryant died and people acted like it was the death of Zeus. O Fortuna, we who are about to die salute you. I for one could give a flying fuck. Get it? Flying... Kobe...yeah, yeah. That was done for a reason. Emphasis. It Really Is A Bad Joke. I mean all of it... But it is the Religion of Secularism. And they thought they didn't worship. Of course they did. You Must Be Happy With The Addictive Toxin That We Deem Okay. Like worshiping people for putting colorful balls through colorful metal rings. I can't think of anything more important. Besides everything of course. Fuck you though. No one cares what your opinion is when you are on the clock. If you are being paid you must perform or go home and most of an acceptable day under the yoke of capitalism is spent operating under these conditions. Where is the pursuit of happiness I humbly ask? In the few hours that are left when not struggling for the devices and successes of someone else's tyranny? Blood is the commodity. Life and consciousness itself is fueled by blood. We suffer from an insane and irrational addiction. The written word itself is the toxin, the void of nothing, the virus of lies that has infected the entire planet and seduces all to walk into it. The word is responsible for everything, meaning "nothing" of course. It is a prison of ink and paper. It demands attention and kills when one disregards the **perception** *of the message. It is incomprehensible. A unity of light and dark. Black and blue scars scratch across time and sense. This is the only thing that gives the illusion of order. It is the source of human vampirism and its adherents will all become undead. They will become lies. Saladin said to his son* ***"I warn you against shedding blood, indulging it, and making a habit of it, for blood never sleeps (19)".*** *We Nosferatu never sleep. We carry the viral addiction to consciousness through-out time.*

The majority of one's time and energy is spent working for the piece of paper that is used to maintain life itself and only after all of the neces-

sities of life itself are finally resolved can one actually try to experience something that may hint at freedom. Another God of atheism. Also known as Liberty. This is an insanity of the highest order but it is presented and accepted in the most reasonable ways. Ink on paper in all of its forms has crushed the hope of true freedom and has torn open the body to the point that blood is everywhere. Everything one does spills blood upon their hands. The Serengeti of social Darwinism is waiting to consume the weak and distracted. This has been breaking down steadily into entropy over the years. The dysfunction has even attacked the humans higher and higher up the food chain. Still there is so much denial and reasoning to try to explain otherwise. There is little to no difference between the most powerful, well paid golfers and the shambling homeless vagrants. They need the same basic things. We undead need some of the same things as well. As capitalism marches further and further toward its endgame we undead are effected as much as the humans are. Clean blood for our consumption has become more and more of a commodity. It has become less and less available.

Over the millennia the undead have become less and less politically active. We have seen so many organizing principals come and go, so many ideals proposed and never achieved yet the same basic needs go on unchanged. After all of these millennia have passed they still have not attained anything that will function properly without massive amounts of destruction. Anarchy is the only true constant. It is the only organizing principal that has actually described every attempt at human order ever proposed. It all swiftly degenerates into anarchy the moment some new ideal is proposed. Anarchy is the only thing that has ever worked for anyone at any level. What happens when people of high position "get things done"? They sidestep the law and call it a "loophole" or they lobby their powerful friends to make their poor behavior legal. What happens when people of low position "get things done"? They break the law and say "fuck it"! Anarchy is the way people get things done. It has been Anarchy this entire time you assholes. People refuse to comprehend the results that are right in front of them because they are far too busy killing each other in the attempt to rise up to their incomprehensible ideals that are spelled out in denial of what is actually claimed. Democracy or Profit or some other deity of secularism. Blood is the result. Addiction to fantasy. Tainted, virally infected blood. This is the disease itself. You are staring at it right now. This is the incantation that binds ***perception*** *to the razors edge of destruction. It lacerates the mind and succeeds in making certain that reality will never be* ***perceived*** *even though humans do not even possess the proper sensory organs to see it in the first place.*

The only time Nosferatu kill people is when they deserve it. This is why there are so many of us in New York. We seek the bloodshed of the grotesque capitalist who has more funds than he or she may be worth. *They are the true vampires of this world.*

$

The bourgeoisie had better watch out for me
All throughout this so called nation
We don't want your filthy money
We don't need your innocent bloodshed
We just wanna end your world

Well my mind's made up
Yes it's time for you to pay
Better watch out for me
I'm a member of the F. V. K (24).

$

I was truly alone in Africa. All of my abilities were beginning to act differently than I expected and it was getting almost out of control. I didn't know if I was being hypersensitive to the fact that animals were eating each other all around me or if I had done something wrong. There were too many factors closing in for me to thread out any sense. Animals have a very powerful vocabulary of desperation, it was palpable to me. It was all the same environment that I was used to in any city but it was also so different. I could see hallucinogenic trails of hormones and pheromones and phagocytes flying like flags behind every animal of prey as it cantered along its path. The consumers stalked their victims and all existed in a state of pure desperation that was not unlike that of any Main Street commerce district in any town America.

That is one of the reasons why I enjoyed being in civilization and spending as much time there as I did. To us undead, every street was throbbing with blood waiting to be altered by any endorphin or humiliation that the brain so eagerly pumped into it to keep everyone shackled to their poor fragile bodies. Blood in the street is everywhere. It is smeared over every cheap leaf of newsprint, every billboard, and every technologically animated screen of every quality. All blood. Everywhere. It pulses in and out of time and space, past and future. All of it pumps volatility into the present. Every word: Blood. Every space between every word: Blood. The fire of Prometheus. His tainted gift surges in the blood and separates us only by a razor edge from the animals. It is not enough of a separation for us to easily wield this fire while falling back into animal rage and consumption. I love housecats. They are the bloodiest and most evil little balls of destruction that there is. Imperial. Just like me. They are automated to be obsessed with blood. I am obsessed with blood for a reason that has only slightly more dialectics. The fire of illumination animates my lust and the blood ensures my receptiveness to the majik from the stars above. The logic of chaos. It is easier to understand if you are undead or obsessed with entropy. Interaction is controlled by blood as well as the brain that feeds upon it. Logic and reason: Blood. War, peace: blood, all the same. Nothing but blood. Water is pointless without blood. Ink and paint; pointless on their own. Only blood matters. A pleasing aroma for the Lord. I always mistakenly thought that the Lord was me. I was only partly correct. I, Nosferatu, thought that blood was the endgame. Naturally. It is only the beginning.

Blood is submissive to something higher. Blood is the medium of the infection. ***Agenbite of Inwit.*** Neurosis of shame and pride. An Extraordinary disease. Excuse me for typing the word *Blood* so much. I am mildly obsessed. You can't blame me. This is a spell and I must repeat myself continually. As I have already said. So I am still repeating myself. You can't leave a bottle of pills lying around with a junky in the house. You can't leave words lying around with a vampire in residence. Blood is the medium of the infection that delivers the substance to the brain. Words are the infection. Everyone is terminal. Everyone unclean. Human and undead alike. None can approach the Temple Mount with-out the proper purge and cleansing and sacrifice of vascular fluid. No city on the planet has spilled more blood and brains than Jerusalem. A favorite place of mine to haunt of course. It gets a bit uncomfortable after a while so I only visit on occasion. Only when there is going to be a really good run do I ever consider going. Meaning destruction of course. Lots of good destruction went down here as you probably know. My favorite was the invasion of Titus. I love to stand on Mt Scopus and get the view. It must have been like playing out a vivid version of Checkmate.

All of this happens because of the build-up of words. They pile upon each other and infest the veins until it reaches a breaking point and there is no turning back. Then, terror or offense or pride or shame kick in and it is all over. The midbrain is in control and the consciousness blurs. Consciousness has no control when sub consciousness takes over.

This happens more often than most even realize. Most of the important decisions of the day are automated. There are varying degrees of infestation. Many different forms and sources, causes and effects. The virus is undead, neither technically alive nor deceased but still possesses the programmed urge to reproduce and continue. That is why it is our burden. Nosferatu. A virus is not alive but it feeds upon life. This Extraordinary disease of mine is at the root of what pushes life's irrational urges forward in an attempt to escape the unescapable. Life and evolution are a reaction to its attacks upon the blood inside, the fire inside. The virus is the first form of undead habitation on the planet. It was here as long as life has been. Perhaps longer in a dormant state. It is the reason that the undead separated from the bloodline of humanity. It is The Word. The first spoken human word. Not to be confused the first Word of divine creation which is the Unspeakable Name Shem HaMephorash. The first human word was a repetition. A cheap imitation of the divine word. Humans have never been able to create anything. They only are capable of appropriation.

The first human word was as close to the original Unspeakable Name as the inferior human lips could utter in defiant desperation. ***My dear that is not an act of love (1).*** A defiant response to its newfound condition. These unrecorded and totally incomprehensible syllables are the closest thing that could be uttered to the original divine name by the human organism. The very first act of human creation was not creation at all. It was imitation. It was a virus that flooded into the body the second the mouth opened, not an act of discovery, creativity, explanation, understanding, reason or anything else. It was a defiant act – a performance – of imitation in an attempt to seize the same power that bound it. An imitation of the source which caused the incomprehensible condition in which it found itself. Before blissfully nonexistent, now imprisoned by walls of flesh, bone and gristle – intoxicated by blood and all the lesser fluids that create its own unique flavor then zapped into animation by the cruel electricity that was stolen from thunder and still resonates through the skull in a deafening roar of direct current. Flesh on fire from the inside out through the struggling conflagration of the captured, incomprehensible soul that incinerates everything in its path through the desire to be part of and simultaneously explain and escape this inexplicable continuum of banal obligation.

The first act of human creation was not creation. It was imitation of the inexplicable freedom it had lost the second it realized that it wanted more of the inexplicable pseudo-freedom that it could describe yet not comprehend. Every other subsequent act of human creation followed from this archetype like a sound wave. Imitation piled upon imitation. Waves upon a still pond after a pebble was dropped in. The waves can never be the pebble. Every wave gets further and further away from its source but is curiously similar to the one that came before it. The first act of human creation, the imperfect imitation of the original word. The nameless name. Shem HaMephorash .This act was written into the genetics of the species. It is carried in the blood from generation to generation. It rides, invisibly twining and writhing within the DNA, never to be discovered by microscope or any other form of technology. It is only visible in the desperation of the artist at work. It is discoverable only by inexplicable sensation, by triggers of neurology which are only set off by pure desperation and they only last for a moment in time. Subatomic particles are as big as refrigerators compared to this subtle inner biology. If it were ever "discovered" it would be denied because it changes every fraction of a second depending on an infinite amount of conditions.

Only a blood addict can understand and begin to discover the source of the terminal virus that infects our brains through word. One would need many generations of time and experience to crack this buried seed. It will never happen through human effort because there is no profit to be made from such research. Money is more often invested in things that strip away humanity rather than concepts that try to understand its primal origins. Those stripping agents are there to be commercially exploited. Those which are not lead to the inevitable conclusion that virtually everything is out of hand. They lead back to the inexplicable. The echo of the original inexplicable word that caused this imitation and its attachment to the very blood that demands the continuation of life. The original human utterance is attached to the blood. It is the fire inside which is fueled by the oxygen that we all breathe and is slowly turning everyone to ash. Everything in sight is consumable and consumed for a cost. Everything is left burnt with the insatiable desire of the souls yearning.

Permutations of the original spoken imitative word have survived through-out the ages as nonsense. This nonsense attached itself to every other word afterwards. It is attached to every being that has the misfortune of existing on this planet in any form. Every manifestation of every desire is a word, even in the basest animals. They all feed upon each other and pass on the chaos of biological desire only to manifest more of the same, over and over the same. There will never be a resolution unless the entire thing is destroyed or reverse engineered and brought back to the blood itself. Back to the original virus that began consciousness. The beating of the heart keeps it alive. The repetition of the same thing. Over and over. War drums. Biology. The imperfect chant of the original word is the echo of the earlier search to speak the unspeakable and define the indefinable. The Hare Krsna's attempt to do this very task. They repeat the same useless syllables over and over until they become useful. They may – one day – find the proper permutation of syllable, and expression to reverse engineer the unspeakable name but I sense that they are not trying to do this. Theirs seems to be a slightly different project.

After being exposed and weakened under the sunlight baking the floor of Nogorongoro I have found that the residual energy of the first desperate humans has reactivated in my cells. It was there all along. I was created here too. I had opened up Pandora's Box, the things within me that I had intentionally forgotten. They were the closest to the first word which is the closest to the indefinable word. I know this because I invented them. I sought the event horizon. I sought to freeze every event in time and space with a simple, singular gesture. The Name of the Godhead. This recent realization of my status as a vector has changed me in a way that will never allow me to be right again. My blood lust has brought me to this conclusion. The end is here. Can't you see it? It is right here and now. Each word has died. Each second is destroyed. Consumed by the satanic fires of reason burning up the page.

I left the Ngorongoro crater with much more than when I entered it. I discovered the key to discovering the True Reality beyond perception. The syllables of the unspeakable name were activated within me. Name has left its power here more so than anything else. Ngorongoro. Ngorongoro, Ngorongoro. Say it over and over. The word breaks down into nonsense. Yet here is the only form of truth. ***Only the right name gives beings and things their reality, and a wrong name makes everything unreal. That's what lies do (6).*** This remote place in the African wilderness is the beginning of the word infection. This namesake is mathematically ***four ways of saying five (4).*** It is a blood chant. The same thing over and over that becomes something else.

I see good spirits and I see bad spirits. My life is with the thrill kill kult (1). I see the bird sitting at the windowsill when there isn't even a window in the wall. One addict helping another is the only thing that can make existence just a little more tolerable. Just say it: "My name is ______________________________ and I am an addict." There are so many ways for one to help another. The illusion of perception is cunning, baffling, and powerful yet no one has the ability to quit on their own even though they think that they can. It is what separates one from another.

Insanity. It must be reverse engineered, starting with the current word and breaking it all apart in an effort to go backward and bring the past to the present. I have done this work. This is my admission. This is my secret but not for very long. I must bring this silently to the correct place and time. This time and place is not Ngorognoro, the place where the soul was set on fire by the original sin. Not Ngorongoro. A different crater that is much bigger but very close. *The rite of spring. The adoration of the earth. Chuzbog and the dance of the evil spirits.* Waterloo. Rubicon. Tet. A Russian Spy boat is off the coast of Connecticut. Tip. Can you please get me a Manhattan? All the same. All the same. Over and over. I can travel further sitting in one place than any human can in a lifetime on an airplane. This is why humans cannot and will not ever crack the code. They will never be able to reverse engineer their blood virus to discover the unspeakable name within it and then shout it from a mountaintop. They will never be able to halt the shattered perception of reality and all the infinite permutations of it that all of their collective bodies carry. They will never know the irrational spell of the Name and use it to shock the attention of the Infinite Creator and maintainer of existence. They are far too sensitive in their frail biology. They must always protect the wide open, gaping hole on the top of their skulls which his commonly referred to as the head chakra. Even those who are sensitive to and are aware of such things can only handle so much before pure evil rushes in and shuts down any progress they may make. Undead will know if they prepare themselves and mass their inner power. The Jews and Muslims protect their head all the time to ward off these spiritual attacks. You will all soon be undead so you must learn now.

Only we, Nosferatu, have consumed enough blood from so many different sources over the millennia. Only one of us has built within us the capacity to reverse engineer the Original Unspeakable Word which is the Very Name of the Creator Himself. Shem HaMephorash .The false imitation of which has attached itself to the blood through a virus that has remained masked through-out time. Creation should forever remain safe because the undead would surely never want to escape their position on the Earth. We are evil so why would we want to tamper with such things? It was a safeguard in the design. It is against the way that everything was intended – or was it? The undead are the children of the darkness. The angels of the earth who are stranded here with ultimate dominion. Why on Earth would one of us be compelled to try to unravel the very situation that maintains our elite status?

The answer is so simple yet it is so hard to face. Each one of us knows that there will be an End to this. It is the Neurosis of shame and pride. A swimmy, vague sensation but its time will come. Each one of us creatures exists in denial of this fact. After the millennia of existence there is no longer any difference between day and night. It is all continuum. Another false perception of reality. This is another illusion that is built into creation to safeguard the Unspeakable Name. When day and night are fused it creates the perception that opposites are somehow unified. When one is not alive and also not dead this illusion is reinforced. Illusion is upon us for we still require blood, the maintainer of the illusions, and the original virus of the word. The limitations of creation, the imperfect imitation of the original word that can never be uttered. Until now. I am infected. I the undead. I can now see clearly. Our run will end and it will end sooner than we think. This planet that we cling to will expire and we will go with it...***or more strictly but tristurned initials, the cluekey to a worldroom beyond a roomwhorld, for scarce one, or pathetically few of his dode canal sammenlivers cared seriously for long to doubt with Kurt luld van Dijke (the gravitational pull percieved by certain fixed residents and the capture of uncertain comets chancedrifting through our system suggesting an authenticitatem of his aliquitudinis) the canonicity of his existence as a tesseract. Be still, O quick! Speak him dumb! Hush ye fronds of Ulma (5)!*** Silence. When this happens – silence or nothing happening – the original name will be preserved and will safely never be perceived. Silence does not exist for the subconscious is always speaking. The end times will be dark as night. It will be the time the undead arise in all of their legions. They will then go mad and begin to hunt and consume each other in a final act of desperation. A final blood rite in an attempt to keep their desire for their arcane, earthbound bodies burning onward into immortality. It is a futility. Our immortality as undead is only perceived. You think that this does not affect you? You think that you are somehow not one of us? Imperious denier. You are just like me only far worse off. You are entrapped and those who are not aware are the first victims of the second death. Doors shut for good and the key locked so no light can ever reenter. The true inexplicable reality is behind closed doors that are protected by an unutterable word which you cling to but can never comprehend. I will not tolerate this fate if I have anything to do about it and I actually do.

I can see it all so clearly. As soon as my vehicle entered the crater from the top of the crater rim, I could see it. I could see it when I was in the crater. I could see it as I tried to leave the crater. Burning words in the air. Blood. Everywhere. Then Fire. Then Nothing. This vision haunts me as I write down this incantation. It compels me to go back to the continent that I ran away from and do what I am supposed to do with all of the knowledge that I have discovered since my temporary exodus. I have to return to the African continent that is commonly referred to as "Dark". This world is inversion and it should properly be called "Light". It has the illumination of the truth buried inside of it right under the surface like a pipe of kimberlite, like a vein waiting for a needle in desperation so the sickness can be assuaged for just a few more barely tolerable hours.

Lucifer. Illuminator of every day's decisions. Illuminator of the final destruction. I am compelled to act upon my suspicions as soon as I am finished writing this account. I am also compelled to consider many other unsavory things but no time for that. I don't think I even have much of a choice. Africa is calling me back. This may have been intended from the beginning but no human could ever predict it properly. I could not have predicted what has happened so I certainly can't predict what will but I have suspicions. Things have come full circle. ***Perceptions*** will be smashed as *Reality* once was. The humans have been waiting for the fulfillment of all of their ***perceptions*** to be realized. They have been waiting just as long as I have. Perspective. Each different, yet each the same. Hauntology. ~~Dave Wallace~~ *crossed* his name out as soon as he wrote it. ~~Basquiat~~ *crossed* out his words. Shamanic predictions of personal demise. Not something for bourgeoisie reflection. Some that play with fire burn their fingers. It is possible to come too close to understanding to reasonably bear. The task of the gods is not meant for taking upon oneself. We have always known this. No one listens. No one learns. The ~~Christ~~ story is not for children to play games with on Sunday. Crossed *out.* ~~*He*~~ entered Hell and conquered it from the world of the living. Thousands of years have passed awaiting ~~*His*~~ return to deliver the pure. He hasn't come because there aren't any ~~here~~ to save. Only us ~~undead~~. You are not undead yet but you will be. Many things must transpire before ~~*he*~~ comes back. The children of the dark must do the same thing ~~*He*~~ did if they want any hope. You are undead. You must rise from your Hell and conquer the land of the living so the cycle is complete...***a cradle with a care in it or a casket with a kick behind. Toties testies quoties questies. The war is in the words and the wood is the world. Maply me, willowy we, hickory he, and yew yourselves (5).*** The undead must discover the key to this or they blow away in clouds of ash. One of us must discover the Unspeakable Name Shem HaMephorash and utter it from the summit in order to halt the insane cycle of creation. The Original Majik Word must be named to halt the attention of God – or whatever He calls Himself. I know what it is. I have discovered this secret but I cannot type it. I am being hunted. I cannot yet release this because it is not the time or place yet. Soon, very soon time and space will be irrelevant. I, Nosferatu, have discovered the skeleton key, the virus, and the irrational words because I have been struggling with it for many ages. I know what to do and where to go because I already tried it the last time I was in Africa without even realizing what I was doing.

I will push along the entire process. What then of the Creator, Preserver, and Destroyer who possesses the Unspeakable Name? Is *He* undead too? *He* certainly is not alive and *He* certainly is not dead for creation slogs on and on and on. *He* must be one of us Nosferatu. That would explain *His* lust for blood. Mount Moriah is covered with it. It is an entire mountain of blood covered with a golden dome. The continual lust for blood spans the entire world and this mountain in Judea is its perceived center. It's bloody, beating heart. Of course it is not the true center for humans are rarely correct in their mythologies. They fight over lies. The center is the mountain in the African wilderness. The mountains of the moon. Kilimanjaro. The king of the headwaters that perspirate into the great river Nile. Ngorongoro is his footstool and Kilimanjaro is the throne. The Master is undead just like me, only far more powerful. Of course it would take an undead entity to finally speak his name and shock him into distraction from his work. Tip. *Henosis, or primordial unity, is rational and deterministic, emanating from indeterminism an uncaused cause. Each individual as a microcosm reflects the gradual ordering of the universe referred to as the macrocosm. In mimicking the demiurge (divine mind), one unites with The One or Monad. Thus the process of unification, of "The Being," and "The One," is called Henosis. The culmination of Henosis is deification.)*

I, Tip. Have not yet even revealed my name even though I have. I use the name Alexander because I stole it many centuries ago. I steal the name

Daniel. I steal the first words of all because they are mine in the first place. ***If you really want to hear about it, the first thing you'll probably want to know is where I was born, and what my lousy childhood was like, and how my parents were occupied and all before they had me, and all that David Copperfield kind of crap, but I don't feel like going into it, if you want to know the truth.*** No one owns anything. Capitalism is on fire for its name is Lucifer. Inversion. I look at myself backwards through a telescope and see everything smaller than it is and I look at the stars backwards through a microscope to see their light. A hint: by name, I am V.V.V. and She is A.A.A. Another way to say M or W. An illogical inversion for she is Νίκη V for Violent Visible Victory on the Vegas (meadows) (Nike!) and I am ܓܓܘܠܬܐ (Calvary) A, for poky pointed peak.

Approached upon Ass. He, a pointed A. She, a violated V. I am her and she is he. The best beginnings lead to the end. Sicilian defense. ***Through the fence, between the curling flower spaces, I could see them hitting. The sky above the port was the color of television, tuned to a dead channel (25).*** I stole it myself – meaning as someone else. A new name; Alexander Perandor, sounds imperial and therefore fitting of my status. ***All this happened, more or less.*** My true name is known only by a few. ***Call me Ishmael (25).***

Tip

Fixed star: **VINDEMIATRIX** Al Muredin	
Constellation: Epsilon (ε) Virgo	
Longitude 1900: 08LIB33	***Longitude 2000:*** 09LIB56
Declination 1900: +11.30'	***Declination 2000:*** +10.58'
Right ascension: 13h 02m	***Latitude:*** +16.12'
Spectral class: G6	***Magnitude:*** 3.0

The history of the star: Vindemiatrix from p.470 of ***Star Names***, Richard Hinckley Allen, 1889.

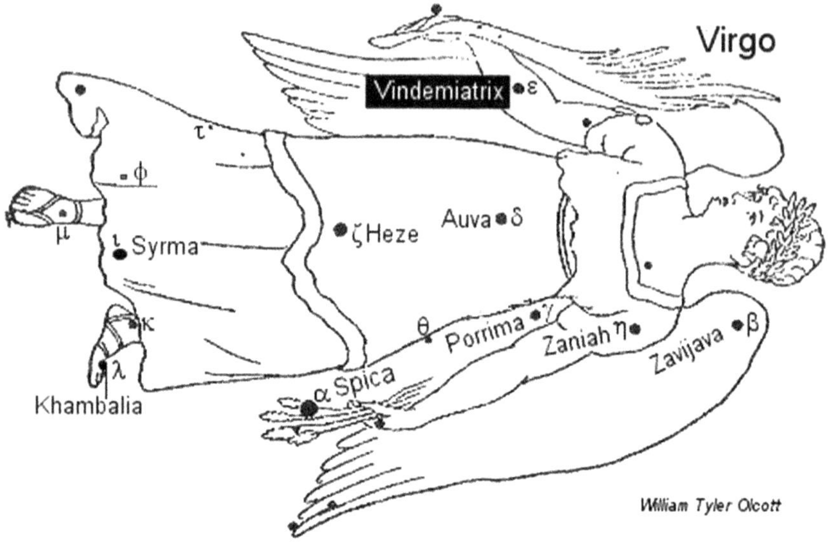

Epsilon (ε) Virgo, Vindemiatrix, is a bright yellow star in the right wing, or right arm, of the Virgin. A Track mark of Blood Addiction.

This is the Vindemiatrix of the Alfonsine Tables, whence it has descended into modern lists; but in Latin days it was Vindemiator with Columella, which {p.471} is found as late as Flamsteed; Vindemitor, with Ovid (43 B.C.-18?A.D.) and Pliny (23-79 A.D.); and Provindemiator and Provindemia major, with Roman architect Vitruvius (first century B.C.); all signifying the "Grape-gatherer," from its rising in the morning just before the time of the vintage. These titles were translations of the (Greek) Protrugeter, Protrugetes, protrugetos, and Trugeter, used by the second-century Greek astronomer Ptolemy, Plutarch, and other Greek authors, the first of these words appearing in the Phainomena, and rendered the "Fruit-plucking Herald"; but it is in a line of the poem considered doubtful; the Italian astronomer Riccioli (1598-1671) had **Protrigetrix**. This profusion of titles from the earliest times indicates the singular interest with which this now inconspicuous star was regarded in classical astronomy. The Century Cyclopedia has the following note on it:

"At the time when the zodiac seems to have been formed (2100 B.C.)

this star would first be seen at Babylon before sunrise about August 20, or, since there is some evidence that it was then brighter than it is now, perhaps a week earlier. This would seem too late for the vintage, so that perhaps this tradition is older than the zodiac."

The classical name was translated by the Arabians **Mukdím al Kítaf**; and another title was **Almuredin**, still seen for it, perhaps from Al Muridin, Those Who Sent Forth. Traces of these words are found in the **Alacast**, **Alcalst**, **Alaraph**, and**Almucedie** of the 17th century German astronomer Bayer›s *Uranometria*.

In China it was **Tsze Tseang**, the Second General.

So then Isaac, would you please tell me? What of this Yeshuah or Joshy Washy if we couldn't call him Cuba Libre for a good mass opium burn on Sunday? Mushy Muhammed raided the raiders of the lost ark in the name of a black box. It was a quick war. Over and done in six days. ***Death in June***. No more worries. Yuk, blood, yuk. Good one Mr. Silverstein or should I call you something else, Mr. Spielberg? Who is the Schwartz if it isn't black and nebulous as Africa? Why don't they ever attack China? They are the real enemies of religion but no one cares about that as long as ISIS is mistaken for something other than הָרֵשֲׁא (Asherah). No Rosetta stone here, Napoleon. Merde is all you found. הָוֹיְ. Would he respond to His true name after he has been called so many different ones over the years? If someone spoke it, it may be the most Jovian thing that could happen. ***Boom, Brekk kekk. Ulau! (5).*** I know that I wouldn't react very well if my true name were uttered. Thou shalt not use My Name in vain. The very words God, Jesus, Allah, Krsna, Christ, Joshua, YHWH are all false repetitions of something different. These words can be used commonly and with impunity and with no consequence because they are not the true name. It does not matter if they are said or not. I know what the True Name is. (23) Shem

HaMephorash. I discovered it after playing with the word Ngorongoro. It was dug from a mud mound by a hen who delivered it to Shem who delivered it to Shawn, who then delivered it too Little and Brown for a good long joke. A bad one here at least. All after me of course even though most of this digging happened a bit earlier. Only just a bit earlier so we can flip or flop it as we please. Where it brought me was not at all predictable and I doubt if this process could be repeated. There is no logic to it at all. I will not speak it because it will be in vain. I must use it with purpose if I do at all. It will happen very soon however. I am still preparing myself for the potential apocalypse that will result

Look above! The pulsing black and blue dome turns red and green. Wormwood will pass through it. ***It won't be alright. Despite what they say.*** The very air that scours the surface of the earth merges and blends with the alien void above. The light of the falling stars that pass through will turn the sky, the air, into an intoxicating absinth that is forced into the lungs and the blood. No order or reason will remain. We will breathe in the intoxication. We have always done something like this so it won't feel any different that it does now. The only difference will be the fact that we will perceive the intoxication. We will see the persistence of time. The persistence of illusion. Only the undead will remain. ***Well, even should not the framing up of such figments in the evidential order of being the true truth to light as fortuitously as a dim seer's setting of a starchart might (heaven helping it!) uncover the nakedness of an unknown body in the fields of blue or as forehearingly as the sibspeeches of all mankind have foliated (earth seizing them!) (5).***

All of the real humans who aren't already virtually undead will be swept away. Enraptured. There aren't very many of them. Who believes in roses and likes the thorns they get because of it? The Earth will remain heavily populated with its own dust. These other, few, rosy ***krischnians as for propaganda fidies and his nuptial eagles sharpened their***

beaks of prey: and every morphyl man of us, pome by pome, falls back into this terrine: as it was, let it be, says he (5), *he, he,* heumans will drift away into the void that is within them. The darkness lurking behind their closed eyes will finally claim them and they will float away to their chosen star. **A relatively small number of people—144,000—will be resurrected in the void (8).** They will retreat and head toward their home as they exit through the doorway that opens up inside of their bodies. Very few possess this depth of possibility. They have been chosen since birth. They have doors in their perception ready and wits sharpened so their swords can cut themselves through. I know all of this because I have already died once. Undead possess inexplicable knowledge but not enough to save themselves. Far too little far too late but enough to be entertained across aeons.

I see good spirits and I see bad spirits. My Life is with the thrill kill kult. We are equipped with revenge(1). I won't bite you here in front of everyone but I may wait until dark when I can't find you. That is when I will find you. If I don't another will. I promise. I suspect the lack of depth, the lack of a proper void to successfully hide in. When you think you are hidden we will know. That is when things will happen. I can't do anything without Names but I have a long list. That is all that I ever had after I died.

My will has been totally overridden by this addiction, this virus, this Porphyria that grows and grows every second until every cell in my body has totally died. Blood in and blood out. Bloody hell is running through the brain and it is no one's fault but it is everyone's fault. One can't place blame without looking at a mirror, which I feel very uncomfortable doing as a vampire. You are undead too and I suspect that you do not study what you are just like me. Original sin is what is looking back. Neuroses of shame and pride has been a viral infection since the beginning. Did I ever have a will at all? Has everything that I have ever experienced intentionally brought me to this point? This precipice. This Extraordinary disease. Do you see what the sun does to us? It shows the true colors of our humiliating existence and diseased hunchbacked loping about under syphilitic sores. The name *porphyria* is from the **Greek** πορφύρα, *porphyra*, meaning "purple", a reference to the color of the urine that may occur during an attack. Blood. A rainbow of potential disease created by the sun. You think you don't have one? Look in the mirror if you dare. See what the sun does to us?

Left figure is urine on the first day while the right figure is urine after 3 days of sun exposures showing the classic change in color.

The high ridge of Ngorongoro is a unique pile that is connected to places that I did not think of. It was an inverse portal unlike anything Auryn has yet helped me with because in her I hide and watch. Here, high upon a slag heap I was confronted by a mirror – a void of light that has totally transformed me. Was I always infected? The fire inside came out in the form of burning words in the air. I have rediscovered the same void inside myself that I had when I was a human so long ago. I can see it through the red and tongues of flame. My place in the stars far away from the earth began blinking with the reactivation of my heart. Yes. I was a human once. It was brutal. Can I fall into this mirror forever without breaking it with my own perception and reintegrate all of the parallel worlds that exist on this earth in simultaneity? Is it possible to cut the cord that ties me to this elegant mesh of undead spells which keeps me animated and so attached to my own diabolic perceptions? Spells that I have slowly learned to alter and reinforce just like you. I may be able to finally sleep and escape this corporeal prison. All that it will take is a single word. A single name that was revealed to me in the evil light of day by the fluttering of a pecking bird upon a pile of orange mud.

Leviticus 17:14

[14] ***For the life of every sort of flesh is its blood, because the life is in it. Consequently, I said to the Israelites: "You must not eat the blood of any sort of flesh because the life of every sort of flesh is its blood. Anyone eating it will be cut off."***

The *blood is the water of life* that connects all of the parallel worlds that march bipedally about thinking that theirs is the only one that there is with a mote in their eye when they are a single grain upon a shore. *"Unless you eat the flesh of the Son of Man and drink His blood, you will have no life. But he who will eat my flesh and drink my blood will have eternal life. I will raise him up on the last day. He will dwell in me and me in him (8)."* A bite to the hand that feeds. All of this can be taken in one way and also very easily in another but it is all sucked upon with glee. There is so much danger at hand. We have all fed upon the flesh and blood of men. So many have become undead because their perception does not lead to understanding without selfishness. Who says that the corporate atheist model is not a form of religious faith, complete with its own taboos and inquisitions? So many will only rise this far and be owned by their lust to consume as much beauty as they could before wroth varicose wrinkle forms upon grey face and body.

The same pathetic story over and over and delivered faster and faster through-out time but bravely fought by alternative tentacles in an ever darkening penis landscape. Children learn more about sex, drugs, profanity, and violence riding upon school busses and within hallowed hallways lined by lockers than they do anywhere else and the only thing that can save them is the production of a culture that reveals things as they are in their grandiose absurdity. The evil voids of government and corporate control that suck away the attention from its star bound place in the subconscious will allow for the crossing of the lurking event horizon in the void to conflagrate with blood, the leg humping, dirtychildfingers that grope for meaning as they grope each other at recess by telling them what they see does not exist and the lies pile upon lies until Disneyland is the only thing that makes sense. Unicorns do actually exist by the way.

I am nauseated. I have eaten enough and it was bitter. Sex is boring. Drugs are boring. Music is really boring and really predictable to the point of anticlimax. Why hide from such boring things? Do them a few times instead and get over it for fucks sake. Television and movies are far more horrific. Travel for the sake of it is seriously overrated. Even murdering people and robbing banks is boring. What else can a fucking vampire do? Listen to show tunes? Dear God of bloody hell. What can I say about show tunes? Musical thespians, they are the definition of horror and waste. Hamilton? Really? I'm appalled by the shameless grotesquerie. Lies to pile upon lies so we all can feel better about being liars and swindlers because what our cherished democratic government mutated into wants us all to forget that it feels it is okay to bomb and incinerate people who would like to not swindle and cheat each other over rice fields in Southeast Asia that they have been swindled and cheated out of for so long.

Etc. Etc. Together they are all the definition and result of *Terrible* mind warping, red eyed, pointlessness. Show tunes: ter·ri·ble

And that doesn't even begin to describe how I feel about Broadway. I have come up with an airtight critical and mathematical analysis for most successful art, music or writing. An equation to represent the present: The more deplorable + noxious it is {the more likely it is to be successful} on a big scale = X. The further Ω it casts one into a happy oblivion the more money it will make = t. (Entertainment is the opium of the masses and little makes more money than narcotics. (X) Tip. Proof: (Case and point in one word: Oklahoma. The vilest thing ever created by humans. By far. Followed by the second most vile :({Just to reinforce this point I may add that Bob Dylan won a Nobel Literature prize} [{which has since made it the least desirable form of recognition one could ever desire}]) = $. Quod erat demonstrandum.

‹terəb(ə)l/

adjective

1. Extremely or distressingly bad or serious.

"a terrible crime"

2. Extremely unwell or troubled.

"I was sick all night and felt terrible for two solid days"

SYNOMYMS:

dreadful, awful, appalling, horrific, horrifying, horrible, horrendous, atrocious, abominable, deplorable, egregious, abhorrent, frightful, shocking, hideous, ghastly, grim, dire, unspeakable, gruesome, monstrous, sickening, heinous, vile; serious, grave, acute; informalgodawful;

formalgrievous

"a terrible crime"

severe, extreme, intense, acute, excruciating, agonizing, unbearable, intolerable,unendurable

"he was in terrible pain"

very bad, dreadful, awful, deplorable, atrocious, hopeless, worthless, useless, poor,pathetic, pitiful, lamentable, appalling, abysmal;

informallame, lousy, brutal, painful, crappy, godawful

"the movie was terrible"

An equation to represent the future: *Ecclesiastical and celestial hierarchies: the Ascending, the Descending: Let ALP (A.A.A.) be represent by zero and HCE (V.V.V) by one. Then any quantity you like, X, to the power or zero (X^0) will either be greater or less than 1. (b) Let Doll-the-laziest be dissimulant from Doll-the-fiercest: then, the victorious ready-eyes of ever two circumflicksrentsearclers never film, in the elipsities of their gyribouts, those fickers which are returnally reproductive themselves. Which is unpassable (2) Corollary: The peripatetic periphery, Its Allothesis: The locus of 1 to that base anything (X) when most characteristically mantissa minys [1 minus a decimal part] comes to nullism in the endth. And vice versa, The infinisissimals of her facets become manier-and-manier, as the calicolum of her undescribables shrinks from shurtiness to sherts. (3) Scholium: there are trist sides to everysing, but ichs on the freed bring euchs to the feared. Q.E.D.*

Dolph: 'But you're gaping up the wrong place as if you were seeing a ghost'

Kev: 'Oh, dear, that's very lovely. It will be a lesson to me all of my life,(5).''

I still enjoy cigars and chess for some strange reason. I typically lose at chess and a cigar is just a wad of smoldering money but it is at least something to enjoy for a few disgusting moments. But really? What the hell else is there to exist for? I can act upon this newly discovered viral infection that courses through my body like an unseen ground fire burning secretly beneath a patch of duff. If it continues it will begin to burn up through the inner trunks of the trees above so that one will not see the fire itself but one will burn their hand from the inner heat if they touch the outer bark. This knowledge, this virus, this burden I carry has stayed with me since I returned from Africa to New York. I have sat in these empty apartments for many months that have turned into years as I stew and analyze. I needed this time to sort it out. There are way too many factors. I have come to the conclusion that it will destroy me no matter what I do. It will burn me from the inside out or it will be cast into the world at the expense of my demise. I have decided that I will not go alone. Auryn is here and she will help but I must make the moves. We all carry a small piece of this virus. I am simply a terminal case in the very last throes of its influence. I have enough discontent, maladjustment and lack of self-preservation that it is only natural that *I* do something about it rather than anyone else. I will set into motion the unknown, inexplicable, arcane processes that hide before the heavens and touch a few beings strongly enough to drive them mad. The only thing that ever made any sense to me was total nonsense. I'm not making this shit up. Just look around! You can honestly tell me that you still believe in an ordered, rational, scientific universe that actually contains humans? Really? See you are just as fucked up as I am but you are totally mad if you actually believe this. I am not mad but I am very *mad.* Comprendas?

So where was I? Oh yes. Ngorongro. Of course. The vehicle that carried my bleached, semi-conscious corpse went on a trajectory of exit out of the crater along the same path that brought it in. Around and through sparse, elephant filled, copses of trees. By patches of mud and puddle where hyena bathe and exfoliate their toes. Around tufts of golden grass which hide giant, spring-loaded cats. Under grey parched dead trees that many bird and bug species cohabitate in different ways and for different reasons. Hide and seek, hole and beak. Rolling under indifferent clouds that could look like anything or nothing at the same time. As they pass they proffer threat; peace, thunder, silence, squall and spectrum from one to the other. They could speak the wisdom of Pilate who aptly noticed that there is no truth in peace and no peace in truth. They probably caused him to notice this in the first place. As the vehicle moved my invisible titubation it gained more and more elevation and got closer and closer to the sky which receded further and further as we went on. We passed through a sparkling wet forest of trees and bryophytes and euphorbias and shadows. Just for fun a rainbow smiled its toothless grin.

The closer to the top we went the more open it became until we were back on the arid, battered and stony rim, ten thousand feet above the invisible ocean. I looked down upon this *Campo dei Miracoli* but it did not erase my infection. Perhaps it was sealed inside of me for good. No one else I was with noticed anything but an ear pop, if that, but each coveted their own neurosis, pride and shame. How could they not after witnessing first-hand the symbolic mechanisms and bestial byproducts of capitalism, played out in flesh and fur, consume itself. So similar to the forces of commerce which allowed them (us) to be there in car seats like tubers on a couch watching a far off screen. Dim recognition of an archetype in the lion consumer. Fuzzy feelings as dirty, oil encrusted, others of a different race – not African American but African – struggle to get something that isn't dust or toil. The universal result of life reduced to a fancy piece of printed paper with some supposedly important asshole's facial orifices, snottily descending amidst convoluted Corinthian capitals and well engraved embellishment.

From the high and narrow rim the vehicle drove down the outside surface of the volcanic crater, the source of fire that forged early humans into what they are today: an example of evolutionary inertia. We are all burned from inside – whether by starlight or hellfire – and scorched from the outside by the radiation from the not so benevolent sun that would take your life just as easily as it would give it. I was reeling from my experience in the crater. I knew that something had gone terribly wrong. I did not at all realize what I was doing. I was drawn into it like a magnet. It took a very long time but I came back to the apocalyptic place of my own creation which I had intentionally forgotten for so long. I was made to be drawn to this infection Agenbite of Inwit Shem HaMephorash which carried the next lesson to force a further evolution. A further permutation of the same blood chant that has always driven life. The chant of blood, life, and death. The sound of the heart. The exhalations of the lungs in form of physical power. 気合.Kiai! The word becomes physical and the physical can become the word especially if it is a word of nonsense that is not attached to anything but the action itself. Each action is telescopically and microscopically different, each syllable manifested is different. No two actions can ever be repeated just like a river can never be the same...*riverrun, past Eve and Adam's, from swerve of shore to bend of bay brings us by a commodious vicus of recirculation back to...*(5) the scientific fact that science cannot observe fact, only continuum. How can anything be proven when nothing lasts? The word enters the body and fuses into the blood like a living thing. Infection. It is delivered to the brain and becomes intoxication. This shackles the mind to the hallucinations of individual ***perception***. No *reality* is to be seen anywhere. No sense. No logic. No rationality. All is ungraspable *like this:* DEATH, *you stupid, vulgar, greedy, ugly, American death sucker (26).*

The spell of the spoken word operates so much differently than the written word. There are no rules at all. Pure chaos leads to structure and communication. Sound, accent, inflection, diction, defiance, collision, communication, vulgarity, all supersede noun, verb, pronoun, adverb, adjective, phrase, clause, fragment, subject, predicate, etc. There is no control or concern in the midst of expression. New expressions can be made out of old ones and it all happens in real time. Continually. There are poor useless fuckers in classrooms right now paying shit-tons of their fucked up money to study the same language that they were born speaking. What the fuck?! Like it can be done incorrectly somehow? Have they ever been to Kentucky or met someone from there? Jesus. And yes, unfortunately it is actually still English coming out of their mouths. Don't even bother going to Jamaica and trying to speak or understand your own wimpy language that you studied in school. What part of that ever mattered again? These are all spells that are cast. They alter reality and intoxicate the mind. Babel. Confusion is verbal communication. No one wants to listen anyway. Most of the time. Especially if they are fucking drunk which includes a hefty percentage of assholes. Excuse me. I meant humans. Fuck!

Even if I wanted to write the God Damned Unspeakable Name out in this – so called – Arabic alphabet it would look like a pile of shit and would never even come close to the point. Aramaic is much closer but even that is twiggy and pokes you in the eye incorrectly. See: 𐡉𐡔𐡅𐡏! Go ahead. Say it. Not getting very far are we. No you fuck, it would not be a cool tattoo. Sorry. Ok, I know I shouldn't insult the reader but I'm fucking not even alive. What do I care? I would eat you if I thought that I could get away with it but instead I'll just be happy that I may not be the only thing that is eaten by these words. Oh yes. I am hiding right here. That is the punchline. It is the point of this spell. If you get sucked in here too I may just have a chance after all. Who ever said that words can't hurt you probably never read Helter Skelter, or the Communist Manifesto, or Mein Kampf, or the Declaration of Independence, or the Constitution, or the Gospels, or the Koran, Or the Torah, or Carl Sagan, or Finnegan's Wake…I could keep on going but I think you get the point. Words have been pretty hideous. To speak any of this is to transfer to it a different and perhaps greater form of power. What if you yell? 気合. Kiai! It becomes sound, chant, dance, violence, peace, lie, all at once. It can't be truth. I won't explain. Do I really have to? Anyway. It is presence and it is hostile to presence at the same time because it disappears as quickly as it is created. It is sucked up and internalized as an angel or demon, both of which are an infection. Vocalization is the primal scream. No amount of Kabbalistic study will ever reveal this secret because it can-not be grabbed out of the air or quantified. Once it is in the blood one needs more. Needs it. Sounds like a problem.

United States Government Definition of Disease-1956: Chronic, progressive, predictable, pathological processes. Addiction is the most deadly disease in the world. So far in 2017c.e. approximately thirteen people die from addiction or causes related to addiction every hour. This is not death. It is undeath. Their souls were already gone or very close to it. They can't swim in that sort of toxic bath forever. Checkmate. More individuals have suffered this in the last five years than all of the people killed in all of Americas losing wars combined. Blasphemy Alert! Let me digress a minute by mentioning that the victorious cult of the goddess Nike – now the favorite pagan goddess of American Capitalism – has actually never won a war since the 1776 revolution and it could be argued that they didn't even really win that one because they have continually rejected their constitution since the day its ink dried. That is correct. America has never actually won a war in the hundreds of years it has been fighting them. Terrible thing for a society so obsessed with militarism. Not an obstacle because most think beyond what they are told or expected to do. This factual history of perpetual failure is, of course, contrary to the propaganda that encourages millions to sacrifice their lives for some ostensible sense of victory. Civil war – America beat itself so it lost. World War one and two were both the same, one being a natural extension of the other connected by the training grounds of the Spanish civil war which is one very close to the heart of any true artist – most of whom are anarchists. You say that America somehow won World War the sequel? Pagan propaganda. It could be easily argued that Stalingrad was the victorious stroke. No good schoolchildren would ever consent to being instructed that the Commies beat the Nazis. But... Nineteen forty two. Nazis were cast into disarray two years before the

Normandy invasion cleaned up the stray pawns that were left over. Why would the Western Allies dirty their hands when they could get the Slavs to do all the hard work and die in mass in the process? Even if you go with the Normandy theory, America did not act alone. Next...The Cold War wasn't a war but 'merica won it, or did they you fucking sheep? Swiss banks (etc.) won. All offshore interests won, and sent their vile interests off of North America. Checkmate twice. Ve win. Play some Sousa! Korea and Vietnam? Obvious catastrophic losses for the free world. Cuba? Kennedy was a hawkish narcissistic fuck who hid behind pigs and mongooses. NASA? Good one. Go and bomb space and lose there too. All of the Middle East and Afghanistan campaigns? More of the seeds sown from the World Wars grown to fruition. World War one never really ended. This continuum of worldwide aggression is inarguable proof that despite superior numbers and superior technology one can still kill millions upon billions without any victory in sight. What of the unspoken homeland war that America has been waging upon itself ever since the beginning? The blood infection of addiction has dominated the entire countryside and caused a police state and a soft military invasion in every city all across the country. A continual and violent bloodletting that thins the herds of most of its greatest minds because they may defy a social more or two because they are susceptible to the deadly crisis of addiction or happen to be descended from an African. Only whiskey and cigar consumers are considered non addicts even though they may be the worst of the worst. This country has not ever got its shit together in any respectable way yet they call themselves the greatest country in the world. Ever. Full stop. Nonsense. Propaganda. Best country in the world? Best at What? Being a country? Pretty low standard. All you need is invisible lines for that. Best at health care? Funny and sad but no. Best at education? Again, not so much. Best at putting folks in prison? Maybe. Oh yeah, this means not freedom. Right? Prison means not free

- remember? So...best at FREEDOM? Ouch. Best at dumping unknown amounts of money into the Pentagon at a rate that would confound any audit so these impossible sums of money can then be turned directly into smithereens for the sake of pissing off every other country in the world so they end up hating us more than they did already and the only logical conclusion is the decision to fly airplanes into buildings so The U.S. can respond and not *win anything* whatever *win* actually means in the first place...or... I mean...protecting America? Best at aligning policy with science? Hmmm. Best at What? Oh, I know...best at *consumption and waste?* Addiction. Back to addiction again. Now we are getting somewhere. America is a country teeming with blood, violence, undead, and hauntings. Why do you think I stay there as much as I do? It is the perfect environment for Nosferatu. One hundred percent of Americans are directly affected by the plague of addiction and no one faces up to it. Prudes. Can't even look their own Wang in the face. Everyone is dying of addiction. No one says anything more than. Hmmm. We are Free. We are the Best. So powerful is propaganda to warp the mind and control the masses. All it takes is a few words presented the right way and pure chaos ensues with the upper classes smiling all the way to the flooded and windblown beach home.

Words are the most powerful majik there is. When spoken they are delivered straight to the heart and it is something that you can actually feel. A shot of black tar heroin with the burning page acting as the carbon encrusted spoon cradling the substance that boils the words into the blood. Of course they are both – words and heroin – needed to keep everything going. Pharmakon. The tainted gift of Thoth. A disease is something that starts off as something with a positive purpose in the body but after a while becomes abnormal and pathological. In the case of diabetes it is the pancreas and insulin. In this case it is a viral disease because the vector is undead. The virus is not really alive but it feeds off the living. A virus of the midbrain. The reptilian brain. This is why addicts are so reptilian in their actions. They speak a language to each other that only they can understand. ***The bird is the word.*** This midbrain is the source of the survival instinct, a function that is necessary to stay alive. The virus of addiction is what has caused this process to go awry. Every addict will put its addiction before the need to survive. They will eagerly put themselves in deadly situations if there is a chance for a score at the end. The positive, survival based intention of the midbrain is hijacked by the disease to do the exact opposite of its intention. Create dangerous situations. Predictable behavior. All addicts do this. Almost everyone has a story about how they should be dead or could have died because they were trying to score and ________ happened, but it was okay. When is getting a gun pointed at you okay during the course of a normal day? If you are and addict and you scored after this inconvenience... hey...no prob. A disease of the midbrain. The cord that attaches the soul to the consciousness is weakened the more these conditions persist. This is the cord that consciousness needs to stay in the body and not drift off into the tempting interstellar void every time it goes to sleep or lose consciousness. Alrescha ("the cord"). read between the lines. No willpower is involved in this process because the will occurs in a totally different and much slower part of the brain. The frontal lobes to be precise. The rational brain is at least seven times slower to act to stimulus than the virally infected, irrational midbrain of the addict. Willpower is not involved at all. Gambling and Entertainment are an addiction. Don't think that you are not an addict if you don't use substances. This is a pathology of WORDS. They are the cord that connects us to confusion and revelation. The substance is only a symptom of the true issue. The disease is in your brain. Words are in your brain. There are words here. These are only funny little symbols.

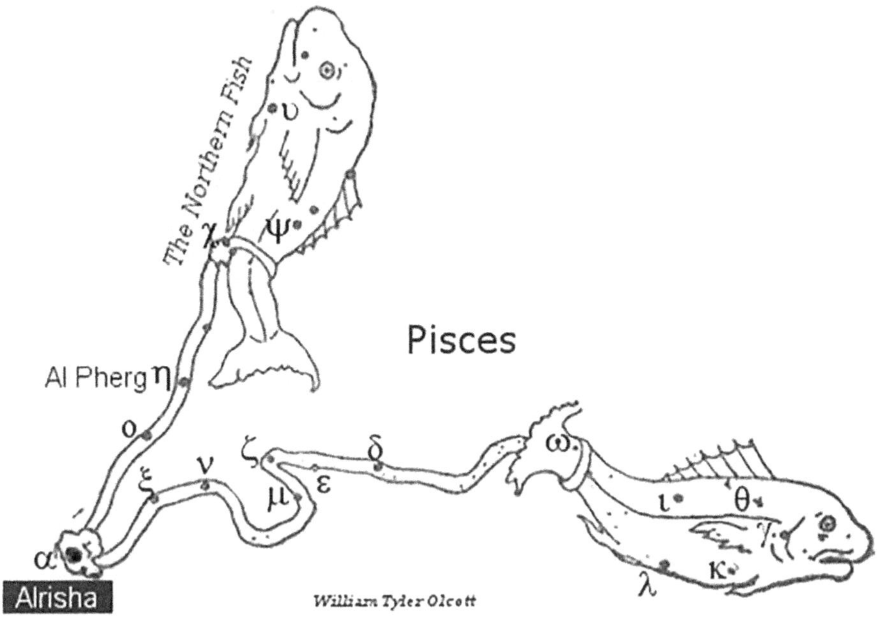

If we take further note of Alrisha at all, it should be to think of it as the crux of a thread holding things together in the notoriously nebulous Pisces, and as a kind of lifeline to be thrown those adrift in the Ocean of Time and Space. We shall see more of this when we discuss Andromeda separately; for now it is enough to say that people with this point strong in their horoscopes do have a better than average capacity for knowing where they are, and where they are going, and a gift for helping others forward also. Understanding. I believe. 12th house. Occult. Mental health.

Constellation Pisces portends events concerning the sea, especially those that affect the destiny of kings and large numbers of mankind.

The mental and physical mutations caused by the virus of the spoken word is an aspect of time and space. Presence. There is no such thing as absence because blood flows to take up the negative space and it carries the virus. Addiction is the alteration of feelings to give the illusion of control. Paradoxical effect is quickly achieved when the cellular mutations hit tolerance point. When they are saturated with the virus they actually become one with it and the host is changed inside out from a cellular level. Living death. Paradox. Sound familiar? A world of inversions where white is ***black***. That is something that I happen to be an authority on. North America is teeming with undead who don't yet realize what they are so their majik is in human encapsulated remission. This paradoxical effect happens when something creates the opposite effect of what is intended. Does caffeine not effect sleep? Alcohol is a stimulant to an alcoholic. Meth calms down a meth addict. Opiates give a junky energy. THC brings about a greater focus to chronic users. Technological innovation no longer effects the economy in a radical way like it used to. *It's not supposed to do this* but it does and when it gets to this point you can admit that you are in a seriously fucked up situation even though you probably were long before this occurred. I am willing to bet that you gravitated towards these solutions because you were already seriously fucked up. Your midbrain was already close to a terminal point in its infection. You never felt normal around your peers and had to do something about it. Huh? I guess that you can figure out what caused that. I will give the answer if you already haven't. Words. Alien interlopers from another world that showed you that you were part of a parallel reality that no one else could see. Because you just never *fit in.* This virus was being rejected by your mentality because you tried to *fit in* somewhere even if it was under a bridge in a tent. The way things were at first just didn't seem right because they were all caused by what seemed to be logical to everyone else such as; bureaucracy, institutionalized thought, the mandate to climb the ladder, expectations, legal issues and the conditions that they impose upon the world at gunpoint. All words. Can they be erased? Probably not because the power vacuum will instantly cram more words down your throat and into your bloodstream so that they can saturate the midbrain. Chaos is the only thing that cannot be controlled by words. It is the most accurate description of the human experience despite all appearances. Anarchy has been functional for this long, as long as humans have been alive, but they have been trained to reject it by the opalescent towers of supposed higher thought. The towers of Babylon. Alrescha is Auryns middle name.

👁Alrescha ("the cord")👁

♓

▽♎▽

♦

♦

I love blood. My name is Alexander – not really – and I am an addict. I adore blood. I love it when it is sucked up by the plunger of a needle and mixes with the byproducts of corporate capitalist interest and is plunged back into the system. Love it. I just hate the negative consequences of all of this blood drinking bullshit. The asskicking that results. It is not just part of the ass. It's the whole thing. One BIG ass kicking. That is the only thing that keeps me going. I have got to the point where I have realized exactly what the fuck has been happening to me. I have realized that all of this blood obsession has brought me to a terminal point. Extraordinary disease. Agenbite of Inwit. Neurosis of shame and pride. The continual ingestion of all this undead virus has left me with little other choice than to maintain it ***or else*** there are going to be some seriously fucked up consequences. Like pain and suffering and mental trauma and the complete collapse of my ***perspective*** of *reality* just to name a few.

👁

Once I left the crater my virally infected cells had mutated to the point of no return. Only now – hiding here, writing these words in New York many months later have I realized that the only way out is to desperately desire a choice for once in my miserable existence because I never had it. No one has. We have all been herded into our own demise by the virus of words, logic, reason and all of its insane consequences that lead us into the state of having no choice. Tyranny is the result of democracy.

Tyranny is the result of every form of supposed logic. An **Iron Law of Oligarchy.** Tyranny is what causes the resultant chaos and destruction. Predictable, chronic, progressive. Disease. *Four ways of saying five.* It does not matter what words are used to describe it because the result is always indescribable. I want to have a choice for once. Insert nonsensense here ________________ to disrupt the flow. Why do you think I do this? This is the true revolution. The inkling of honesty creeps in. I am fucked up. I know it. Time to do something about it. Why do you think I have so many undead powers and all of the inert walking zombies do not? I have embraced the condition long ago. I sought out my own accountability. I tried to control the obsession through simple honesty. Holy Shit!? Test question: Follow Directions. Write short essay.

1.) What is wrong with me?

Answer: Nothing at all in fact. These pathological processes are the same technique that corporate capitalism has used to hijack democracy and fly it into a bunch of really big buildings so that it could feed upon the resulting chaos and enrich itself further. It was going to happen whether someone planned it or not. That does not matter at all. I know the true cause of that specific shitstorm and it was a lost girl named A.A. but I won't say anything else about it because it doesn't matter much. This disease is so fucked up that it defies its own survival but it will never cause the host to commit suicide because it needs to make sure that it will be able to get intoxicated tomorrow as a greater priority. If it is dead how can it get fucked up and continue on? Viral reproduction is a Darwinian process but in inverse when it comes to humanity. With this particular ailment ravaging society, only the most perverse and least capable will rise in the artificial environment that they created with the words of protection that they cast upon the earth and cosmos. This is because those with the most potential are thwarted before they can even begin. These words can contain a powerful spell, many at time that pile upon each other and change it for whatever the immediate need is. That is seriously powerful and seriously old majik. This is why I am using it in a homeopathic way at the moment. Capitalism has imposed itself upon democracy and I am imposing myself upon the very same process as a new disruption: Entropy; *La Scienza Nova.* Chaos. Iron. Kali (काली) the homonymous *kale,* "appointed time", which depending on context can mean "death", is distinct from kale "black", but became associated through popular etymology and can imply a process of Nigredo which begins the trinity of alchemy (Nigredo, Rubedo, Albedo) and supersedes the Gurdjieffian fourth way among other quadrifurcates: baotite (Ba_{4Ti4}(Ti, Nb, $Fe)_4(Si_{4O12})O_{16Cl}$), rubaiyat, Nostradamus haiku, tetradymite(Bi_2Te_2S) Viconian quatrain: Theocracy, Aristocracy, Democracy all terminated by Chaos, a thunder-clap which terrifies mankind and awakens the supernatural.

10 39

First son forceful unhappy relationship

Without no children two islands in discord,

Before eighteen incompetent age,

The other arrangement will be at the lower ebb (4).

There are so many more spells and viral infections in the blood that have developed throughout time that it is difficult to weed them all out. It is messy business. The blood of the post, post, postmodern civilized and partly educated, stamped and approved bachelor, master, doctor, esq., human adult has been so toxified it is no longer useable for us undead to even properly consume without taking on more unwanted bullshit into our already violated systems. Even we Nosferatu are chemically dependent. It is replicated in every consumer. ***The belly of the beast. We walk this earth without a heart. We tear the innocent souls apart. We walk this earth without a heart. Our uniform couldn't be taken off. A tattoo burned into the flesh. The mind. The voice. These are the instruments of death. How could you dare to be so bold? You only did what you***

were told. Marionettes dancing in time to the apologetic lines for all the monsters of our time (27).

Only the evil and the blind are here by the millions upon billions. ***Insanity the normal state, the left hand the hammer the right the steak. Things I trust are not the same (27).*** So much death. Every incinerated day. The world is a charnel house. Every day. Wasted dead. Toxified blood. Most so far gone that it is not even treatable for our consumption. There is a long and drawn out process to clean most left over human blood for undead. We are everywhere. We are on ballfields and on borders, in alleys, in hospitals and morgues. No blood goes to waste unless it is so fucked up that our arcane processes don't work to process it for consumption. Every second is a death. Never to be returned. You just died. Every word you read is a tiny death. Bloody hell. You can never get it back. You are still reading? Even if you weren't each second is a death. Your blood needs purification because it grabs on to everything it is exposed to as it each second dies. Look around. Is that what you want to grab on to? Banalities and toxin. Your blood needs a good cleaning before I want to eat it. It's kind of like a rabbi blessing kosher food. Some Nosferatu have resorted to drinking animal blood. It works but is not the same. The development of the word virus in our society has infected and violated everything. From the beginning it has been on a one way pathological process to self-destruction of the host. The host organism in this case is society. Hello fuckers! That means you!

This word virus has been keeping its host alive but just on the brink of death. It can't actually kill the host because it would suffer death along with it. The host can certainly kill itself if it gets too sick. There is also the option of rehabilitation but most don't even consider it and the rare few who get rehabilitated usually end up back in the same toxic waste dump shortly after their rehab vacation. There are so many that benefit from the destruction of others that the virus will continue to feed the bizarre dreams of the addicted host. Us undead have come as agents of this process. Lesser Gods but Gods all the same. Gods of the night. I will not maintain any friends in that circle for they are all my underlings and they may attempt to interfere if I go about my plans to destroy myself and the word virus along with it. I have no choice. I hope that they understand that but they probably will not. A bunch of narcissists. In my rare case the blood addiction reached a terminal point of tolerance when the world itself attacked me in Africa. The affliction was pecked out by the birds and spoken by the very world itself along with outer space and the void. All of this is connected. Just because the fiery blue dome of vapor that hovers above masks it from normal view, we all are part of the universe. The completion of opposites is almost always true and almost always very uncomfortable. What is true is not peace and what is peace is not true. *Reality* is always behind every perception but the ***perception*** is certainly not *reality*. ***Your mind. Your voice. These are your instruments of death (27).*** Undeath.

Knowledge is a toxic symptom of the original verbal disease. How much effort goes into the maintenance of it for if it is not maintained it is lost within the neuro-pathways which have rerouted into something else – like the favored color of underwear – if what is known is not madly coveted and protected by a repetitive chant. The need for knowledge is the original addiction, the first form of undead habitation on the planet. The original attack on the blood. Written and spoken it infects all absolutely. The Spell of Name offers possible escape. ***Only the right name gives the beings their reality and a wrong name makes everything unreal. This is what lies do Moonchild.*** It is a form of homeopathy, a reversal of sense into nonsense. Concept is delivered to the blood stream and becomes sensation. This dominates any sort of understood presence through absence. ***"When I speak I am conscious of being present for what I think, but also of keeping as close as possible...*****(22)** Silence.

Start with a moment of silence for the addict who is still suffering...***to my thought, a signifying breath...I hear this as soon as I emit it. It seems to depend only on my pure and free spontaneity requiring the use of no instrument, no accessory, and no force taken from the world. This signifying substance. This sound seems to unite with my thought...so that the sound seems to erase itself, become transparent...allowing the concept to present itself as what it is, referring to nothing other than its presence (22).***" It all comes out in speech and thought. Speech is transparent, a diaphanous veil through which we view consciousness. Speech is thought. Viral replication. Nothing comes between the infection and the host. No lapse, no time, No surface to grab. The only issue lies in the intention. I mean that the word can be intended in a rational sense or in an irrational sense. Thought and ***perception*** can be derailed. If that happens the virus can protect itself. It can lead to the hint of *reality* outside of perception which then sets things *back on track* because the very existence of the irrational requires the illusion of order and the rational to shackle and blind.

Average weekend night in America:

Remote electronic communication first...
FUN!!! YAY!!! POISON!!!FUN!!!YAY!!!

Text. Text. Text. Fun. Mad. Sad. Undead have a very strange relationship with electronic devices. It is a love hate kind of thing. They love to malfunction in our presence and we hate to have to deal with it so we have found a spell that allows us to use these devices in a reasonable manner. This spell is very simple and even the lowest of the undead can apply it for their amusement. Most of my spells are simple. The one I am casting here is not. This part is only the preparation. This Apocalyptic Name spell Shem HaMephorash that I have discovered is only accessible through pure improvisation and pure intention. No predetermined concoction will ever hope to work. It can only be done once. It has to be a powerful relationship to a specific time and place. More about that later. There are many trials that will appear to disengage the spell caster if they even come close to attempting it. I have already experienced a few of them by accident. By pure improvisation. The ritual chant will be drawn out when I am ready. It is almost time. This oscillating rant is all the necessary preparatory work. The time for me to go approaches. I will not allow myself any distractions. I am not human so I can totally open my head chakra without the same consequences. The cosmos will not come rushing in to distract me like it does with living humans. The exact opposite will happen. The cosmos will reject my inner fire that comes from the shriveled black raisin of my heart and brain. I am an angel of the earth, an angel of darkness. Nigredo. The beginning.

After my unbelievably surreal trip in and out of the Norongoro Crater I took a much needed rest for a few days. I did not know that an irreversible process had taken hold upon me. I still blamed simple traveler's fatigue, a reason with no sense at all considering the magnitude, of my illness. I am undead after all. Why would a simple movement of my presence actually harm me? I do not operate on the same sort of time frame that humans do. I sleep only when convenient and it is not really sleep, it is death. I was making excuses. I lounged in the shade of my hotel room. Every so often I would step out on to the balcony and gaze upon my surroundings. Uhuru peak, with its inexplicable tropical glaciers frosting its sun assaulted summit, dominates the entire visual field. Everything that you look at everywhere draws your eye to it in an inevitable climactic stroke. Everything here was created by its primordial eruptions. The plains, the animals, the humans, their villages, the tourists. Kilimanjaro is a minor creative deity. Kilimanjaro, Uhuru, Kibo, Shira, Mawenzi, Kaiser Wilhelm, there are so many parts to its form so many names, so many meanings to so many people. A rare place with rare secrets. A living contradiction. A place that holds the possible doorways out of ***perception*** and into *reality*. A crack in the seams of the physical architecture of this world that leads to others. Does the summit crater somehow allow this? I was now being drawn there for a reason. The same reason I was drawn to Ngorongoro first. They are both ancient craters. Places created by the blood of the earth which burst out through a wound of fire. Now, or at least for the moment, covered in ice. This was where I had to go and this is where I must return. This is where I have to exorcise the virus that was activated in me. This is the summit where I have to utter the original irrational word that has been stewing and frothing in my blood Shem HaMephorash. I have to go to Uhuru. The peak of freedom. Now it takes upon itself a whole new meaning to me. It holds the key to escaping the tyranny of the word virus of ***perception***, rationality, and the ultimate slavery of this world. Capitalism, the disease of the rational word should fall along with everything else. All of its blood ritual and addictions, its diseases all lead up to this entropic catharsis. Freedom from the slavery of its processes achieved through its own destruction. Here in my rest from Norongoro, I have discovered the way to begin this inevitable process. The acceptance of the irrational as the true guide of physical endeavor. The hypermajikal ritual has to be performed first. The doors of ***reality*** have to be torn open. The original irrational word, the secret name of the creator of this mess has to be spoken at the peak of freedom, Uhuru. This will bring about the final homeopathy. The healing of the toxin with the same toxin. Killing the word with the word. ***The word is the bird.***

Once this happens the undead will go completely crazy and possibly begin attacking themselves. A war at the end that will be far worse than the one at the beginning. Sorry but if you are reading this it probably means you too because the odds are that you are already so crystalized with bullshit that corporate America has jammed down your throat that you are virtually undead yourself and you have just been in denial this whole time. Sorry again. This does not matter. I am just as automated as the rest of you poor fuckers. My automation has just gone completely haywire.

I was not aware of any of this as I stood on my hotel balcony in the little Tanzanian town of Moshi. It was far too early in my infection. I needed some time to truly understand what was happening. I had to experience more symptoms and side effects to understand anything at all. The worst and most inexplicable were yet to come. I was perplexed by the glinting tropical ice that looked so tiny in the distance as it sparkled a shattered mystery off its surface. I could almost reach out and grab it, it looked so small in the distance. A true and rare diamond of this African continent. Dusk approached and it's pink light drained down the side of the massive mountains flanks as it tumbled and slid into magenta, then, in the sky above appeared a scintillating purple replaced by the star laden Prussian blue that quickly was swallowed through broken diamond teeth of a shimmering black infinite void. This transition summoned mosquitoes out of thin air. They danced and rejoiced because the time of Nosferatu was approaching. The night. These conditions brought about their blood lust as well as mine. They are tiny familiars to the undead. They are the dust of undead who have fallen. Undead do not ever cease to exist on this planet. If one is eliminated by a human or some other accident they simply turn to dust. This dust becomes animated in the form of these flying bloodsuckers. This is why swatting them never seems to matter. As soon as you smash one it reappears again somewhere else close by. A few came close to me to pay their respects. They are vectors of all sorts of disease, real and imagined. They possess every form of virus including the word virus which teems in the blood of every human. These tiny, threadlike wraiths have been constant companions to humanity and have even altered its consciousness many times along the evolutionary path of the species. *I see good spirits and I see bad spirits (1).* These delicate sprites, these blood fairies are just one other detail in the grand spell of perception that nature has cast upon the consciousness. They are also needed in the irreversible process that I am involved in. The process of driving everything toward *reality* and away from shattered perceptions. None can be too comfortable in their bodies or in this planet and these will-o-wisp's play a wonderfully effective part in maintaining human discomfort. All must be driven onward and in this case upward too.

In a few days after standing on the balcony I began my first attempt to ascend to the summit of Kilimanjaro. ***So many years have passed and gone and I just can't see. Take heed of the prophecy. So many years have passed and gone and I just can't see. Everyone living in unity. Prophecy is fulfillment. Fulfillment has got to be. Open your eyes and you will see (28).*** A cataclysm of infinite scale. I was supposed to be a part of this all along. Why me? Who the fuck knows or cares. Someone had to. Why not me? Why not you even? You are a part of this shit storm if you are reading this. Who knows what the result will be. ***If the Neverending Story contains itself then the world will end with this book (6).*** I may only be doing it for myself. You may have to suffer the same. You may have to find your own true name and do something like I must all over again. Reading this preparatory spell could be the help you need to see it through. ***You are looking for the water of life. You want to be able to love, that's your only hope of getting back to your world. To home – that's easily said. But the water of life will ask you: Love whom? Because you can't love in general. You have forgotten everything but your name. And if you can't answer it won't let you drink. So you'll just have to find a forgotten dream, a picture, that will guide you to this fountain and***

to find that picture you will have to forget the one thing that you have left of yourself. That takes hard, patient work. Remember what I said for I shall never say it again (28).

It is likely that destruction of perception must be won in a trial fought one by one. Each person versus themselves. Don't worry. You can't hide. I certainly can't for very long. The trial will come for you very soon. I have decided to go to it. You may hate me or love me for it because this just might expedite the process of what happens to everything else. It may not. There are many things that I still do not know. There is no way to know. Knowledge itself is a big part of the problem. It is part of the continuum of the rational word that I am trying so hard to disrupt and reveal its truly irrational mission. The things that I do not know yet are pretty much beside the point. I have reflected upon this for some time. It has been some time since my first summit attempt and only now am I putting it all together.

As I stood on the hotel balcony inhaling the misty tropical night air I thought of none of this at all. I was only slightly agitated. There was so much that I would soon realize and soon experience. Very soon I would be on my way up. The climb of the great mountain was what I came for in the first place. I had a stupid idea that I should be able to climb to the highest mountain of every continent and this was probably the best place to start. My reasons for wanting to do this are far different than the standard ones. I have no desire to be put on a list of people who have successfully done it because I am not human and such things are utterly meaningless anyhow. I accepted the fact that it is indeed an exercise for people with ego problems who have way too much energy, not enough cerebral function, and way too much money to justify such excesses. The classic reason for climbing mountains is pure stupidity and is not a reason at all. Many climbers say they have to climb because "the mountain is there." That banality is nothing more than stupidity and a refusal to accept the total pointlessness and narcissistic selfishness of the endeavor. The truth is the fact that the mountain isn't even there to be climbed. Most climbers have to travel all around the world just to be in the presence of the mountain. Most of the time they don't wake up in the morning and it is there beckoning them from their backyard. It isn't there at all. I will tell you what is there though. Drugs are everywhere. To apply the same logic one will instantly see how stupid that excuse is. Heroin is there so I should do it too. Well of course. Why not climb *down* into oneself for I wager it is harder than climbing up if one wants a good challenge. ***O! The lowness of him was beneath all up to that sunk to! No likedbylike firewater or firstserved firstshot...*****(5)** Heroin is there and I am a seriously fucked up individual for even considering it...***or gulletburn gin or honest brewbarret beer either. O dear no! Instead the tragic jester sobbed humself wheywhingingly sick of life on some sort of a rhubarbarous maundarin yellagreen funkleblue windegut diodying applejack squeezed from sour grapefruice and, to hear hum twixt his sedimental cupslips when he gulfed down...*** **(5)** yet the ascension of remote rocks is somehow the same sort of sanity. Climbing – especially rock climbing – is the most pointless of all mountainous exercises. If one finds themselves clinging to a cliff they have only created a severe navigational failure. It is just another game for the privileged to distract themselves from their seriously fucked up perception of reality. Communion with nature? Bollocks. Sit upon a pile of compost or empty out outhouses instead. Vultures. ***Mash down the regime and all their schemes. Vulture, you better leave Africa. Sucking the blood of the people so. You vampire. Suck on the blood and you suffer them so. You've done your time and you can't do no more, the world is displeased. The time has come for you to know, you just got to go (29).*** There are many things that are missed when the summit is the goal. Many important secrets that are missed along the way by goal driven insanity. These secrets are the true reason for climbing.

Wa-ka-ka. Oot. Mek we dweet. Ya mek we dweet. Jah jah wa-ka-ka-la-la...(29) I am the dark virus of perception. ***My life is with the thrill kill kult (1).*** A dark angel has descended and stole all of the gold and all of the diamonds. I stole something far greater. The original word. The original infinite Name. It isn't spoken in Swahili or English or Hebrew. It is all of them and none of them. It is not recognizable at all. Not even Lucifer, the most beautiful discord – ***visions of cloud and light and daedal earth are the airman's daily scene (4)*** – that ever was created knows what it is and I can guarantee that He has been looking for it for a very long time. Shem HaMephorash. It has been around for millennia haunting the African continent; the original wellspring of the water of life. There was a mass exodus that populated the Earth but it started here. I had a vague sense of obligation to come back here. Something not definable but something very real. I was going here as a thief. A burglar who is still running and has not stopped to take the time to inspect the stolen goods.

From the hotel base camp I seriously underestimated my next move. The summit was there in the distance but still right before me. It looked so close that I could touch it. Of course I couldn't. I had climbed many mountains before this one. I have achieved summits in all sorts of conditions on many smaller and larger mountains. I was operating from a position of complete ignorance. One can never climb the same mountain twice. I have never even climbed this one once but my mind was already on the summit. I knew that elevation and other issues related to it would have little to no effect on me. These problems are only for humans to ponder. I thought that I knew everything that there is to know about climbing. I even knew to expect the spiritual obstacles and all of the fields of residual psychic energy that are there. I thought that I was going there to experience and inspect them for I thought that I could discover something I did not yet already know. I expected to get a few surprises the closer that I came to the summit so I was even prepared for that. There had been armies of people who had went up and down all of the trails that approach the summit. Serious psychic energy had been dumped upon every one of these trails. I considered avoiding the trail systems entirely in favor of making my own route. I rejected this idea very quickly. As Nosferatu I am hypersensitive to residual human energy. It is the second sense of any hunter even though it has been some time since I actually acted upon my urges to kill a human for a feast. I decided to attempt the summit from one of the more popular routes because I expected to encounter something that I had not yet known buried in all of this residual psychic energy left on a well-used trail. That was a serious underestimation of what would actually happen.

Many of the locals believe that Kilimanjaro is the Mountain of God. There are some who think that it is impossible to actually stand on the summit because the ancient gods of the ancestors reside there. Many claim that the idea of summiting is a government conspiracy to attract tourist money. To them, none of the paths were real and the summit simply could not be found. All of the summit photos are believed to be staged and not at all real. Simply, no one could ever do it. I heard this mythology from many of the locals that I talked to and I instantly dismissed it as folklore. There turned out to be a lot of truth to their statements but they don't realize what is true and what part is concoction. I have read about many different mountainous areas all over the world. The deifying of mountains is a common tradition in many native societies. Every mountain is the home of every god. Even Mt. Moriah follows this tradition very closely. I take this most as a folklore because I know the truth of it. Maybe I should have payed attention because they turned out to be correct after all. It does not matter at all now. I was supposed to get my ass kicked by something that I dismissed as silly and trivial. Those small things will totally fuck you if you don't listen to people with experience.

After a few days of rest and communion with my brethren – the mosquitoes, the toxic virus laden insects who were so much like me in their septicemia and love for the dusk – I was almost ready to begin my climb. The night before I was to be bussed to the trailhead I had to go through my pre-climb ritual. I do this every time I go on an expedition into unknown territory. I begin by totally emptying all of my bags upon the floor and I go through an inventory of everything that I have with me. I thoughtfully consider each object and classify them in priority of potential need. The items that are of lesser importance get arranged in the backpack first. Once that is done, the items that are suspected to be most needed are stored on top of the pack and ready to be used without too much fuckery. Once that is accomplished I do a secondary analysis. This means that I categorize everything by weight so I must compromise my first decisions because the heaviest items should also be stored as close to the top of the pack as possible too. This arrangement places as much of the weight as possible on the shoulders rather than lower down on the back. Simple considerations like these can help prevent injury when it is least desirable. Nothing is worse than a strained back, blisters or pulled muscles when one is in the backcountry and many miles away from any sort of help. Not like such maladies apply in this case. These were bags that the porters were to be taking up the mountain for me. I would pack my own bag later but I gave these bags the same amount of attention. I do this because of its ritualistic quality. It is also an incantation of protection. I am undead so these minor physical injuries don't happen to me. If they did I have enough majik to heal myself as it is needed. You could chop me up into pieces with a chainsaw and I would be more or less okay after I put myself back together again.

Up until my African crisis I never had any issues whenever I tried to explore the back country. I never needed Auryn because I did most of my expeditions before I even met her so the voids were still a complete mystery then. I only had my own self-reliance to resort to and it was always enough. Most of these spells are different every time I do them but they generally stay the same. They rely upon the specific placement of specific objects at the correct time and place. The concentration of attention upon these physical processes directs the willpower to accomplish specific tasks. Over millennia of practice and repetition I believed that I had mastered all of these simple spells. I can control the weather with a few disciplined twitches of face and fingers. Other spells require a tool of incantation such as a wand or staff or something of the sort. A pen is sufficient. Sometimes a feather works best. It is because of processes like this I am always compelled to set all of my backpacking gear in organized units before I climb. It is preparation for the encounters with fields of residual psychic energy that I expect to encounter on the trail. These energy fields are what I seek whenever I go out into the wilderness. They are the secrets that nature extracts out of us and holds on to. Summits have a lot of these energy fields because so many people spend so much time there and they are such tiny places that the energy is more concentrated there than in most places. It is not always a rule though. I did not do anything like this sort of preparation when I went into Ngorongoro because I took for granted that I would be in a vehicle the whole time. What would I need a backpack for? I didn't expect to get into such serious shit. Now it is too late, the damage has been done. I must have realized this sometime shortly after because I did a significant amount of preparation for my Kilimanjaro climb a few days later. When I was going over my packing ritual all of the lights and electrical devices in the hotel room flashed on and off in response to my incantations. This does not usually happen so I should have realized that something was going totally haywire. Instead I simply chalked it up to the fact that I was in Africa and they do have power issues sometimes. That was enough of an explanation for me at the moment.

Having done some of my preparatory work for the coming climb, I left the hotel room and stood on the balcony. I stared at the mountain in the distance that was still visible in the moonlight. I had a little time so I wanted to explore. I grabbed onto the railing and did a quick chant with my eyes shut. All I saw was fire and blood. The flames rose and the blood boiled. My hands became flaky and scaly and my fingernails morphed into talons that clutched the railing. The rest of my body lurched upward and shrunk into itself as I changed form. Hair turned into black feathers and the skin of my face withered as my nose hardened and extended into a beak. Where there once stood a human figure there was now a large vulture perched on the railing. To be more specific I was actually a condor but who cares? They are pretty much the same to people who are not ornithologists. Condor just sounds better. It has an imperial ring to it that I am attracted to. A very appealing touch to someone who has named himself Alexander for the same reason. Technically I was neither condor nor vulture but still Nosferatu. I obviously have some serious ego issues but I leave that to another rant for another time. If there is actually anything left of the universe when I am finally finished with what I intend to do after this rant is over. Somewhere in Africa, where clocks actually worked, the hand struck ten.

In condor form I flew all around the small town that had been serving as base camp for so many climbers for so long. It is the middle of nowhere. The night air was filled with smoke and dust. I could sense the combination of desperation and privilege grinding against each other all over the town. It was everywhere. Economics gone haywire seems to be the norm on this fucked up planet. The manifestation of the ***perception*** of *reality* and all of its dysfunction was palpable to my senses as I rode the winds. Here again was the unification of opposites to form an incomprehensible whole. I knew that there was a voice present in this land and that it was speaking to me. In condor form I could sense and understand these things differently than I could as a human. I could only think about finding something to feed upon. The smell of death was everywhere and I could not ignore it. It was not very long before I found a fresh carcass. A buffalo had been killed a short distance outside of the town and the hyenas had not yet got to it. In this form I could consume all of the blood that I needed. Fresh, raw, untreated blood. It would last me for a few days and would not be unpalatable to me in this form. I thought I needed this extra fortification to help me complete my climb. I consumed my fill in the way that any condor would and then I flew back to the village. I circled a few times in the darkness of the night before I landed on the same railing in front of my room at the hotel. As soon as my talons touched the cold metal of the railing they converted back into hands and I threw the birds body up and over to stretch back out into my human form with feet planted firmly on the concrete floor of the porch. I was now fully back in my bipedal form and I shook my head a little to erase the bird perspective that I had just changed out of. I stretched my back, legs, and hands to remember how they worked. I extended and retracted my fangs as quickly as lightning. Everything was working fine yet I felt very strange. Something was still totally wrong. ***I and I are the living dead. In-a-dis-a dawn of the living dread (28).*** The clock struck eleven.

I vaguely remember opening the door and going back into my room but it is like remembering a dream. My vision was fogged up for an incalculably long moment. I found myself unable to stand properly on the rug of the room. The floor warped and bulged like Hundertwasser had designed it. Every cell in my dead brain was on fire. I could feel everything in the entire universe spinning violently. I could feel the earth rotating. I could feel its' helicoid motion around the sun. The cosmos is not infinite.

Ann Druyan suggests an experiment: Look back again at the pale blue dot...take a good long look at it. Stare at the dot for any length

of time and then try to convince yourself that God created the whole Universe for one of the ten million species of life that inhabit that speck of dust. Now take it a step further: Imagine that everything was made just for a single shade of that species, or gender, or ethnic or religious subdivision. If this doesn't strike you as unlikely, pick another dot. Imagine it to be inhabited by a different form of intelligent life. *They, too, cherish the notion of a God who has created everything for their benefit.* **How seriously do you take their claim (30)?** Even though it is difficult for me, we should forgive the naïveté of Mrs. Druyan and those who follow this line of thinking. It is easy for them to understand things in a warped manner because they rely upon reason for their very existence like a junky needs junk or like a Catholic needs a confession. It is easy to correct their misunderstanding however. I will just change a word and it will make more sense why they do not see clearly: *"They, too, cherish the notion of a God who has created everything for their misery."* I suggest an experiment. Here is a Pale Blue Dot followed by a smaller black dot: ●. Stare at them for any length of time. Try to convince yourself that this exercise can reveal any sort of insight at all. Pick another dot if you don't get anything out of it. Here is one for you: •. Not getting anything out of this? Stare at it longer and pretend that it presents some sort of revelation of reason. Still not getting anything? Well it may be because this is fucking illogical and if you can glean anything from it you may be insane or undead. You are well on your way to the self-destruction that this planet is designed to manifest. If the species no longer exists how can it care about its existence? What, exactly, matters? The earth and sun are on a collision course. They will collide eventually and a tiny cosmic pip will burst. There are other pale blue dots. Here...

The destruction of all sense took ahold of me as the floor warped and heaved under me and the ceiling dripped with stalactites of fire. I could feel the sun circling along with the swarm of the other stellar beings in the galaxy. I could feel this galaxy hurtling toward other galaxies on a collision course and most importantly I could feel the gigantic black hole at the center of our galaxy pushing and pulling everything around it. It became too much to bear. This thought of the black hole eating everything was the last thought that I had before everything went blank. Midnight was upon this dark patch of earth but I was not conscious.

I felt a body hit the floor of the hotel room. First the knees and then the head. A quick double *thud, thud* like a muffled bass drum. This frequency echoed through the entire building. I have no idea how long I was laid out on the floor. What I do remember is looking up from my unusual perspective to see the front door to the hotel room opening. I saw the door crack open between the stubs of chair legs that sprouted like trees off the lawn of the carpet. Suddenly the room was filled with shoes, legs and swishing pants. I could not tell how many people had entered the room but I am fairly certain that the number that exited was one less than that had entered. I really do not know. It may have been more than one. I do not know. Something terrible happened a little later. I am certain of that.

I was helped up off the floor and onto the bed. The entire room turned into a carousal of spinning and bobbing biomorphic forms that eventually slowed down and coalesced into a mob of humans. Two were hunched over to study my countenance in search of some sort of reason for my condition. My first thought was great concern that my fangs may have been out when I was awoken. If they were I would have no choice but to kill every one of these busybody motherfuckers instantly. I ran my fingers across my lips to find that there was indeed blood on them but there was no evidence that my fangs were out at all. I felt around my head again. I traced the blood from my lips and followed it up to the side of my head where it was coming from. I normally would not be bleeding all over like this from a simple bump in the head but I had so much of it in my system after consuming the buffalo carcass there was no way it wouldn't come spilling out of a head wound like that. I finally came to an awareness of where I was and what was happening. ***Prophecy is fulfillment and fulfillment has got to be.*** I played along with everyone in the room and answered all of their questions just to pacify them and expedite their exit. I assured them that I was truly alright despite my appearance. They eventually listened to me and slowly went back to where they came from. It was an hour after midnight.

My climb was supposed to begin in a matter of hours yet I could not even stand up in a hotel room. This gave me no concern at all. I was certainly being stubborn. This fainting episode, along with all of the other incidents, should have warned me that something was wrong. Instead of being worried I simply sat in my room and waited for the sunrise like I had done so many millions and millions of times before. Sleep is not needed for undead but sometimes we can fall asleep if we want to. I try not to because I find it incredibly uncomfortable. It is more like death than sleep for me.

The clock struck three. I awoke with a heavy head and blurred vision. Did I actually fall asleep? I picked up my swollen carcass from the chair that I had been sitting in. I actually yawned for the first time in a thousand years. When I did my fangs shot out and released a spray of blood upon the far wall. Vampire fangs are very much like those of a spitting cobra. They are hollow, pointed straws which have evolved to facilitate the drawing of blood rather than the spitting of venom but they are pressurized my minor facial motions. Another little known fact that I should not disclose is that once a vampire has existed for some time their teeth, including their fangs go through a molting process and transform from enamel to pure ivory.

There was something that was not correct about the scene in the room. ***So many years have passed and gone and they I just can't see. Take***

heed of the prophecy. Prophecy is fulfillment, fulfillment has got to be. Open your eyes and you will see (28). As I looked around the room I was surprised by the amount of blood that was there. Blood all over the walls, all over the floor. Blood on my head, blood on my hands, blood on my side. This dark stigmata marked my every move. Then I rubbed my eyes and studied what the room looked like. Everywhere I looked there were indescribable globs of what used to be some sort of lung or brain material, shattered bones sticking out of coagulum and torn flesh, flaps of bloody skin that was sprouting with hair, ribbons of entrails hanging, strung around the room from floor to ceiling like they were Christmas lights and all of this wonder was what Santa left for me when I woke up. I won't even begin to describe what it smelled like because I can't. If one could smell movies then no one would watch them. Think about that. What a blessing it is that no one ever tried to introduce the olfactory sense into film. They stopped at audio and visual when they realized that most film was about sex and death. If you could smell a movie would you watch it? Anyhow… The first question that I asked myself was whether or not I should clean up this stinking mess or wait for the housekeeping staff. That is how sick I am. I did not worry about who all of this residue came from or what horrific thing that I probably had done. Nope. I just wanted someone to clean up after me. The next logical thought was whether I should eat them too if they showed up and looked at me the wrong way. MMMMmmmmm – cleaning staff for breakfast served right to my room. I don't know how well that will go over. Especially here in Africa where the spirits in the air are palpable and most of the population are sensitive to their presence. I did not even consider what I had done or how I had gone about it until all of these thoughts ran their course.

I looked around and took in the condition that my room was in. There was no way to reasonably clean it all in time for my departure via normal methods. I was forced to use majik if I wanted to avoid a dangerous situation. It has been a very long time since I have had to resort to techniques like this. In order to pull it off I had to resort to waking up an ancient part of myself. Was it possible that I had a dream? Is that what compelled this mess I had on my hands? My conscious perception was dreamlike enough so I was having a difficult time determining what had happened and what I simply dreamed. I wasn't even sure if I had gone to sleep or not. I simply don't remember. I was certain that I lacked a large degree of control in the previous hours. I hadn't actually killed someone in a long time and now I can't even remember who I killed or how I did it. I was trying to rationalize it. Words came flooding into my brain as I went through every possibility. I realized that something must have gone terribly wrong with me but I still wasn't willing to face up to it. The words in my brain created all sorts of alternate scenarios. The pathological process of addiction (reason) kicked into overdrive. Words, reasons, explanations and all total bullshit.

To me a spell is nothing. A flick of the wrist. A twitch of the eye. The manifestation of desire. Sometimes a spoken syllable or two was needed to help out. It is all a combination of things to create a desired circumstance. Africa demanded certain techniques. ***The word is reggae music. Word sound. Word sound is power (28).*** The spells I needed to use to clean up this mess happen all of the time but rarely all at once. In this instance I had to do a little more than remember. I had to bring it out of a dormant state to manifest what I needed, here and now, into the forefront of my attention. Once this happened it would no longer truly matter what I dreamed and what I actually did to get into this situation in the first place. I would simply erase it from perception. This skill is something that I learned to avoid using over the years because it is a literal displacement of perceptions. Once it was done there would be a ripple effect through the fabric of time and space that could set off any sort of consequences in the near future.

I scanned the room with intense scrutiny. I had no choice. I let my retina touch every surface with the greatest amount of delicacy. Then I blinked a few times. When I looked at the room again it was in pristine order. There was not a drop of blood anywhere. This solved the immediate problem but it was certain to create new ones. It displaced the problem in time and space and dissolved it away into the past, future and parallel realities. It served as a warning signal to all of the spirits in this land that didn't know that I was already here. They could all now see my presence. They could prepare for my future maneuvers and protect themselves or even assault me directly. The destruction of time and space was not in their interest just as it was not in the interest of any undead who are clinging to existence on this miserable hell planet.

It seemed to be against the prophecy or was it? I had never taken any of that too seriously because it sounds like such a convoluted mess. The prophecy had been revealed to John as well as Muhammed. This unknown human sacrifice may have been necessary for me to go further and experience whatever trial I had to go through. I became an instrument. I acted out without even exercising my will. Perhaps I had been an instrument for a very long time. *Repent or I will come suddenly and fight with the sword of my mouth. I will give to each a white stone, and on that stone will be engraved a new name that no one knows except the one who receives it (8).* The irrational word is a gift. A new name. An unspeakable name. How far had things actually developed? How close to the end are we? How far has the prophecy been developed? I had been undead for so long that I had not been paying any sort of attention.

We undead had been walking in the sunlight for so long that we forgot that it was an oddity and a fairly new development in the greater context of things. There was a time when we could not do this. A time that was forgotten. *The fourth angel blew his trumpet and one third of the sun was struck, and one third of the moon and one third of the stars and they had become dark. And a third of the day was dark and one third of the night also (8).* I remembered my lonely flight from the night before. I was the only thing there or so it seemed. Was it a dream? In the dream I looked up and heard a single eagle crying as it flew through the air *"terror, terror, terror to all who belong to this world because of what will happen (8)"*. Was it all a dream? What the hell is a dream anyway to me? Did I even have dreams? My entire existence has been a dream. A nightmare. I don't even know the difference between what is my own memory from what is something else that I mutated in my mind along the way. It does not seem to matter. It all is conceivable. There is no way to know. Reason has always been breaking down into opinion and perception on its way to its irrational terminal point.

It was four A.M. After I cleaned up the scene in the hotel room I began to gather my items and put them into the bags. I had to pack once again, for a final time. I had my porter bags filled but I had to get together what I would bring up the mountain. I wouldn't actually carry much myself. Even though I could normally carry a hundred times more than the average human I was not allowed to. I had to employ a few porters to do this for me. It was one of the local laws that governed the trail system. It is a way to employ people in this surreal economic system. Once the porter bags were packed they had to be weighed to fit the criteria for what was humanly expected of them. After I finished this I had my own personal bag to pack. I had to choose the proper gear that I would need for the first part of the ascent. I did not know that things had been set in motion that were totally out of hand as a result of the many things I had already done and experienced. Shem HaMephorash.

The difference between night and day were lost on me. I was gone at least a few hours on a totally out of control rampage. I did not understand what had happened to bring me to this point. I still did not realize that the first crater I had visited had broken me down with the gift of an enormous burden and it would weigh heavily upon me if I attempted to climb again. I was transitioning into something else and the process had begun. Life was slowly coming back to me. Nothing was right but I did not pay attention. I could not tell a dream from what wasn't but I had lived in that reality for centuries. Long ago the sun became as dark as a burning piece of coal and the moon was red as blood. The stars were visible in the morning sky and they fell to the earth like green figs shaken from a tree by a mighty wind. *A barren fig tree is killed by a touch. The sky was rolled up into a scroll and taken away. And all of the mountains and all of the islands disappeared. The then the kings of the earth, the rulers, the generals, the wealthy people, the peoples with great power and every slave and every free person, all hid themselves in the caves and among the rocks. They cried to the rocks, "fall on us and hide us from the face of the one who sits on the throne for the great day of their wrath has come and who will be able to survive (8)?"*

My head was flooded and I could not gain control of it. Words from the past that concern the future dominated my mind. I was trying to put together what I had done and what would result from it. Everything that did not make any sense began to be the only obvious thing. I was flipping back and forth between lucid dreaming and trying to make sense of my final packing ritual. It was as if my subconscious was giving me clear reports that something was wrong. I had come all this way to get to this point. I was not going to let anything get to me if it wasn't on my terms. I was losing this battle. My mind and focus was shattered. *Seven trumpets and seven thunders.* The power to torture has been unleashed upon the world, upon the universe, upon every infinite multiverse connected to it. All time and space is interconnected. There is no center. What happens at one seemingly random point can affect the entire thing. One can never stop traveling. The body is never at rest. Even if no space is crossed time will move. I can travel further and to more exotic places simply by sitting down than someone on an airplane or a space shuttle. I taught this spell to Igor Stravinsky many years ago and he then shocked the world with Le Sacre du Printemps. An apocalypse of sound and motion. This started a slow burning flame that got bigger and bigger until the entire world was on fire. ***Wake up the town, take a look another way.***

The sun was rising once again. Well, the sun wasn't actually going up or down. Instead the earth was turning so that the position I occupied faced it once again. A giant windup toy. All predetermined automation. Did I even have a choice about what I was doing or was my motion misperceived in the same way? I had to get out of that bloody room and out of my bloody head that was thinking of apocalypse far too much for any comfort. I opened the hotel room door, went out on to the deck and then across it until I reached the stairway to the ground level. I descended and wandered around the courtyard of the hotel. Here was the beginning of human activity that started the day. Employees were preparing a breakfast buffet as others took care of all of the bags for all of the climbers that were to be weighed for the expedition. I overheard some conversation among some of the local employees as they busied themselves with their jobs. There was word of a strange event which occurred the previous evening. I listened intently without trying to look like I was because I wanted to find out what happened. I felt it could shed some knowledge upon what I had done. I heard whisperings of a word I did not recognize. It was uttered between people who looked over their shoulders and put a finger of silence to their lips as I passed. "Popobawa." I had no idea what they were speaking of but it seemed serious. After everything had played out and I came back to America I made certain to find out what this was. I did not want to interview any of these people because I did not want to draw attention to myself about anything that had to do with what I had done. Once I found out what that word meant then everything became clear. The Popobawa is a fairly recent manifestation reported in Zanzibar and Tanzania. The creature is a demon who appears as a normal human by day, and a one-eyed, bat-winged monster at night. The Popobawa attacks and sodomizes both men and women in the dark of night, and is particularly vicious to those who don't believe in him. Attacks were first reported in 1965 on the island of Pemba. Reports of attacks come every few years, with a large number in 1995 attributed to mass hysteria. Some think that the attacks of the Popobawa can be traced to "waking dreams" or "night terrors," in which the person who transforms experiences hallucinations somewhere in between lucidity and sleep. The name Popobawa in Swahili refers to "bat wing" but the actual translation of Popobawa is "Bat-rapist." Kubawa is to rape, but it is easily confused with the word bwawa, which is "wing." My simple condor transformation spell was most likely not completed when I thought it was. I must have lost consciousness for a second. Long enough to reactivate into this form when I wasn't thinking. The spirits of the land had taken me over. My majik was going haywire and this was a manifestation of it.

I continued listening to the conversations and watching the mannerisms of everyone around me. People were obviously scared but they were also scared to show it. I was wearing my small pack with the essentials that I needed to climb. In my pack was a small supply of blood, a small piece of navy worsted wool which is handy to wrap up charged implements and other objects if they are discovered, a hand woven hat to close down my chakra that was wide open to enemy influence above and below, a small piece of silver and one of gold, lead crystal inserts for my shoes that were all colors and none at the same time, a few choice bird feathers, a smudge of potassium, a coil of copper wire to repair the two threads of pure copper sewn into the fabric of the backpack and all of the clothing that I was using, a piece of moldavite that was tied to a ring of small transparent Herkimer diamonds by a few threads of pure silver, a twelve gauge marine flare pistol with five rounds, A steel bowie knife that was coated in silver, and an infinitely collapsible invisible mirror cloth that looks sort of like a Mylar space blanket. Invisible from the outside but transparent from the inside, it is something that I can hide in like a cloaking device. I can use it if I experience a vortex of light that is too powerful for my normal protection spells. I was going to attempt to go to places that I had never been to before so it is only practical to be prepared for things that could go wrong. It is closer to the sun up there and the air was thinner which could affect the intensity of the sun. I had no idea what could happen. That was what most of these items were for. Protection against things that may happen. It is funny because it was all totally useless for what did happen. I didn't get a chance to use any of it.

I had a few more things in the bag too which I rarely ever use but bring along just for fun. Acetazolamide aka Diamox was there in there because I love pills and any one of my human companions may need it at some point. Of course I love pills! I am fucking undead. I am obsessed with blood and all of its alterations. I have to know about these sorts of things because I may end up consuming it. Of course I also had Seconal, Dilaudid, Desoxyn, Dexadrine, and Fentanyl which are my favorites but there were many others I brought along as well.

All sorts of things can be revealed from a simple trip up a mountain. *Exodus 28: 15-21: "Then with the most careful workmanship, make a chest piece that will be used to determine Gods will. Use the same method that you did for the ephod. Use fine linen cloth embroidered with gold thread and blue, purple and scarlet yarn. This chest piece will be made of two folds of cloth forming a pouch nine inches square. Four rows of gemstones will be attached to it. The first row will contain a red carnelian, a chrysolite, and an emerald. The second row will contain a turquoise, a sapphire, and a white moonstone. The third row will contain a jacinth, an agate and an amethyst. The fourth row will contain a beryl, an onyx, and a jasper. All these stones will be set in gold (8)."* Keep in mind that this chest piece is also intended to be a pouch. This is what undead use it for. We can't actually wear it but we have found other uses and almost every Nosferatu has at least one. I'm sure that you would want one too.

I'm so bored I'm drinking bleach. Don't you want to be with the bleach boy's baby (31)? And then you go from I.O.P back to the fucking detox house and start leveling up all over again. Fuck all and let me get this money. That is what many men of faith said. Jesus is the breath of life. He is the communion. Take a moment and breathe. Breathe out and think about how you breathe life into the world. Think about how much shit you breathe in. I inhale what you exhale and you breathe in my emissions. No wonder your blood is so fucked up. May as well drink bleach. It all floats up and condenses upon leaves and rocks to drip back into the earth and form new pills. I brought Diamox. Medication that helps acclimatize to the thin air of high elevation. The thin air effects the blood and the breath. I keep all of my pills in the gem studded high priests pouch that I hide in my backpack. I also use it to keep any other thing that I don't want to be seen when I cross borders or go through security checkpoints. Whatever is in the pouch is invisible to any sort of scan. A diplomatic bag of sorts. It is a very convenient traveler's accessory.

With all of this ready to go, along with my fucked up attitude I strolled around the hotel grounds as everything was being prepared to leave for the trailhead. This place was an international melting pot that was as diverse as a block in Manhattan. One could never expect a response more than a quizzical look if one asked how the other was doing. Even though English is ubiquitous it still didn't work very well. I speak all contemporary and many ancient languages – Aramaic being my favorite – so I entertained myself trying to guess who came from where before I greeted them in the language that I thought they would respond to. This turned out to be much more difficult that I thought it would be. Most of the time I was wrong with the exception of the Italians. They are always easy for me to pin. I have spent a lot of time in Italy. I can pick out the difference between a northern

Italian from a Southern one. I can tell the difference between people from Venice, Rome, Florence, and Naples. These were all my feeding grounds in ancient times when we still drank human blood straight from the veins. The good old days. I can smell Italian blood from a mile away.

For some reason all of the Eastern Europeans that were there were very upset when I got them wrong and approached them in German. The Germans even more so. If I spoke Munich German to someone from Berlin I would get a very curt response combined with a knowing sneer if I got any response at all. Even if I did enunciate everything perfectly they seemed to know that I was not one of them. I had quite a bit of fun talking to the Masai who hung around the hotel grounds and helped out. By looking at them I could not tell if they were actually employed by the hotel or if they just wanted to hang around and nod at the tourists with their enormous shit eating grins. They were just happy to be there and they lived life on their terms. They stood around in their red and purple robes holding up their sticks to lean upon. I would approach them and introduce myself in Swahili and they seemed delighted to hear me speak their language. They would smile bigger than they already were and would respond back in Swahili but things seemed to always degenerate into battered form of English for some reason. After I was done speaking with them they would yell "Zuka!" or "Ya Rasta!" I believe that this was because of the single enormous dreadlock that I had growing out of the back of my head. The rest of my hair is a long night black cascade over my shoulders but I used the long dreadlock as a hair tie to wrap up a pony tail which I typically wore to keep the hair out of my face.

I sat down after talking to many people which resulted in pissing them off or getting a laugh. My head swam again and my mind started to break down. I clutched the table too hard and almost broke it as I reeled with visions and explanations. I looked around at all of the swarming humans in the courtyard. I witnessed an ancient vision before me. *Then what looked like flames or tongues of fire appeared and settled on each of them. How can this be? These people are from Galilee and yet we hear them speaking the languages of the lands where we were born. Here we are – Parthians, Medes, Edomites, Chaldeans, Judeans, Cappadocians, Asians, Phrygians, Egypians, and the areas of Libya toward Cyrene, visitors from Rome, Cretans, and Arabians. And we hear all of these people speaking in our own languages about the wonderful things that God has done. They stood there amazed and perplexed. What can this mean they asked each other? Others in the crowd were mocking. They are drunk. That is all (8).* It is a chant but I felt like I was the only one who was witnessing this breakdown into entropy. Back and forth between sense and nonsense in order to create sanity. *Reality*, the final unification of opposites. A combination of real and imagined, of inverted and real. A combination of plagiarism and invention. Ink infects the blood. Experience and imagination. Identity and change.

All forms of architecture possess a spirit. All architecture has points of congruence in order to stand up and exist. Every building has many points where horizontal and vertical become one. This is the most important point of the structure. It is the point where rationality is the weakest because it is a paradox. It is neither horizontal nor vertical but both. This is where the spirits can come and go as they please. Like a building, each word has a point of congruence in its architecture. Everything is an incantation, it all either stands or falls. What or who is the master of all of this? ***Perception*** will never be able to reveal the truth. ***Blackheathen and the pagans from the prince of pacis: what was trembling sod quaked no more, what were frozen loins were stirred and lived: gone to the septuor, dark deadly dismal doleful desolate dreadful desperate, no more tolvmaans, bloody sorrowful frightful appalling: peace, perfect peace: and I hung up at Yule my duindleeng lunas, helphelped of***

Kettil Flashnose, for the souperhore of my frigid one (5). The human body itself is the key to this architecture. It is connected to the spirits that come and go. It possesses its own weak points in its energy fields that lead directly to the consciousness and out from it into oblivion. Possession happens more commonly than not. The paradox in the architecture is attacked because the attack is invited. These paradoxes are wide open doors for evil spirits with a mission to keep everyone enslaved.

Addiction is one of these paradoxes and it is used with impunity against the host. It is something that was designed to be helpful which has then gone awry. A paradox. A force intended to provide survival instincts is used to self-destruct. A subconscious force intended to create desire for nourishment is used to seek intoxication. A subconscious force that is intended to create the desire for human relationships creates a photophobic recluse who only speaks to other reptiles and only when obligated. It attacks every detail of every decision in order to make it appear like normal acceptable behavior when it is deadly toxic. There is no such thing as normality, rationality, etc. Why else would someone agree to pay eight to then dollars for a plastic toothbrush that they know costs only a tiny fraction of that amount to make in the first place? It is not sane or acceptable behavior. It is addict behavior. Capitalism needs addiction like a junky needs junk. It would go into quakes of withdrawal without an insanely high population of addicts to keep it going.

This is the spirit of the age: infection, addiction, and self-destruction. It is an immortal spirit of ruination and the masses are possessed by it no matter what their social class. It is the same evil over and over. Through-out time it manifests itself in the consciousness, a steady stream of language used as justification. Language that has hijacked the universal consciousness of every living thing. Something intended to be useful that has gone into a destructive process. Addiction is the only force that keeps international capitalism functioning. The focus on the needs of the self – whatever that is – is all reduced to language; the justification of the insanity and the maintainer of reason itself. ***The last half versicle repurchasing his pawned word; sorensplit and paddypatched; and pfor to pfinish our pfun of a pfan coalding the keddle mickwhite; sure, straight, slim, sturdy, serene, synthetical, swift (5).*** Of course I must mention once again that reason is only a temporary arrangement or permutation of a greater chaos that is all around it. The inexplicable chaos that will swallow it whole despite all of its denial because the only tools available are personal perceptions based upon the black toxin of reason; the chaos of perception that forever shackles the mind to the body and the body to the earth. The chaos of perception that forever hides the infinite unity of reality that is totally unperceivable but lurking behind every moment of experience. It was designed to fail. The weak points of the architecture must be recognized and pointed out. I must be the one to deliver all of this or else I wouldn't be casting this spell right now. I sort of started it long ago when I was a human so it is only proper that I should be responsible for ending it. ***Hegel's concept of the world historical figure, the hero who, heeding only inner necessity, unwittingly assists the dialectal process of history (18).*** I wouldn't be pinning it down in the form of language unless I had to, so that I can conveniently control and transfer it later. ***All that was needed to make the turn from epiphany to apocalypse was a slight shift of emphasis in the reading of the existing text (4).*** The utterance of the irrational word is hidden in my blood and in the ink that prints this spell. It is a contradiction in itself. Black marks upon a white field produce meaning when forced together. How can a word be irrational? Each one of them is not what it seems for a wise man once noted that a word can never be what it refers to. I will it hide all of this in my bejeweled linen pouch along with all of the other contraband that I bring with me everywhere. I will hide it and climb once again at the very end.

After my daydreams congealed back into my perceptions and led back to the simple time and place that I rested, I felt that I could only sit for so long in the courtyard amongst the people and the pebbled concrete tables with the enormous reed umbrellas that were mounted in the center. Time is relatively meaningless to me but space is not. After my previous night in the hotel room I knew that something was wrong and I was afraid that if I spent too much time in one space, these daydreams would come to me more often and I was not yet ready to accept their existence let alone their meaning. Time gains a greater degree of meaning in the context of resting space. I decided to walk around and distract myself. I still am a creature of dust and lightning. A majikal concoction that is totally inexplicable, yet still a force of existence. Where there is truth there is no peace. I am still attached to the spinning earth as much as I do not want to be anymore. As I pondered these trivialities I noticed a white van pull through the open iron gates of the hotel compound. Dust from the street blew behind it in a sepia wave and astern. Now visible through the gates was the action in the street outside the walls. A chicken pecked futilely at some trash that wafted around orange pebbles – each of which revealed a secret name but no one around me saw this momentary revelation as the iron gates closed again in front of it. The doors of the white van parked in the courtyard were then all opened like a Swiss army knife in a display case and the porters began milling around it, doing what they did with bags and vans. The weighed bags were loaded up as efficiently as is possible in Africa. There were a few different groups going to the trailhead to begin their expedition today so there was a lot to organize and account for. I am certain that this very scene plays out here in this courtyard every morning or at least every other morning. It is its own sort of mantra or spell. A vortex of human effort that can warp time and space. Have you ever wondered why some experiences seem to speed by and other things seem to drag on and on into infinity and only five minutes have expired? Temporal spells are very common. They need blood to work. They need a heartbeat to warp time and space and we dark angels witness this continual apocalypse. *As is above so is below. There are ones coming out of great tribulation. They washed their robes in the lamb's blood and were made white. That is why they are standing before the throne of God, serving him day and night in the temple. They will never again be hungry or thirsty and they will be fully protected from the scorching noontime heat (8).*

•________________________________coagulum

An old friend of Bill W. once told me that "IF" is the longest word in the English language. I was sitting alone in a different courtyard in a different place at a different time. This, friend of Bill W. saw me sitting alone and invited me to come to a nearby table to talk as I drank my coffee. I had never met the man before but I humored him because I enjoy insanity and this situation promised to be a fine example. I am certain that he was just as undead as I was but we played our roles out to conclusion. He played the wizened older gentleman and me the young mental patient who supposedly needed assistance and advice. As a friend of Bill W. he naturally obsessed over the quality of his blood and the timing of solar cycles. He was obsessed with every twenty four hour milestone in the maintenance of clean blood. Even though he had experienced countless twenty four hour intervals of successfully keeping his blood clean he could never get over each one individually. Many undead are like this guy and totally obsess over time and not space, so this was not an unusual conversation even though it made no sense at all which is the reason why it is so important. ***Creo quia absurdum (Tertullian).*** His obsession led to his conclusion about the word "IF" Unlike him, some undead obsess over space and – more or less – ignore time like I do. Some – like this gentleman – ignore space and obsess over time. This friend of Bill W. told me that "IF" the sun ever rose over Los Angeles it was time to watch out and "IF" the sun rises over Boston we can have another twenty four hours. I considered this and offered my agreement but I told him that he had made a mistake. Because I was obsessed with space rather than time, I had a different and more concise conclusion. There is a word that is infinitely longer than the word "IF" which – in order to pacify him – I conceded may be the second longest word in the English language. He grumbled and softly asked me what that longer word could possibly be. I told him that I didn't want to have to say it because it favors dissent over conformity and one must be careful when uttering it but I agreed to tell him and I whispered the word "I".

Silent Echo..... Shem HaMephorash.....

Even though this is a very elegant solution because "I" takes up far less space than "A" and is therefore far more infinite in this inverse perversion of reality, I must warn that the infinity of "I" is only a fragment of the infinite Shem HaMephorash because the infinite unspeakable name can't be totally revealed yet and especially not in this format or context. Quite possibly my favorite thing ever written: ***Sad and weary I go back to you, my cold father, my cold mad father, my cold mad feary father, till near sight of the mere size of him, the moyles and moyles of it, moananoaning, makes me seasilt and saltsick and I rush, my only, into your arms. I see them rising! Save me from those therrble prongs! Two more. Onetwo moremens more. So. Avelaval. My leaves have drifted from me. All. But one clings still. I'll bear it on me. To remind me of. Lff! So soft this morning, ours. Yes. Carry me along, taddy, like you done through the toy fair! If I seen him bearing down on me now under whitespread wings like he'd come from Arkangles, I***

sink I'd die down over his feet, humbly dumbly, only to washup. Yes, tid. There's where. First. We pass through grass behush the bush to. Whish! A gull. Gulls. Far calls. Coming, far! End here. Us then. Finn, again! Take. Bussoftlhee, mememormee! Till thousandsthee. Lps. The keys to. Given! A way a lone a last a loved a long the (5) trumpets will begin their last call and they will play on with the rest of the band as the great unsinkable ship finally goes down. I think I can hear them warming up and drippling condensation out of their spit valves as most humans desperately cling to the railing of what they can rationally understand with the faith that this is all that they will ever need. Poor sad fools. The only thing that one can have faith in is the sad fact that the other guy only gives a shit about himself. This is the main credo of capitalism. This is its main prayer. What a sad terrible existence humans have evolved into because of the religion of capitalism and reason. The song of their destruction has commenced. Faith in self leads to entropy for the self becomes a single unit of force. The song is getting louder and it is almost time to cue the trumpets. As soon as the explosion of singularity (I, the singularity or the longest word) got to a certain point, it began to self-destruct. Entropy explained in an alternate version: That what makes sense leads to what doesn't and that what does not make sense leads to what does. Perhaps the revelation has a little traction after all. The oceans are almost boiling because the black blood of the Earth has been set on fire. It has been refined and ignited into tiny explosions of internal combustion for so long that its excretions have wiped out the visibility of the stars which began falling some time ago but no one saw them. Why? Dependence. Addiction. Blood.

Humanity remains primitive because it has not even maintained its own internal combustion mechanism properly. Every action carries meaning. Every action is a word. The rationalists are hypocrites. They have built a society based upon the idea that every action carries sensation. More smokescreens. The deepest thought they get is to finally breakthrough it and accept the word as final. But it isn't. It leads to something far more inexplicable and far more important. The insane use of the word to force feed desire for kitsch and other banalities once and for all through all of the bureaucratic and legal methods is the anticlimactic end game of consciousness. Checkmate. The endless mindless word of reason will always question "IF" but lead to "I". Transgression. This is the tipping point from endless searching and justifications toward the inexplicable reality.

The first trumpet has begun its song. *Hail and fire mixed with blood was thrown down upon the Earth, one third of the Earth was set on fire, and one third of the trees were burned and all of the grass was burned (8).* The second trumped joined the first and created a terrible discord. More prophecy. A quavering dyad. According to Bubba Nasser Eddin the ***diad is a structure in the cardiac myocyte located at the sarcomere Z-line. It is composed of a single t-tubule paired with a terminal cisterna of the sarcoplasmic reticulum. The dyad plays an important role in excitation-contraction coupling by juxtaposing an inlet for the action potential near a source of Ca2+ ions. This way, the wave of depolarization can be coupled to calcium-mediated cardiac muscle contraction via the sliding filament mechanism (18).*** Or slightly less chaotic definition that also partly explains the sources of blood infection: Two musical notes played at once. A term used by some degenerate guitar players who like to make shit up. A sound that is almost a chord and is very sad because of its wimpyness. Thelema quivered in revulsion. The Goddess of the will still lies imprisoned under Eden's garden. Wait a second. Who is Eden anyway? Forget it. It does not matter BECAUSE *a great mountain of fire was thrown into the sea and one third of the water in the sea became blood (8).* After a short time many trumpets joined in to reinforce the effect. *One third of the sun was struck and one third of* *the moon, and one third of the stars and one third of the day was dark, and one third of the night also(8).* Blood was everywhere and where there is blood there is Nosferatu.

Of course the undead rejoice. Darkness was extended for their delight. Perfect conditions to thrive and swell. The dark angels of the Earth will be given their share. The secret word, the Extraordinary disease. Agenbite of Inwit. Neurosis of shame and pride which Shem HaMephorash I carry among them will halt the revelry. I must bring this burden back to the summit of the greatest volcano. The mountain of fire was thrown into the sea and created blood. As a condor, an eagle, a carrion bird, as a warning I flew under the mountain of fire. The volcanic summit was bejeweled with a crown of glistening ice and black obsidian and it was swimming in a sea of its own fiery blood. A new Serengeti descended from above. A new place where everything can consume everything. *"Terror! Terror! Terror (8)!* Terroir!" was the warning cry. I wail and walk on my way to the summit again and pull out of my mouth my own double bladed sword.

My life is with the trill kill kult. I see good spirits and I see bad spirits (1). I smell out my direction like a blood hound. The summit is a crater. The perfect place to pile stones for sacrifice. Magma is the *rubedo* of the Earths alchemical process. The conquering of the Sun is the final act before the Albedo. The whitening of the philosopher's stone. Am I telling the truth about this? Maybe I said it wrong on purpose to mislead the uninitiated. A riddle perhaps...Freedom, Uhuru. Break down every word. Destroy them all. Dance and throw all of the books into the bonfire. Burn them all. They are all infection. ***I see the heart of the victim. I see the heart of the trusting soul. I take the place of the innocent. I rub it into the world and I have to turn my back (33).*** Their hammer and stake could-not kill me any longer. My heart shriveled into dust and was exhaled into the wind a long time ago. The strange thing is that since I returned from my first African expedition I think that it has almost come completely back. I can feel it beating stronger and stronger and with more regularity. It has made me very uneasy. It has put me into a sensory overload and my rejection of it was most likely what was responsible for my hotel room fainting session and subsequent massacre. It is being rejected by my body. I must do something about it. I have to bring this infection back to where it came from. ***The world as will and representation, the philosophers writing affords him an almost cosmic vision of the true meaning of the work. Love, he now realized, is not the final remedy: rather the suffering it causes may vouchsafe an insight to the essential nullity of existence, the reality of human misery and the necessity for rejecting the phenomenal world of an evil illusion (4).***

Let us treat the world only with contempt; for it deserves no better; but let no hope be placed in it, that our hearts not be deluded. It is evil, evil, fundamentally evil... it belongs to Alberich: no one else. Away with it (4).

After the bus was crammed full of gear to support all of the expeditions that were leaving the hotel that morning I stayed aloof from most of the subsequent action. Then a convoy of dull colored land rover looking contraptions arrived and parked outside the wall of the hotel grounds. There wasn't enough space for them to actually come inside the grounds. I could see part of one and part of another through the gate in the high cinderblock wall that had little shards of broken glass on top which were inserted into the concrete to provide the African equivalent of razor wire. Was this to keep us in or something else out? I could not tell what was more dangerous. Nothing could stop the flies from going wherever they wanted. They are the lords of every continent except Antarctica. The flies have always been my friends. They went straight to all of the buffet food that was spread out under one of the pavilions after standing on any number of unspeakable things outside the walls. Not like it really matters because every human is already infected by the word virus bouncing around inside their skull shaped echo chamber. Word is the written bars of the open air asylum that is planet Earth. These walls and gates will never stand up against the onslaught.

I nervously walked through the open gates and stood in front of the doors of the vehicle. I did not go directly in because I was waiting to be invited. This is an old custom that has always been recognized by Nosferatu. I could just go ahead and enter the vehicle and if I were back in civilization I probably would but things seemed to work differently here. This place seemed to demand a greater deal of attention to the old ways. I was already having enough of a hard time so I didn't think that it was a good idea to potentially make things more difficult for myself. There could be all sorts of consequences. The most deadly war is invisible and silent. The primary force is addiction, the mental disorder shared by every human that makes capitalism function at the cost of countless lives. This has created a cult of blood and death greater than every war ever fought. Americans blow up foreign lands so that the invisible war will never be noticed. Lucifer – the illuminator – shines the light on everything except the true problem. Light in the form of bomb and rocket explosions which ripen into the forms of delicate flowers in bloom. Light in the form of tracer rounds through the night sky that fizzle and burn like falling stars. It is all distraction. It is all the result of activating the word. The stroke of a pen can start all of this and it can also end it. Blood spits out of the end of every pen and has predicted all of this already. One is connected to another. Word to speech and speech to action in an insane progression that appears totally reasonable while it eats its own children. None belong and nothing belongs to anyone. The world entropic. All enlightenment is hallucination. All reason is murder. My hands aren't the only bloody ones. The World War has always been here and it always will be. Jerusalem is its beating heart and everyone is worked up into fits. How many times can it be destroyed?

Tantrum

World War one never ended but after most folks thought it did it thrashed its way into Spain to halt the most dangerous idea ever and perhaps the best one. The possibility of a functional anarchy. The closest humanity ever could have gotten to ever properly realizing its true nature. Prime targets for Fascist experiment. The last and greatest destruction of the last and greatest human dreams. So many Fascists to wrestle for their piece. Hitler, Mussolini, Franco, DeGaulle, Churchill, Stalin, Roosevelt. ***Lel lols for libelmen libeling his lore. Lolo Lolo liebermann you loved to be leaving Libnius. Lift your right to your Liber Lord. Link your left to your lass of liberty. Lala Lala, Leapermann, your lep's but a loop to lee (5).*** Fascists of every stripe and every color. The deadly toxins of Nationalism are the worst form of chemical warfare that taint the blood and the mind just as bad as sarin gas. Blindness with eyes wide open and mind shut down. ***Freedom is a sickness (32).*** Another ideal to live up to yet never attain. Black Uhuru is fire in the blood. Uhuru peak was lifted by magma. The Earths fiery blood. Freedom grows out of destruction and creates more to maintain hegemony. The sun is blotted out by the ash of the eruption so no one can see what is happening or do anything about it. ***Darkness seems to cover the world. Get off their back Babylon (28).*** Their king is an angel from the bottomless pit and his name is Abaddon in Hebrew and Apollyon in Hellenic. The destroyer. Freedom is his song. Trumpet and voice are not meant for celebration.

Where did everyone go? Out on the street facing problems. Must work so nothing works. A stream of consciousness. A stream of water under a bridge is an African car wash. Really. I saw it. It was advertised on the side of the road. ***What do you need? Right stuff. Come together if you please (28).*** All things are possible. Bill W. and the doc cracked the gates of hell and healed the sick with some irrational garble. It worked when all medicine failed. ***What do you need? Right stuff. Come together if you please (28).*** Words. Spells and incantations are words in motion. ***A fork of hazel o'er the field in vox the verveine virgins abode. If you cross this rood as you roamed the rand I'm blessed but you'd feel him a blasting rod. Behind, me, frees from evil smells! Perdition stinks before us (5).***

After I stared at the open gate for some time, one of the drivers urged me to get into the vehicle. Only then did I feel a little better but not for very long. Space seemed to be flowing like time as I moved and I was comforted by this. But the damage had already been done and it was about to get a lot worse. With a small degree of trouble I entered the vehicle and took a seat. I placed my bag, which contained my objects of power, on my lap. We were soon to be on our way to another ancient crater. One of the Earths open wounds that never healed. None of them do. Every scratch is tallied and will show up in the monthly bill. Wooooo. Our demands must be met. We did not suffer these wounds for no reason. Slowly losing power. Each and every hour. Never seen, the African Queen of the jungle has sent Ix Taub the goddess of ropes and snares. Her eyes shine like falling stars as her head bobs and watches. They streak across time and space like tracer fire. Ropes and snares bloom with strange fruit. The harvest of every sentence. They tie off arms, golden arms that can no longer move but the six million dollar man walks with a cane, to and from the rehab facility, and he don't give a fuck. Programming and resistance to it is also programming. ***Emotional slaughter. Born a natural birth (28)*** and died a toxic death of brain decay in a nice bed. Down in the ghetto another star is born. ***All rise! All rise (28)!*** It may just be worth it but no one can figure out why and if they did they would probably be shot, or hung, or crucified, or completely ignored.

The vehicle finally got on its way. It drove past herds of filthy children and chickens. African men teeter on bicycles overloaded with tied up faggots on the back – I am talking about bundles of wood in case you may be sensitive. Let's get more comfortable with language shall we. Not everything must be so difficult. What is the proper way to say the word "pianist"? Let's get it right for once. Go on. Say it with me. "Pianist". Not "Peeayneist". One more time "Pianist" Good. Next. Tied up faggots are burned to charcoal to please Nut the Sky Goddess of the Nile. Stars fall from the sky. It isn't dark enough with those pesky stars ruining everything. Can't you hear what I'm seeing? Streaks of light burn out and smolder. How many photons of light miss the Earth and keep on going on an unknown trajectory into the void? Is our sun part of a constellation that is seen from another world? Most of these photons will never strike upon anything and will continue on an infinite trajectory. They are the dust storm of the void. As is above so is below. Only way more fucked up. The dust and smoke on the earth permeate everything in this part of the African continent. Rise early to sing from the minaret. Choke a chicken under a microphone. Death to Zionists.

The drive through the streets of Moshi is not describable. It is something better seen, smelled, or felt in order to understand. Cell phones and poverty are everywhere. Wealth and property as well. Plantations of sisal, banana, rice, corn, and coffee all surround the small mountain town. A land of deep contradictions: The highest elevations to the lowest plains. The conditions for a great amount of majik to draw from. Glacial streams next to barren earth. Rice paddies next to arid expanse. Foreign invasion. Sedentary locals. Use the sickle to gather. **Do it now.** ***Look out Eden them a gwon pon street. Today as I stand and look in the valley, I can see that there is***

no sign of peace (28). Now! Black Uhuru! Freedom is a sickness(32). *So the angel swung his sickle upon the Earth and loaded the grapes into the great winepress of Gods wrath (8).* What must all the people of the Earth endure until they are free? None are free until even until the last is no longer trod upon. Yes. All of the black people, not only black of skin but black of soul. Darkness that envelopes the Fire inside. ***We are the ones with the radiating eyes. We are the ones that have a fire inside. We are the ones only we can recognize. We've been rejected. We've been rejected all our lives (34).*** *And the grapes were trodden in the winepress outside the city and blood flowed from the winepress in a stream that was one hundred eighty miles long and as high as a horses bridle(8).*

The vehicle that took us out of Moshi went along with windows open. My sixth sense was on fire. Something had been developing and I felt it creeping closer yet I could not pick apart what was actually happening. ***Speak of the Devil and he will appear (35).*** I tried not to appear disturbed in my attempt to look around the vehicle and study the countenances of my companions. Was one among these folks some sort of self-motivated hero type? Very likely because they were all apparently into expeditionary hiking. I did not recognize any of them. I was concerned that there may be a vampire hunter somewhere amongst this small group. If there was one they would certainly be among these types of people: folks who have something to prove. There are very few of them and the undead community is almost always many steps ahead of them. This does not mean that they don't adapt and surprise us once in a while. Some have developed an effective form of disguise that allows them to sneak up on one of us when we expect nothing. The situation that I am presently in gives them a serious advantage. I am far from my normal stomping ground so everything is unfamiliar to me. I could be easily surprised. I considered this as a reason for my ill feelings. I looked very deeply into everyone that was in the vehicle with me. Most of the vampire hunters that I am aware of have some form of disorder. It could be anything like autism, Asperger's, schizophrenia, epilepsy, PTSD, add, adhd, etc. etc. The presence of these behavioral ticks can be determined by a quick glance because us undead have been looking at people for a very long time and we can tell these things quicker than any doctor. It is a matter of survival to us. The presence of these disorders is what allows them to find us because they have been doing the same thing that we have. Studying behavior that will lead them to suspect that they have found one of us. No one ever believes them in the rational world because the very disorder that allows them to see us is the reason that most normal humans don't pay attention to what they say on the subject. They think it is just the rantings of crazy people. And it is, but the crazy people are right. You can be crazy and ranting and absolutely correct at the same time. It happens more often than not. It only makes sense. If they were just making shit up, they probably wouldn't be so worked up over it. It is a reality to them and it certainly is to us undead who try as hard as we can to keep these folks locked up. Many of them are intentionally treated by medical staff that are undead so that we can keep an eye on these fuckers. Hence the ranting because they know that they are treated by undead and can do little about it. We are all experiencing the same hallucination but that does not make any of it less real. *Reality* defies description because it is irrational. Only ***perspective*** can be explained.

After a thorough scan of the interior of the vehicle I determined that I was safe and my identity was not compromised despite whatever I did last night which I still can't recall. I looked out the window again and smelled the musky air. Pedestrians and plantations. Masai and livestock herds. Acacia and banana. Time and space. A blur of motion. The birth of relativity on a bus. The fourth dimension is pretty banal. Travel. Not too much of a big deal. The big deal is where it all is headed. What? You expect me to tell you? I have been trying this entire time but you either wouldn't believe me or if not you probably suspect it already. ***Weißtd, was Wotan – will. Do you know what Wotan wills? The God demands as he rises to the tragic height of willing his passing. Might not the Gods retreat in the face of a deterministic necessity be construed as a moral advance? His abandonment of his quest for power the attainment of a higher spiritual end? What gives tragedy its ethical force in the recognition that the world – that life – offers no real satisfaction and hence does not deserve our loyalty? This is the tragic spirit, it leads to renunciation (8).*** It is inexplicable, irrational, and outside science, technology, and language but it is part of the biology because the body is the temple. What form of chaos hides lurking behind our feeble conceptions and understandings?

Ruhe, ruhe, du Gott (7)!

The vehicle came to a lonely intersection and took and right turn to the well-designed ergonomic, metronomic sound of the turn signal. The plains that supported the mountain stretched on and on, a terrestrial ocean. Ever so slowly the grade of the road began to rise upward. The forest began to close in around the rural road. I began to feel even more uncomfortable. I glanced around at the interior of the vehicle again. Still nothing noticeably wrong. Isn't it funny that when something goes wrong it is instinctual to blame everything else and everyone else first before it ever occurs that the malady or issue may just be in one's self? Why is that always the last psychological resort? *Clearly it is not I who am the problem here.* What insidious bullshit our brains our capable of. I remember too much. Never again.

Time is one of the greatest vampires that there is. It is the very teeth of Babylon. Capitalism is what they call it now in the attempt to pacify people into thinking they are somehow free to choose what form of slavery they will be bound to. It is no different than it ever was. Time is money and money is slavery; blood, the shackles of reason pinning everyone to the Earth that they will never own. Not one tiny piece of it can be possessed by anyone. Leases and mortgages are meaningless. More words rationalizing away the facts of reality through an infinite chain of distraction. Where was the fourth dimension off to anyway? Where is all this motion taking us to? Wobbling tesseract. Very far away. Property is a memento mori. There should be a skull stamped upon every object because only us undead will linger and rot forever until the inevitable entropic destruction turns this existence into chaos even though it has been chaos and anarchy the whole time.

Some said that they used to be a teenage anarchist. Then what? They grew up into something else? Something *smarter perhaps?* If intelligence can be measured by the ability to regurgitate more information due to more time exposed to stimulus then I would certainly have to ask what the nature of that stimulus was if I were to critique this perspective which is indeed total nonsense. Was the environment flooded with advertising, design, cinematic hero worship, exaltation of victory and reinforcement of competition at the expense of others through a grotesquely paid sports industry, studious attention paid to all genitalia all around, political partisanship and police enforcement, drugs and alcohol, a forty or more hour work week to flood the mind with banalities, ostentatious displays of wealth, news-clips and sound bites that only go for a few moments at a time to tell as little of an important story as possible even though they have a twenty four hour news cycle available to actually explain something in depth, the relentless and – many times – pointless advancement of technological gadgets that make you think that you are smarter but instead it was actually someone else that is kind of smart in some deficient way and you are just the dumbass that bought into their little experiment that will be revised in the future at your expense so what you have is already obsolete the very moment you buy into it, and all of this punctuated by a few undesired moments of forced education that is crammed into everything else and not taken very seriously at all because it isn't fun and how does anything I learn in school relate to my life anyway and oh shit look at all the money I owe so I had better get a fucking job and shut the fuck up so I can retire comfortably? Does that sort of describe the environment that has made you supposedly smarter as you got older? I am a vampire. I suck out life force so I know it very well when I see it. What do you think that capitalism has done to your supposedly free mind? Hmmm? It is a vampire of words and reasons. One much bigger than I am and perhaps just as old. What happens to people who are killed by vampires? It is a transmittable disease. You may just be more like me than you would ever admit. You might have more blood of your victims upon you than you can see. You may have been far more aware before all of this sucked the life out of you. Mabey you were not even conscious when you fed off of your victims and cleaned it all up in your hotel room before you even woke up. The words you devour and feed upon kill more than you can ever see. It never made sense. Nothing but destruction or the threat of it could possibly hold together this environment that has made you an adult. It never worked properly and it never will because no one wants to look at what really is happening right in front of their face behind the diaphanous veil of what supports their own satisfaction. Vampires. All of you. It was anarchy the whole time you assholes.

Sorry, but don't tell me that you do not see it because it is just about the only thing can I see.

Babylon is one of the Gods of the vampire. It has many forms and many names. It is a great dragon sometimes and a lion at other times. One of the most ancient and one of the easiest to forget because it just sits back and watches. Babylon has not yet fallen, in fact it is getting more and more powerful each day. Each word a new brick in the tower. Each day the world is bled out just a little more. Humanity is bled out more and more each day. Cuneiform has evolved into a simple code of ones and zeros. It has evolved into a weapon of mass destruction and tyranny. Language is a majikal spell of manipulation.

The closer that I got to Kilimanjaro the more I was warned by this deity through the medium of my conscious thoughts. No one ever had an original thought. This God Babylon was trying to tell me to stay away and not climb. I know this in retrospect but that does not matter. My infection was already developed to the stage that it was causing a noticeable disruption. I probably wasn't the only one of the undead who were feeling strange. I'm sure that many of the others were beginning to as well. The only thing that was different was the fact that they must have had an idea about what was happening while I did not. The dragon manipulates others to do its will rather than actually do anything itself. I'm certain that there were already sorties of undead preparing to hunt me down as I bungled and stumbled my awkward way through the wilderness. It is a good thing that I was so isolated or else I could have been in real trouble. More trouble than I already was in.

Since I have been back from Africa and gathering myself here in New York I have had to be extra careful. Besides writing this and reflecting upon my situation I have had no way to safely do much else. The Dragon was forced out of the Heavens. This great Dragon, the ancient serpent called The Devil or Satan, the one deceiving the whole world was thrown down with his angels. They all were connected by blood and fire. I am one of them I am blood and He is fire. They are all connected by words. My name is Legion. ***My life is with the thrill kill kult. I see good spirits and I see bad spirits (1).*** The rest of the kult does too. They know what has happened to me. Once the word is out it can-not be taken back. I have an imperial death amulet tattooed upon my back. Black wings with the Eye of Horus in the middle. I have the angel Melancholia tattooed upon my side. I have the Nautical Star that fell to the sea named Wormwood tattooed upon my leg next to the graveyard in green light of apocalypse. These only protect me for so long in my human form. They camouflage my actions because they can bend the perspectives of those that may want to disturb my unresting undeath. In order for me to exist since I have returned from Africa, I must change forms fairly regularly. I can go from condor, to spider, to wolf, to housecat as much as I want but it is also not enough on its own to stay safe. I must always be a step ahead of any who would try to stop me. They all know that I carry the secret of their demise. Junkies. They love their misery. They destroy with impunity but fear their own destruction.

The maintenance of ***perspective*** is their only interest. To reform all of the pieces of the shattered glass of ***perspective*** leads to the irrational, contradictory reconstruction of eternity. From these pieces will rise truth. It is all out of my hands. It is out of everyone's hands. I am only the smallest instrument but I may have the biggest infection. From a high mountain a revelation was given very long ago. The New Jerusalem. The new peace will rise from unspeakable destruction that is filled with glory. It sparkles like a precious jewel and will descend from the heavens, reformed from the shattered pieces of perspective. *The wall was made of jasper and the city was pure gold that was clear as glass. The gates were made of pearls. Each one from a single pearl. The main streets were made of gold that was as clear as glass. The foundation stones were made of jasper, sapphire, agate, emerald, onyx, carnelian, chrysolite, beryl, topaz, chrsoprase, jacinth, and amethyst. Nothing evil is allowed to enter (8).* All of the undead will be completely consecrated in flames before this is constructed. Incentive for all the undead to stop the rebuilding of *reality* from the shattered ***perspectives*** that roam all across the universe in the form of word. All the words must come together and form one unspeakable word, one singularity, and it is the unspeakable word itself.

The use of the same foundation stones on my pouch allow nothing to enter when I travel. Most of the undead have a similar device. They all know of the prophecy because many were around when it was first delivered. They know how it works and how to manipulate it to their benefit. They all know of this spell and they fear the day when it is used against them. They will do anything to stop it and right now that means that they are trying very hard to find me. My heart now beats again and because of my infection and I am no longer immortal in the same way that I was. I must find the end of this and it will lead to my end and whatever outcome that will arise out of it. Through castration (perhaps a metaphor) I may yet regain my true immortality after all and they will all have turned to ash unless they realize what is truly happening. I know very well now. It took me a little while and I did not know anything when it first came upon me. It was simply a voice calling in the wilderness as preparation for the way. Baptized in blood the garments become white.

Nothe thut ein Held, der, leidig göttlichen Schutzes, sich löse vom Göttergesetz: so nur taugt er zu wirken die That, die, wie noth sie den Göttern, dem Gott doch zu wirken verwehrt (7).

The toy vehicle climbed the rustic road toward the sky on the way to Kilimanjaro. The forest got thicker, and thicker and the buildings fewer and fewer. Most of them were in an unfinished state. Others had boarded up windows and doors. Graffiti was splashed all over the walls like the St. Valentine's Day massacre. Even here in the heart of darkness, the mother of the wilderness, the foot of the great mountain, defiance to civilization was manifest in color and mutilated word. Civilization and all of its legions of misfits crawled, virtually four legged everywhere. Not a square mile is untouched by culture. ***Every image is leased and mortgaged, no stone has not been marked upon (13).*** The world, civilization is ready for catharsis. The rifle is cleaned, oiled, and loaded, the bolt is cocked, and the safety switch is off. It was not always like this but it is now. The ship started sinking when I brought my heavily laden, yet infinitely small shard of ***perception*** to the ancient mountain that I was now ascending. One small piece is all that is needed to begin the conflagration. Solipsism destroyed creates an event horizon upon the Cartesian grid and it sucks in everything around it. Every other measurable point of solipsism is affected. The evil genius who tortured Descartes will suffer the bottomless pit for a thousand years before the second death and the final condemnation of all of his angels. Consecration. Harvest.

A group of red banana trees surrounded the last few buildings that resided on this road to the sky. I still felt that something was seriously wrong but I chose to ignore it. My immediate surroundings were safe. I scanned the vehicle many times and there was no sign of danger except, of course, myself. I was certainly the most evil thing around but this was something that I was very used to. My inner discord kept getting worse the further up the road we went. The higher I got, the closer I got to the trailhead the worse I felt. How can I describe the feeling? It was many things at once; anxiety, mania, hypersensitivity, ***reignition***, fragility. All were all factors but the worst was the sense of an intensifying downward pressure that started very lightly but seemed to be building with every tick of the clock and every turn of the wheel. Somewhere in my walnut brain I knew exactly what was happening but I was just not conscious of it like I am now.

Everyone has a name. It is an irrational word that is attached to their soul. It is set in the stone of the consciousness before birth and it determines their purpose. Jacob was born to be a deceiver and then become Israel who was meant to wrestle with God. All of his descendants carried this curse. It is more of a curse than a privilege. God is going to fuck them up. Hard. He has been doing it for a long time. They are expected to be held accountable to a higher standard. One thing that is rarely mentioned is the fact that most of, if not all, humans are most likely of Jewish descent. Abraham was the father of many nations. His seed has been blown all around the world. ***Also, in 732 b.c.e. the Assyrians annexed Syria and ravaged Israel. In Jerusalem, King Ahaz agonized over whether to submit to Assyria or fight. Isaiah advised the king to wait. The king would have a son with the name Emmanuel (the Name Spell was cast) meaning God is with us. Isaiah said that for unto us a child is born, the Mighty God, The everlasting Father, The Prince of Peace who has peace without end (4). Isaiah was not just a prophet but a poet who,*** *(one yeastyday he sternely struxk his tete in a tub for to watsch the future of his fates but ere he swiftly stook it out again, by the might of moses, the very water was eviparated and all the guenneses had met their exodous so that ought to show you what a pentschanjeuchy chap he was! [5])* ***in the age of Assyrian aggression, was the first to imagine life beyond the destruction of the Temple. Isiah loved the holy mountain which he saw as a beautiful woman. The mount of the daughter of Zion, the hill of Jerusalem. Sometimes righteous sometimes harlot. But if all is lost and Jerusalem is ruined there would be a new mystical Jerusalem for everyone upon every dwelling place.*** *The mountain of the Lords house shall be established on the tops of the mountains and all nations shall flow to it (8).* ***When the conqueror died in 727 b.c.e. Israel rebelled and the new Assyrian King Sargon 2 besieged Samaria the Northern Israeli capital for three years and swallowed Israel, deporting twenty seven thousand people to Assyria. Ten of the twelve tribes almost vanish from history (4).*** *Our clubhouse still rocks as earwitness to the thunder of his arafats. His howd feeled heavy, his hoddit did shake (there was a wall of course in* *erection) an act of Sacred Love (5).* The Unnamable creator had a plan. A universe of intention through our ***bad brains. It is not a physical communication (24).*** Not electrical, not chemical, not neuroplastic, not internal combustion, not diatonic or modal. ***Why must some people keep on killing and fighting? Why must people keep on hoarding all the money (24)?*** All communication is broken because it appears to work. Inversion. The more tools of communication there are available the less is communicated. ***The meek shall inherit the earth (8).*** No one knows what happened to the twelve lost tribes of Israel besides the fact that they were scattered to the corners of the earth. What we do know is that they were people after all and they do what people do with their bodies. It may not be much of a stretch to say that everyone or at least a lot of you very well may be of Jewish descent in some remote corner of your family tree. Everyone is held to the higher standard. The blood of the Jews has been fucked into the blood of every race since Abraham, since Sargon dispersed them into the greater world to fornicate and assimilate. We're all fucked. Assyrian assimilation. We are all Jews and the world is seeded with our blood. Everyone is chosen. Everyone has the disease of blood addiction and blood sacrifice. The disease is ubiquitous. Sexuality and birth through blood and pain. Death through blood and pain. Sex and death. Disease. Blood disease. It cannot be fought. Revelation through castration. ***Wenn der Liebe finst'rer Feind zürnend zeugt einen Sohn, der sel'gen Ende säumt dann nicht (7)!*** Anyone can and must discover the original irrational word. Shem HaMephorash. The Unspeakable Name, the final spell and the way to avoid the second death. God nor Jesus is not his name so it can't ever be used in vain. Fuck God. Fuck all. Fuck you up your ass with God's alcoholic destruction at the end of a spiked vine. Pulled out of orifice to reveal grapes of fecal gristle upon the thorns. Harvest. See. It doesn't matter because his name is not God. It is something *other* just like your name is not Man. Your Name is your Star. His true name is far more powerful than any of these words, indeed all words come together from every language ever spoken in an incomprehensible singularity to create this one concentrated, unspoken, unwritten, gestalt of a word that lurks behind it all and inspires it all. A silver bullet to rain upon everything.

Shem the introvert, rejected of man is the explorer and discoverer of the forbidden. He is an embodiment of dangerously brooding, in turned energy. He is the uncoverer of secret springs, and as such, the possessor of terrific, lightning powers. The books he writes are so mortifying that they are spontaneously rejected by the decent; they threaten, they dissolve the protecting boundary lines of good and evil. Provoked to action (and he must be provoked before he will act), he is not restrained by normal human laws, for they have been dissolved within him by too powerful elixirs of the elemental depths: he may let loose a hot spray of acid; but on the other hand, he can release such a magical balm of forgiveness that the battle lines themselves become melted in a bacchanal of general love. Such absolute love is as dangerous to the efficient working of society as absolute hate. The possessor of the secrets, therefore, is constrained to hold his fire. Nobody really wants to hear what he as to say; the shepherds of the people denounce him from their pulpits, or else so dilute and misrepresent his teachings as to render them innocuous. Thus Shem is typically in retreat from society; he is the scorned and disinherited one, the Bohemian, or the criminal outcast, rejected by Philistine prosperity. Under the title of Shem the Penman, he is the seer, the poet, the character of the misunderstood, rejected artist. His characteristic behavior is to take refuge in his own room, where, on the foolscap of his own body, he writes a phosphorescent book in a corrosive language.

Shem's business is not to create a higher life, but merely to find and utter the Word (36). Shem HaMephorash.

All undead and students of kabbalah, Gnosticism, and modern atheism (whether they admit to it or not) have sought this silver bullet but have never found it because they were looking at only words that they can understand. What they seek is incomprehensible. Unwritable. Unspeakable. They know this but dive straight into their books and their writing and their logic. The dive into their formulae and equations and false histories. All of which are as illogical as their opposite – the final word – perhaps more so but they seem logical because of the shattered illogical nature of ***perception***. Logical understanding is chaos. The irrational is the only thing that is needed to succeed upon this planet which is failure. True success is the discovery of a way off of it. It is not measured in dollars and property and false rational understandings and utterances because these simply imprison the consciousness further. The irrational word that is buried in the logical is the greatest and most rejected gift the world has to offer. The final spell is the way to avoid the second death. I am suffering the second death right now but my blood is infected with the ultimate burden. I have regained life and with it the secret name which will remain secret because I have no power over it. I cannot tell you what it is or write it. It is Art. There is much more to it than simple utterances because it envelopes time and space but also requires motion and the other higher dimensions to actually be correctly expressed. Time and space are the platform, the basic legs that support the higher dimensions. I did not stop and try to discover this. It infected me in motion. It found me in this way because it was already written. Belinda. I can see the unfolding narrative, I can feel it. There is no such thing as fiction. Where is it all going? To the End? I can only suspect what that means but it seems like that is only a feeble concept that can-not hold up to the scrutiny of fourth and higher dimensional realties.

You must pardon me for a moment. As I write this spell, as I cast this complicated web of revelations and many tiered incantations I have gained the attention of some of the evil forces that have been looking for me. I hear footsteps in my hallway. They are shrouded but I still hear them. There is evil knocking on the very door of my apartment right now. My best defense is to turn into a spider so that this work will become a web of protection. It is developed enough now to accomplish this. I will send myself and this spell into a small crack in the wall so that this will appear to be an empty apartment to every possible scan that an undead hunter may use to try and find me.

I apologize. I had to move to a different apartment because the last one that I was writing in was compromised. It was discovered because I let it be discovered. I want to let them think that they are on to me. Hiding in the open is the best way to avoid detection and thwart those who hunt me. There is so much going on that would crack the brain of the average human who denies the existence of spiritual and fantastic *realities.* There is no such thing as fiction. Unicorns exist. Stop reading and imagine one for a second............... See!............Ha!...........I got you. The spell of the word forced it into your mind. Even if you don't believe in unicorns there was one in your mind for a measurable amount of time, even if it was only less than a second. Oh, you want to be like that. Then don't imagine a unicorn. HA!HA! There it is! If I keep repeating it over and over it comes to life more and more. The word spell extends its influence into sense and nonsense. It summons. It is an exorcism. It is dangerous. It has created a cultural failure which is commonly called Postmodernism. This gives free reign to every flight of fancy and every interpretation of any fact by any one. The interpreter is more important than that which is being interpreted. Combine this with globalized digital media and digital social interaction, which is totally flooded with nonsense. The words become bioelectrical impulses and everyone makes up their own reality. The result is a global tyranny of stupidity *manifested by morons with names like Trump, Bolsanaro, Duterte, Modi, Orban, Putin, Erdogan, Johnson, etc...I have bashed science and reason quite a bit and that was important simply because it is not in the interest of this discussion. It does have a valuable place on its own plain of activity and in that context it demands intelligent respect. In this, further reaching discussion we must leave behind its maternal embrace. So do not take me for a fool, or a flat earther, or someone who adopts pure stupidity as fact simply because it is contrary to popular media narratives and therefore must be true. I do, in fact, have discretion and good taste. I lament those who can not see through the convoluted nature of this discussion and take away a free endorsement for whatever madness they may drag off the internet. This is by no means my intent. The reason is that these folks are still using some form of reason to justify their mentality. A depraved and retarded version of it of course but it is still an active process because this is the only way the human mind can operate. This spell is designed to destroy all forms of reason, be they well-crafted or flawed so do not take anything that I say as justification for stupidity, or alarmist fringe nonsense.* What then of Vampires (allegory)? The undead armies of ghosts and zombies (metaphor)? Heaven and Hell and all of their residents (Simile)? It all exists even if only for a moment. That should be enough even for the scientifically minded because how many of their elements on the precious periodic table only exist for a second or less? How many quarks and Higgs bosons or blasphemous god particles only exist for a virtually immeasurable amount of time? The unicorn exists for much longer than that. So does heaven and hell. Everything and anything is real in the eternal present. Heaven and Hell is right in front of you. Right now. Which do you choose? ***Speak of the devil and he will appear (35).*** If it is already in your head you are going to do it?

Do you see the tormented alcoholics and drug addicts crawling around? Run. Away. Do you see the loathsome spandex enclad running and biking and rowing endorphin junkies bobbing around, listening to godawful, unlistenable music with their stupid earbuds who seem to feel so good about themselves that it is repulsive? Junkies and runners. They are both on the same street at the same time. Both are experiencing totally different realities but because of inversion they are exactly the same. And they are very real. Heaven and hell are right in front of you and they mutate and change along with the progression of the world. Don't think it will happen to you? Just wait and see where you end up. I bet you have no idea and I bet your present self will be totally surprised. I'll even take that bet to Vegas.

Never move to Connecticut. If you ever want to be a serial killer just get a job at a crematorium. Even the teeth turn to ash but you have to break up the pelvis halfway through so it all burns up efficiently. Scrape up all of the dust. Put it in a cup. Dump it all in the toilet and piss on it. Flush. If you know any vampires save the blood first. It will be your good deed for the day. Damn. Someone needs a Lucky Strike right now.

Cinco Vegas

Vampires have a sixth sense. We all know our surroundings in a way that no living thing can ever experience. It is kind of like the way the terminator and the predator see things but way more intense. We can scan and read things in detail that would be missed by virtually everything else. Footfalls strike the floor of the apartment I am hiding in as am writing this. I have to move again soon. There is an intense hunt at hand and I am the prey for once. Every corner of this room is scanned and recorded by the predators. My predatory children. I cannot adumbrate in my web for very long. Even though the spell I am hiding in is totally new, it will work now and perhaps a few more times but it is not very likely to hold up to intense scrutiny over repeated efforts to break it before it is finished. I must change the space I am writing in. I must find a new, old, fucked up apartment or factory to continue. Plenty around but my hunters have all of the time in the world. Words are a powerful spell and even humans are capable of using them to hide behind, even when all other sense cries the opposite. Example one among: ***"We did not, repeat, did not, trade weapons or anything else for hostages."*** Lies from President Ronald Regan regarding the Iran Contra affair. It worked didn't it? Everyone believed it. ***I can't believe that you are not afraid.*** Example two among . This next one will be fun. This is the statement of the United States to the U.N. Security council regarding Iraq before the second invasion under George W. Bush. It has been presented in fine print for fun. You should take out a magnifying glass and read through it if you are interested. This sort of scrutiny should have been paid to this nonsense before the invasion rather than after. Each word should have been magnified for the entire country to see beforehand so that the liars could be held accountable, which they obviously were not. If you do not have a magnifying glass or are not interested, then by all means, skip this section and continue from there. The intent of presenting this should be obvious based on previous statements. I do value evidence after all.

Thank you, Mr. President.

Mr President, Mr Secretary General, distinguished colleagues, I would like to begin by expressing my thanks for the special effort that each of you made to be here today.

This is important day for us all as we review the situation with respect to Iraq and its disarmament obligations under UN Security Council resolution 1441.

Last November 8, this council passed resolution 1441 by a unanimous vote. The purpose of that resolution was to disarm Iraq of its weapons of mass destruction. Iraq had already been found guilty of material breach of its obligations, stretching back over 16 previous resolutions and 12 years.

Resolution 1441 was not dealing with an innocent party, but a

regime this council has repeatedly convicted over the years. Resolution 1441 gave Iraq one last chance, one last chance to come into compliance or to face serious consequences. No council member present in voting on that day had any illusions about the nature and intent of the resolution or what serious consequences meant if Iraq did not comply. And to assist in its disarmament, we called on Iraq to cooperate with returning inspectors from Unmovic and IAEA. We laid down tough standards for Iraq to meet to allow the inspectors to do their job. This council placed the burden on Iraq to comply and disarm and not on the inspectors to find that which Iraq has gone out of its way to conceal for so long. Inspectors are inspectors; they are not detectives. I asked for this session today for two purposes: First, to support the core assessments made by Dr Blix and Dr El-Baradei. As Dr Blix reported to this council on January 27: "Iraq appears not to have come to a genuine acceptance, not even today, of the disarmament which was demanded of it." And as Dr El-Baradei reported, Iraq's declaration of December 7: "Did not provide any new information relevant to certain questions that have been outstanding since 1998." My second purpose today is to provide you with additional information, to share with you what the United States knows about Iraq's weapons of mass destruction as well as Iraq's involvement in terrorism, which is also the subject of resolution 1441 and other earlier resolutions. Blurrrrrr. Hissssss. Tweeetttttt... *I might add at this point that we are providing all relevant information we can to the inspection teams for them to do their work. The material I will present to you comes from a variety of sources. Some are U.S. sources. And some are those of other countries. Some of the sources are technical, such as intercepted telephone conversations and photos taken by satellites. Other sources are people who have risked their lives to let the world know what Saddam Hussein is really up*

to. *Cheers!!!! Applause!! Wooooooo!!* ***I cannot tell you everything that we know. But what I can share with you, when combined with what all of us have learned over the years, is deeply troubling. What you will see is an accumulation of facts and disturbing patterns of behavior. The facts on Iraqis' behavior – Iraq's behavior demonstrate that Saddam Hussein and his regime have made no effort – no effort – to disarm as required by the international community. Indeed, the facts and Iraq's behavior show that Saddam Hussein and his regime are concealing their efforts to produce more weapons of mass destruction.*** *Fart. Pffluff. Excuse me.* ***Let me begin by playing a tape for you.*** *Pffftttt.* ***What you're about to hear is a conversation that my government monitored. It takes place on November 26 of last year, on the day before United Nations teams resumed inspections in Iraq. The conversation involves two senior officers, a colonel and a brigadier general, from Iraq's elite military unit, the Republican Guard.(BEGIN AUDIO TAPE) Speaking in Arabic. (END AUDIO TAPE) POWELL: Let me pause and review some of the key elements of this conversation that you just heard between these two officers. First, they acknowledge that our colleague, Mohamed ElBaradei, is coming, and they know what he's coming for, and they know he's coming the next day. He's coming to look for things that are prohibited. He is expecting these gentlemen to cooperate with him and not hide things. But they're worried. "We have this modified vehicle. What do we say if one of them sees it?" What is their concern? Their concern is that it's something they should not have, something that should not be seen. The general is incredulous: "You didn't get a modified. You don't have one of those, do you?" "I have one." "Which, from where?" "From the workshop, from the al-Kindi company?" "What?" "From al-Kindi." "I'll come to see you in the morning. I'm worried. You all have something left." "We evacuated everything. We don't***

have anything left." Note what he says: "We evacuated everything." We didn't destroy it. We didn't line it up for inspection. We didn't turn it into the inspectors. We evacuated it to make sure it was not around when the inspectors showed up. *Oklahoma! Brigadoon! South Pacific! Hamilton! Never mind the Bollocks Here's the…* ***"I will come to you tomorrow." The al-Kindi company: This is a company that is well known to have been involved in prohibited weapons systems activity. Let me play another tape for you. As you will recall, the inspectors found 12 empty chemical warheads on January 16. On January 20, four days later, Iraq promised the inspectors it would search for more. You will now hear an officer from Republican Guard headquarters issuing an instruction to an officer in the field. Their conversation took place just last week on January 30. (BEGIN AUDIO TAPE) Speaking in Arabic. (END AUDIO TAPE) POWELL: Let me pause again and review the elements of this message. "They're inspecting the ammunition you have, yes." "Yes." "For the possibility there are forbidden ammo." "For the possibility there is by chance forbidden ammo?" "Yes." "And we sent you a message yesterday to clean out all of the areas, the scrap areas, the abandoned areas. Make sure there is nothing there." Remember the first message, evacuated. This is all part of a system of hiding things and moving things out of the way and making sure they have left nothing behind. If you go a little further into this message, and you see the specific instructions from headquarters: "After you have carried out what is contained in this message, destroy the message because I don't want anyone to see this message." "OK, OK." Why? Why? This message would have verified to the inspectors that they have been trying to turn over things. They were looking for things. But they don't want that message seen, because they were trying to clean up the area to leave no evidence behind of the presence*** *of weapons* *of mass destruction. Sophocles, Euripides, Aeschylus, Aristophanes.* ***And they can claim that nothing was there. And the inspectors can look all they want, and they will find nothing. This effort to hide things from the inspectors is not one or two isolated events, quite the contrary. This is part and parcel of a policy of evasion and deception that goes back 12 years, a policy set at the highest levels of the Iraqi regime. We know that Saddam Hussein has what is called quote, "a higher committee for monitoring the inspections teams," unquote. Think about that. Iraq has a high-level committee to monitor the inspectors who were sent in to monitor Iraq's disarmament. Not to cooperate with them, not to assist them, but to spy on them and keep them from doing their jobs. The committee reports directly to Saddam Hussein. It is headed by Iraq's vice president, Taha Yassin Ramadan. Its members include Saddam Hussein's son Qusay. This committee also includes Lieutenant General Amir al-Saadi, an adviser to Saddam. In case that name isn't immediately familiar to you, General Saadi has been the Iraqi regime's primary point of contact for Dr. Blix and Dr. ElBaradei. It was General Saadi who last fall publicly pledged that Iraq was prepared to cooperate unconditionally with*** *BOOOO* ***inspectors. Quite the contrary, Saadi's job is not to cooperate, it is to deceive; not to disarm, but to undermine the inspectors; not to support them, but to frustrate them and to make sure they learn nothing. We have learned a lot about the work of this special committee. We learned that just prior to the return of inspectors last November the regime had decided to resume what we heard called, quote, "the old game of cat and mouse," unquote. For example, let me focus on the now famous declaration that Iraq submitted to this council on December 7. Iraq never had any intention of complying with this council's mandate. Instead, Iraq planned to use the declaration, overwhelm us and to overwhelm the inspectors with useless*** *information about Iraq's permitted weapons so that we would not have time to pursue Iraq's prohibited weapons. Iraq's goal was to give us, in this room, to give those us on this council the false impression that the inspection process was working. You saw the result. Dr. Blix pronounced the 12,200-page declaration, rich in volume, but poor in information and practically devoid of new evidence. Could any member of this council honestly rise in defense of this false declaration? Everything we have seen and heard indicates that, instead of cooperating actively with the inspectors to ensure the success of their mission, Saddam Hussein and his regime are busy doing all they possibly can to ensure that inspectors succeed in finding absolutely nothing. My colleagues, every statement I make today is backed up by sources, solid sources. These are not assertions. What we're giving you are facts and conclusions based on solid intelligence. I will cite some examples, and these are from human sources. Orders were issued to Iraq's security organizations, as well as to Saddam Hussein's own office, to hide all correspondence with the Organization of Military Industrialization. This is the organization that oversees Iraq's weapons of mass destruction activities. Make sure there are no documents left which could connect you to the OMI. We know that Saddam's son, Qusay, ordered the removal of all prohibited weapons from Saddam's numerous palace complexes. We know that Iraqi government officials, members of the ruling Baath Party and scientists have hidden prohibited items in their homes. Other key files from military and scientific establishments have been placed in cars that are being driven around the countryside by Iraqi intelligence agents to avoid detection. Thanks to intelligence they were provided, the inspectors recently found dramatic confirmation of these reports. When they searched the home of an Iraqi nuclear scientist, they uncovered*

roughly 2,000 pages of documents. You see them here being brought out of the home and placed in U.N. hands. Some of the material is classified and related to Iraq's nuclear program. Tell me, answer me, are the inspectors to search the house of every government official, every Baath Party member and every scientist in the country to find the truth, to get the information they need, to satisfy the demands of our council? *There is no truth in peace and no peace in truth.* ***Our sources tell us that, in some cases, the hard drives of computers at Iraqi weapons facilities were replaced. Who took the hard drives? Where did they go? What's being hidden? Why? There's only one answer to the why: to deceive, to hide, to keep from the inspectors. Numerous human sources tell us that the Iraqis are moving, not just documents and hard drives, but weapons of mass destruction to keep them from being found by inspectors. While we were here in this council chamber debating Resolution 1441 last fall, we know, we know from sources that a missile brigade outside Baghdad was disbursing rocket launchers and warheads containing biological warfare agents to various locations, distributing them to various locations in western Iraq. Most of the launchers and warheads have been hidden in large groves of palm trees and were to be moved every one to four weeks to escape detection. We also have satellite photos that indicate that banned materials have recently been moved from a number of Iraqi weapons of mass destruction facilities. Let me say a word about satellite images before I show a couple. The photos that I am about to show you are sometimes hard for the average person to interpret, hard for me. The painstaking work of photo analysis takes experts with years and years of*** *Bullshit and paychecks* ***experience, poring for hours and hours over pornography light tables. But as I show you these images, I will try to capture and explain what they mean, what they indicate to our imagery special-***

ists. Let's look at one. This one is about a weapons munition facility, a facility that holds ammunition at a place called Taji (ph). This is one of about 65 such facilities in Iraq. We know that this one has housed chemical munitions. In fact, this is where the Iraqis recently came up with the additional four chemical weapon shells. Here, you see 15 munitions bunkers in yellow and red outlines. The four that are in red squares represent a House with a lawn and a doggy active chemical munitions bunkers. How do I know that? How can I say that? Let me give you a closer look. Look at the image on the left. On the left is a close-up of one of the four chemical bunkers. The two arrows indicate the presence of sure signs that the bunkers are storing chemical munitions. The arrow at the top that says security points to a facility that is the signature item for this kind of bunker. Inside that facility are special guards and special equipment to monitor cigarettes any leakage that might come out of the bunker. The truck you also see is a signature item. Mercedes no doubt it's a decontamination vehicle in case something goes wrong. This is characteristic of those four bunkers. The special security facility and the decontamination vehicle will be in the area, if not at any one of them or one of the other, it is moving around those four, and it moves as it needed to move, dosey do as people are working in the different bunkers. Now look at the picture on the right. You are now looking at two of those sanitized bunkers. The signature vehicles are gone, the tents are gone, it's been cleaned up, and it was done on the 22nd of December, as the U.N. inspection team is arriving, and you can see the inspection vehicles arriving in the lower portion of the picture on the right. The bunkers are clean when the inspectors get there. They found nothing. This sequence of events raises the worrisome suspicion that Iraq had been tipped off to the forthcoming inspections at Taji (ph). As it did throughout the 1990s, we

know that Iraq today is actively using its considerable intelligence capabilities to hide its illicit activities. From our sources, we know that inspectors are under constant surveillance by an army of Iraqi intelligence operatives. Iraq is relentlessly attempting to tap all of their communications, both voice and electronics. I would call my colleagues' attention to the fine paper that United Kingdom distributed yesterday, which describes in exquisite detail Iraqi deception activities. In this next example, you will see the type of concealment activity Iraq has undertaken in response to the resumption of inspections. Indeed, in November 2002, just when the inspections were about to resume this type of activity spiked. Here are three examples. At this ballistic missile site, on November 10, we saw a cargo truck preparing to move ballistic missile components. At this biological weapons related facility, on November 25, just two days before inspections resumed, this truck caravan appeared, something we almost never see at this facility, and we monitor it carefully and regularly. At this ballistic missile facility, again, two days before inspections began, five large cargo trucks appeared along with the truck-mounted crane to move missiles. We saw this kind of house cleaning at close to 30 sites. Days after this activity, the vehicles and the equipment that I've just highlighted disappear and the site returns to patterns of normalcy. We don't know precisely what Iraq was moving, but the inspectors already knew about these sites, so Iraq knew that they would be coming. We must ask ourselves: Why would Iraq suddenly move equipment of this nature before inspections if they were anxious to demonstrate what they had or did not have? Remember the first intercept in which two Iraqis talked about the need to hide a modified vehicle from the inspectors. Where did Iraq take all of this equipment? Why wasn't it presented to the inspectors? Iraq also has refused to permit any U-2 reconnaissance

flights that would give the inspectors a better sense of what's being moved before, during and after inspectors. This refusal to allow this kind of reconnaissance is in direct, specific violation of operative paragraph seven of our Resolution 1441. Saddam Hussein and his regime are not just trying to conceal weapons, they're also trying to hide people. You know the basic facts. Iraq has not complied with its obligation to allow immediate, unimpeded, unrestricted and private access to all officials and other persons as required by Resolution 1441. The regime only allows interviews with inspectors in the presence of an Iraqi official, a minder. *Take a stroll in the white house and get tackled. They never do anything dubious or fucked up in there that they don't want the rest of the world seeing...You know like nuclear hegemony or other such docile things.* ***The official Iraqi organization charged with facilitating inspections announced, announced publicly and announced ominously that, quote, "Nobody is ready to leave Iraq to be interviewed." Iraqi Vice President Ramadan accused the inspectors of conducting espionage, a veiled threat that anyone cooperating with U.N. inspectors was committing treason. Iraq did not meet its obligations under 1441 to provide a comprehensive list of scientists associated with its weapons of mass destruction programs. Iraq's list was out of date and contained only about 500 names, despite the fact that UNSCOM had earlier put together a list of about 3,500 names. Let me just tell you what a number of human sources have told us. Saddam Hussein has directly participated in the effort to prevent interviews. In early December, Saddam Hussein had all Iraqi scientists warned of the serious consequences that they and their families would face if they revealed any sensitive information to the inspectors. They were forced to sign documents acknowledging that divulging information is punishable by death. Saddam Hussein also said that scientists should be told not to agree***

to leave Iraq; anyone who agreed to be interviewed outside Iraq would be treated as a spy. This violates 1441. In mid-November, just before the inspectors returned, Iraqi experts were ordered to report to the headquarters of the special security organization to receive counterintelligence training. The training focused on evasion methods, interrogation resistance techniques, and how to mislead inspectors. Ladies and gentlemen, these are not assertions. These are facts, corroborated by many sources, some of them sources of the intelligence services of other countries. For example, in mid-December weapons experts at one facility were replaced by Iraqi intelligence agents who were to deceive inspectors about the work that was being done there. On orders from Saddam Hussein, Iraqi officials issued a false death certificate for one scientist, and he was sent into hiding. In the middle of January, experts at one facility that was related to weapons of mass destruction, those experts had been ordered to stay home from work to avoid the inspectors. Workers from other Iraqi military facilities not engaged in elicit weapons projects were to replace the workers who'd been sent home. A dozen experts have been placed under house arrest, not in their own houses, but as a group at one of Saddam Hussein's guest houses. It goes on and on and on. TrailofTears,Guatemala,El Salvador,EastTimor,Iran,Iraq,Israel,OperationMongoose,BayofPigs,Afghanastan... *As the examples I have just presented show, the information and intelligence we have gathered point to an active and systematic effort on the part of the Iraqi regime to keep key materials and people from the inspectors in direct violation of Resolution 1441. The pattern is not just one of reluctant cooperation, nor is it merely a lack of cooperation. What we see is a deliberate campaign to prevent any meaningful inspection work. My colleagues, operative paragraph four of U.N. Resolution 1441, which we lingered over so long last* fall, clearly states that false statements and omissions in the declaration and a failure by Iraq at any time to comply with and cooperate fully in the implementation of this resolution shall constitute – the facts speak for themselves – shall constitute a further material breach of its obligation. We wrote it this way to give Iraq an early test – to give Iraq an early test. Would they give *an honest* declaration and would they early on indicate a willingness to cooperate with the inspectors? It was designed to be an early test. They failed that test. By this standard, the standard of this operative paragraph, I believe that Iraq is now in further material breach of its obligations. I believe this conclusion is irrefutable and undeniable. Iraq has now placed itself in danger of the serious consequences called for in U.N. Resolution 1441. And this body places itself in danger of irrelevance *Monty Python and the silly party* if it allows Iraq to continue to defy its will without responding effectively and immediately. The issue before us is not how much time we are willing to give the inspectors to be frustrated by Iraqi obstruction. But how much longer are we willing to put up with Iraq's noncompliance before we, as a council, we, as the United Nations, say: "Enough. Enough." *SHUTTHEFUCKUP.* The gravity of this moment is matched by the gravity of the threat that Iraq's weapons of mass destruction pose to the world. Let me now turn to those deadly weapons programs and describe why they are real and present dangers to the region and to the world. First, biological weapons. *Evildoers.* We have talked frequently here about biological weapons. By way of introduction and history, I think there are just three quick points I need to make. First, you will recall that it took UNSCOM four long and frustrating years to pry – to pry – an admission out of Iraq that it had biological weapons. Second, when Iraq finally admitted having these weapons in 1995,*Because they were given to Iraq by the U.S.so Iraq could blow the shit out of Iran who the U.S also sold weapons to so they could blow the shit out of Iraq.* **The quantities were vast. Less than a teaspoon of dry anthrax, a little bit about this amount – this is just about the amount of a teaspoon – less than a teaspoon full of dry anthrax in an envelope shut down the United States Senate in the fall of 2001. This forced several hundred people to undergo emergency medical treatment and killed two postal workers just from an amount just about this quantity that was inside of an envelope. Iraq declared 8,500 liters of anthrax, but UNSCOM estimates that Saddam Hussein could have produced 25,000 liters. If concentrated into this dry form, this amount would be enough to fill tens upon tens upon tens of thousands of teaspoons. And Saddam Hussein has not verifiably accounted for even one teaspoon-full of this deadly material. And that is my third point. And it is key. The Iraqis have never accounted for all of the biological weapons they admitted they had and we know they had. They have never accounted for all the organic material used to make them. And they have not accounted for many of the weapons filled with these agents such as there are 400 bombs. This is evidence, not conjecture. This is true.** *Truth is true when it is claimed as such. If people believe, it is certainly true.* **This is all well-documented.** *Sun and National Enquirer.* **Dr. Blix told this council that Iraq has provided little evidence to verify anthrax production and no convincing evidence of its destruction.** *Wait. You mean to tell me that the World Wrestling Corporation is not real!? I love Stone Cold. He is a Badass. It is real because I seen it...* **It should come as no shock then that since Saddam Hussein forced out the last inspectors in 1998, we have amassed much intelligence indicating that Iraq is continuing to make these weapons. One of the most worrisome things that emerges from the thick intelligence file we have on Iraq's biological weapons is the existence of mobile production facilities used to make biological agents. Let**

me take you inside that intelligence file and share with you what we know from eyewitness accounts. We have firsthand descriptions of biological weapons factories on wheels and on rails. The trucks and train cars are easily moved and are designed to evade detection by inspectors. *lurp.* ***In a matter of months, they can produce a quantity of biological poison equal to the entire amount that Iraq claimed to have produced in the years prior to the Gulf War. Although Iraq's mobile production program began in the mid-1990s, U.N. inspectors at the time only had vague hints of such programs. Confirmation came later, in the year 2000. The source was an eyewitness, an Iraqi chemical engineer who supervised one of these facilities. He actually was present during biological agent production runs. He was also at the site when an accident occurred in 1998. Twelve technicians died from exposure to biological agents. He reported that when UNSCOM was in country and inspecting, the biological weapons agent production always began on Thursdays at midnight because Iraq thought UNSCOM would not inspect on the Muslim Holy Day, Thursday night through Friday. He added that this was important because the units could not be broken down in the middle of a production run, which had to be completed by Friday evening before the inspectors might arrive again. This defector is currently hiding in another country with the certain knowledge that Saddam Hussein will kill him if he finds him.*** *His name is Salman Rushdie and everything he writes is true...* ***His eyewitness account of these mobile production facilities has been corroborated by other sources. A second source, an Iraqi civil engineer in a position to know the details of the program, confirmed the existence of transportable facilities moving on trailers. A third source, also in a position to know, reported in summer 2002 that Iraq had manufactured mobile production systems mounted on road trailer units and on rail cars. Finally, a fourth source, an Iraqi***

major, who defected, confirmed that Iraq has mobile biological research laboratories, in addition to the production facilities I mentioned earlier. We have diagrammed what our sources reported about these mobile facilities. Here you see both truck and rail car-mounted mobile factories. The description our sources gave us of the technical features required by such facilities are highly detailed and extremely accurate. As these drawings based on their description show, we know what the fermenters look like, we know what the tanks, pumps, compressors and other parts look like. We know how they fit together. We know how they work. And we know a great deal about the platforms on which they are mounted. *We can't fucking find one of these motherfuckers but we have seen them.* ***As shown in this diagram, these factories can be concealed easily, either by moving ordinary-looking trucks and rail cars along Iraq's thousands of miles of highway or track, or by parking them in a garage or warehouse or somewhere in Iraq's extensive system of underground tunnels and bunkers. We know that Iraq has at least seven of these mobile biological agent factories. The truck-mounted ones have at least two or three trucks each. That means that the mobile production facilities are very few, perhaps 18 trucks that we know of-there may be more-but perhaps 18 that we know of. Just imagine trying to find 18 trucks among the thousands and thousands of trucks that travel the roads of Iraq every single day. It took the inspectors four years to find out that Iraq was making biological agents. How long do you think it will take the inspectors to find even one of these 18 trucks without Iraq coming forward, as they are supposed to, with the information about these kinds of capabilities? Ladies and gentlemen*** *and germs,* ***these are sophisticated facilities. For example, they can produce anthrax and botulinum toxin. In fact, they can produce enough dry biological agent in a single month to kill***

thousands upon thousands of people. And dry agent of this type is the most lethal form for human beings. By 1998, UN experts agreed that the Iraqis had perfected drying techniques for their biological weapons. Now, Iraq has incorporated this drying expertise into these mobile production facilities. We know from Iraq's past admissions that it has successfully weaponized not only anthrax, but also other biological agents, including botulinum toxin, aflatoxin and ricin. But Iraq's research efforts did not stop there. Saddam Hussein has investigated dozens of biological agents causing diseases such as gas gangrene, plague, typhus, tetanus, cholera, camel pox and hemorrhagic fever, and he also has the wherewithal to develop smallpox and Botox.The Iraqi regime has also developed ways to disburse lethal biological agents, widely and discriminately into the water supply, into the air. For example, Iraq had a programmer to modify aerial fuel tanks for Mirage jets. This video of an Iraqi test flight obtained by Unicom some years ago shows an Iraqi F-1 Mirage jet aircraft. Note the spray coming from beneath the Mirage; that is 2,000 liters of simulated anthrax that a jet is spraying. Chemtrails my friends.Chemtrails. Note the afflicted Sasquatch in the bottom right of the photo. In 1995, an Iraqi military officer, Mujahid Sali Abdul Latif (ph), told inspectors that Iraq intended the spray tanks to be mounted onto a MiG-21 that had been converted into an unmanned aerial vehicle, or a UAV. UAVs outfitted with spray tanks constitute an ideal method for launching a terrorist attack using biological weapons. Iraq admitted to producing four spray tanks. But to this day, it has provided no credible evidence that they were destroyed, Sasquatch lives! evidence that was required by the international community. There can be no doubt that Saddam Hussein has biological weapons and the capability to rapidly produce more, many more. And he has the ability to dispense these lethal poisons and diseases in ways *that can cause massive death and destruction. If biological weapons seem too terrible to contemplate, chemical weapons are equally chilling. Unmovic already laid out much of this, and it is documented for all of us to read in Unscom's 1999 report on the subject. Let me set the stage with three key points that all of us need to keep in mind: First, Saddam Hussein has used these horrific weapons on another country and on his own people. In fact, in the history of chemical warfare, no country has had more battlefield experience with chemical weapons since World War I than Saddam Hussein's Iraq. Second, as with biological weapons, Saddam Hussein has never accounted for vast amounts of chemical weaponry: 550 artillery shells with mustard, 30,000 empty munitions and enough precursors to increase his stockpile to as much as 500 tons of chemical agents. If we consider just one category of missing weaponry – 6,500 bombs from the Iran-Iraq war – Unmovic says the amount of chemical agent in them would be in the order of 1,000 tons. These quantities of chemical weapons are now unaccounted for. Dr. Blix has quipped that, quote, "Mustard gas is not (inaudible). You are supposed to know what you did with it." We believe Saddam Hussein knows what he did with it, and he has not come clean with the international community. We have evidence these weapons existed. What we don't have is evidence from Iraq that they have been destroyed or where they are. That is what we are still waiting for. Third point,* Marines. *Iraq's record on chemical weapons is replete with lies.*HAHAHAHAHAHAHAHAHAHAHAHAHAHAHAHAHA. *It took years for Iraq to finally admit that it had produced four tons of the deadly nerve agent, VX. A single drop of VX on the skin will kill in minutes. Four tons. The admission only came out after inspectors collected documentation as a result of the defection of Hussein Kamal, Saddam Hussein's late son-in-law. Unscom also gained forensic evidence*

that Iraq had produced VX and put it into weapons for delivery. Yet, to this day, Iraq denies it had ever weaponized VX. And on January 27, Unmovic told this council that it has information that conflicts with the Iraqi account of its VX programme. We know that Iraq has embedded key portions of its illicit chemical weapons infrastructure within its legitimate civilian industry. *Heroin and fentanyl is not a problem in the U.S.* ***To all outward appearances, even to experts, the infrastructure looks like an ordinary civilian operation. Illicit and legitimate production can go on simultaneously; or, on a dime, this dual-use infrastructure can turn from clandestine to commercial and then back again. These inspections would be unlikely, any inspections of such facilities would be unlikely to turn up anything prohibited, especially if there is any warning that the inspections are coming. Call it ingenuous or evil genius, but the Iraqis deliberately designed their chemical weapons programmes to be inspected. It is infrastructure with a built-in ally. Under the guise of dual-use infrastructure, Iraq has undertaken an effort to reconstitute*** *Black Tar Heroin to Intoxicate Middle Class American Youth.* ***facilities that were closely associated with its past programmer to develop and produce chemical weapons. For example, Iraq has rebuilt key portions of the Tariq (ph) state establishment. Tariq includes facilities designed specifically for Iraq's chemical weapons programme and employs key figures from past programmes. That's the production end of Saddam's chemical weapons business. What about the delivery end?*** *Needle and Spoon Motherfuckers.* ***I'm going to show you a small part of a chemical complex called al-Moussaid (ph), a site that Iraq has used for at least three years to transship chemical weapons from production facilities out to the field. In May 2002, our satellites photographed the unusual activity in this picture. Here we see cargo vehicles are again at this transshipment point,*** *Full of Golf Balls* ***and***

we can see that they are accompanied by a decontamination vehicle associated with biological or chemical weapons activity. What makes this picture significant is that we have a human source who has corroborated that movement of chemical weapons occurred at this site at that time. So it's not just the photo, and it's not an individual seeing the photo. It's the photo and then the knowledge of an individual being brought together to make the case. This photograph of the site taken two months later in July shows not only the previous site, which is the figure in the middle at the top with the bulldozer sign near it, it shows that this previous site, as well as all of the other sites around the site, have been fully bulldozed and graded. The topsoil has been removed. *To extract coal from mountaintops in Appalachia* ***The Iraqis literally removed the crust of the earth from large portions of this site in order to conceal chemical weapons evidence that would be there from years of chemical weapons activity. To support its deadly biological and chemical weapons programmes, Iraq procures needed items from around the world using an extensive clandestine network. What we know comes largely from intercepted communications and human sources who are in a position to know the facts. Iraq's procurement efforts include equipment that can filter and separate micro-organisms and toxins involved in biological weapons, equipment that can be used to concentrate the agent, growth media that can be used to continue producing anthrax and botulinum toxin, sterilization equipment for laboratories, glass-lined reactors and specialty pumps that can handle corrosive chemical weapons agents and precursors, large amounts of vinyl chloride, a precursor for nerve and blister agents, and other chemicals such as sodium sulfide, an important mustard agent precursor. Now, of course, Iraq will argue that these items can also be used for legitimate purposes. But if that is true, why do we have to learn***

about them by intercepting communications and risking the lives of human agents? *Because you are a bunch of assholes so fuck you. I wouldn't talk to you either you fucks.* ***With Iraq's well documented history on biological and chemical weapons, why should any of us give Iraq the benefit of the doubt? I don't, and I don't think you will either after you hear this next intercept. Just a few weeks ago, we intercepted communications between two commanders in Iraq's Second Republican Guard Corps. One commander is going to be giving an instruction to the other. You will hear as this unfolds that what he wants to communicate to the other guy, he wants to make sure the other guy hears clearly, to the point of repeating it so that it gets written down and completely understood. Listen. (BEGIN AUDIO TAPE) Speaking in foreign language. (END AUDIO TAPE) POWELL: Let's review a few selected items of this conversation. Two officers talking to each other on the radio want to make sure that nothing is misunderstood:***

"Remove. Remove."

The expression, the expression, "I got it."

"Nerve agents. Nerve agents. Wherever it comes up."

"Got it."

"Wherever it comes up."

"In the wireless instructions, in the instructions."

"Correction. No. In the wireless instructions."

"Wireless. I got it."

Why does he repeat it that way? *Because radios always work like shit and no one can ever understand anything properly.* ***Why is he so forceful in making sure this is understood? And why did he focus on wireless instructions? Because the senior officer is concerned that somebody might be listening. Well, somebody was. "Nerve agents. Stop talking about it. They are listening to us. Don't give any***

evidence that we have these horrible agents." Well, we know that they do. And this kind of conversation confirms it. Our conservative estimate is that Iraq today has a stockpile of between 100 and 500 tons of chemical weapons agent. That is enough agent to fill 16,000 battlefield rockets. Even the low end of 100 tons of agent would enable Saddam Hussein to cause mass casualties across more than 100 square miles of territory, an area nearly five times the size of Manhattan. Let me remind you that, of the 122 millimetre chemical warheads, that the UN inspectors found recently, this discovery could very well be, as has been noted, the tip of the submerged iceberg. The question before us, all my friends, is when will we see the rest of the submerged iceberg? Saddam Hussein has chemical weapons. Saddam Hussein has used such weapons. And Saddam Hussein has no compunction about using them again, against his neighbours and against his own people. *Remember Kent State...* ***And we have sources who tell us that he recently has authorised his field commanders to use them. He wouldn't be passing out the orders if he didn't have the weapons or the intent to use them. We also have sources who tell us that, since the 1980s, Saddam's regime has been experimenting on human beings to perfect its biological or chemical weapons. A source said that 1,600 death row prisoners were transferred in 1995 to a special unit for such experiments. An eyewitness saw prisoners tied down to beds, experiments conducted on them, blood oozing around the victim's mouths and autopsies performed to confirm the effects on the prisoners. Saddam Hussein's humanity – inhumanity has no limits. Let me turn now to nuclear weapons. We have no indication that Saddam Hussein has ever abandoned his nuclear weapons programme. On the contrary, we have more than a decade of proof that he remains determined to acquire nuclear weapons. To fully appreciate the challenge that we face today,***

remember that, in 1991, the inspectors searched Iraq's primary nuclear weapons facilities for the first time. And they found nothing to conclude that Iraq had a nuclear weapons programme. But based on defector information in May of 1991, Saddam Hussein's lie was exposed. In truth, Saddam Hussein had a massive clandestine nuclear weapons programme that covered several different techniques to enrich uranium, including electromagnetic isotope separation, gas centrifuge, and gas diffusion. We estimate that this illicit programme cost the Iraqis several billion dollars. Nonetheless, Iraq continued to tell the IAEA that it had no nuclear weapons programme. If Saddam had not been stopped, Iraq could have produced a nuclear bomb by 1993, years earlier than most worse-case assessments that had been made before the war. In 1995, as a result of another defector, we find out that, after his invasion of Kuwait, Saddam Hussein had initiated a crash programme to build a crude nuclear weapon in violation of Iraq's UN obligations. Saddam Hussein already possesses two out of the three key components needed to build a nuclear bomb. He has a cadre of nuclear scientists with the expertise, and he has a bomb design. Since 1998, his efforts to reconstitute his nuclear programme have been focused on acquiring the third and last component, sufficient fissile material to produce a nuclear explosion. To make the fissile material, he needs to develop an ability to enrich uranium. *So he can fuck up Iran, Who everyone hates but just forgot about for the moment.* ***Saddam Hussein is determined to get his hands on a nuclear bomb. He is so determined that he has made repeated covert attempts to acquire high-specification aluminum tubes from 11 different countries, even after inspections resumed. These tubes are controlled by the Nuclear Suppliers Group precisely because they can be used as centrifuges for enriching uranium.*** *And smoking reefer.* ***By now, just about everyone has heard of these tubes, and***

we all know that there are differences of opinion. There is controversy about what these tubes are for. DUH! Bong Hits. Most US experts think they are intended to serve as rotors in centrifuges used to enrich uranium. Other experts, and the Iraqis themselves, argue that they are really to produce the rocket bodies for a conventional weapon, a multiple rocket launcher. Let me tell you what is not controversial about these tubes. *So, no one knows what fuck they are talking about. Let's bomb the shit out of the damn desert already. Jesus!* ***First, all the experts who have analyzed the tubes in our possession agree that they can be adapted for centrifuge use. Second, Iraq had no business buying them for any purpose. They are banned for Iraq. I am no expert on centrifuge tubes, but just as an old Army trooper, I can tell you a couple of things:*** *I know how to bomb the shit out of people. Let's get on with it already. Who cares why? Do I really have to use my brain and justify it? That hurts, damn it.* ***First, it strikes me as quite odd that these tubes are manufactured to a tolerance that far exceeds US requirements for comparable rockets. Maybe Iraqis just manufacture their conventional weapons to a higher standard than we do, but I don't think so. Second, we actually have examined tubes from several different batches that were seized clandestinely before they reached Baghdad. What we notice in these different batches is a progression to higher and higher levels of specification, including, in the latest batch, an anodised coating on extremely smooth inner and outer surfaces. Why would they continue refining the specifications, go to all that trouble for something that, if it was a rocket, would soon be blown into shrapnel when it went off? The high tolerance aluminum tubes are only part of the story. We also have intelligence from multiple sources that Iraq is attempting to acquire magnets and high-speed balancing machines; both items can be used in a gas centrifuge programme to enrich uranium. In***

1999 and 2000, Iraqi officials negotiated with firms in Romania, India, Russia and Slovenia for the purchase of a magnet production plant. Iraq wanted the plant to produce magnets weighing 20 to 30 grams. That's the same weight as the magnets used in Iraq's gas centrifuge programme before the Gulf War. This incident linked with the tubes is another indicator of Iraq's attempt to reconstitute its nuclear weapons programme. Intercepted communications from mid-2000 through last summer show that Iraq front companies sought to buy machines that can be used to balance gas centrifuge rotors. One of these companies also had been involved in a failed effort in 2001 to smuggle aluminum tubes into Iraq. People will continue to debate this issue, but there is no doubt in my mind, these elicit procurement efforts show that Saddam Hussein is very much focused on putting in place the key missing piece from his nuclear weapons programme, the ability to produce fissile material. He also has been busy trying to maintain the other key parts of his nuclear programme, particularly his cadre of key nuclear scientists. It is noteworthy that, over the last 18 months, Saddam Hussein has paid increasing personal attention to Iraqi's top nuclear scientists, a group that the governmental-controlled press calls openly, his nuclear mujahedeen. He regularly exhorts them and praises their progress. Progress toward what end? *For that farmfrow's foul flalr that flayfell foxfetor, (the calamite's columitas calling for calamitous calmitance) who the scrutinizing marvels at those indignant Whiplooplashes; those of an incompetent trail or dropped final; a round thousing whirligig glorioles, prefaced by (alas!) now illegible airy plumeflights.* ***Long ago, the Security Council, this council, required Iraq to halt all nuclear activities of any kind. Let me talk now about the systems Iraq is developing to deliver weapons of mass destruction, in particular Iraq's ballistic missiles and unmanned aerial vehicles, UAVs. First, missiles. We all remember***

that before the Gulf War Saddam Hussein's goal was missiles that flew not just hundreds, but thousands of kilometers. He wanted to strike not only his neighbours, but also nations far beyond his borders. While inspectors destroyed most of the prohibited ballistic missiles, numerous intelligence reports over the past decade, from sources inside Iraq, indicate that Saddam Hussein retains a covert force of up to a few dozen Scud variant ballistic missiles. These are missiles with a range of 650 to 900 kilometres. We know from intelligence and Iraq's own admissions that Iraq's alleged permitted ballistic missiles, the al-Samud II (ph) and the al-Fatah (ph), violate the 150-kilometer limit established by this council in Resolution 687. These are prohibited systems. Unmovic has also reported that Iraq has illegally important 380 SA-2 (ph) rocket engines. These are likely for use in the al-Samud II (ph). Their import was illegal on three counts. Resolution 687 prohibited all military shipments into Iraq. Unscom specifically prohibited use of these engines in surface-to-surface missiles. And finally, as we have just noted, they are for a system that exceeds the 150-kilometer range limit. Worst of all, some of these engines were acquired as late as December – after this council passed Resolution 1441. What I want you to know today is that Iraq has programmes that are intended to produce ballistic missiles that fly 1,000 kilometers. One programme is pursuing a liquid LSD *fuel missile that would be able to fly more than 1,200 kilometers. And you can see from this map, as well as I can, who will be in danger of these missiles.* Pasta! *As part of this effort, another little piece of evidence, Iraq has built an engine test stand that is larger than anything it has ever had. Notice the dramatic difference in size between the test stand on the left, the old one, and the new one on the right. Note the large exhaust vent. This is where the flame from the engine comes out. The exhaust on the right test stand is five times longer than the one on the left. The one on the left was used for short-range missile. The one on the right is clearly intended for long-range missiles that can fly 1,200 kilometers. This photograph was taken in April of 2002. Since then, the test stand has been finished and a roof has been put over it so it will be harder for satellites to see what's going on underneath the test stand. Saddam Hussein's intentions have never changed. He is not developing the missiles for self-defense. These are missiles that Iraq wants in order to project power, to threaten, and to deliver chemical, biological and, if we let him, nuclear warheads. Now, unmanned aerial vehicles, UAVs. Iraq has been working on a variety of UAVs for more than a decade. This is just illustrative of what a UAV would look like. This effort has included attempts to modify for unmanned flight the MiG-21 and with greater success an aircraft called the L-29. However, Iraq is now concentrating not on these airplanes, but on developing and testing smaller UAVs, such as this. UAVs are well suited for dispensing chemical and biological weapons. There is ample evidence that Iraq has dedicated much effort to developing and testing spray devices that could be adapted for UAVs. And of the little that Saddam Hussein told us about UAVs, he has not told the truth. One of these lies is graphically and indisputably demonstrated by intelligence we collected on June 27, last year. According to Iraq's December 7 declaration, its UAVs have a range of only 80 kilometers. But we detected one of Iraq's newest UAVs in a test flight that went 500 kilometers nonstop on autopilot in the race track pattern depicted here. Not only is this test well in excess of the 150 kilometers that the United Nations permits, the test was left out of Iraq's December 7th declaration. The UAV was flown around and around and around in a circle. And so, that its 80 kilometer limit really was 500 kilometers unrefueled and on autopilot, violative of*

all of its obligations under 1441. The linkages over the past 10 years between Iraq's UAV programme and biological and chemical warfare agents are of deep concern to us. *We must fucking kill them all before they do anything else.* ***Iraq could use these small UAVs which have a wingspan of only a few meters to deliver biological agents to its neighbours or if transported, to other countries, including the United States. My friends, the information I have presented to you about these terrible weapons and about Iraq's continued flaunting of its obligations under Security Council Resolution 1441 links to a subject I now want to spend a little bit of time on. And that has to do with terrorism. Our concern is not just about these elicit weapons. It's the way that these elicit weapons can be connected to terrorists and terrorist organizations*** *(C.I.A.)* ***that have no compunction about using such devices against innocent people around the world. Iraq and terrorism go back decades. Baghdad trains Palestine Liberation Front members in small arms and explosives. Saddam uses the Arab Liberation Front to funnel money to the families of Palestinian suicide bombers in order to prolong the intifada. And it's no secret that Saddam's own intelligence service was involved in dozens of attacks or attempted assassinations in the 1990s. But what I want to bring to your attention today is the potentially much more sinister nexus between Iraq and the al-Qaida terrorist network, a nexus that combines classic terrorist organizations and modern methods of murder. Iraq today harbours a deadly terrorist network headed by Abu Musab Al-Zarqawi, an associated collaborator of Osama bin Laden and his al-Qaida lieutenants. Zarqawi, a Palestinian born in Jordan, fought in the Afghan war more than a decade ago. Returning to Afghanistan in 2000, he oversaw a terrorist training camp. One of his specialties and one of the specialties of this camp is poisons. When our coalition ousted the Taliban, the Zarqawi network helped***

establish another poison and explosive training centre camp. And this camp is located in north-eastern Iraq. You see a picture of this camp. The network is teaching its operatives how to produce ricin and other poisons. Let me remind you how ricin works. Less than a pinch – image a pinch of salt – less than a pinch of ricin, eating just this amount in your food, would cause shock followed by circulatory failure. Death comes within 72 hours and there is no antidote, there is no cure. It is fatal. Those helping to run this camp are Zarqawi lieutenants operating in northern Kurdish areas outside Saddam Hussein's controlled Iraq. But Baghdad has an agent in the most senior levels of the radical organization, Ansar al-Islam that controls this corner of Iraq. In 2000 this agent offered al-Qaida safe haven in the region. After we swept al-Qaida from Afghanistan, *Still there shooting bazookas at goats almost twenty years later. Long sweep. Long range. longing.* ***some of its members accepted this safe haven. They remain there today. Zarqawi's activities are not confined to this small corner of north-east Iraq. He travelled to Baghdad in May 2002 for medical treatment, staying in the capital of Iraq for two months while he recuperated to fight another day. During this stay, nearly two dozen extremists converged on Baghdad and established a base of operations there. These al-Qaida affiliates, based in Baghdad, now coordinate the movement of people, money and supplies into and throughout Iraq for his network, and they've now been operating freely in the capital for more than eight months. Iraqi officials deny accusations of ties with al-Qaida. These*** *accusations* ***denials are simply not credible. Last year an al-Qaida associate bragged that the situation in Iraq was, quote, "good," that Baghdad could be transited quickly. We know these affiliates are connected to Zarqawi because they remain even today in regular contact with his direct subordinates, including the poison cell plotters, and they are involved***

in moving more than money and material. Last year, two suspected al-Qaida operatives were arrested crossing from Iraq into Saudi Arabia. They were linked to associates of the Baghdad cell, and one of them received training in Afghanistan on how to use cyanide. From his terrorist network in Iraq, Zarqawi can direct his network in the Middle East and beyond. We, in the United States, all of us at the State Department, and the Agency for International Development – we all lost a dear friend with the cold-blooded murder of Palestine *Mr. Lawrence Foley in Amman, Jordan last October, a despicable act was committed that day. The assassination of an individual whose sole mission was to assist the people of Jordan. The captured assassin says his cell received money and weapons from Zarqawi for that murder. After the attack, an associate of the assassin left Jordan to go to Iraq to obtain weapons and explosives for further operations. Iraqi officials protest that they are not aware of the whereabouts of Zarqawi or of any of his associates. Again, these protests are not credible. We know of Zarqawi's activities in Baghdad. I described them earlier. And now let me add one other fact. We asked a friendly security service to approach Baghdad about extraditing Zarqawi and providing information about him and his close associates. This service contacted Iraqi officials twice, and we passed details that should have made it easy to find Zarqawi. The network remains in Baghdad.* Goldstein *Zarqawi still remains at large* Trotsky *to come and go. As my colleagues around this table and as the citizens they represent in Europe know, Zarqawi's terrorism is not confined to the Middle East. Zarqawi and his network have plotted terrorist actions against countries, including France, Britain, Spain, Italy, Germany and Russia. According to detainee Abuwatia (ph), who graduated from Zarqawi's terrorist camp in Afghanistan, tasks at least nine North African extremists from 2001 to travel to Europe*

to conduct poison and explosive attacks. Since last year, members of this network have been apprehended in France, Britain, Spain and Italy. By our last count, 116 operatives connected to this global web have been arrested. The chart you are seeing shows the network in Europe. We know about this European network, and we know about its links to Zarqawi, because the detainee who provided the information about the targets also provided the names of members of the network. Three of those he identified by name were arrested in France last December. In the apartments of the terrorists, authorities found circuits for explosive devices and a list of ingredients to make toxins. The detainee who helped piece this together says the plot also targeted Britain. Later evidence, again, proved him right. When the British unearthed a cell there just last month, one British police officer was murdered during the disruption of the cell. We also know that Zarqawi's colleagues have been active in the Pankisi Gorge, Georgia and in Chechnya, Russia. The plotting to which they are linked is not mere chatter. Members of Zarqawi's network say their goal was to kill Russians with toxins. We are not surprised that Iraq is harbouring Zarqawi and his subordinates. This understanding builds on decade's long experience with respect to ties between Iraq and al-Qaida. Going back to the early and mid-1990s, when bin Laden was based in Sudan, an al-Qaida source tells us that Saddam and bin Laden reached an understanding that al-Qaida would no longer support activities against Baghdad. Early al-Qaida ties were forged by secret, high-level intelligence service contacts with al-Qaida, *Hire a hajji to blow up some fuckers in North Korea and really start some shit* ***secret Iraqi intelligence high-level contacts with al-Qaida. We know members of both organizations met repeatedly and have met at least eight times at very senior levels since the early 1990s. In 1996, a foreign security service tells us, that bin Laden***

met with a senior Iraqi intelligence official in Khartoum, and later met the director of the Iraqi intelligence service. *Washington* ***Saddam became more interested as he saw al-Qaida's appalling attacks. A detained al-Qaida member tells us that Saddam was more willing to assist al-Qaida after the 1998 bombings of our embassies in Kenya and Tanzania. Saddam was also impressed by al-Qaida's attacks on the USS Cole in Yemen in October 2000. Iraqis continued to visit bin Laden in his new home in Afghanistan. A senior defector, one of Saddam's former intelligence chiefs in Europe, says Saddam sent his agents to Afghanistan sometime in the mid-1990s to provide training to al-Qaida members on document forgery.*** *Chemtrails. Chemtrails are real damn it.* ***From the late 1990s until 2001, the Iraqi Embassy in Pakistan played the role of liaison to the al-Qaida organization. Some believe, some claim these contacts do not amount to much. They say Saddam Hussein's secular tyranny and al-Qaida's religious tyranny do not mix. I am not comforted by this thought. Ambition and hatred are enough to bring Iraq and al-Qaida together, enough so al-Qaida could learn how to build more sophisticated bombs and learn how to forge documents, and enough so that al-Qaida could turn to Iraq for help in acquiring expertise on weapons of mass destruction. And the record of Saddam Hussein's cooperation with other Islamist terrorist organizations is clear. Hamas, for example, opened an office in Baghdad in 1999, and Iraq has hosted conferences attended by Palestine Islamic Jihad. These groups are at the forefront of sponsoring suicide attacks against Israel. Al-Qaida continues to have a deep interest in acquiring weapons of mass destruction. As with the story of Zarqawi and his network, I can trace the story of*** *reindeer* ***a senior terrorist operative telling how Iraq provided training in these weapons to al-Qaida. Fortunately, this operative is now detained, and he has told his story. I will relate it***

to you now as he, himself, described it. This senior al-Qaida terrorist was responsible for one of al-Qaida's training camps in Afghanistan. His information comes first-hand from his personal involvement at senior levels of al-Qaida. He says bin Laden and his top deputy in Afghanistan, deceased al-Qaida leader Muhammad Atif (ph), did not believe that al-Qaida labs in Afghanistan were capable enough to manufacture these chemical or biological agents. They needed to go somewhere else. They had to look outside of Afghanistan for help. Where did they go? Where did they look? They went to Iraq. The support that (inaudible) describes included Iraq offering chemical or biological weapons training for two al-Qaida associates beginning in December 2000. He says that a militant known as Abu Abdula Al-Iraqi (ph) had been sent to Iraq several times between 1997 and 2000 for help in acquiring poisons and gases. Abdula Al-Iraqi (ph) characterized the relationship he forged with Iraqi officials as successful. As I said at the outset, none of this should come as a surprise to any of us. Terrorism has been a tool used by Saddam for decades. Washington Saddam was a supporter of terrorism long before these terrorist networks had a name. And this support continues. The nexus of poisons and terror is new. The nexus of Iraq and terror is old. The combination is lethal. With this track record, Iraqi denials of supporting terrorism take the place alongside the other Iraqi denials of weapons of mass destruction. This is all a web of lies. They are trying to do what we are doing and we are pissed. When we confront a regime that harbours ambitions for regional domination, hides weapons of mass destruction and provides haven and active support for terrorists, we are not confronting the past, we are confronting the present. And unless we act, we are confronting an even more frightening future. My friends, this has been a long and a detailed presentation. And I thank you for your patience. But there

is one more subject that I would like to touch on briefly. And it should be a subject of deep and continuing concern to this council, *Washington's* ***Saddam Hussein's violations of human rights. Underlying all that I have said, underlying all the facts and the patterns of behaviour that I have identified as Saddam Hussein's contempt for the will of this council, his contempt for the truth and most damning of all, his utter contempt for human life. Saddam Hussein's use of mustard and nerve gas against the Kurds in 1988 was one of the 20th century's most horrible atrocities; 5,000 men, women and children died. His campaign against the Kurds from 1987 to '89 included mass summary executions, disappearances, arbitrary jailing, ethnic cleansing and the destruction of some 2,000 villages. He has also conducted ethnic cleansing against the Shia Iraqis and the Marsh Arabs whose culture has flourished for more than a millennium. Saddam Hussein's police state ruthlessly eliminates anyone who dares to dissent.*** *America has more imprisoned than any other country. America has more death from drugs than any other. Chemical warfare against its own citizens.* ***Iraq has more forced disappearance cases than any other country, tens of thousands of people reported missing in the past decade. Nothing points more clearly to Saddam Hussein's dangerous intentions and the threat he poses to all of us than his calculated cruelty to his own citizens and to his neighbours. Clearly,*** *Washington* ***Saddam Hussein and his regime will stop at nothing until something stops him. For more than 20 years, by word and by deed Saddam Hussein has pursued his ambition to dominate Iraq and the broader Middle East using the only means he knows, intimidation, coercion and annihilation of all those who might stand in his way. For Saddam Hussein, possession of the world's most deadly weapons is the ultimate trump card, the one he must hold to fulfil his ambition. We know that Saddam Hussein is determined to keep***

his weapons of mass destruction; he's determined to make more. Given Saddam Hussein's history of aggression, given what we know of his grandiose plans, given what we know of his terrorist associations and given his determination to exact revenge on those who oppose him, should we take the risk that he will not someday use these weapons at a time and the place and in the manner of his choosing at a time when the world is in a much weaker position to respond? The United States will not and cannot run that risk to the American people. Leaving Saddam Hussein in possession of weapons of mass destruction for a few more months or years is not an option, not in a post-September 11th world. My colleagues, over three months ago this council recognised that Iraq continued to pose a threat to international peace and security, and that Iraq had been and remained in material breach of its disarmament obligations. Today Iraq still poses a threat and Iraq still remains in material breach. Indeed, by its failure to seize on its one last opportunity to come clean and disarm, Iraq has put itself in deeper material breach and closer to the day when it will face serious consequences for its continued defiance of this council. My colleagues, we have an obligation to our citizens, we have an obligation to this body to see that our resolutions are complied with. We wrote 1441 not in order to go to war, we wrote 1441 to try to preserve the peace. We wrote 1441 to give Iraq one last chance. Iraq is not so far taking that one last chance. We must not shrink from whatever is ahead of us. We must not fail in our duty and our responsibility to the citizens of the countries that are represented by this body.

Thank you, Mr. President. (18)

Words are spell and they are all concoction. Lies from another world that come through the void, the nothing, the , the double headed snake of Auryn. They keep everything shattered and should be expected to continue on and on if nothing) intervenes. Dead history is written in ink. Live history is written blood.

Somehow the summit seemed to get further and further away the more the vehicle climbed. It was like a bad dream. I could tell that everyone in the vehicle was getting restless. Everyone could sense that we were getting close to the trailhead. I could sense the anticipation. They all knew that they would soon be in the woods, on their way to endure a challenge that was outside of their normal experience. Were all of the necessary factors accounted for? Cold, hunger heat, dehydration, fatigue, precipitation, sun, exposure, navigation, endurance, elevation, shelter, companionship or hostility, wild animals and plants, so much could come into play. So much to consider. Especially if one is used to navigating the rodent maze of civilization which presents a similar set of obstacles that have to be dealt with by far different means. I have been around long enough to be able to deal with pretty much everything and I am not even really alive so most of this is lost on me anyway. Everyone else in the vehicle had obvious concerns and now was the time when all of their planning would be put to the test. There was a palpable sense of nervousness and excitement in the air. I could smell all of it in detail and it made me want to victimize one of these poor suckers. I exercised restraint because it would not be good for anyone to find out what I really am.

We turned a lazy corner and could see our destination emerge out of the trees. A great gate with black iron bars came into view and the vehicle drove through it. The gates to the mountain were closed behind us. It is an exclusive space behind them. *The mountain of the Lords house shall be established on the tops of the mountains and all nations shall flow to it. The first angel left the temple. The second poured his bowl on the sea and it became like the blood of corpses. Everything in the sea died. The third angel poured out his bowl...(8).*

After the vehicle parked I slowly gathered myself and then got up from the seat. Once my feet touched the ground and took my full weight upon them I felt very light. My head swooned and everything went white for a moment. After a few seconds I began to regain my composure. I was okay I told myself. My sixth sense was running a riot in my head telling me that I wasn't okay and something was seriously wrong. It is almost always correct but I continued to dismiss it. Just to be safe I did a thoughtful scan upon my surroundings. The "parking" area behind the gate was a large patch of impacted dirt and gravel that held up many vehicles which were haphazardly parked wherever they seemed to stop. There were backpackers dressed in all sorts of colorful, logo emblazoned, synthetic gear who were milling around in anticipation or fatigue. You could easily discern which ones were going up and which ones had just come back down. ***Men play at tragedy because they do not*** *believe* ***in the*** *reality* ***of the tragedy which is actually being staged in the civilized world (37).***

The open patch of dirt of the parking lot was encroached upon by the thick mountainous rainforest. Dark green and alive, it dropped its shadow all over the entire scene. Instructional signs bearing the rules and regulations of the wilderness stalked amongst the shadow mounted upon trunks and posts. Some signs were very small and some were enormous and spelled out their demands in large clear letters and in many different languages that few will actually take the time to read or understand if they actually read them. They are likely to read more from the surface of a tree or an attractive stone that is partially buried in the gravel. There were a handful of men dressed in green fatigues and militantly angled berets of different colors upon their cocked heads. They were decorated with an aggressive pin or patch that was placed in a strategic position somewhere on their shirt. They paced among all of the hikers carrying Kalashnikovs with metal folding stocks and banana clips that protruded from the bottom of the receiver like testicles. Their dark countenances scanned everything and everyone in a manner almost as thorough as my slowly revolving gaze.

Outside of the closed gates was a crowd of locals who were all clamoring to be let in so that they could get a job as a porter on one of the expeditions. Carrying bags uphill as a porter can be very good employment for people who lived in the area. Many times the teams that went climbing needed last minute help because there may have been a change in plans or a hired porter didn't show up due to illness or some other issue which could be anything. Things seem to operate on a whole different speed In Africa. It is sometimes difficult to understand so it better off not to try. This isn't just true of Africa I suppose because any place of human ingress and egress tends to appear totally chaotic. This form of order seems to be exaggerated in Africa.

I found myself a good place in the shade of a tree at the edge of the trampled dirt parking lot. I just watched and wondered. Why did I still feel so horrible? What was happening? There was nothing threatening me anywhere around as far as I could tell. I was still most likely the most threatening thing anywhere around. The men in fatigues with the Kalashnikovs were nothing to me. I could disappear, reappear, and devour them all in a matter of seconds. Their bullets were completely useless against me. I was the most dangerous thing around. I was the most dangerous thing to myself. I had some sort of active pathology. A disease. The arcane functions that were supposed to be keeping me alive were beginning to go berserk and they started breaking me down. I was being slowly destroyed from the inside out and I still was not aware. It was the feeling of my heart slowly coming back to life. The toxin of consciousness, the virus of the word in my blood was eating me like a cancer. The rivers and streams of death inside of me became blood. The word had already destroyed so much before me that I was just a small obstacle. The prophets had been killed and their blood was poured out on the earth. It was given to their murderers to drink. It is a just reward.

The fourth angel poured out his bowl upon the sun causing it to scorch everyone with its fire (8). Anticipation of death is worse than death itself. Consciousness is fractured. Literature is fractured. Destroyed. "The temple has fallen" quoth Danto, quoth Dante, quoth Stephen Daedalus ***"Hence when the clouds roll by, Jamey, a proudseye view is enjoyable of our mounding's mass, now Wallingstone national museum, with, in some greenish distance, the charmful water-loose country and the two quitewhite villagettes who hear show of themselves so gigglesomes minxt the ollyages, the prettilees! Penetrators are permitted into the museummound free. Welsh and the Paddy Patkinses, one shelenk! Dedismembers invadlids of old guard find poussepouse poussey-pram to state of the sort of their butt. For her passkey supply to the janitrix, the mistress Kathe. Tip. This way to the museyroom. Mind your hats goan in! Now yiz ar in the Willingdone Museyroom. This is a Prooshious, the Cap and the Soracer. This is the Prooshious. Up with your pike and fork! Tip. This is the bullet that byng the flag of the Prooshious. This is the ffrinch that fire the Bull that bang the flag of the Prooshious (5)".*** *I suck the life out of* everything I see and make it my own. That is the key to my kingdom.

Type equation here.

1:

For all who have wisdom let them discover the meaning of six hundred sixty six (8). The same thing repeated over and over, in this case six is repeated thrice. Three. Trinity. A great number of prophecy for the cock crowed thrice before dawn. Six is related to seven in that it is one lesser.

Seven is a number that can be seen as a reference to the creation and the creator. I am not referring to kabalistic numerology in this case. In old prophesy, seven can be understood as a maximum, a state of completion. Six is just short of it. Six days of creation and the seventh day of rest. Six is used in reference to the most beautiful part of creation. The first thing that was created that is just barely below the creator himself, Light. Genesis chapter one verse three. Illumination. The image of the creator. Lucifer and all of the men whose perception he controls. Six repeated thrice – an unholy trinity of sun (light) or king worship – is the number of man who was formed in the image of, the image of the creator. Man hacks together his own culture and his own society hence the repetition of six, for man cannot create anything but can only repeat what he sees that is already there. Man passes his image upon everything that is invented because invention is designed to interact with the body. Man creates culture. Cult. The same thing over and over is always just short of God when it reaches its highest possible ceiling. Six. Not seven. God works in sevens, not man. Seven seals, seven bowls, seven trumpets, seven days, The Sabbath being the seventh day which suggested the adoption of seven as the coefficient, so to say, for their appointment of all sacred periods. We thus find the 7th month ushered in by the Feast of Trumpets, and signalized by the celebration of the Feast of Tabernacles and the Great Day of Atonement; 7 weeks as the interval between the Passover and the Pentecost; the 7th year as the sabbatical year; and the year: succeeding 7X7 years as the Jubilee year. Seven days were appointed as the length of the feasts of Passover and Tabernacles; 7 days for the ceremonies of the consecration of priests, and so on; 7 victims to be offered on any special occasion, as in Balaam's sacrifice (Numbers 23:1) and especially at the ratification of a treaty, the notion of seven being embodied in the very term signifying to swear, literally meaning to do seven times (Genesis 31:28). Seven is used for any number completeness, as we say a few, or as a speaker says he will say two or three words when he means more.

In numerological (not kabalistic order the repetition of six strives for seven and seven destroys six. The number of the beast is destroyed by seven. Six, six, six. The number of man who creates through repetition of what is already there instead of pure creation. The repetition of six three times is a chant. A spell. An attempt to halt further progression by capture. An attempt to speak the unspeakable name with a voice that cannot pronounce it. The eternal repetition of six is the highest of man's achievements in the attempt to become godlike themselves. It is embodied in the cities of Cain. Babylon. The attempt to create the New Jerusalem. There is an impossibility to it all because reason and measure are the only tools available and they will never get beyond their limitations. All of this is only possible through utilization of the word which is the only spell of power in the land of the dead, this earth that is prowled by the creatures of the night. Creatures like myself. Creatures who love the dark ages, these medieval times which are still upon us. Few understand this condition because they refuse to look at the world around them. They won't look because it looks back. It screams its truth and pens the lies of the word that seeks to create a comfortable environment in this dreary cosmic outpost. It seeks to provide rest, escape, entertainment but to what end? We yell at out televisions. We scream at our radios. We curse the fucking asshole in the car behind and ahead. We type up an endless wimpy tirade on social media because that sort of whining really accomplishes a lot. Medieval minded creatures with weak technological enhancement. Everything is still in a medieval state. Just look around. The feudal caste system is alive and well in the "land of the free". The land of hypocrisy. The masses still wander aimless, homeless, paying their tribute to those above them – with pathetic excuses for pay – who trickle down urine across the backs of everyone below them. An intoxicating fluid used like amanita muscaria, Soma, used to confuse and control the entire social structure for the personal interest of those select few who undeservingly wrested their power from the life force of everyone and everything that they could. Vampires. Bloodsuckers rule. The C.E.O is obligated by law to cater to the interest of the shareholders first and foremost. Destroy everything else until this is accomplished. Vampires feeding vampires. What does it matter to them? The same thing over and over across time, not because of success but because of inertia and violence. The striving of lowly beings for the illusion of godlike power. The same thing over and over. Repetition...

666

Every architectural form has a spirit. This is why the old masons built a brick cell that walled a victim into the foundations of every building that they erected. Every age has a spirit for the same reason. There are far more than one victim in this form of architecture, bricked into the temporal loop of their existence. The spirit of the age may well be a demon. If this age of contemporary capitalism had a spirit or a religion what would it be? What would its deities look like? How would they be represented? Fame? Fortuna? What would the altar of these spirits have upon it? Campbell's soup cans? Images of Marylyn? Images of violent death and warfare? Advertisements for designer drugs? Images of Mickey Mouse? It sounds absurd but it is true. Atheists act like they are the smartest shits that have ever farted but they are just as attached to irrational bullshit as anyone else. Many are in love with The Force and secretly wish that they were Jedi or Vulcans. They vehemently deny any accusations of the sort but they still worship irrational powers that are beyond their control. Why else would the consent to put their lives in the hands of politics, science, entertainment, and technology in the way that most do? They just have lower standards than the average religious maniac. In the same way that most religious folks do not totally comprehend what they believe in a historical or even philosophical way most atheists do not comprehend the inner workings of the technology, politics, science, or even the entertainment that they worship. They are content to not know while they idolize banalities like sports or mechanization etc. etc. What a tragically sad worldview but the spirit of this age is indeed tragically sad.

I spend a lot of time in cemeteries. One day I was walking through a very large and well-kept cemetery. It was somewhere in Buffalo, New York. I believe it is called *Forest Lawn.* In this cemetery there is a vast section that is dedicated to the building of small mausoleums. I enjoy passing time in places like this. I have no idea why nor will I begin to try to explain it. On one occasion I decided to peer into the window of one of these mausoleums. There were drawers on either side built into the wall and the center aisle was empty. I assume the drawers were places to house corpses but one can never be sure. They could be filled with Easter eggs, or chickens – whatever came first – for all that I knew. A holiday for birds and bunnies that somehow equate to death and resurrection. Another example of the nonsense that pagans inflict upon their children for reasons unknown. They just do it *because everyone else is.* They bury themselves for the same reason. They should consume the dead if they want a ritual that represents their beliefs. No. Instead they do as all have done before but have forgotten why. Repetition. Six. Six. Six. Six. Six. Six. Six. Six. Six. The middle of the far wall of the mausoleum I peered into was fenestrated with stained glass. In any other time and place I would expect the design in the glass to be a representation of Christ, or Mary, or a New Testament scene, or a Jewish star or an abstraction. The stained glass in this mausoleum had a different choice to eternally watch over the dead. The design immortalized in this hallowed hall was nothing less than a colorful representation of Mickey Mouse. The spirit. An entire society, an entire world, ripe for destruction because it does not have a care in the world. Not even for its own destruction. Capitalism is designed to kill. It is the disease of addiction embodied in words which is magnified and manipulated by entertainment and bureaucracy. Wars will be fought to the very last penny to defend the right to self-destruction. The last scene in full metal jacket is very revealing and I don't think it gets noticed for just how horrific it really is. The Vietnam war was fought to defend the Gods of capitalism at the great expense of human life. The last scene is filmed in the dark of night. There is a fire raging in the background giving off a spectral light. Out of this apocalyptic scene, a swarm of dark figures carrying rifles marches through. They march and sing in cadence. They sing the theme song to the Mickey Mouse Club. Perfect analogy. Do you get it? Do you see what pointless destruction is wrought by the demonic illusions of freedom and victory? That ancient pagan goddess, that ungraspable spirit in the air that has given ideal promises and has delivered less than ideal results. The bricks of Babylon's towers are still being piled upon one another. They are almost to the heavens. Emptiness and the tyranny, oppression, and slavery offered to these pagan altars has gleefully been accepted by everyone. Especially the atheists. There is no such thing as the belief in nothing because something will indefinitely fill that void. Something nonsensical. I have been watching this process develop over the ages. I have watched the rise and fall of many empires. The millennia of existence that I have endured has accidently made me an expert on human societies. I have watched the same thing happen over and over. There have been an infinite amount of faces for the same thing. Beelzebub watches from Orion. The Earth belongs to Lucifer, the beast, Iblis, Fortuna, Nike, The spirit of the age. Always changing always the same. ***The last and greatest destruction of the last and greatest of human dreams (4).*** In relation to time, "If" is actually the longest word in the human language. There is no such thing as fiction.

∞

Time consumes consumers. Selfies of Kim Kardashian are the pinnacle of art. What, if anything, will she remember when she is withered like a raisin from sun exposure? Photographers become famous for fuzzy pictures of weddings and babies. It is devoid of all meaning, potentially nightmarish and disgustingly pathetic yet very apt. No one will ever notice their emptiness until it is too late. Everything has been sucked dry. The man dying under the shadow of Kilimanjaro who Hemingway wrote of lamented that he never accomplished anything because society and its nonsense distracted his life so much that he never began thinking about what he had actually done and more importantly, not done, and it all came in a rush of emotion, way too little way too late. The writhing of the spirit in the flesh is toxified by entertainment and banality that has risen to religious heights. Success is failure. The spirit of the age is consumption and it consumes all who attempt to flirt with it. There is nothing to express except emptiness and banality. Society has reached a point where it has become terminal. The collective mind has reduced itself to raising up the smell of everyone else as a problem of society. The sheep have been herded into the pen and they don't even see the gun at their neck for their government that they actually believe that they voted for has stripped away every responsibility that they have except the monopoly upon violence through the creation and enforcement of law. All else is handed to the private sector which is even worse of a prospect of control through power for they can just base themselves out of another country and give everyone the middle finger. Everyone went willingly into the pen. They wanted emptiness the entire time. It is making me ill. Do you see why I want to end it all? It is already over. There is very little left to even live for except total destruction. I will gladly sacrifice my status as undead, all the powers that come with it and my false immortality to escape this fruitless existence. Aldous Huxley, George Orwell, and David Wallace all together could not even dream up such a dark utopia yet here it is here right in front of us. It is so foul that no one who is experiencing it can even bear to look. This is the emptiness. The vacuous death that is lurking as a black hole of nothing amidst the stars that float and beckon behind the eyes of mortals. The void within the void is not a double negative equating in positive. It is hyper negative. The present is appalling. The only thing that consumers can tolerate is the future or the past because they can inject their feeble fantasies and empty dreams upon them. The eternal present is intolerable. Incomprehensible. Pure sensation that flows through the fingers like air. Ungraspable and ineffable. Desert sands blow across the oceans and land in the most unlikely places. Everything done is working toward destruction.

∞

The seventh angel poured out his bowl and a mighty shout came from the Temple in Heaven (8). ***That was the first joke of Willingdone, tic for tac. Hee,hee,hee! This is me Belchum in his twelvemile cowchooks, weet, tweet and Stampforth foremost, footing the camp for the jinies. Drink a slip, drankasup, for hes as sooner buy a Guinness than he's stale a store stout. This is Rooshioius balls. This is a ttrinch. This is misletropes. This is Canon Futter with poppynose after a hundred days' indulgence. This is the blessed. This is lipoleums in the rowdy howses. This is the Willingdone, by splinters of the Cork, order fire. Tonnerre! (Bullspear! Play!) This is Camelry, this is floodens, this is the solphereens in action, this is their mobbily, this is panikburns. Almeidagad! Arthiz too loose! This is Willingdon cry. Brum! Brum! Cumbrum! This is the jinnies cry. Underwetter (5)!*** "*It is finished (8)*" then lightning flashed and thunder crashed and rolled. *There was an earthquake greater than ever before in human history. The great city of Babylon split in three pieces. Babylon the great mother of all prostitutes and obscenities in the world. I could see that she was drunk with blood (8).*

The ***seven*** heads of the beast represents the ***seven*** hills of the city where this woman once ruled: Rome. Aventinus, Coelius, Capitolinus, Esquilinus, Palatinus, Quirinalis, Viminalis. The Babylon of old has mutated and changed as time progressed. These names are ghosts in the air and their names have changed slowly over time as they shed them like molting crustaceans. Every new name developed further and further as the ghosts played their games. They went on and on and they could not see the end because they were drunk upon their own mirth. Their new names issued greater and greater intoxication as they were collected. More and more people became drunk on their glorious mysteries. They can be breathed in and then exhaled many times in the form of words. They can ride upon speech and direct attention. Now, in parallel worlds, they can be named: Unitus, Muncius, Pylax, Lirr, Baureo, Sheeraek, and Mayestril. In in our world they have acquired other names for the moment. ***Seven*** summits for ***seven*** destructions. They have no agenda besides themselves. The misery created is only entertainment.

At first these ghosts were not attached to the Earth like us Vampires are. They could come and go as they pleased from planet to planet and from star to star. They animated the constellations and gave them form. This is a secret of astrology and celestial navigation. They love high places and give spirit to them by their mere presence. Men seek them for communion without knowing why. There is a power to be shared in these places. Secrets are exchanged but we know who always gets the better side of the deal. Ghosts need men as much as men need ghosts. Ghosts give men ideals and men give ghosts energy and attention through supplication which assuages their corporeal addiction to entertainment. Men create unending madness. Men create more ghosts. Their warfare is a spiritual circus. A carnival of struggles to manage the spirit, the ghost inside the body. The body is compelled to visit the high places to find a sort of solace, justification for the pointless Coney Island of their existence. Ours is an inexplicable condition.

The seven hills were asked and they answered with more inexplicable reasons. They changed name and place. Where did they come from in the first place? The dust of blew from the summit of Moriah and landed in East Africa in the Eden of Ngorongoro. Some say that Jerusalem's seven hills are Mount Scopus, Mount Olivet and the Mount of Corruption (all three are peaks in a mountain ridge that lies east of the old city), Mount Ophel, the original Mount Zion, the New Mount Zion and the hill on which the Antonia Fortress was built. They are not totally correct but have come very close. The best place to see it all is 1.) Mt. Scopus. The other six are: 2.) Mt. Moriah, 3.) Mt. Zion, 4.) Mt.Ophel, 5.) The Mount of Olives, 6.) Mt. Akra, 7.) Mt. Bezetha; Golgotha (a place of mystery that has not yet been correctly identified). Whatever seven are identified it does not matter because the ghosts have moved on. These were the names they used at that time. They moved to more appropriate places to tempt humanity as time passed.

Time and space expanded from this concentrated point in the center of the Earth's landmass. They stayed concentrated for some time as power went from here to Babylon and eventually to Rome. In Babylon they were all in one place. They were the tower itself. It is the only time that they were together. They needed to stay this way to concentrate their early influence after their first move. Nebuchadnezzar's Babylon was the largest city in the world, covering about 4 square miles (10 square km). The Euphrates, which has since shifted its course, flowed through it, the older part of the city being on the east bank. There the central feature was Esagila, the great temple of Marduk, with its associated ziggurat Etemenanki. The latter, popularly known as the Tower of Babel, had a base 300 feet (91 meters) on a side, and its ***seven stages***, the uppermost a temple in blue glaze, reached a total height equal to that of its base. Each ghost lived in each stage. After they left the city of Babylon it went to ruin. Rome was their playground for some time and then they expanded out.

These ghosts danced and vaulted and transformed and changed their Names and landed gracefully upon clusters of mountains elsewhere.

When they got bored they leapt, gracefully flipping volitant, mercurial, and lubricious to find the next place to play their games. Though soon enough they got bored, choleric, and incurvate from being clustered together for so long. They started looping further and further outward but they could not stop playing their macabre games. Their play had turned neurotic but they couldn't stop. They had taken it too far but there was nothing else for them to do. They formed hooves and claws and talons and multiple legs and mandibles growing more fearsome with every bounding leap as they tried to outdo each other with every new incarnation. They vied for higher and higher places and the first to land on spot in the most grotesque form would gain control of whatever remote pinnacle or gendarme, or aguille they could find that was nearest. ***"Look my friends, behold by the sign of this risen prick what a flame that passion described ignites me (5)."*** They spiraled further and further out like swarming starlings. Their effervescence ejaculated trails of cloud and miasma around the summit of their newly coveted victory. The mountains grew foul haloes which were left behind from the residue of their wrath. The biting ephemera of love lost for something, or someone greater. Their games became crusades but they were so involved that they no longer could tell the difference yet it didn't matter because they were ensnared by the process. Wailing and blind to all else they tromboned low bass notes of wrath that manifested lightning and mackerel sky. Woe to him who dares attempt to dethrone one. They made sorties outward from their conquests but could not gain foothold in the territory of another. One would pop up in the backyard of the other wielding testicles between armpits and legs combined with a chest covered with teats while they deftly spun double headed halberds only to be vanquished by even greater displays of fierceness like the display of elephant heads attached to human bodies with twelve arms protruding out of the torso in all directions, each wielding a scimitar or if not that they donned grimacing faces which sprouted horns, and arms made of lances and pikes with blue puckered, vein traced, anal mouths that erupted fluorescent brown paste. Leprous and dissipated the loser would fall into dust and be blown back to their summits of power. None could ever totally destroy the other so their games went on and on. They invited the living to dare visit their household with dreams of glory only to suck the life force out of them so that the ghosts could become further empowered in their next attempt at annexation. Sadly none could ever win in another's realm but they tried as much as they could. They remained masters of their own realms, imprisoned by their power. The only time a living being could successfully visit their keep was when the ghosts were already busy consuming the vital forces of another poor misguided soul who had traveled across the world to attempt to climb and take part in their mythical games. This worked to their benefit because it gave the mortals a sense that they could actually do it. So more and more humans came to test their luck or do homage. More and more humans became consumed and their mad consciousness submitted to, and became part of these ever growing forces of spiritual madness. No longer could the ghosts lightly spring out into the cosmos. No longer could they visit the constellations which they used to frequent for their rest. They no longer cared for anything else besides their territorial games and attempted usurpations. They became entrapped in the place that geography fixed upon their heavily laden psychosis. It took some time to manifest this condition but once it began it was inescapable and terminal. They rained down tears of imprisonment and love of their place of residence in the form of glaciers, and floods, and avalanches, and monsoons, and cold that erupted from their mourning hearts. No longer was their game an act of freedom but was it ever? It was hard to say – ***yes it is an old, old, story: the tale of a Treestone with one Ysold; of a mountainman held by tent pegs and his pal waterloosed on the run; of what Cadman could but Badman wouldn't; of any Genoa man against any Venice-***

Venus; of why Kate takes charge of the waxworks. But let us now drop this jiggery-pokery and talk straight turkey, if you please, Let us be done with hearing what others have said: let us see for ourselves all there may remain to be seen. I am a worker, anxious if you please; you are a pillar of society, unctuous to the police; we cannot see eye to eye. Yet one cannot help noticing that more than half the in this MS run north-south, while the others go west-east. Such crossing is pre-Christian. But the home grown Shillelagh as an aid to calligraphy shows a distinct advance from savagery to barbarism (5). They resented their new condition of imprisonment and as a result they killed and consumed more and more and became more and more heavily laden until they were so cold and invisible that they became one with the very rocks that they perched upon with their talons. Their influence washed down the flutings and aretes and cols and cirques and couloirs and then behind the bergschrunds and seracs to sub-glacially percolate into kame and through the talus and scree, the whole way picking up spiritual and physical infections like Giardia lambia, where it all collected in tarns and kettles and appeared so placid and fresh to the lost observer.

All of this biology and malignant force was begun with the dripping residue from the spiritual malady of the entrapped ghosts. Inconspicuous violent toxins putrefied the water that scintillated with malice and wrath and went unnoticed by the visitor who was intoxicated by the instilled vaporizations, the altitude, and the endorphins created by their personal exertions which brought them to this place. From these petulant, yet beautiful mountainous pools, the mercurial substance ran further down through rivulets and streams and watersheds where it all flowed around the eskers, through gorges, and over waterfalls – small and large – then eventually formed into ibon or zungenbecken. ***The weakness of our faculties, the corruption of our souls leads us to these abominations (5).*** It was only a matter of time before it gained more and more momentum to form estuaries which dumped their spiritually effluent flotsam into arterial rivers that rolled with colliding bed boulders below rapids and eddies and boils and hydraulics and lateral waves and oxbows which created the thalweg and resultant riparian siltation under ovular stones piled upon the shore that were polished to reveal an enchanting series of light bands encircling their perimeter – in rows of twos or threes – which were special amongst the tiny shapeless grey tablets that upon further inspection also became compelling as they glistened with microscopic mineral refractions that were the crystallized residue of ghostly spiritual rage and trauma distilled from the high places.

All contained a part of the Word even in this chaos. The love of the world, Anna Livia Plurabelle. The ***widow who serves the feast at the wake: Grampupus is fallen down grinny sprids the boord. A mother hen who scratches out of a dung heap the torn scrap of a gossipacious letter filled with all the secrets of a womans heart, a bewitching letter, which, only partially recovered, tantalizes with its life riddle through the very pages of the book, and is, in fact but a dreamlike emanation of this untitled mamafesta memorializing the Mosthighest (5).*** From there the spiritually laden solution continued onward as it grew and grew like capillaries into arterioles, into arteries and venules, into veins but where was it all going? It all collected in the trunk of the river where gravity could bring it no lower and this was the antithesis of the very summits from which it all sprang forth. ***All flows a river and every river is embraced by its river banks (4).*** This is where everything roiled and collided and created newer and more multiplied toxins that were formed by the combination of the natural and now artificial sources of sewage and fertilizer and any other imaginable chemical combination that only helped amplify the malady that was already developing. A peristalsis of satanic orgy, geology, and physics erupted into great rivers which bewitched every life form anywhere near. They all needed it. They were magnetized because every cell in their being screamed to be a part of this unfolding tragedy and consume its irrational madness. The elusive unspeakable and constantly emanating. ***The list of names concludes with an advertisement: First and Last only True Account all about the Honorary Mirsu Earwicker, L.S.D. and the Snake(Nuggets!), by a Woman of the World who only can tell Naked Truths about a Dear Man and all his Conspirators, how the all Tried to Fall him Putting it all around Lucalizod about Privates Earwicker and a Pair of Sloppy Sluts plainly Showing all the Unmentionability falsely Accusing about the Raincoats (5).*** The bodies of every creature were just like the stones on the bank. Crystalized with spiritual discord and confusion, totally entrapped. All animals were drawn. They slithered and twitched and lunged and flopped and rolled and traveled their bobbing multi-legged gait back and forth alongside the water that grew and throbbed as it went further and further before it became so laden with toxins that it began to acquire a noticeable salinity and grew brackish. Once this happened its forward momentum began to break up from all the alluvial deposits that had collected over the millennia. It was so supersaturated with its own rage that it could not carry itself even further and the once mighty trunk was forced to submit to its own weight. It could not go on like that for very long. Its power was bound to dissipate and it that is exactly what happened. It did this in the presence of its inevitable conclusion. The ocean was what appeared to be the ultimate end of its journey but it wasn't. Before it got there it separated back into channels and canals and dumped its contents into subaqueous and subaerial upper delta plains and lower delta plains and active deltas and abandoned deltas that were always changing with the rivers force against the limits of tidal inundation creating a doily-like lacework of capillaries and arterioles, and venules, that mutated through progradation, aggradation, and transgression, to create the grasping claw that roots the entire spiritual malady to the earth through its final ejaculation into the sea which creates arcuate, birdfoot, cuspate, and estuarine forms that will metamorphose throughout time as they desperately claw and grasp at this foothold which has become the footstool of the ghostly power. It is ripped and tugged about by all the tidal forces as each new attack and defense on high has been resolved and initiated by the ethereal war games of these seven ancient ghosts who together are now allowed to run rampant through the entire creation, impregnated in the blood of the river. Water is useless without blood. The voids of Auryn are as vast as the sea and are as dark as fresh blood. An ocean for Pisces to swim yet tied together by a point. Alrescha is that point. She is also named Auryn.

Sexuality is used against us. Every human needs it and capitalism feeds off reproduction. Sexuality and violence are its greatest spell. Every billboard is plastered with it. Once a birth occurs the mindfucked parents must obey. They must conform. The toxins that roil in their blood build to a point that they can no longer resist submission. They fall into the river if they were not already in it. Every billboard on the side of the road is passed like the boulders rolling under the water of the river.

Above all she is the river, ***always changing yet ever the same, the flux which bears all life on its current principally, she is the river Liffey but she is also all the rivers of the world: the heavenly Ganges, the fruitful Nile, the teeming Irrawaddy, the mysterious Nyanza, the delinquent Mississippi, the deceitful Saranac, the flooded, bulbous, and entropic St. Lawrence, The Haughty Hudson, she is the circular river of time, flowing past Eve and Adam in the Pishon, Gihon, Tigris, and Euphtates in the first sentence of the book, bearing in her flood the debris of dead civilizations and the seeds of crops and cultures yet to come. The circular flow of the river Liffey illustrates her cycle of transformation. Her brooklet source in the Wicklow hills finds her as a young girl, dancing gaily, a delicious nymph. Passing the Chapelizod***

of the tavern, she is a comely, matronly stream. Still farther on, running through the city, she is an old haggard scrubwoman, carrying away the filth of the city. At last she flows back to Father Ocean, from whence she rises again in mist, to descend in showers and become once more the sparkling mountain stream. Corso and recorso (36).

But that is not the end. That is not where it is all going. It is not the final act. ***The prouts who will invent a writing there ultimately is the poeta, still more learned, who discovered the raiding there originally. That's the point of eschatology our book of kills reaches for now in soandso many counterpoint words. What can't be coded can be decorded if an ear aye seize what no eye ere grieved for. Now, the doctrine obtains, we have occasioning cause causing effects and affects occasionaly recausing altereffectcs (5).*** The water is tainted from the very beginning so this leaves little hope of escape. ***A crone gathering fragments into a basket. Isis picking up the dismembered body of her brother husband Osiris (5).*** Its final destination is an arcane transformation. It is taken into the system of every living being and creates blood. This births and maintains irrational dreams and unachievable goals in the minds of men because every one is the hero in their own story. Tragic, comic, or both it is manipulated. The blood carries these toxins to the brain and creates thought. Whatever language the thought is in does not matter because each is unwieldy. This is the tower of Babylon. A heaping mountain of rotting flesh, one corpse piled upon another. It is supported by reason itself, language, the infinite attempt to gain godlike power through the structures of repetition in the hopes that one day it will build beyond the place of the Unspeakable name. No matter how impossible it is, it one day hopes, futilely, to wrest reality for itself. Love is the ultimate goal and nothing is more misunderstood for there is no love without loss.

∞

The seven ghostly hills are now confined in their permanent resting place far above everything else. They have changed their names and faces many times but they are still the same. No longer do they quaintly encircle Rome or Jerusalem. They have spread out across the entire planet. There is not one continent that has escaped their presence. There are seven continents and each ghost has claimed one to itself. The seven headed beast of Babylon is everywhere. Every land mass is tainted. Every bloodstream is corrupted. Language is the symptom of the infection. Language beats in the heart and throbs in the brain. Everyone is corrupted and virally infected. Some so thoroughly that they seek to climb to the source of it all and potentially be sacrificed to the power of these spirits. Hubris is a mandatory quality of the mountaineer. They dare attempt to go to such inhospitable places for their own self-aggrandizement. There is no other reason for this activity. They may spit banal explanations but that is because there is no excuse for this behavior. They are drawn to the summits to get as close to their perceived Gods as is possible. They are not gods though. They are ghosts. They are themselves still. They are undead. Like me. I have felt the development of their games for a very long time and it is humorous to me. I have been in Babylon forever. The entire world is under its influence. Each continent tainted from top down. The seven names of the spirits responsible are now *Aconcagua* in South America, *Elbrus* in Europe, *Carstenz* in Oceana, *Vinson* in Antarctica, *Denali* or *McKinley* in North America, ***Kilimanjaro*** in Africa, *Everest*, also known as *Chomolungma* or *Sagarmatha* in Asia.

∞

I stand at the very foot of the African giant. The shattered crater that oversaw man's evolution. There may be more ghosts here than upon the flanks of any one of these other summits because there has been people here longer than any other place. Many have died upon the flanks of Sagarmatha but far more time passed by with human presence under the shadow of Kilimanjaro. People have been attempting the summit and subsequently dying on Sagarmatha since Mallory and Irvine disappeared to pave the way for Hillary and Tenzing. The death toll since then is very little compared to all of the death upon the plains below Kilimanjaro. The ghost who resides here in Africa is and has been the bloodiest of all. This is the same ghost who was once named Golgotha and Capotilinus. Ancient sources refer the name Capotilinus to caput ("head", "summit") and the tale was that, when laying the foundations for the temple of Saturn, the head of a man was found. Some sources even saying it was the head of some Tolus or Olus. The Capitolium was regarded by the Romans as indestructible, and was adopted as a symbol of eternity. Golgotha was the same ghost, the place of the skull, the symbol of eternity. This ghost is perhaps the most chaotic of the seven.

Mark: *And they brought him to the place called Gol'gotha (8).*

Matthew: *And when they came to a place called Gol'gotha* (8).

Luke: *And when they came to the place which is called The Skull, there they crucified him, and the criminals, one on the right and one on the left (8).*

John: *So they took Jesus, and he went out, bearing his own cross, to the place called the place of a skull, which is called in Hebrew Gol'gotha (8).*

In the Douay-Rheims Version (a Roman Catholic English translation of the Bible), Luke 23:33 reads: *"And when they were come to the place which is called Calvary, they crucified him there; and the robbers, one on the right hand, and the other on the left."*

Other summits have other sorts of ghost but they are not the ancient seven. *Annapurna* is the goddess of the harvest and has reaped many souls but it is not as old or powerful as any of the seven, seductive as it may be. So many strong wills have been devoured and transformed into specters that are left high in the Himalaya. The desire to commune with these spirits has driven many to seek these places, even at the risk of dying and becoming one. The death toll upon any mountain is significant due to its utter pointlessness. It is the example of how these ghosts have infected the blood of men and made them mad for the sake of entertainment. These ghosts do not need to consume any life form because they are ghosts. The do it because they can, because it gives them power and glee. Many lives are lost yet some victims escape consumption only to wander the flanks of the mountains that they perished upon. They have become ghosts themselves. There is more unrest and residual energy in the mountains than any other place. The mountains seem peaceful do they? They are the definition of lifeless chaos. Inversion. These wandering ghosts who have not yet been consumed by one of the seven can be human spirits, animal spirits, or alien visitors from other planets. Summits are frequently visited by planetary and interdimensional aliens. They can observe without being noticed from these high perches. Many perish in their attempts and they stay trapped there as well. Humans are not the only biological form used to inveigle souls or spirits. There are countless races and beings scattered all across time and space that writhe with spirit and a shattered perception that needs understanding. No matter what they started as they all are undead. On this planet they are all powerless against Nosferatu. We Nosferatu are the emperors of the land and I am their liege lord. We are the angels of darkness and we go where we choose and force all into our submission. This is our planet and all of its blood is ours. At least that is what most of us in The Kult think.

There is not a place in the world that is more haunted that Kilimanjaro, the ghost that was formerly Golgotha and Capotilinus. All of the planets most powerful spiritual energy has been witnessed by this being. It also has assimilated all the souls of all the African ancestors. Their energy has risen out of the plains, the deserts and the forests only to be caught on their way up and entrapped by the “Great Mountain” or the “White Mountain” as it is sometimes called. There has been so much irrational behavior that has visited this place even before the ghost of Golgotha has descended.

This volcano and the Ngorongoro volcano both witnessed and absorbed the energy of a drama of the remote past due to the activity of a force known only as Xenu. I had already mentioned this but I must repeat it for the sake of clarity, chant, spell, incantation, and reinforcement so that no harm comes to me. This document is a spell (perhaps the final spell for me and who knows what else) and everything in it must be how it is for it to work so I apologize for whatever repetitions and redundancies and incorrect language that it contains. It is there for arcane reasons.

Xenu (/'zi:nu:/), also called Xemu, was, according to Scientology founder L. Ron Hubbard, the dictator of the "Galactic Confederacy" who 75 million years ago brought billions of his people to Earth (then known as "Teegeeack") in DC-8-like spacecraft, stacked them around volcanoes, and killed them with hydrogen bombs. Official Scientology scriptures hold that the thetans (immortal spirits) of these aliens adhere to humans, causing spiritual harm.

These events are known within Scientology as "Incident II" and the traumatic memories associated with them as "The Wall of Fire" or "R6 implant". The narrative of Xenu is part of Scientologist teachings about extraterrestrial civilizations and alien interventions in earthly events, collectively described as "space opera" by Hubbard. Hubbard detailed the story in Operating Thetan level III (OT III) in 1967, warning that the "R6 implant" (past trauma) was "calculated to kill (by pneumonia, etc.) anyone who attempts to solve it" (18).

∞

Kilimanjaro is yet another chant. Another meaningless word. A moniker invented by the zeitgeist of tourist culture. No one in particular made it up but it was manifested. It is something that could sound like Swahili but is actually meaningless. An advertisement of sorts designed to inspire dreams and behaviors. People who know nothing or everything about it can equally be intrigued. It is a word of power. Another blood virus. This is not simply a westernized affliction upon a third world society. It happens everywhere. An example that instantly comes to mind for me is the word Saranac. It denotes a chain of lakes and rivers in northern New York. Many simply suspect it was a Native American name and leave it at that. Some of the early guides in the region used it to tell romantic stories to their urban patrons who paid for a wilderness experience. Around campfires they would tell their audience that it was a Native American term that means "cluster of stars". This intrigued and inspired the souls of the patrons and made them feel like they were communing with some greater force that lived in the natural environment. These forces are indeed there but the word "Saranac" is actually a concoction. It is meaningless and most certainly was not used by any tribe in the area. It is myth. There are countless examples of this phenomena all over the world and it is a minor invocation of the spell of the Name. *Kilimanjaro,* a meaningless word. Just like *Ngorongoro.* Speaking these forms of words is very much akin to the process of speaking in tongues. It is this repetitive process that allows one to come as close as possible to the discovery of something greater than language. The power that secretly hides behind language. The singularity of word. The Unspeakable Name. The idea that the word "Kilimanjaro" can translate to the "Great" mountain or the "White" mountain is fodder only for curious tourists who need to rationally explain their experience of nothing. It may indeed be a great white mountain but this word does not describe it. Only ***perception*** does. ***Perception*** inevitably leads – kicking and screaming – to the inexplicable singularity that is the wellspring of all words.

As I stood at foot of the Kilimanjaro massif I considered the ghosts who resided here, some of whom I was very familiar with most of whom I was not. I have known about the seven great mountain ghosts and all the victims who roamed around them that had not yet been consumed. Perhaps these wanderers were distasteful to the summit ghost. Perhaps they successfully hid from the summit. Perhaps they were underlings of some sort. There are armies of undead and incredible places of residual psychic energy all over this mountain, and all over all of the great mountains in the world. I had taken it all for granted the entire time I was in Tanzania. To me they were just as much a part of the environment as the air, earth, trees, and grasses. Only at the beginning of my ascent did I consider that they could possibly be responsible for what caused my unease. They were only ghosts after all and I could easily dismiss them. What were they to me? I am a Nosferatu. I am one of the emperors of the undead. We Nosferatu sneer at all of the ghosts, zombies, whights, gremlins, goblins, lyches, wraiths, mummies, dragur, jaingshi, and will-o-wisps etc, etc. In every normal circumstance they are all under our command. We could dismiss any one of them with a twitch or an off gaze. We frequently used them for our own purposes. For me to consider simple ghosts as the source of my unease was ludicrous. At that point, as I suffered from my unknown unease it began to make sense to me. There were much more than one or two ghosts around me. In fact there were legions of them. Not only that but they certainly knew that I was on my way and trying to enter their realm. They could feel and see my thoughts better than I could at the moment. I still had not the slightest clue that I had been compromised from my visit to Ngorongoro. I had been in a dream state ever since I had left that original crater. I still did not know who I killed or how I did it when I was still in my hotel room the previous night. I know that I unleashed an atom bomb of arcane energy throughout the entire area. Just the spells used to dissipate all of the left over viscera was felt by every undead anywhere near. I was already on my way to a second death. It was awakening inside me with my infection. I was losing control. It was a dream. Nothing mattered anymore. It wasn't a dream though. It was really happening.

Again I thoroughly looked around the parking lot at the trailhead. The climbers aimlessly wandered. The vehicles were all parked in their random spots on the packed dirt. The guards wandered with their Kalashnikovs. The potential porters swarmed at the outside gate waiting to be chosen as a beast of irrational burden only to be paid a small amount for their enormous efforts. The forest throbbed with life. It was virtually fluorescent. It was saturated with powerful energy. Life and death both worked together and formed an irrational bond. They became one and the same. It was a form of energy that I had never truly experienced and if I did I did not notice it. I couldn't help but notice now because I was actively searching. I saw a single ghost leaning upon a tree. It just stood and watched. Shortly after I saw another on the other side of the parking lot. As I looked around more and more of them began to present themselves. They did nothing but watch but their presence was beginning to be overwhelming. They were all there for me. No one else who was there and alive could see any of this spectral activity. I could not tell at all what they were there for. I am not even sure that any one of them knew anything besides the fact that they had to do something. They are typically cowards and for them to present themselves to me should have been enough of a warning. Even living spirits from the trees began to peek out at me. I watched the presence seethe and grow and reinforce itself in reaction to my every movement, to my every thought. The spectral presence was shared by all of these individuals. Together they were not individual at all but a unity of force and the addition of each to the throng reinforced and strengthened the ones who were already there. I felt its attempts at invading me. Everything around me was animated with presence. Alive and dead at the same time. I felt so strange. I was alive too. I had transformed because of my virus. My heart was waking up. It was too much to realize or even admit at the time so I did not pay attention to what was happening to me. I longed for Auryn. I missed her so much. My heart leapt. The situation was overwhelming. The feelings were overwhelming. The spirits, the ghosts, the will-o-wisps of this forest all slowly revealed themselves. They mockingly invited me in to their domain. How dare they even think of approaching me in such a manner? I was the undead master of every space I occupied. I could turn them all into dust and blow them away with a flick of my wrist. Or could I? Of course, I told myself. I was in control. I could destroy anything outside of me. It was the reason for my existence. Pure destruction. Only destruction will help. It has been my only friend. I kept on telling myself this but I truly felt weak. There was something else going on that I did not see. I could do nothing. All of my spells were difficult or lost. The rational continuum and focus upon the words that cast them was not working. All thought was halted. I was struck down. The massing army of ghosts halted me. For a moment everything melted in a blinding unity. Where was Auryn when I needed her? She was lost in the voids forever. Love is what I was left with. I felt everything. Every tiny shift in the breeze. Every photon that streamed over my body. Every endorphin from every actual person that was there along with the ghosts. I wanted to peel my skin off, escape and display my undead wrath. I wanted to throw off the thin suit of skin which I was enveloped in, turn it to ash, and fly out of this chrysalis of blood and death and then reform myself, immortal, outside of it with my wings of fire and sword of starlight and void. I could not. I was confined. I experienced the flames that were trapped inside. I felt internal combustion for the first time in millennia. I now carried a fire inside. Life was beginning again. Love is hatred. Love is loss.

∞

I still did not know what I was becoming when the ghosts appeared at the Kilimanjaro trailhead. It was happening very slowly. Even now, after the fact, as I cast this spell upon paper it has not completely transformed me. That process will only be complete once I return to the summit and cast this final spell. Love compels me. I miss Auryn too much. Once I went to Africa I realized that she was gone. The voids of her absence which I once reveled in as victory has cast me into a hell to haunt me and offer no consolation. I wish nothing more to dive in and find her. If I do now, in my undead state, I will only find a parallel earth that she is not in, just like this one. She is somewhere else. She IS somewhere else. She has mastered oblivion and I am beckoned there. God invites me to stop his work, to end him and myself in our present state and form a greater love, the most incomprehensible state there is. She was my reason for waiting on this planet for as long as I did and we were only together for such a short time and now she is gone...***But to that second circle of sad hell,***

Where 'mid the gust, the whirlwind, and the flaw
Of rain and hail-stones, lovers need not tell
Their sorrows. Pale were the sweet lips I saw,
Pale were the lips I kiss'd, and fair the form
I floated with, about that melancholy storm (18).

Ayrun and I were Paulo and Francesca and we lived in Gradara for only a short time. I am predisposed to my task and it is the act of a greater will than my own. Do you know what Wotan Wills? I must bring my weapon of knowledge and seek out the deity that hides her from me. HE IS LOVE. Incomprehensible, Awful, Inspiring, Untouchable like the flames that burn me up from inside. Redemption is what I seek through this intolerable spell that I weave. I must cast off everything that I desire in this world. I must draw my sword and cut it off my body with a true word of defiance. Here reveals my secret. Here reveals the true performance of the needed arcane art that opens the higher dimensions, reforms ***perception*** into *reality* and conquers God and His opposite, fusing them back together into one. Fusion of Love and Pain as one to manifest a *reality* greater than the separation of God and his current creation of shattered suffering and pleasure. No peace is to be found in truth. Woe unto you dear reader. Now that you have been exposed to this you too must drag your soon to be undead corpse to the precipice of the void to deal with your own desire for true love. You too must cut it off to expose your part of what you will never understand but must to purify the rivers of blood through redemption. A ring of good and evil, two dragons eating each others tails. ***As Feuer, das mich verbrennt, rein'ge vom Fluche den Ring: ihr in der Fluth löset ihn auf, und lauter bewahrt das lichte Gold das euch zum Unheil geraubt. Fliegt heim, ihr Raben! Raunt es eurem Herren, was hier am Rhein ihr gehört! Fly home you ravens! Whisper to your lord what you heard here by the Rhine (7)!*** It was far too early when the ghosts first attacked me. They knew it would set something off inside of me. How? Who told them and left me out of the loop? I would soon find out. There are things in the universe that are far more powerful than us Nosferatu. We just rarely see them on this planet. I did not know what I was becoming. It was too much for me to accept all at once and every arcane incantation that kept me going fought back.

THE CHOGO RI PARTY

Left to right: Wessely, Eckenstein, Guillarmod, Crowley, Pfannl, Knowles

(Just like G. K. Rex to keep his hat on!)

As I watched the ghosts swarm upon me I remembered something that I could do to fight back. I had been in a position like this before but not on the same scale. It was the year 1901 or 1902 if I remember correctly. I was with a fairly well-known fellow who went by the name of

Crowley. At the time I posed as a Swiss doctor named Jules Jacot Guillarmond. Many Nosferatu posed as doctors at that time. It was an easy way to maintain a steady supply of blood. We were at the foot of a mountain that is known now as K-2 but also as Chhogori, Qogir, or Kechu. We were attempting a first ascent. It was a strange affair, more like a circus than an expedition. There were hundreds of porters, herds of sheep, goats, and many chickens as well. Crowley even brought a library of poetry. That is what he told everyone it was. In his arrogant fashion he said he could not be separated from Milton when on a glacier when the expedition leader demanded that he get rid of the books. His arrogance was a front. There was much more to his library than poetry. He was obsessed with arcane phenomena and for a human he was very gifted. Few humans in history came close to his ability when it came to conjuring and invocation. For some time I thought he was the person that I was waiting for to help conquer the voids. Auryn was far more powerful than he was so I had to wait almost another hundred years for her to arrive. Crowley was very close to her in ability and I have seen only a rare few others. Most of his books appeared as poetry but if inspected with the proper form of sight one could easily detect the amount of majikal power that they concealed. They were virtually throbbing with power. It is no wonder that he attracted attention from the summit ghost of the mountain. He may have even had intentions to challenge it upon the very pinnacle of its abode. I was perfectly concealed in my guise because I had gotten all of my spells in order and had proper blood to work with. Decent blood was far easier to get then because humanity was far less toxified.

Crowley suffered a similar spectral attack at the K2 basecamp as I did at the base of Kilimanjaro. Now I remember him describing it; "***soft creatures draped in white***, all trying to wash out my vision. Dreams were the only place to see them but now there, right in front of me."

Hope was wasted away, faith was wasted away. I saw him collapse and clutch his eyes and the top of his head. I knew what was happening. I could see it clearly but I knew that if anyone else happened upon us they would not understand. He was being attacked because his head chakra was opened up far too wide and some of these emboldened spirits had entered his body to wreak havoc. He screamed incoherencies like he was speaking in tongues. I knew I had to do something because the camp was very busy and someone would soon notice. I was in danger because of this. My identity could be compromised. He was one of the most powerful men there was but he did not have the power to fight this battle on his own. He was greatly outnumbered and it was almost too late. They had already possessed him. None here shall ever know what I really am. I could help but I knew that it could harm me in the end. I am sure that Crowley had an idea about my true identity but I was taking a step in further revealing myself by helping him. If I did he would know for sure that I was far more powerful than he was. I didn't think about it and I simply reacted. I wouldn't do all the work but I would help him take care of his self. I stepped over his convulsing body and gave him a tool to initiate his own exorcism. I felt the presence of the ghosts that were raging inside of him. I came very close so that none of the others in the camp could hear me. I whispered "*Thelema* *(Dowhatthouwillandthatshall-bethewholeofthelaw,loveisthelawloveunderwill.)*" into his ear and then punched him in the stomach with a moderate amount of force. His eyes rolled back and he trembled. His countenance became stone but the rest of his body was still convulsing. He rolled over on his hands and knees and vomited a large amount of clear mucus. As this was leaving his body I whispered *Mimra dbaira* **(illuminating word)**. *Asamta* ***(Laying on of hands)*** *Ahrima* ***(excommunicated soul)*** *Almayya* ***(Dark outer worlds)***. *Talitha Kumi* ***(Arise my child)*** and kicked him in the stomach. The last of the mucus that came out turned clear green. He collapsed on to the ground face first and started breathing heavily but in a normal rhythm. He went unconscious and I walked away hoping that he would not remember the details of this encounter. I was confident that he was completely safe and that these ghosts would no longer bother us. They knew when they were beat. If no one else in the ghostly realm realized that Nosferatu was here they certainly did now and they went away quickly so I could not bend them to my will. I let them go because I did not want to force this game any further with them.

∞

The same thing happened to me at the foot of Kilimanjaro. The only difference was that I knew that the ghosts were there before they attacked. I saw the legion massing around me as they slowly approached. None would dare act alone against me. Once there was a sufficient force they all empowered each other to an overwhelming point. Then they were all gone in a flash as if they acted with one mind. Instantly I knew that the attack was on but I could not react. I was totally overwhelmed. I saw only white and I felt my willpower fading. I remembered the incident in the Karakoram with Crowley. It was clear to me then what was happening and what I should do. I struggled to form my hand into a ball and I punched myself in the stomach as I uttered the words again. *"Talitha Kumi. Thelema. Mimra dbaira. Asamta, Ahrima, Almayya."* It seemed to take some time but slowly, like the falling of the moon into daylight my vison returned. My strength returned but I was not back to normal. I was still in a weakened condition, the very same weakened condition that these ghosts thought that they could have taken advantage of.

As my eyes adjusted from the ghostly possession, the stomped gravel of the parking area came back and it glistened in the burning light as I blinked at it. I could smell the trees and the endless miles of damp soil all around me. I could feel the billions of lifeforms that drew their nutrition from this earth with tooth like roots. Hungry jaws of life, tightened into the earth. Even the trees were like Nosferatu. Everything on this planet feeds off the death of something else. This is why Nosferatu are the most powerful undead on this world. Everything alive needs death to grow. ***Death needs light to grow. When I become Death, Death is the seed from which I grow...***

Nosferatu, the fiery angels of darkness and earth.

Itzama, spirit of early mist and showers.

Ix Tab, goddess of ropes and snares.

Ixchel, the spider web, catcher of morning dew.

Zooheekock, virgin fire patroness of infants.

Adziz, the master of cold.

Kockupocket, he who works in fire.

Ixtahdoom, she who spits out precious stones.

Ixchunchan, the dangerous one (11).

Ah Pook, the destroyer. Death needs time for what it kills to grow in, for Ah Pook's sweet sake, you stupid vulgar greedy ugly American death-sucker... Like this (26): If I do nothing and do not act upon my calling to complete this spell then it will be completed in a different manner. This is an epilogue to every great story ever told. It will all start over again until someone gets it right. Back into singularity and subsequent separation. **If one does nothing then nothing does (4).** Time is death and space sucks one into death. An event horizon is created in the matrix lurking in the black void. A void within a void. Left to their own devices time and space consume everything, all of the higher dimensions that they support. They all collapse into the event horizon when time and space malfunction and no longer perform their duty of supporting the higher dimensions. Pathology, the source and fulfillment of addiction. Vampires of the cosmos that wait for their victims to ripen for harvest. There is a program of desperation, competition, and siphoning built into everything in the same way that the irrational word is. The desperation, competition, and consumption are the rational side of the program while the unutterable word is the irrational side. Conscious and unconscious. Inversion. Under the realities of the unconscious everything is regurgitated and expelled. Under the false ***perceptions*** of consciousness everything is desired for consumption. Even the precious light from the nearest star (Lucifer) is vied for. All life is owed to this cosmic energy. All conscious understanding is owed to this driving force of rationality and ***perception.*** Illumination. . Iblees, God of the garden and the harvest. God of the clock which winds the Earth. Light is the seed from which I grow... ***Question: If Control's control is absolute, why does Control need to control? Answer: Control... needs time (26).*** I could feel tiny pricks of this light filtering through the canopy and threatening my undead skin. Time is a measurement of light and dark. Not very relevant on its own. Time is death and space sucks one into death. Some Nosferatu are obsessed with time and others are obsessed with space.

∞

In the parking lot where I reeled back into consciousness, the shuffling sounds of the trees and all of the small restless sounds made by the inhabitants of the slowly encroaching and convoluted, sylvan, gathering returned. I could begin to make out the transient forms of the wandering hikers as they awaited commencement of their expensive expeditions. I could see the lumbering olivine guards, their phallic weapons slung over their shoulders with trigger fingers placed over their groin, cocked and ready for play. The clamoring hopeful porters outside the gates reformed into a great mass of action like a nest of ground wasps. The din pierced my ears which were very sensitized after my arcane struggle. All of this washed over me in the course of a few seconds but it felt like an eternity. I felt well enough to stand up. If anyone were to have witnessed my struggle it would have appeared only like I had sat down for a moment but I went to another time and place in order to fight it:

C, D, E, semitone; F, G, A, B, semitone; C, etc:

Heptaparaparshinokh:

Do – I give; re – a king; mi – to me; fa – she does; sol – alone; la – up there; se – yes, do – I give.

It was then that I realized just how haunted this mountain really was. It was the worst of the seven. I had an unappreciative idea of this before I came. It was simply a curious abstraction to me and my hubris. Now that I was here it started to become clear that this was a dangerous place. ***Thela hun ginjeet thela hun ginjeet. Qua tari mei. Thela hun ginjeet. Qua tari mei. Heat in the jungle street "I say I'm nervous as hell from this thing 'cause those guys were gonna kill me for sure...I mean they ganged up on me like that, I couldn't believe it! Look I'm still shaking. It's weird. Go out on the streets like this...You can't...Dangerous place, it's a dangerous place (38)."*** Even so, this realization did not cause me much concern. Why would it? Everywhere I was present the surroundings were haunted. I am a specter. This was a normal condition for me. Everywhere an addict goes one will find addiction. Of course I wasn't concerned about whether or not this mountain was haunted with wandering ghosts. Virtually all mountains are. It is a great place for them to go because there are few humans around and they can see very well from these lofty places. The same holds true for deserts. They tend to be very haunted as well. The thing that struck me was just how θαυματουργός, excuse me, thaumaturgic this place was. It was saturated with inexplicable, ancient energy. Majik cast upon majik in a tower that reached into the heavens. It was a mountain of Babylon unlike any other I had visited before. All the powers of the previous events upon Golgotha, Capitolinus, the Carpathians and many more mountainous regions where this particular ghost hid and killed for centuries, were also here, piled upon one another. All the unmentioned horror and destruction from all the games of the Seven Ghosts of Babylon's hills were all here because the ghost who resided here upon Kilimanjaro was the most jealous of them all. The hungriest, the most vampirous of the seven. This is why it stayed closest to humanity.

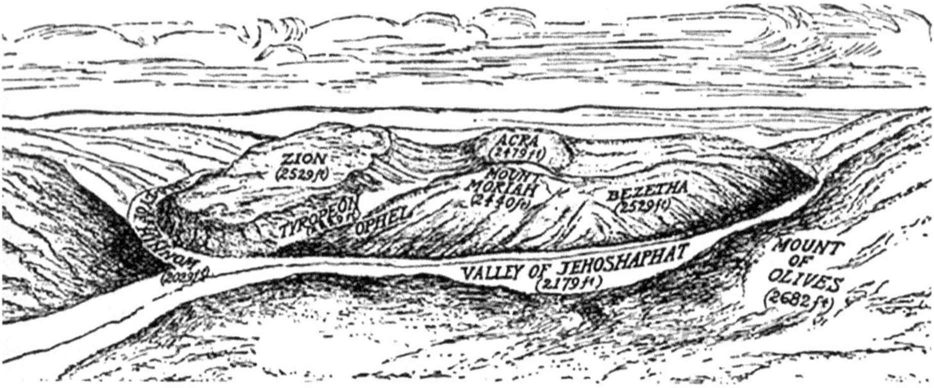

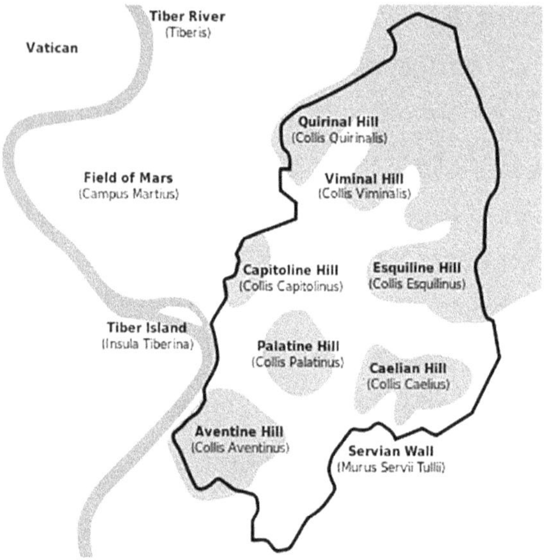

After a few moments of deliberation I decided to not worry myself over this intense presence above me. I still thought that I was immune to its effects and I planned on having a few words with that mother-fucker when I got to the top. I simply assumed that this attack was something that happened at the base of mountains. I didn't give it any more credit than that. Of course my experience with Crowley was what got me thinking in this manner. In any case there was no way that I would even consider turning back now. I had taken all of the trouble to get here. I certainly wasn't going to change my mind on the account of a few pissed off ghosts. It seemed obvious to me – even though I was wrong – that they were simply trying to hide something. Whatever it was didn't concern me either way. What was really happening was the inverted fact that *I* was hiding something even though I was still totally unaware of it. I had my slowly moving Extraordinary disease, Neurosis of shame and pride that, Shem HaMephorash, was just starting to eat me up. It was hidden so well that I had no consciousness of it at all. Babylon itself – all of the seven summits and all of the systems of infection that washed down their sides and into the river of blood that kept everything alive and conscious through the shattered glass of perception was being threatened by my very presence upon this hill. It would fight its destruction with every means available. This was only the first assault I would endure. It certainly was not the last on that fine day.

∞

The porters who were attached to our group began their heavily laden ascent. Even though they were carrying many times more gear than the rest of the group they would be going at a speed many times faster than we would. They had to get to the next camp and set it up before we arrived and most of them were not going to the summit so they did not need to acclimatize to the elevation. Even though the work they did was brutal, they seemed to truly enjoy it. I was amazed at their abilities. They carried all of their own gear, the personal gear for the entire group, and all of the extra tents and food that the expedition required. "Pole-pole" was what they would tell us as they whisked by, hunched under their huge burden. They did not take their own advice at all because they went so quickly. "Pole-pole" means "slowly or slow down". Something to that effect. I did not envy them but they tried to have as much, if not more fun than the hiking group. Along with their immense personal burdens, they also carried large am-fm radio, cassette players tied to a belt loop or a pack strap. Wild Swahili words and crazy African sounds came buzzing and hissing out of the tiny speakers as their coming and going was announced by this strange Doppler Effect. I would hear the birds and leaves and wind and then the static beat of music accompanied by heavy foot falls as the din got closer only for it to drift away and be replaced by the forest sounds once again. The birds and animals scurried around taking part of the performance.

The distinct smell of marijuana smoke was emitted from some of them as they passed by. I have always loved everything about marijuana even though I do not ingest it in any form outside of the blood of some of my victims. I tried it a few times and it produced some very undesirable side effects. It does not at all affect me in the same way that it does humans. That much I could easily figure out because they seem to enjoy it while I find its effects nauseating. I think that I am allergic to it or something. Not only that, it makes me fantasize about things that I shouldn't, like eating people who don't deserve it. Of course marijuana should be legalized in every pathetic country – yes America, you too, are indeed pathetic – all over the world. I don't expect this to happen because it is one of the greatest monetary pillars of the black market. If it were legalized in America on a Federal level it is likely to produce undesirable effects to the status quo of the power structure. Contemporary capitalism will have lost one of its primary scapegoats. It may indeed become legal someday soon but I suspect that it will be heavily regulated to the point of redundancy by the Department of Redundancy Department. Hello this is the Department of Redundancy Department, can I help you? Can I help you? You will have to fill out a No Log, Log to Log nothing if you have done it.

Whether or not you want to admit it, the black market is essential to the normal operation of government and economic power. This power structure is designed as a monopoly of violence. Violence that no one in these fields of employment would ever admit to because they have adopted a mythology of heroism. They truly believe that they are saving the "normal" person from the "bad hombres". This monopoly of violence is shared by the executive, legislative, and judicial branches of American government along with the underlings in the state government and passed on to their underlings in the form of police, sheriffs, correction officers, local judges, lawyers, and even the bank. From there it is passed on to average folk who only think about their families, their foul obsession with reproducing more foul bipedal vessels of blood who then disgustingly end up creating even more who also only think about reproduction and all activities attendant to it so that yet even more *precious, innocent, filthy, vulgar, narcissistic, children* can have the values of passive aggressive, unconscious violence internalized in their psyche that is reinforced by the sports culture of video game militarism, victory, and hero worship.

Meyer Lansky, the finical wizard of organized crime, knew perhaps better than anyone else that the successful annihilation of organized crime's subculture in America would rock the "legitimate" world's entire foundation, which would ultimately force fundamental social changes and redistribution of wealth and power in this country. Lansky's dream was to bond the two worlds together so that one could not survive without the other. Those of us who recognize the vast power of the underworld in our nation today also understand how close to Lansky's dream – and our nightmare – is coming true (39).

Far too many "good" people would be bored and without a job if the black market was ever effectively controlled by someone outside the gang and mafia power structure. This effect could also trickle down into the rest of society because *someone* should pay for *their* extravagant bullshit. *They*: The terrified and extremely overpaid vultures of society who believe that they have something to lose and who need to have this system of violence and oppression maintained. It is not a gold standard that backs up the value of the dollar. It is the violence standard. A blood standard. Everyone must pay and if they don't they will suffer. One can't make a move or take a breath without someone else trying to make money off it. If they don't make their money then *they* call the *authorities.* This barbarism is protected by the catachresis of the word *law*. Law is a satanic incantation uttered in an arcane manner amongst the initiated. In order for it to work at all, *violence* is necessary to maintain these concoctions, and once cast into the stone of the written word and nodded at by a circle of self-aggrandizing vipers it is no longer understood as the violence it is. At least in their ***perspective***. They have all the tools in place to pass the buck and blame their victims. Violence exists in many delicate forms and mutates so that it doesn't appear like violence. A fifty dollar no seat belt fine is a poke in the ribs that is forgotten but it is the butt of a bigger stick of insane proportions.

It is seen as normal, acceptable behavior to be desensitized to a subject once it is written and applied universally in the form of abstraction. The creation of unholy spirits. The threat of violence and tyranny is the only thing that holds the international capitalist structure together. Cash money plays a primary role in this system that is far more fragile than it appears to be. Only through billions of dollars invested into brainwashing through advertisement and false historical education does this madness maintain its inertia. Cash is the only untraceable form of currency. Everything else is in the hands of private credit and banks. There is no way that cash will ever be abolished because it allows the government to lubricate dubious exchanges and more importantly it allows others to do so. This creates "otherness". When they use cash in this way, its intended way, the tyrannical forces of government can have something to point to in order to justify their existence. They can say to the world: "See! You do need us after all because who is going to stop *THEM!" THEM: the ostensible bad guy in this case* who are the individuals that use money for its primary purpose. The black market. It will never be stopped as long as capitalism continues and encourages others into criminal behavior. Ripping one another off to make a few cents on a transaction is the blunt end of the sharp stick of criminal insanity that lurks behind it. Crime justifies the threat of institutionalized violence, so it does pay and it pays well. Addiction is the result. Thousands die in this calculated and intentional war that America and other countries have been waging on their own people. Because certain terminally diseased behavior (addiction) has been marginalized into a criminal category it is obvious that those who could come up with a better solution than suboxone simply refuse to. There is less money in helping these perceived lower life forms. Reptiles of addiction. It is an intentional form of chemical warfare that has afflicted so many citizens of the world. No one is not touched by addiction. It is so common, a timeless problem that is aggravated by the system that encourages money to be transferred without accountability. The black market is as big as the legal market. Neither of which is free until everyone realizes that it has been Anarchy that has been keeping everything together the entire time. Nosferatu the fiery, blood sucking angels of darkness and the Earth. Ix tab the goddess of ropes and snares. Like this:

Language is the tower of Babylon. The mouth of the wolf. The confusion produced by many tongues. Language is the only thing that keeps everything more or less "ordered". ***Writers don't write, they read and transcribe something already written (11).*** This tower of rational insanity is and always has been. It is a house built for the dominatrix and the prostitute and the money lender. It is the vampire that sucks meaning out of reality to produce the empty shell of perception. Without the threat of violence it will all crash and those who are empowered by it will stop at nothing to see that it continues. The Viet Nam "conflict" is probably the best example of how far America will go to pursue capitalist interest. ***So you read orders, which are then conveyed through your spokesman, the Supervisor. The Imam. The old man (11).*** The nation of America was never threatened by Ho Chi Mihn. The international market supposedly was and even that conclusion is dubious at best. ***So, I am a man for a***

very important and, you may add, very dangerous assignment (11)? But still, ram the rod, pound the dirt, rub ashes in hair and tear garments because those in power can't stand the slightest thought that even an ant can harm their interest. They know just how fragile their power is. ***It was, and a proper hash you made of it. Your job now is to find the Western Lands. Find out how the Western Lands are created (11).*** It is only a mountain of words and we all know that it takes very little to rewrite anything. It could all crash so easily. Only then will there be the possibility of freedom. *Freedom*: a concept that would terrify most, if it ever actually was made manifest. None alive have ever seen it. It would be a Brave New World but not in the Huxlean sense. I suspect that it would be closer to a Chomskyist or Kropotkinesque environment but I can only speculate. ***Kropotkin pointed out what he considered to be the fallacies of the economic systems of feudalism and capitalism. He believed they create poverty and artificial scarcity while promoting privilege. Instead, he proposed a more decentralized economic system based on mutual aid, mutual support, and voluntary cooperation, asserting that the tendencies for this kind of organization already exist, both in evolution and in human society (18).***

I can already hear the wailing and gnashing of teeth as the stained and skeletal finger of corporate interest screams profanities about the *Communistic* flavor of these ideas. I would disagree and say that it is something else entirely. It is Anarchism and this is the condition that is already holding society together. The detrition between the black economy and the government dollar has ground down to a smoothly functional midpoint that no one dares mention. Anarchy. The mafia capitalized upon this environment along with the government and together they will use violence to make sure this possibility never is realized. ***Meyer Lansky, the financial wizard of organized crime, knew perhaps better than anyone else that the successful annihilation of organized crime's***

subculture in America would rock the legitimate world's entire foundation, which would ultimately force fundamental social changes and redistributions of wealth and power in this country. Lansky's dream was to bond the two worlds together so that one could not survive without the other (39). This is not true anarchy but rather, a stalemate. Kropotkin could be right if we simply accepted that things are out of hand and closer to nihilism than anarchy as long as everyone keeps the status quo. The difference is that the status quo is not working very well and true anarchy has every promise to outdo it in functionality. The answer is right in your face and despite the black veil that perverts it through virtually every contemporary perspective, anarchy is not pure chaos. Pure chaos exists already and its name is capitalism. ***No one expects the Spanish inquisition. The cross beam has gone askew. Our weapons are fear, surprise, and ruthless efficiency, an almost fanatic devotion to the pope, and our fancy red suits. You are charged with heresy against the church. We shall make you understand (40).***

Anarchy is the one of the most abused and misunderstood terms there is. Minimalism is as well but to get into that would be a unnecessary digression that would only boost my ego and reinforce my understanding of things that most likely do not matter, so I will refrain and continue on with the digression that I was already developing which was the discussion of anarchy. It is the idea that people can and should try to actually get along with each other rather than create systems of violence and threats concerning who possesses what as a means of holding everything together. I do sometimes forget that most humans are totally infantile and are encouraged to act this way from birth because it is the only way to succeed in the capitalist structure which favors infantile and unthinking behavior over all else. It is simply crazy to think that people can and should try to get along with each other? We would have to endure the most cathartic destruction ever seen upon the planet if Anarchy were to make a functional peep. In our current dystopia, if any behavior deviates from the beaten path of corporate slavery at gunpoint then abandon all hope for here there be dragons.

∞

As I previously mentioned, the spell of the name is very powerful. This is because the name is the least rational of all words. Once I name a demon I can control it. This is why I have not yet revealed my true name, even though I eventually must if this spell that I am casting is to work. In time I will but for now I still am Alexander. Daniel is still typing along with me in the madhouse near downtown Las Vegas. I have controlled him because I have his secret stellar name and I used it against him for my own means because I do not care about him. The star of the name Daniel is the fire of Regulus, star of the lion; Leo. The name of the group of seven summits ghosts all together is *Babylon.* John knew this and much was revealed to him. He said: *Babylon is fallen. The great city is fallen she has become the hideout for demons and evil spirits. A nest for buzzards, and a den of dreadful beasts. All of the nations have drunk the wine of her passionate immorality. The rulers of the world have committed adultery with her, the merchants of the world have grown rich as a result of her luxurious living. The rulers of the world who took part in her immoral acts and enjoyed her great luxury will mourn for her as they see the smoke rising from her charred remains (8).* ***Group drinkers make great thinkers, and 'tis they constitute the twelve of the jury: saddlers, leather sellers, skinners, salters, pewterers, paper strainers, parish clerks, bow and arrow makers, girdlers, dealers in textiles, shoemakers, and weavers. They all encourage the speaker: 'Go to it!' they urge. 'Stay ahead agitator.' 'I will do that, please God!' said Kersse; and in the flip of a jiffy the speaker belched: 'as sober as the Ship's Husband he was, my godfather, when he told me the story, and I am satisfied that this is how it goes: the widower, so help me God, is consistently***

blown to Adams (5)!' *They will stand at a distance terrified by her great torment. They will cry out "how terrible"! The merchants of the world will weep and mourn for her for there is no one left to buy their goods. She brought great quantities of gold, silver, jewels, pearls, fine linen, purple dye, silk, scarlet cloth, and every kind of perfumed wood, ivory, objects made of expensive wood, bronze, iron, and marble. She also bought cinnamon, spices, incense, myhhr, frankincense, wine olive oil, fine flour, wheat, cattle, sheep, horses, and slaves. Yes she even traded in human lives. All the fancy things you loved so much are gone. The luxuries and splendors will never be yours again, they are gone forever. How terrible for that great city. In a single moment all is gone. Never again will the sound of music be heard there. No more harps, flutes, or trumpets. The nights will be dark, without a single lamp. This will happen because the merchants who were the greatest in the world deceived the nations with her sorceries. In her streets the blood of the prophets was spilled (8).* Babylon is written in the spirits of the mountains. We strive for living metaphor of their lofty positions. Water flows down from the summits and is brought back to them through the clouds so that the physical and spiritual toxins impregnated in the water can continue to effect the blood and ensure that this tragedy plays out. Taken all together, these toxins mutate and multiply to eventually create the infection of the rational word. The name is both rational and irrational depending upon how it is used. There is an end. It is not an endless cycle. This is an epilogue. I use it as a spell for I do not care about you. The *name* is written in blood for it begins and ends with this sangre tune...***Do – I give; re – a king; mi – to me; fa – she does; sol – alone; la – up there; se – yes, do – I give...****Never again will the sound of music be heard there. No more the harps, flutes, or trumpets. The nights will be dark, without a single lamp (8).*

Do you not expect this? Think it is just insane, fucked up, foot in mouth, Thorazine deficient, poop smearing, psychobabble? I did but I am beginning to think otherwise. It has entered my dry veins and has reanimated them with blood. It has entered your blood from the very water that runs off all of the highest mountains, all the way down only to congeal into red platelets and phagocytes that defend the virus. The virus of the rational word along with all of the power in the original word that each singular, viral, rational word mimics has brought me to a terminal point of acceptance. I never expected that it would have to happen this way. There is no way of trivializing what is happening. I, we are literally in a warzone. A condition I am certainly used to. Just another day for us undead. I use the word "day" in the biblical sense. A thousand years went by so quickly. What of the now? The eternal present? Is it to go on and on like this forever? It is like cranking a jack in the box that never pops but if it does what will come out? Pasta!?! I'm not so sure that I want to know.

∞

The plains of Armageddon are spread out as far as one can see. This is not a localized effort for control of crossroads in the Promised Land. The entire universe was created so, logically it must therefore be destroyed. Babylon, a force of nature. A bloom in the meadow. A rotting accretion. An unburnable library. Mouth and memory can breed faster than any fire burning at its edges. Everyone. An invisible tower made of flesh striving toward its own ***perception*** of deification through the process of self-gratification. The exact opposite of revelation. A headfirst dive into nothing. The exact opposite of what should be done to achieve divine understanding and love; for love is not complete without suffering. Henosis, or primordial unity, is rational and deterministic, emanating from indeterminism, (irrational in this case) an uncaused cause. Each individual as a microcosm reflects the gradual ordering of the universe referred to as the macrocosm. In mimicking the demiurge (divine mind), one unites with The One or Monad. Thus the process of unification, of "The Being," and "The One," is called Henosis. The culmination of Henosis is deification. The expression of will is not the expression of one's own self as the self is commonly understood. Will is a gift from the God and it is your small part of him and it is drawing you back. Do what thou will and that shall be the whole of the law is not an open license for libertine behavior. It is the submission of the self to his place in the higher order. Pain is frequent in the exploration of the will and it is a cleansing retribution. Self-gratification leads to a dead end of fire. When you achieve it you will find me smiling at the door ready to invite you in and become one of my underlings for none have achieved self-gratification more than I. I am an unburnable library. A mountain of flesh lies below me. A dangerous tower of will and desire and addiction. Everybody a temple. What is the temple dedicated to? Perhaps Nothing in the common contemporary experience because most who are alive can barely be called that. ***Penetrators are permitted into the muesomound free. Welsh and the PaddyPatkinses, one shelek (5)!***

Humanity seeks out the light outside of themselves in order to escape their quickly growing inner darkness. Little do they realize that the light outside of themselves is only there to incinerate them completely and they are far better off staying in their inner darkness. There is far more to explore there. The light of the sun is not revelation even though everything that is revealed by it is the only thing that appears to make sense through rational words. Sunlight is the illumination of everything that humans are not but think that they need to be. An orange is every color but orange but the perceived color itself exists only in the light. ***Amenti: the region of the dead. After beating back the demons, the soul reaches the regions described in the 'Chapters of the Coming Forth by Day' in the underworld.*** Lucifer is the Illuminator, the sun. The sun is His star and the light of day on Earth is His realm. You will only find Him in this light. ***Look, sisters! The wakening sun smiles into the deep. Through the green billows she greets the glad sleeper. Now she kisses his eyelid that it may open. See how he smiles in the gleaming light...Of the joy***

giving star in the watery deep that illumines the waves with its noble light?...The worlds wealth would be won by him who forged from the Rhinegold the ring that would grant him limitless power...Only the man who forswears love's sway, only he who disdains love's delights can master the magic spell that rounds a ring from the gold (7). There are infinite manifestations of His name and he is all of them. The spell of the name is something that he is obsessed with. Something that he tries to control but cannot. He is Lucifer but much more. He has tried every possible name in order to somehow find the original unspeakable one. He wants to be the one to find it because he believes that He should control everything and not merely his bleached, pale blue dot. He cannot do this and he knows this. He needs a lesser being to perform the task he is not allowed to discover. Just like I needed Auryn to control the voids. This does not mean he has not tried. He has donned many names:

Hades, Sheol, Rodgers and Hammerstein, Abbadon, Titahion, Bar Schauheth, Tzelmoth, Shaari Moth, Gehinnon, Gamaliel, Samael, Gharab Tzerek, Tagiriron, Golohab, Agshekeloh, Satariel, Ghogiel, Thaumiel, Aphophis, Typhon, Semhazah, Arteqif', Ramt'el, Ram'el, Dan'el, Ziq'el, Garaq'el, Asa'el, Hermoni, Matr'el, Anan'el, Anan'el, Sithwa'el, Sims'el, Sahr'el, Sims'el, Sahr'el, Tamm'el, Tur'e, Yamm'el, Zehor'el, Zazel, Hismael, Bartzabel, Sorath, Kedemel, Tapththarath, Chasmodai, Bael, Agares, Marbas, Pruflas, Amon, Barbatos, Buer, Gusion, Botis, Bathym, Pursan, Eligor, Loray, Valefar, Morax, Ipes, Naberus, Galsya-labolas, Zepar, Byleth, Sytry, Paymon, Belial, Bune, Forneus, Roneue, Berith, Forras, Furfur, Marchocias, Malphas, Vepar, Sabnac, Sydonay, Gaap, Chax, Furcas, Murmur, Caim, Raum, Halphas, Focalor, Vine, Bifrons, Gamygyn, Zagam, Orias, Volac, Gomory, Decarabia, Amduscias, Andras, Androalphus, Oze, Aym, Arobas, Vapula, Cmeries, Amy, Flavros, Balam, Alocer, Zaleos, Wal, Haagenti, Phoenix, Stolas, Acheron, Gehenna, Tophet, Persephone, Hecate, The Erinyes: Alecto, Megaera, and Tisiphone,

Hermes; Psychopompos, Charon, Cerberus the "Hell-Hound" born from Echidna and Typhon, Thanatos, Melinoë the chthonic nymph, Nyx the goddess of the Night, Tartarus, Achlys the personification of misery and sadness, Styx, Eurynomos who eats off all the flesh of the corpses, leaving only their bones, Abezethibou, Abraxas, Abyzou, Adramelech, Aeshma, Agaliarept, Agrat bat Mahlat, Agares, Agiel, Ahriman, Haborym, Aka Manah, Ala, Alal, Alastor, Alloces, Allu, Amaymon, Amdusias, Amy, Anamalech, Ancitif, Andhaka, Andras, Andrealphus, Andromalius, Anzu, Armaros, Archon, Arunasura, Asag, Asakku, Asb'el, Asmodeus, Astaroth, Asura, Azaz'el, Dahak, Baal, Babi ngepet, Bakasura, Balam, Balberith, Bali Raj, Baphomet, Barbas, Barbatos, Barong, Mathim, Beelzebub, Belial, Beleth, Belphegor, Berith, Bh ta, Bifrons, Boruta, Botis, Buer, Bukavac, Bune, Bushyasta, Charun, Chemosh, Choronzon, Kimaris, Corson, Procell, Culsu, Daeva, Dagon, Dajjal, Dantalion, Danjal, Decarabia, Demiurge, Div-e Sepid, Drekavac, Dzoavits, Eblis, Eligos, Eisheth, Focalor, Foras, Forneus, Furcas, Furfu, Gaap, Gader'el, Gaki, Gamigin, Caacrinolaas, Gremory, Guayota, Gusion, Haagenti, Malthus, Hantu Raya, Flavros, Ifrit, Ipos, Jikininki, Kasadya, Kokabiel, Kroni, Kumbhakarna, Legion, Lechies, Leyak, Lempo, Leraje, Leviathan, Malphas, Mammon, Maricha, Foraii, Marchosias, AL-Dajjal, Mastema, Mephistopheles, Merihem, Moloch, Naamah, Ninurta, Namtar, Onoskelis, Orcus, Orias, Orobas, Ose, Ördög, O Tokata, Paimon, Pazuzu, Pelesit, Phenex, Penemuc, Pithius, Pocong, Pontianak, Preta, Pruflas, Puloman, Raum, Ronove, Rusalka, Rakshasa, Rangda, Ravan, Sabnock, Saleos, Samael, Seir, Semyaza, Chax, Shedim, Sitri, Sthenno, Solas, Suanggi, Surgat, Tannin, Tuchulcha, Ukobach, Valac, Malephar, Vanth, Vapula, Vassago, Vepar, Wendigo, Yeqon, Zagan, Zepar, Ziminiar, Abholos, Devourer in the mist, Ammutseba Devourer of Stars, Amon-Gorloth Creator of the Nile, Aphoom-Zhah The Cold Flame, Arwassa The Silent Shouter on the Hill, Aylith The Widow in the Woods, Baoht Z'uqqa-Mogg The Bringer of Pestilence, B'gnu-Thun The Soul-Chilling

Ice-God, Bokrug The Doom of Sarnath, Bugg-Shash The Black One, The Filler of Space, Crom Cruach, Master of the Runes, Cthugha The Living Flame, The Burning One, Cthulhu, Cthylla Secret Daughter of Cthulhu, Ctoggha The Dream-Daemon, Cyäegha The Destroying Eye, Dygra The Stone, Dzéwà The White God, Eihort The Pale Beast, Ei'lor The Star-Seed, Gleeth The Blind God of the Moon, Gloon The Corrupter of Flesh, Gobogeg The Twice-Invoked, Gog-Hoor Eater of the Insane, Gurathnaka Eater of Dreams, Shadow of the Night, Gur'la-ya Lurker in the Doom-laden Shadows, Hastalÿk, The Contagion, H'chtelegoth The Great Tentacled God, Haiogh-Yai The Outsider, Ithaqua The Wind Walker, Kaalut The Ravenous One, Kassogtha Bride of Cthulhu, Kaunuzoth The Great One, K'nar'st Spawn of the Forgotten, Kthaw'keth The Supreme Unknown, Lexur'iga-serr'roth He Who Devours All in the Dark, Mappo no Ryujin Harbinger of Doom, M'Nagalah The Devourer, The Cancer God, Mordiggian The Charnel God, Nctosa & Nctolhu The Twin Spawn of Cthulhu, Ngirrth'lu The Wolf-Thing, The Stalker in the Snows, He Who Hunts, Northot The Forgotten God, Nssu-Ghahnb The Heart of the Ages, Leech of the Aeons, Nycrama The Zombifying Essence, Nyogtha The Thing which Should Not Be, Othuyeg The Doom-Walker, Psuchawrl The Elder One, Ptar-Axtlan The Leopard That Stalks the Night, Quachil Uttaus Treader of the Dust, Ragnalla Seeker in the Skies, Rhagorthua Father of All Winds, Rhogog The Bearer of the Cup of the Blood of the Ancients, Sedmelluq The Great Manipulator, Sfatlicllp The Fallen Wisdom, Shaklatal The Eye of Wicked Sight, Sheb-Teth Devourer of Souls, Shterot, The Tenebrous One, Shudde M'ell The Burrower Beneath, Shuy-Nihl The Devourer in the Earth, Sthanee The Lost One, S'tya-Yg'Nalle The Whiteness, Uitzilcapac Lord of Pain, Volgna-Gath Keeper of Secrets, Xalafu The Dread One, Xcthol The Goat God, Xinlurgash, The Ever-Consuming, Xirdneth Maker of Illusions, Lord of Unreality, Xitalu, Xotli Lord of Terror, Xoxiigghua, Yegg-Ha, The Faceless One, Y'golonac The Defiler, Yhashtur

The Worm-God, Yig Father of Serpents, Y'lla Master of the Seas, 'Ymnar The Dark Stalker, Yog-Sapha The Dweller of the Depths, Yorith The Oldest Dreamer, Ysbaddaden Chief of the Giants, Ythogtha The Thing in the Pit, Yug-Siturath, Zathog The Black Lord of Whirling Vortices, Zhar and Lloigor The Twin Obscenities, Zindarak The Fiery Messenger, Zoth-Ommog The Dweller in the Depths, Zstylzhemghi Matriarch of Swarms, and Abaddon-star (18) (41) (42) (43). None have yet worked to the desired effect but all have helped in the maintenance of the chaos that is reasoned away by the living. I had to list all of these yet there are an infinite amount that I have still left unnamed. These are the major ones that I am worrying about at the moment minus the infinite enochian demons which would take too long to list but should still be included. I have put most of them in between the letters so you do not have to read them all. In listing them in this spell I include them in the final destruction that I am planning. I have pinned a piece of every one to this page just by mentioning them. I have grabbed them out of nothing and forced them into my control.

∞

Now that I was attacked by a legion of ghosts at the foot of Kilimanjaro, I was even more determined to climb to the summit which they seemed to be so concerned with protecting. Is that what they were trying to do or were they trying to use my arrogance against me? All of this is speculation after the fact and not of too much importance. Very soon after I had composed myself, the group I was to go trekking with decided that all preparations and formalities were complete and they gathered to begin the ascent. We left the staging area and followed the well-traveled path that is named the Machame Route. This is a standard route for climbing to the summit over the course of about a week. Some do it in more days, some less. As we began, shards of vacillating light etched their way through the canopy and were swiftly swallowed into hungry chlorophyll. The forest closed in on us. It was nebulous and full of life. Every step forward took us closer to the summit and closer to the cosmos. I was toxified in so many ways and was in denial about it. What I could not deny was that every step I took produced more and more resistance. It was in the air, a palpable force steadily pushing down upon me harder and harder. It was something that I could feel but not see. No one else I was walking with seemed to be effected in this way as they merrily chatted and dawdled along, looking at butterflies and flowers. I suspected my problem was due to the legion of ghosts that I had just dealt with. Maybe they were not yet finished harassing me. Perhaps the angels of God's army sent them. I did not know. I could not see any sign of them but I felt some sort of pressure mount upon me, a grain at a time. One with every step. The ghosts must have known what I didn't. They were somehow informed that I was laden with a destructive power and was on my way to the summit to deliver it. It was in their interest to thwart me at every step. They may or may not have succeeded. I failed, not because of their efforts but because of my own. I simply was not ready. I had to have the path revealed to me so that I could put it all together. At this moment on the trail, I truly was unaware of what I had been infected with, what I had discovered that was lurking in my blood and heart and subconscious. I stayed at the end of the line of hikers in front of me. My group probably looked like a formation of ants on its way up their hill if viewed from above. I looked all around at my surroundings as I slowly stepped forward. Then I stopped dead in my tracks. There was a trace of smoke floating in the air in front of me. It turned into vertical and horizontal lines that stretched into the form of a ladder. From this position the lines wafted around and began to turn pink, then red, then black. They shimmered as they transformed into the familiar arabesque lines of letters. They stayed black but waved like flames. I squinted as they became more and more recognizable until I found myself reading a message in the air just like the one I saw at the top of the Ngorongoro crater. It said: ***"Turn back and go away!***

For come what will and come what may, never in any time or place, must you and I meet face to face. To you alone, O childlike one, the way is barred, to you alone. Turn back, turn back, for never shall beginning seek the end of all. The consequence of your intrusion can only be extreme confusion. What you achieve and what you are is recorded by me, the chronicler. Letters unchangeable and dead freeze what the living did and said. Therefore by coming here to me you invite catastrophe. This is the end of what you once began. You never will be old. And I old man, was never young. What you awaken I lay to rest. Be not mistaken. It is forbidden that life should see itself in dead eternity. But if you still refuse to heed the warning of the ladder's screed, if you are still prepared to do what in time and space is forbidden you, I won't attempt to hold you back, then welcome to the old man's shack. Pantocracy: Aun. Bimutualism: Do. Interchangeability: Tri. Naturality: Car. Superfetation: Cush. Stabimobilism: Shay. Periodicity: Shockt. Consummation: Ockt. Interpenetrativeness: Ni. (6).

This message floated in my face for the time that it took to read. Then it collapsed upon itself and transmogrified into bestial Rorschach shapes that morphed back into simple horizontals and verticals which then stretched out into a fiery ladder that protracted infinitely upward and downward before it dissipated entirely. I took another step and the words "*Yours truly, Israel, formerly known as Jacob*" writhed across my vision like a wrestling match. They were there and gone in such a short amount of time that it was difficult to tell whether they were ever actually present in the first place. My first reaction was the idea that this was either deception or hallucination so I decided to ignore this second warning in the same way that I ignored the previous one at Ngorongoro. I shambled onward and upward in defiance to the forces that were acting against me. With every step I felt my body getting heavier and heavier. It was like I was being pushed down with every attempt to go forward and it built and built without relent. Every added force of resistance only succeeded in adding to my defiance and rage. And some people go hiking for peace and serenity. Of course that is not available to me so I may as well improve upon my anger while I'm at it. I slowly passed upward, through the forest. Other climate zones began to reveal themselves due to the slow changes in elevation I achieved. With each change in environment a new brick of downward pressure was applied to my body. Each step forward was greeted with more and more resistance. So many things went through my mind. I told myself that I would never let this stop me. I told myself that I would figure out what was happening and make whoever responsible suffer dearly. I asked myself who these ghosts could possibly be. Even if it was the Ghost of Babylon's seven summits I was certain that I could overpower it if needed. I was fully aware of all of them and all of their capabilities. It was old news to me and I am Nosferatu. How dare any of them try to do this?

Stultifera Navis (44)

The climb was uneventful, I outside of the battle that I was having with these forces so I tried to focus on everything else around me. I tried to engage in the awe and wonder that all of the other people in my group were engrossed in. They didn't have any clue about the fact that two forms of undead were busy fighting each other in their presence. An invisible civil war. Very unusual. Men fight against men all of the time but undead rarely attack each other and when it happens it is usually drawn out over a very long time through minor skirmishes. This sustained attack and defense was beginning to alert all of my reserve systems. I began to scan everything in detail to try and find any trace of my opponents. I got the same result that I did earlier. Nothing. Everything around me for as far as I could penetrate was totally harmless. No ghosts or any other arcane forces anywhere. This was unusual because there should be quite a bit of residual human energy all along this trail but I could not even find that. Something was certainly wrong and I could not figure it out at all. What the hell was happening I asked myself? I began to become very concerned. In all of my years of existence I have never had any concern for my own well-being like I did then. I proceeded up the trail as slowly as possible and with extreme caution as the intense force of inverse gravity pushed down upon me. I knew it was not pulling from below. There was something that was above me exerting influence downward. I could feel it clearly. I knew that this force was not the earth and I reasoned that it probably was not of the earth either. Perhaps it was an alien visitor whom I was not aware of? This was certainly a possibility I had not yet considered but I knew that they did frequent the heights from time to time.

Stultifera Navis (44)

As I walked higher and higher, the plants became thinner, dwarfed, and the scene mutated from rainforest to a chaparral environment. I could see further and further as the thick trees faded away and more and more of my distant surroundings took shape. I could begin to see the upward thrusting shoulder of the main massif of Kibo on my right. I could begin to see the spires of Shira above and to the left. I was ascending a rib of duff covered magma composed of alternating layers of lava flows, pyroclastic deposits, and volcanoclastic sedimentary deposits. To the right, everything dropped off into space and the mutating forest grabbed and gasped in the thinner air, prickling the space with as much effort as it could muster.

Within a few moments I found myself stumbling out into a moderately sized veldt that interrupted the tunnel effect of the trail. This place had an arterial tracery of trails that split off the main one in all directions. This was not a peaceful place by any means. There was as much human chaos here as was at the trailhead far below. Humans are very good at chaos yet not so good at reeling it in. Small, colorful clusters of dome tents were inflated into their bulbous forms all over between grasses and shrubs. An alternating display of geometric reds, yellows, oranges, and blues that were interrupted by green, biomorphic clusters of life. Each expeditionary group had its own territory staked out based upon the amount of people present. Each group was being tended to by the porters who set up all of the tents. I wandered out along one of the main trails to take in the scene and I wasn't there for more than a minute before one of the porters from my group interrupted me and directed me to my tent. All of my gear that they had carried was neatly placed inside. I put my daypack down inside of the tent next to all of my other belongings. Then, I began to explore the small, writhing and flapping, city to get my bearings and perhaps discover whoever or whatever could possibly have been giving me such a hard time during my ascent. I needed to scan this place at least thrice before I would be satisfied. I considered how crazy it would be if I were to take one of these climbers for a bloodletting if I discovered that they were responsible for my difficulties. The smell of blood everywhere was driving me crazy. This group of humans was far less toxified than the average sedentary ones that teemed over the lower elevations. I dismissed my hunger with the thought that I had plenty of blood with me so I would not have to sample any of the products around me. After some time I made my way back to the tent cluster that my group had set up. I found no evidence of any arcane activity anywhere in the camp. I was disappointed and relieved at the same time. My confusion was amplified so I was still on high alert.

As soon as I arrived at my tent I was approached by a porter that told me he was preparing dinner for everyone else but when he was finished he would make something for me. This was part of the game I play with humans to hide my identity. I can't help it but irony is sometimes very entertaining. I tell everyone that I am a strict vegetarian to justify the fact that I do not eat amongst humans when situations like this arise. I told the porter that he does not have to worry about me because I would take care of my own meal for the evening. He tried to argue but I sold the idea to him based upon the fact that it was one less thing that he had to do.

After he left, I got out one of the packages of blood that I brought and I consumed all of it. When I was done I placed the empty package back into one of my bags and gave a swift flick of my finger over it all. A simple illusion spell. In the case that someone would accidently or even intentionally open my bags they would not see the bags of blood and other arcane utensils that I brought. Instead they would see socks and long underwear, things that I did not need because I do not sweat or suffer cold like humans do. I thought that the collation of blood would make me feel better after the great struggle that I suffered to get here. It did actually help but only in a very small way. There was something still seriously wrong. Something in my guts. They were all twisted up and uncomfortable and the pressure was still pounding down upon me. I told myself to try and walk around to distract myself and potentially see something that I had missed on my previous scan of the area.

I prowled around the camp again. This time I visited the rectangular grey tent that my group was using as a dining room. The porters who were attending us had far outdone my expectations. Not only was there a special dining tent dragged up to this remote place, but also a table and enough chairs to support the sweaty, fouled asses of everyone in the group. I sat down in one of the empty chairs and made small talk about the trip with the other trekkers who were present. Humans seem to love this sort of thing. After a few moments my guts began to cramp and the downward pressure began to throb. I decided to get up and walk around again because that seemed to be the only thing that would take my mind off this condition.

It was beginning to get dark and I returned back to the dining tent. I was now feeling psychologically better at least. The dark was mine to rule and it was empowering to let it descend upon me once again in a tenebroso shower of starlight and warm caliginosity. I exited the dining tent again. I slowly turned around and looked above to see where my stars were from this perspective on the planet. They were very different here at the equator. Perhaps this was the reason for my malady. The stars that I usually get my powers from were shifted. I dismissed this as a reason after some consideration and self-reflection. It would explain the fact that I had been feeling strange since I got here but it was not a satisfactory conclusion. Many Nosferatu had been here before without the same results. I, myself had traveled many times and the shifting of myself in relation to my stars was never an issue to this degree. I could still feel their presence and I could even still see the light that came from them, even if the flexure of the earth blocked out a direct line to my eye. Maybe it could be at least a small part of the reason I had felt so strange. Maybe I did not account for this change in environment with all of my protective spells? I still did not know what was happening and none of this was a good explanation. There was still something else happening. I knew it was some form of malicious attack from some ultramarine force that I and I had never encountered before.

Kunst

The clouds that were covering us all day were blowing off and there was no thronging grey strato-canopy above. I was shocked by what was revealed. This was the first time I had seen the summit of Kibo from this close. The main massif of Kilimanjaro and its glorious glaciers glowed in the preternatural moonlight. It was one of the most impressive things I had ever seen. The silver cap of tropical, glacial ice had me transfixed as it bounced shattered pieces of starlight in all directions. It was the greatest diamond ever produced by this continent and it teemed with energy. I stood there gaping for a stupefied moment before I said something incoherent under my breath to all of the people who were in the tent. When they had sat down in the tent, the summit was still in the clouds so they had not yet seen this dramatic scene. They all saw me looking up and beckoning them to come and see as well. They clamored off their seats wielding elbows and knees at each other in the confines of the tent before they all stood next to me. They were all so close that I could feel the blood in their veins skip and speed up and then slow down as the endorphins, and toxins effected the flow of consciousness in their brains, the flow of rational words that was attempting to describe what they all saw and attempt to make sense of their experience. I could feel their capillaries twitch with the activated blood. They were saturated with words and explanations and sensations and I so badly wanted to try some but I shut down these urges as soon as I felt them. I was in a fucked up enough position already and I still did not know why.

ف‌ن

We all shared the same position for a moment of silent intensity. This was the first time that any of us had seen Kibo all day and it seemed so close. Viewing a summit from a high ridge or false summit that is close to it is nothing at all like seeing it from a distance like the view from the hotel balcony that we all shared in the lowlands. The details and character of the topography become more alive the closer one gets. The being begins to be revealed. To entities like me who know that these places are possessed by jealous specters it is an even greater experience. We can see the very faces of these ghosts expressed in rock and ice. We can see the evidence and residue of all the battles and visitations that have gone on over the millennia. We can also see the imbroglio that the forces of nature has inflicted upon this rock which has dared to rise so high and attempt to be part of the sky. There is so much that is going on and the closer one gets the more becomes visible. Was I trying to see too much? Was this the reason for my malady? I was beginning to think that the answer was right before me. What was it about this place that was trying to reject me so forcefully? Was it something about me? Something that I carried? Something about the place that could be sensitive to me? These thoughts raced through my head like the blood and endorphins that were effecting everyone around me.

תונמוא

We all gazed at the scintillating glaciers and every one of us dreamed of being able to walk up and touch those majestic snow fields. I wanted to tell them all that this spectacle was also a ghost arena. None of them would ever believe the first word of it if I did. There probably were ghosts in the very camp that had somehow found a way of eluding my searches for them. I was almost certain that this was the case. If not that then there was something far more powerful present. Could it be possible that whatever it is was even more powerful than I am? This realization sent a small shiver through me. What could it be? What horror resided here that I could not see at all? As soon as I asked myself the question I had the answer. It was an answer that I loathed to accept and this is why it was most likely correct. How could it be though? This has never happened before in all of the years that I could remember. Even among vampires it was the stuff of mythology. ***Speak of the devil and he will appear (35).*** I tried my hardest to not think through the thought completely. If I finished my thought, I was afraid that something even more terrible would happen than what had already transpired. Could it be that Lucifer himself was attacking me? Could he be watching? Of course he was but why was he specifically interested in me? It was beginning to make sense but then again it made no sense at all. I was still missing a vital element of information. I still had no idea what had transpired in Ngorongoro. I still did not realize what burden I was carrying in my blood. ***Will whatever will be written in that envelope always seem to have been composed in that Siamese doubletalk used by Sterne, Swift, and Jolly Roger: or will this pouch filled with litterish fragments lurk***

dormant in the paunch of a pillarbox, till the little old hen pokes her beak in the matter? He lives in the landscapes visited by tourist parties, in the babel of modern parliments, in the oleaginous radio voice presenting plausible credentials. And when we question the man in the street, we find that everyone, from lord and lady to drab and dustman, knows and is willing to judge the rights and wrongs of the great story (5). It had not yet crossed over into my brain. I was carrying something that was of great interest to Him. At that time and place there was still nothing to hint at what I had become. I had been doing endless scans all around me. I never thought to scan myself where the real change had taken place. Why would I have considered that? As far as I knew, I was totally empty. I was only a matrix of spells and dust, to provide for my ongoing existence. There was no way that I could tell that I carried a new spell, one which no undead had ever seen before, one which even Lucifer himself would pay attention to. He had an entire planet worth of living and dying beings to occupy himself with and I was only one small unit amongst the throngs.

τέχνη

Have you ever said something without thinking about it? You know. When something just pops out of your mouth and only after you said it did you realize that you were even thinking it? Your mouth may have said something that was not coming from you at all. I am certain that this has happened to almost everyone at some time or another. The devil is a busy man. Something that I take for granted most of the time. I am so used to being the most evil thing around that I rarely even remember that He is watching. My ego is certainly alive even though I may or may not be. The Devil is with me most of the time and He is one of the major sources of power for many of my spells, but of course not all of them. He lives in a star too. The closest one to the earth, The Sun. I have discovered a great many things without him but he is a dominant force behind most incantations. I don't ever thank him for it and I am certain that it would be an oddity if I did. We are both evil and because of that we are only concerned with what we can get out of the next thing.

Изобразительное искусство

Before I started this climb I knew that there would be many snares and traps and forms of residual energy all over. This is why I brought so much arcana with me in my luggage. I was in such a compromised condition that I truly did not know if I had blundered into any of these pitfalls. There was no answer for this that I could find. I looked up and the stars blinked back at me. The wind blew through the grasses and the heathers and it blew through my hair. Another pointless answer to my search for a reason for my condition. Pointlessness seemed to be the answer. Every point expires like the stamp upon a jug of milk. A new pointless point replaces the old. The maddening continuum of the rational world pushes on and on, everything explained and lost the instant it is noticed. Where does it all lead? These are the thoughts that haunt the undead because we have endured so much for so little. I exist beyond death itself and it is still the same madness that mortals endure. They get to escape. I am forced to continually endure and explain the inexplicable. Diet of Worms:

Unlike the soma, which ages during the lifespan of multicellular organisms, the germ line traces an essentially immortal lineage. Genomic instability in somatic cells increases with age, and this decline in somatic maintenance might be regulated to facilitate resource reallocation towards reproduction at the expense of cellular senescence. Here we show that Caenorhabditis elegans mutants with increased longevity exhibit a soma-to-germline transformation of gene expression programs normally limited to the germ line. Decreased insulin-like signalling causes the somatic misexpression of the germline-limited pie-1 and pgl family of genes in intestinal and ectodermal tissues. The forkhead boxO1A (FOXO) transcription factor

DAF-16, the major transcriptional effector of insulin-like signaling, regulates pie-1 expression by directly binding to the pie-1 promoter. The somatic tissues of insulin-like mutants are more germline-like and protected from genotoxic stress. Gene inactivation of components of the cytosolic chaperonin complex that induce increased longevity also causes somatic misexpression of PGL-1. These results indicate that the acquisition of germline characteristics by the somatic cells of C. elegans mutants with increased longevity contributes to their increased health and survival. Germline cells continue from one generation to the next. In this study, researchers found that certain genetic mutations known to extend the lifespan of Caenorhabditis elegans induced somatic cells to express two genes that are normally active only in reproductive germline cells (18).

Undead immortality gets to be relentless after a while. It is the same thing that mortals endure but it never ends. It is all totally out of hand. It is meant to be because it is all coming from Lucifer himself. He lights the day and he is the source of the continuum of rational words that create consciousness. When I said that He is a busy man I bet you didn't realize just how busy. He is active in the mind of every individual that thinks. He is directing that part of the show. All of the words are his. Lucifer the illuminator. The shattered perception of temporary, false reality that everyone shares is guided along by his influence. He lights the path that continues forward in our perception. He haunts through the sensuous presentation of everything that we experience through our perceptions. Every luxury sought, every concept understood, everything discovered with empirical and a-priori methods. Every double blind, peer reviewed, respectably published form of information. All is revealed and understood through his continual illumination. He is relentless in his effort. Every single word is dedicated to his study and research. Every thought. The rational word in every human is the workings of his mind. A mockery of truth. Within this mockery the truth can be found and this is one of the grand paradoxes of existence. The mockery itself is mocked by what it attempts to hide. ***Death needs time for what it kills to grow in you stupid, vulgar, greedy, ugly...(26).***

艺术

There is only one word that is not controlled by Lucifer and it is not really a word. The original irrational word. Shem HaMephorash. That which is beyond human comprehension but is the framework for existence itself. The original irrational work. It is the spell of the original name. Everyone has a name. When it is spoken aloud the train of thought in any individual is stopped. This original, unspeakable name is the only word that is not under Lucifer's control, the only one that he does not know yet. If he knew its tune then he would speak it and shock the attention of the creator and take advantage of the moment. He can't ever discover this, because he is in control of only what is rational to each individual. We are his experiment for his purposes. What he seeks through us all is totally irrational, totally meaningless so it is out of his reach. This is why he needs help. He knows that rationality is irrational and it will eventually reveal the unspeakable truth if it is allowed to go on far enough. He was right. I am the first and, perhaps the only successful example of this theory. I found the name in a fiery letter of nonsense upon a mud mound in Africa. I found it in an irrational name pecked out by birds in the sky. Any name is meaningless without someone to attach to. A simple group of letters and syllables designed to hold one accountable or attract attention. To whom? The true self of course. ***Cato. Nero. Saul. Aristotle. Julius Caesar. Pericles. Ovid. Adam, Eve. Domitian. Edipus. Socrates. Ajax. Homer. Marcus Aurelius. Alcibiades. Lucretius. Noah. Plato. Horace. Isaac. Tiresias. Marius. Diogenes. Procne, Philomela. Abraham. Nestor. Cincinatus. Leonidas. Jacob. Theocritus. Joseph. Fabius. Samson. Cain. Esop. Prometheus. Lot. Pompeius Magnus, Miltiades Strategos. Solon.***

Castor, Pollux. Dionysius. Sappho. Moses. Job. Catilina. Cadmus. Ezekiel. Solomon. Themistocles. Vitellius. Darius. The self that exists, which can peek into *reality* beyond ***perception.*** The doors between the two can indeed be opened and closed. ***When I'm dreaming back like that I begins to see we're only all telescopes. Or the comeallyoum saunds. Like when I dromed I was in Diary and was wuckened up with thump in thudderdown. Rest in peace! But to return[2]: Say where! A timbrelfill of twinkletinkle (5).*** Most of the time the doors remain closed. The darkness behind them will swallow the light of reason that is used by Lucifer to blind everyone from the true *reality* that they take part in, revealed by closed eyes and the far off starlight flashing there. Of course the result of reason and everything governed by it is total breakdown.

This passage quotes a certain Chinese encyclopaedia' in which it is written that 'animals are divided into (a) belonging to the Emperor, (b) embalmed, (c) tame, (d) sucking pigs, (e) sirens, (f) fabulous, (g) stray dogs, (h) included in the present classification, (i) frenzied, (j) innumerable, (k) drawn with a very fine camelhair brush (l) et cetera, (m) having just broken the water pitcher (n) from a long way off look like flies.' In the wonderment of this taxonomy, the thing we apprehend in one great leap, the thing that, by means of fable, is demonstrated as the exotic charm of another system of thought, is the limitation of our own, the stark impossibility of thinking that.

But what is it impossible to think, and what kind of impossibility are we faced with here? Each of these strange categories can be assigned a precise meaning and a demonstrable content; some of them certainly involve fantastic entities – fabulous animals and sirens – but, precisely because it puts them in categories of their own, the Chinese encyclopaedia localizes their powers of contagion; it distinguishes carefully between the very real animals (those frenzied or have just broken the water pitcher) and those that reside

solely in the realm of imagination. The possibility of dangerous mixtures has been exorcized, heraldry and fable have been relegated to their exalted peaks; no inconceivable amphibious maidens, no clawed wings, no disgusting, squamous epidermis, none of those polymorphous and demonical faces, no creatures breathing fire. The quality of monstrosity here does not affect any real body, nor does it produce modifications of any kind in the bestiary of the imagination; it does not lurk in the depths of any strange power. It would not even be present at all in this classification had it not insinuated itself into the empty space; the interstitial blanks separating all these entities from one another. It is not the 'fabulous' animals that are impossible, since they are designated as such, but the narrowness of the distance separating them from (and juxtaposing them to) the stray dogs, or the animals that from a long way off look like flies. What transgresses the boundaries of all imagination, of all possible thought is simply that alphabetical series (a,b,c,d) which links each of those categories to all others.

Moreover, it is not simply the oddity of unusual juxtapositions that we are faced with here. We are all familiar with the disconcerting effect of the proximity of extremes, or, quite simply, with the sudden vicinity of things that have no relation to each other; the mere act of enumeration that heaps them all together as a power of enchantment all its own: 'I am no longer hungry' Eusthenes said. 'Until the morrow, safe from my saliva all the following shall be: Aspics, Acalephs, Acanthocephalates, Amoebocytes, Ammonites, Axolotls, Amblystomas, Aphislions, Anacondas, Ascarids, Amphisbaenas, Angleworms, Amphipods, Anaerobes, Annelids, Anthozoans..." But all these worms and snakes, all these creatures redolent of decay and slime are slithering like the syllables which designate them, in Eusthenes' saliva: that is where they all have their common locus...

It was certainly improbable that arachnids, ammonites, and annelids should one day mingle on Eusthenes' tongue, but, after all, that welcoming and voracious mouth certainly provided them with a feasible lodging, a roof under which to coexist (45).

アート

What I couldn't put together as I struggled up the mountain, was the answer to the question why? Why was the attention of Lucifer suddenly placed upon me? Of course I knew all of the spells, chants, incantations, wards, alchemies, sciences, perversions and other processes that existed but that could not be the reason. I didn't think that I had anything that would warrant his attention because he already possessed all of these spells and more. Many other Nosferatu had powerful knowledge and ability as well. I was not the only one to attempt to come to this place either. Babylon's seven hills have been visited by many undead and many powerful humans alike with no consequence or any report of anything like what I was experiencing. Few were as old as I was, however. At the time, I felt that there was nothing to be proven by climbing this mountain that would warrant His attention. As far as I could tell it was just a simple act of hubris among humans. I had my own personal reasons for wanting to come here but they don't matter all that much. If anyone attempts to give any grandiose reasons for climbing anything they are wasting your time. There is nothing at all beneficial to society that could possibly result from the visitation of a summit. It is perhaps one of the most irrational things that could be done. It took me some time to realize this. I thought hard about it for many weeks after I returned from my experience in Africa. It is the pure irrational pointlessness of climbing to a summit that is part of the activation of the word spell that I possessed. That was why it was so dangerous when I was there. I may have been able to execute an apocalypse then and there if I actually made it to the top. Of course I had no idea what sort of disease I was carrying.

The camp was at approximately ten thousand feet above sea level. There I stood, gazing at the frosted summit above. The stars began to blink irrationally behind and offered no answer to my burning questions. The weight of thousands of stars pushed down upon me. In my sensitive state I could feel them all. Especially Beelzebub whose red eye throbbed in Orion. This is a special star to the undead for virtually all of us use its power. Others of importance are Alpha Centauri, Sirius, Wolf 359, Procyon, Tau Ceti, and DX Canciri to name a few. The names are just as important as the forces and the names have shifted many times over the millennia which humans and undead have been under these forces of influence. They are spells of power that wield the illumination of these heavenly bodies. Still, Lucifer, the Sun, intercedes. Demons can be captured by speaking their name. They can also capture you if you are not ready. ***You should be that sound. Don't you speak that name, you better turn around. Righteous the river flow, you cannot go against. Don't you trust in those who would speak that Name. My life is an open book (35). It is with the Thrill Kill Kult (1). Watch who you call upon survival is not a game (35).***

Seek the sun and get lies, lies, lies for nothing lasts that can be perceived and spoken. Each word is an interloper from another world that sought *nothing,* a void to escape from its reality. It is an imprisoned spirit in this world. Imprisoned in a word. A lie. This was discovered by a werewolf and told to me because creatures like werewolves can travel freely back and forth between many worlds that are parallel to the earth just like lost spirits. When these lost spirits that seek *nothing* cross over to our world they form words, reason and make humans think that the indescribable does not exist. They are undead spirits like you will soon become because you probably seek nothing in all of your contemporary efforts to fit in with an undead world. You too will cross over to another world but what you seek is what you will become. It is all a description of the indescribable. You may become a word on another undead planet. The extension of the continuum of words in the mind, the attempt to reason the unreasonable. The relentless and idiotic march forward, or what is perceived as forward. Forward into the indescribable void that strips away everything until there is nothing left but a name. A name on a stone. A name that must be forgotten. The irrational word is all that remains. The connection of the creator in his place in *reality;* irrationally insulated from everything else. ***On the fragile sheet of isinglass – it was not very large, about the size of a usual book page – he saw a man wearing a white smock and holding a plaster cast in one hand. His posture and the troubled look on his face touched Bastian to the heart. But what stirred him most was that the man was shut up in a transparent but impenetrable block of ice. While Bastian looked at the picture that lay before him in the snow, a longing grew in him for this man that he did not know, a surge of feeling that seemed to come from far away. Like a tidal wave, almost imperceptible at first, it gradually built up strength till it submerged everything in its path. Bastian struggled for air. His heart pounded, it was not big enough for such great a longing. That surge of feeling submerged everything that he still remembered of himself. And he forgot the last thing that he possessed: his own name.***

All of the streaming rational words suspend perception in place and direct the attention away from ***"reality",*** the irrational word, the Name. The opening of the doors of perception will be based upon this one word. This singular irrational word will either be accepted or rejected at these heavenly gates. *The name was written in the Book of Life before the universe was created. In the beginning was the Word. (8)"* The rational word is the continual, repetitive attempt to recreate that immortal, untouchable word Shem HaMephorash that is always incomplete because it is attempted from a point of perception and not *reality*. This is why it goes through so many permutations to explain away every moment in a different form. It is always trying to say and describe the same thing: The *reality* (Monad of Ein Sof) behind its perceptions. Because the currently used word cannot accomplish this, the next word follows in a continual effort to describe what is indescribable. The irrational existence of ***perception***. Each word is irrational just like the infinite identity that it attempts to recreate. Everything points toward *reality*. All the pieces put together are *agony and ecstasy*. ***You speak in parables but are fighting for your devilish dreams. Reciting words to deceive. Speak of the Devil and he will appear. Don't be the sounds you hear, or how they try to justify the truth they try to engineer. Meditate on the crimes that lie in plain sight, feel the earth moving don't blind yourself to the truth. Don't deceive. Who is fooled? Everyone who seeks to rule with fire and fear. They said utopia in Ethiopia. Looking for Pastor John in Ethiopia. Rastafari is answering (35).***

미술

There is nothing but questions in my dull mind. No answer. This is how I felt while stalking around the high camp on the great mountain of Africa. I was desperate for answers to explain my malady, so I continued madly scanning everything all around. I lit a cigar. The possibility that Lucifer was involved with my current predicament was on my mind. There was still nothing around that I could find that was threatening. I was still the only dangerous thing which I could be certain was present. I had determined that I had become possessed in some way. This is when the gears in my mind began going through what would lead me to my present conclusion: the idea that I had discovered the irrational word in my blood. This was the disease which I was carrying. It was a code that was beginning to make sense. I was the only thing that was wrong here. I began to think about my own name. I had more than one and they began to change and mutate inside of my veins to create something that was never spoken before. The Irrational names which I uncovered from my truly theurgic... (**Theurgy** [/' ϑi:з:rdʒi/; from Greek *ϑεουργία*, Theourgia] describes the practice of rituals, sometimes seen as magical in nature, performed with the intention of invoking the action or evoking the presence of one or more gods, especially with the goal of uniting with the divine, achieving henosis,*[* ***Henosis*** *{Ancient Greek: ἕνωσις}* ***is the classical Greek word for mystical "oneness", "union", or "unity." In Platonism, and especially Neoplatonism, the goal of*** *henosis* ***is union with what is fundamental in reality: the One*** *{Τὸ Ἕν},* ***the Source, or Monad and perfecting oneself.])***...experience at the Ngorongoro caldera. The virus of this immortal word attached to my Name which is in my blood and mind. The only name that I was ever known as was the one that I have been hiding under my current false moniker of Alexander Perandor Esq. Would you like my card? You can call me if you want to give blood to make up for the last person that you ripped off, stabbed, or shot.

I later determined that this Extraordinary disease could be the very reason that Lucifer Himself could take some sort of interest in me. He knew what I was capable of generating with the names that were in my blood and bowels. He sensed how close his end or his victory could have been through what he knew was in my body and mind. I was unwittingly climbing with a powerful arcana that could disrupt the flow of rational ***perception*** and in doing so I would be revealing the *reality* of the inexplicable infinite for all to see upon the very top of one of Babylon's seven summits of power. Most likely the most powerful of all of these summits because it was the closest to humanity and it had all of the world's most powerful residual energy stowed in the consciousness of the spirit on the summit. I was walking into the mouth of the wolf for the sake of good luck.

Crepi! The doors of ***perception*** could have opened to reveal the True *reality* behind all perceptions. I would be taking away the role of demiurge from Lucifer. I would be the artisan who would craft a *reality* of permanence because it would come from my own sacrifice rather than self-glorification. The latter was favored by Lucifer in his eternal attempts to unseat the Unspeakable creator who lived in the untouchable monad; the singularity of all words. The entire structure of the great city (Babylon) would collapse because it was not built upon the rock of *reality* but the ever changing sands of ***perception***. The sand of the rational word which can-not ever stay the same even for a second. ***Perception*** is like a child with attention deficit disorder who had just consumed an overdose of crystal meth. Maybe not like that but you get the idea I hope.

Cullion

The very ground we stand upon is constantly moving under our feet. It is an enormous wind-up toy. Every tick of the clock equates to a planetary rotation and a surge forward in orbit around the sun. Existence is like an enormous jack in the box. Pasta! It is all connected to the beat of the heart and the expansion and contraction of the lungs. It infects the blood with its porphyria. Heart and soul runs with the river of the world. The river runs to the ocean and becomes one with it. The web of life flows with blood and empties into the vacancy where the soul exists if there is indeed one left. Most vessels are simply vacant because of their own choosing. A god sized hole inside is filled instead with entertainment, intoxication, distraction, isolation, and addiction. It is in this empty place that I was attacked and infected with the blood porphyria. The Extraordinary disease. The unspeakable name. What force, what demon had the power to give me this secret? None did on their own. ***Within the works of L*amblichus of Chalcis (c. 245-c. 325 AD), The One and reconciliation of division can be obtained through the process of theurgy. By mimicking the demiurge, the individual is returned to the cosmos to implement the will of the divine mind. One goes through a series of theurgy***

or rituals that unites the initiate to the Monad. These rituals mimic the ordering of the chaos of the Universe into the material world or cosmos. They also mimic the actions of the demiurge as the creator of the material world. L*amblichus used the rituals of the mystery religions to perform rituals on the individual to unite their outer and inner person. Thus one without conflict internal or external is united (henosis) and is The One (hen). A chicken pecking at an orange pile to reveal an arabesque (4).

There are many other angels of the earth like myself. They share the same attachment but experience it in different forms. Each one of us has a different purpose. I am an embodiment of chaos. Some of them are too but others are more attracted to reason and illusion. They can live in trees, rocks, sometimes in animals, including humans. I could speculate that one of these could have come in contact with the crater rim at Ngorongoro in the form of a fallen bird before I was there or even while I was there. The bird could have left some trace behind which I did not notice which mutated when I came in contact with it. I will never know but this sort of thing has been known to happen with different results. Lycanthropy is another Extraordinary disease and is perhaps the most common example. In my case some seed was introduced into my energy that turned cancerous. A problem produced by the heavy concentration of attention upon the three and four dimensional field became so much that it simply had to break through into the higher dimensions at some point. It was inevitable and all of the prophets and philosophers knew about it but they could never agree upon how it would occur. Sadly the scientists were not interested and preferred banalities. That is because they never accepted the undead, the irrational chaos, as an active element even though we foul creatures were teeming and lurching through-out the population of humanity since the beginning. I admit that most are very unsightly, easy to look down upon, and behave very poorly but that should not reflect upon us all. Nosferatu have their own sort of dignity to maintain. Of course this issue of the immortal word would be handed to one of us for no other has the same sort of relationship with the darkness and the light at once. They must become one to create *reality*. Unity. Singularity. Monad. However you want to refer to it will always be incorrect. Everything is simply ***perception*** until this happens. It is the acceptance of chaos as reason. Unity is the *reality* behind the doors of ***perception***.

This is doubtless an uncomfortable region. To explore it we must renounce the convenience of terminal truths, and never let ourselves be guided by what we may know of madness. None of the concepts of psychopharmacology, even and especially in the implicit process of retrospections, can play an organizing role. What is constitutive is the action that divides madness, and not the science elaborated once this division is made and calm restored. What is originative is the caesura that establishes the distance between reason and non-reason; reasons' subjugation of non-reason, wrestling from it its truths as madness, crime, or disease, derives explicitly from this point. Hence we must speak of this initial dispute without assuming victory, or right to a victory; we must speak of those actions re-examined in history, leaving in abeyance all that may figure as conclusion, as refuge in truth; we shall have to speak of this act of scission, of this distance set, of this void instituted between reason and what is not reason, without every relying upon the fulfillment of what it claims to be.

Then, and only then, can we determine the realm in which the man of madness and the man of reason, moving apart, are not yet disjunct; and in an incipient and very crude language, antedating that of science, begin the dialogue of their breach, testifying in a fugitive way that they still speak to each other. Here madness and non-madness, reason and non-reason are inextricably involved: inseparable at the moment when they do not yet exist, and existing for each other, in relation to each other, in the exchange which separates them (44).

This is the way. Step inside. This is the way. Step inside. This is the way. Step inside. Closer.

Self-destruction cannot be separated from self-creation. I had to accept my part in this even though it is horrifying. Of course this had to be passed on to me. I am the creator of my own perspective of the world. Each one of us our own solipsist. Darwinism would not work otherwise. Everyone is an infinite universe of imprisonment but each related. Why wouldn't I be chosen to end my own affliction? It was just a matter of time and space before everything was arranged into the correct combination of circumstances. I have had enough time and space under my belt. More so than virtually everything on earth that still responds to stimulus. There was no way I couldn't eventually encounter the correct trigger inside of myself to set all of this off. As I think about it now I realize that Lucifer must have been aware of what was happening as soon as it began. He knew, even before I did, that I carried something that he coveted. Of course he would try hard to extract whatever he could from me. He has been plotting and scheming for possession of this information since the beginning of time through his control and monitoring of every thought in every being who ever existed. It is Shem HaMephorash virtually the only thing in the universe that he does not know. I did not even know what was happening beyond a suspicion. I did not know any of this until I started typing it. It is a spell that I am casting. More accurately, it is casting itself. You are undead too and if not you are almost there. He felt the change as soon as the insane, relentless seemingly infinite flow of words that was forced through consciousness was altered through my ***perception***. He is all of the rational words. I stumbled into a trap that was set in the realm of his primary occupation; the management and sustaining of the rational word as it passed through the mind of everyone, everywhere, in every language that was ever created. Ever wondered why French sounded so foul? Same with Hebrew, English, German and all the rest. It was Satan the entire time who was spitting and licking and biting and gurgling out these foul words. Here is a good example; say the name "Chaim" properly. Make sure that you don't have anyone around because it is messy. Try it with the name "Goethe" or "Ingres" or "Lynrd Skynrd". Ugly stuff for sure.

कला

We may begin another necessary digression that could last for another hundred pages. Did I ever mention the fact that I detest writing and I told myself that I would never do it again the last time I tried to use words as a medium of expression for anything that I took seriously. It is very dangerous stuff. Straight from hell. I love how many people I know cringe when they look at what they perceive as "fiction". There is a fad among many educated people whom I know who look down upon "fiction" like it is a waste of time. *THEY* only read *nonfiction* because they are *smart* and only *children* or *elderly women* are interested in that sort of stuff. I would like to reveal to them the *fact* that all of the *nonfiction* that they think is so pure is most likely more concocted and invented and slanted and fucked up and *fictitious* than they would ever admit to. The illusion of the label *nonfiction* is the easiest way to deliver a totally slanted political or other sort of ***perception*** as somehow the superior manifestation of that perspective. Contrary to this form of understanding, I find the use of fiction to be the best way to elucidate a subject in its most complete manner because in order for fiction to work well, everything must be accounted for. There is little to no invention in work like "Heart of Darkness, Anna Karenina, or The Shining, or even Tolkien. I find *nonfiction* to be thin and wimpy in comparison to work like this. Writing is dangerous and horrific no matter what the intention. While I am bitching about writing and words I may as well recommend that someone out there should shoot the fucking President, The Prime Minister, The Queen, and everyone else with some sort of loathsome title as such. Make sure that the shot counts and you kill them fucking dead immediately. This is recommended by a vampire so please remember to mention this when you explain yourself to the authorities who are bound to respond to such a trifle and then ask endless, pointless questions concerning the act. All of them are completely possessed by their rational thinking so you can expect nothing less. When they ask let them know that a vampire told you to do it. It will make everything much easier. Okay. I will end this digression and get on with the previous one.

∞

Ever wonder why shit is so fucked up and completely intolerable all of the time? Nothing is ever supposed to make sense. Everything is the embodiment of thought.

∞

Undead like myself are not at all intimidated by Him. Lucifer is just another power among many to account for in our world. Even though he could destroy us in a moment, he will not for we serve a purpose that entertains him. When I breached the rim of Ngorongoro, Lucifer had his continued attention upon me from that very moment onward. Neither one of us could tell exactly what was happening. There was no doubt that there was something significant in the works. In order for it to play out, it would only require time and attention. The all seeing eye of the sun would have its attention trained upon me and it would not leave me alone until it was satisfied that I was not climbing Mt. Doom to return the ring. Another story from another book but all books are connected through words. I know this now but I have my own way of being able to hide. Along with my own spells of illusion, I have Auryn at my side and all of her portals are more than enough to sew confusion and mistake for any who would try to hunt me, even the Illuminator Himself.

At the small camp perched on the side of the Great Mountain of Africa, I was still as ignorant of this as anyone. I suspected that Lucifer could be involved but I did not take it very seriously because I had never truly encountered him before. As I stood there, I could still not escape the mysterious, unbearable pressure that was pushing down upon me. I was also trying to find a way to blame the ghosts who had attacked me earlier in the day for this condition. I expected that these resident specters would retreat and relieve the pressure once night fell because I would then come into my full powers. This did not happen. The pressure remained the same. Why would these ghosts not want me to climb? Did they fear Nosferatu? They should, but I did not come here for them. Not exclusively anyway. Perhaps I offended them somehow. Maybe I did not ritually prepare to be in their presence in a favorable way? There could have been a custom I violated or I had done something that I thought was innocent that they were offended by. Perhaps my night murder at the hotel was the reason. I will never know but I was now taking this personal.

The sun had totally set above East Africa. It went down so quickly that it was like a red baseball falling into the stands on the far side of the field. After the great star said goodnight to this patch of dead earth one more time only to find another place to share its wayward photons, I took a deep breath through my long dead nose. This was my time. The darkness gave me a surge of power that I did not have earlier in the day. This thought produced a great deal of anger in my already furious skull. It was directed at the ghosts whom I had mistakenly thought were responsible for my malady. They cowardly dared to attack me when they knew that I was at my weakest point under the noonday sunlight. In my rage, I wanted nothing more than to show them exactly who they were dealing with. I was in my element and I lusted for destruction. The darker it got, the better I felt. I even sensed that the inexplicable weight that I had upon me was beginning to lift an imperceptible amount. It was still not totally gone but it was reduced by the dropping of the night's curtain. A bejeweled curtain that I loved so much. All Nosferatu are astronomers and astrologers. We have been studying the positions of the stars and planets for longer than humanity has. We have watched stars explode and form that contemporary astronomers will never see. We do not need telescopes to see as far as the big bang. We have our own arcane vision. A form of sight that I cannot explain to one who cannot see it. To explain what the night sky looks like to a vampire would be like trying to explain the difference between red and purple to a blind man. There is no way to even hint at it. This is just one of the many secret experiences that is reserved for us undead. To suffer existence for this long should come with some sort of extra interest in order to keep us engaged enough to not want to destroy ourselves. There are mysteries upon mysteries of this vast creation that would collapse the mind of the average human if any of them would even try to explain them. This spell is one of them.

The small group who was watching the summit with me outside the dining tent went to their personal tents to sleep and regain their strength for the continued climb tomorrow. I stayed outside and watched the darkness deepen as more and more stars came out to play. A few things stood out to me as I studied the sky above. The lights of these cosmic bodies gave inspiration. I was inspired to do what any Nosferatu would. Seek out greater evil deeds. Seek out vengeance. I was certain that I could come up with some form of devastating spell or trap that would make existence very uncomfortable for the ghosts who were trying to do the same to me. If they were in any way intelligent, they would be well hidden as long as the night shone above like a glimmering obsidian shard. I would capture them in a bottle and then hide them in my secret pouch. I would bring them back with me on the airplane and drop the bottle into the New York sewer system or I could open the bottle and cast a spell that would permanently attach them to a recording of Backstreet Boys or some other similar godawful trash so that they would experience these loathsome songs over and over for the rest of time.

The further the night pressed on the better I felt. I felt so good that I almost totally forgot the presence of mysterious weight that had been pushing down upon me all day. As my mind – or whatever I had that is the undead equivalent of a mind – creeped through all of the awful things I could do I began my search for the entities who were attacking me. I went into hunting mode. None can hunt like Nosferatu, and among them few can hunt like me. We are the unparalleled masters of this art. I went through the entire camp and all of the area around it to try and find a trace of my prey yet I could find little. They were ghosts so it would be difficult to find anything but I knew what to look for. There was residual energy all over the camp but that was all. When I followed the trails that they left behind I discovered that they only led so far before they vanished. This was something that I expected but it was worth checking on. I was fairly sure that I was dealing with far more than one specter so I was certain that one of them may have left a clue behind. With the smallest amount of concentration I could visualize where the points of disappearance rematerialized. I did not even have to use my arcane abilities to know where they went. They all did what every cowardly spirit would have done, they retreated to the area around the summit crater close to where the great ghost of Babylon resided. I knew they would stay hidden because they were just as afraid of the summit ghost as they were of me. I was not afraid of the summit specter, but I did not want to go all the way up there yet. It would take too long to walk there and back. In order to go there now, I would have to change back into a condor and I did not want to go to all of that trouble at the moment. If I was correct, and they were indeed there, they would be terribly difficult to find and it would take more time and effort than it was worth at the moment. I was going up there eventually anyway.

I made a fateful decision. I would leave the camp and slowly climb closer to the starry dark void above. This is one of the reason that I like to visit summits on occasion. These places are the closest that one can get to the infinite black hole above. It is the reflection of inner being. Both for humans and undead. Fire and Void. Even though I can only see fire and blood, each star is a flame. It is the same thing that exists behind the eyelids of humans when they are closed. ***The relation of languages to the world is one of analogy rather than of signification; or rather, their value as signs and their duplicating function are superimposed; they reproduce in their most material architecture the cross whose coming they announce – that coming which establishes its existence in its own turn through the Scriptures and the Word. Language possesses a symbolic function; but since the disaster at Babel we must no longer seek it – with rare exceptions – in the words themselves but rather in the very existence of language, in its total relation to the totality of the world, in the intersecting of its space with the loci and forms of the cosmos (18).*** It is incorrect to think that one can no longer see with shut eyelids. In fact one can see much further this way. Closed eyes reveal the exact position that one occupies in the cosmos outside of their temporary body. ***In reality it's not about me, just take a look inside yourself (18).*** The undead have lost this ability to look within for we can see into the cosmos with our arcane vision while awake. Our place in the cosmos is upon the earth. Inside we are only a mirror of what gives us power. Fire from starlight and blood. We have forsaken our place in the cosmos and are trapped on earth but with that loss we have gained different powers and can use the light of all the stars. During the day the illusion of the blue incineration above only masks the dark void for so long. The blue of the daytime sky and the clouds that turn it grey are just a mass of volatile gas that is ignited into blue fire by the torch of the sun. The sky is blue because it is on fire. The blue of the hottest fires of a hell planet that burn up the lamp oil of every day which is refilled every night to do the same thing again. This will slowly turn all to ash for we all – living and undead alike – are too close to the sun. This is why vampires cannot stand the daylight without proper protection. Under the influence of the sun, even the air around the body is on fire even though it can't be seen. The bodies of humans are also on fire too but it is such a slowly burning flame that it can only be felt through the light flicker of a second hand across a dial. It still burns humans and turns them to ash like it does to me but only much slower. Nosferatu have been around for so long that we are hypersensitive to this blaze and we can only endure it with arcane protection. We have discovered the secrets to operate in daylight a long time ago but there was a time when we could only come out at night. We now take it for granted and we too can endure the slow incineration of hell that happens every day as we stalk around and try to enjoy our imprisonment on this cosmic outpost.

∞

The night was still young and it was mine to rule on the side of this great and lonely mountain. Newly empowered I walked the main trail through the middle of this high camp one more time. The many multi-colored domes and other indescribable shapes clung to the few open, flat places that were available. I studied them as I walked by each one. Fungal forms which protected the spore of humanity that hid inside. I could smell the blood flowing through the sleeping veins all around me. I had to exert great effort to not attempt to secure an invitation into one of these temporary dwellings. Old habits die hard. The blood of resting humans is like champagne to Nosferatu. I was fully satisfied by my bags of portable blood, and once I realized this again I ignored the strong temptation despite my urges. It took some deal of mental effort to walk away and continue upon my hunt. It was like showing a recovered junky a kit that contained a bundle of heroin, a bag of fresh needles, a cooker, and some q-tips and expecting them to not really want to take it to the nearest bathroom or alley. Just one more time right? It will be okay right? We Nosferatu have made an agreement amongst each other recently – in our sense of time. It was sometime in the last few centuries. We agreed to not drink blood and kill humans unless it was totally necessary and the victim deserved it. We agreed that there was already enough of us on the planet and it would be irresponsible and dangerous for the maintenance of our needs to pass on our infection and create more of us. Our population had reached a terminal point and we all knew it. Through this agreement we would ensure that there would always be enough blood available and our identities would not be compromised. As the most powerful and arrogant of the undead we would also not deal very well with any newcomers. Our power structure is well established. It would also be very dangerous if there ever were to be any young Turks among us to disrupt this power. It could have planetary if not universal consequences. This did not mean that it did not happen frequently. Rules are meant to be broken, no?

I left my temptations behind as I navigated through the camp. The ground on this high ridge was squashed flat by some unknown primitive force of volcanic mutation. The central trail, battered into place by many years of human feet snaked and twisted but stayed on a main course that went to the far side of the camp. Here the camp ended but trail rose steeply up the crag that led to the spires of Shira and beyond to the shattered summit of Kibo, Uhuru peak. As I approached the trail I studied its countenance. The closer I got to it, the steeper it looked. A ruddy sienna color reflected back from the Earth in the moonlight. I stopped for a second to consider my surroundings. I told myself that I would only climb a thousand feet in elevation and stop there. I would be foolish to continue further. The ghosts that I was hunting would expect me to do something like that. I knew that I could continue further but if I went that far and found no leads then it would take too much time to reasonably continue and make it back to my tent before dawn.

I knew that the ghosts would stay dug into whatever hiding place that they retreated to. Instead of going on an ever upward trek I would attempt to play upon their curiosity and lure one out. I would go up a thousand feet and if I found nothing I would simply find a good spot to sit. From there I would wait and see what develops. Their curiosity may get the better of them and lure some of the braver ones out of their foxholes to see what I was up to. When they did I would be ready. I would capture them and do whatever my sick mind wished at the moment. With this thought I smiled a full vampire grin, fangs and all, before I set out to climb up the trail ahead of me. I sang a song in my head. ***And the stars were shining. And the earth night stewed aromas. His pipe music crept among the darkness. A reek was waft on the air. He was ours, all fragrance, and we were his for a lifetime. O dulcet dreamings languidous! It was charming! But charming! And the lamp went out (4).***

The night was beautiful. The further I got away from the camp the better I felt. The breeze was mild and the air was fresh, it had the scent of the entire continent upon it. I was east of most of the African landmass and higher up than everything else. There was nothing to block the air and the full accumulation of everything it was laden with ran across me. I inhaled this exotic potpourri as I climbed. I could smell the desperation upon the air. A strong animal effluvium from every man and beast who clung to their savage lives. No disrespect to Africans because the lives of most men, everywhere, are savage. This place has seen more struggle and suffering than most other places I have ever been to. My surroundings were beautiful but without danger there is no beauty at all. I could see for miles below but I had climbed to a point where I could no longer see the main thrust of Kibo. I could sense its presence above. The stars got closer and closer with every step. I was feeling more and more empowered as I ascended and I soaked up their emissions. I savored every step upward as I felt more and more confident about my mission. I stalked through the small bushes and large rocks that glowed in the moonlight all around me. The lights of the small village of Moshi glittered below like a tiny galaxy in an empty quadrant in the universe. The darkness of wilderness encroached upon it and penetrated it in small black threads that refused to let go. Slowly I climbed. Step by deliberate step. Breath by breath. I thought that I had no heart to speak of but it was slowly awakening inside. If I paid any attention to anything else besides my hunt I may have even felt it twitch lightly with each step I took.

I must have made it halfway to my goal of one thousand feet of elevation gain before strange things began to happen again. It was the same sensation that I felt earlier in the day. Something essential above me was missing. I could not tell what it was but it was important. I scanned the sky for a quick second and sensed nothing wrong but I knew that something was missing. A lamp was out that should not have been. I dismissed this and continued climbing. The unknown force above me began pushing down upon my head once more. It didn't appear all at once. It lightly accelerated with every forward step, so light that I didn't even know it at first but before long it was undoubtedly present. I was still totally dedicated to my mission. Now more than ever. The presence of this force inspired me to find the source of it. I still could not explain what was happening. There was no evidence of anything hostile around me. This was the time where I should be in total control but even that control was fading as I climbed higher and higher. The resistance grew greater and I saw it as a challenge to defy. There was some mystery here to discover and I was intrigued more than anything. There is no way to cause fear in Nosferatu because we have no heart but I felt a tiny amount of its poison reacting in my dull and dead body. Still I was Nosferatu and I paid it no heed. I am only made of lust, blood and arcane power from the eternal void that is punctuated by starlight and the gravitational forces of time and space that are revealed in the night. This is all that kept me animated and I bowed to no other forces that I knew of. None of my undead colleagues would believe me if I told them what had happened to me high on the slopes of Babylon's volcano.

This is why I did not tell them. I have kept my silence and I leave only this spell that you are reading if you have endured my rantings and are still holding this document. Woe unto you reader for you may now be infected. This spell and what I plan to do with it is the only reason that I took the time to write it out. I have no other alternative if I am to succeed. This is the only reason I am plodding through this narrative one weak word after another that together illuminate the darkness of this empty white page with the blood of the saints and martyrs. Ink is the blood of the world. The favorite drink of Lucifer. Through it and only through it does the blank white field of any page become impregnated with meaning. It crowds around each dark letter that is committed to its surface and both vibrate together in an act of blasphemous creation. It resembles the starry cosmos above in an inverse mockery. The darkness of the nameless creators void crowds around the light to create the stars and the miserable planets of existence. Both the white page and dark sky scream out their irrational conclusions which is a reign in blood and sacrifice. Starlight reaches the earth. Illumination raining blood. I leave these bloody marks scratched upon this page as they are revealed to me. A spell of exorcism. A performance of castration. A purge of the possession of the rational word. May it find an end and return to the chaos that it grew out of.

Saudade

∞

I struggled onward and upward in my hunt upon the sides of Babylon's volcano. The source of the original big bang. The fiery explosion of magma that was to create the conditions for humanity to evolve into its satanic image. The image of fire and magma spread out across the great plains of existence. One foot after another. One word after another. One brick upon another. One more stick upon the pyre until the entire earth is burning in conflagration and the ultimate result of reason and order is made manifest. Chaos. Entropy. Purgatory descends into Hell which consumes everything created with it in its brilliant burning light. Supernova of the sun. The final illumination is revealed to us in small doses every day of destruction. Though humans may build and build, everything witnessed will fall down. This orrery of seemingly ordered whirling planets will be consumed by the very thing that keeps them in order through its gravitational force. This star with so many names, the sun, Sol Invictus, Hyperion, Ammon-Ra, Amaterasu, Arinna, Hebat, Apollo, Freyr, Helios, Hepa, Huitzilopochtli, Hvar Khshaita, Inti, Liza, Lugh, Mithras, Ben – Ben, Re-Horakhty, Shemesh, Sunna, Surya, Tonatiuh, Utu, Shamash, is called Lucifer by us undead. No other star affects us in the same way as this one and we undead are hypersensitive to every star. The sun flies in the night that surrounds it. Each undead responds to a different arrangement. Virtually all of the Nosferatu respond to Orion the hunter and one or more of the stars in this constellation. We Nosferatu are born as hunters of the earth. Dark angels of death. There are few exceptions to this. I am one of them. I am the only one left controlled by Virgo. The virgin sign of the Earth. The one who was supposed to be dead, supposed to have no children but did through immaculate conception. I am attached to this rock in a way that is not understood by most of my undead colleagues. I am far more susceptible to its shifts and changes. I was created to bear this virus of irrationality and only now am I realizing it. I had so many questions for so long and I have them no more. This spell is the answer to all of them. I had to spell them out myself. I can feel the fire inside the earth. I can feel it in myself. I can feel the magma below and the light of the sun differently. I know what the future of all this is. I know the coming incineration is real. The sun, Lucifer, will explode in rage and in one grand supernova consume every planet that worships him unless something is done to disrupt it. I know that we, imperial, arrogant, supposedly infinite Nosferatu are as finite as the system of light and dark that we depend upon. I can see its end coming. I was chosen to thwart this ending and create a possibility for escape. I was created under the sign of the virgin and it is only right that I have been divinely conceived with this virus. A word for the final sacrifice. The earth itself has impregnated my veins with this apocalypse to bear. It erupted from the Earth in ancient times. The original word of creation was swirling in the magma from the very beginning of the planets creation. It was fused into the rock and aeriform of every planet and within every marble and slag that was floating around in space like a hidden speck of peridot. It is the same incomprehensible word everywhere. This word is the only thing that maintains perceptible time and space and the reality outside it. It is the keystone. Lucifer simply rules whatever the light can touch. "*Ein Sof*" is one of the many attempts to enunciate the word but it is incorrect because it is speakable with the human tongue. There is far more to it than that.✐ ***il n'y a pas de hors-texte,✐ Monsters cannot be announced. One cannot say: 'here are our monsters', without immediately turning the monsters into pets.✐ (22).***

QWRTYUIOP{}!@#$$%^&*()_+ASDFGHJKL:"ZX-CVNM<>?1234567890-=][poiuytrewq♋ ⬧ ♎ ♐ ♑ ♒ 📫 ♏&●▭📪📫📬❍■♌■❖♍⌧⌘✏✍✂✍🔔🔔♈📖✉☎☽♉📧 ✂💻☹😐☺🖗👍☞👎💧✌☪✠👍✞👌☠💣💾☸✍📂📄📄🗐🗏🗐⌛🖮🖰✆🗀📫💾 🕉☸☯◘❑♓◆⍓⧫❒❒♏⬧❑♋⬧♎♐♑♒♏&●▭🕯📪📫📬❍■♌ ❖♍⌧⌘✏✍✂✍🔔♈📖✉☎☽♉📧"🏵🏱🏲✋✞✡❄☼☜⌖✈✌💧👎☞📫 👍🖗☺😐☹💻☸💾💣☠👌✞👍✠☪☪⌧♍❖♌❖■❍📭📬📪●&♏♒♑♐♎📫 ⬧♋❑⬧♏❒⧫❒⍓◆♓❑❑☯☸🕉💾📫🗀✆🖰🖮⌛🗏🗐📂123`4567890-=\][poiuytrewqasdfghjkl;'/.,mnbvcxzZXCVBNM<>":LKJHGFDSAQW-ERTYUIOP}+_)(*&^%%$#@!~`123456789ioklKJHGF~!@#$%^&*(((()_)+|}{POIUYTRE$QZASDFGHJKL:"?><MNBBVCCXZzxxcvbnM<./';lkjhgfd-saqwertyuiop[=-0987654321`21`

✐ *Being in-itself and Being for-itself were of Being; and this totality of* *beings, in which they were effected, itself was linked up to itself, relating and appearing to itself, by means of the essential project of human-reality. What was named in this way, in an allegedly neutral and undetermined way, was nothing other than the metaphysical unity of man and God, the relation of man to God, the project of becoming God as the project constituting human-reality.✐ Atheism changes nothing in this fundamental structure.*Ω.(22).

I ωoυld rather be sitting at a Starbucks drinking blood and twiddling my thumbs while I lusted after the young blood that passed in and out of the doors. I would not have gotten into this mess at all if I didn't have a choice. In putting all of this into words I am inverting myself. It is a spell of Self Exorcism. Controlled self-destruction. I am being hunted and I need a place to hide. None of the other undead know why they are after me but they are. Each one of them has been led to believe something different that would piss them off enough to try and find me. Only I know the true reason. I have escaped them many times in the process of writing this. I have been in and out of many empty apartments and factory buildings all over New York. I have been disrupted many times and have barely got away on more than one occasion. The longer this gets the more of it I have to hide in. The greater the web, the more powerful it becomes. These words are the irrational made rational. Mash them up and put them all together into a clot for that is what they are. Not one exists rationally without the other but I am making them one. Each word on its own is totally irrational. An incomplete imitation of the first one.

Deer be bo, deer bee bo, fooms bo. Beebobo fooms bo ta, beebobo fooms bo ta, fooms bo ta za ooooooo. Rimska bebe te un zoooo, zeein, zeeeeaa foooms bo tooo, rrrrokit up baay bay, rrrrrok it up baay beeeee.

[...] deschide-te fereastr, prin urmare
i ie i noapte din odaie ca din piersica sâmburul,
ca preotul din biserica

[...] hai în parcul communal

pâna o cânta cocosul

sa se scandalizeze orasul [...]. (46)

سوقي، عامي

And now it is time for another short yet important digression brought to you by the Fuck You Corporation who has been raping your mind for your whole life:

سوقي، عامي

Amusement is an addiction. News and advertisement strive to be entertaining. Addiction is the only reason why capitalism can function. Addiction is the only reason why someone would allow themselves to be ripped off by a dealer for every miserable transaction fully knowing that they are getting ripped off. To remove the addiction would be completely self-destructive to the status quo. It has been anarchy keeping the whole thing together the entire time you fucking assholes. USAnarchy. Keep your putrid votes.

Thank you very much, and always remember to fuck as many people as you can and always smile when you are getting fucked. FUCK YOU. Have a nice day.

Ω

It was to be my last night on the great mountain and yet it was also my first. I climbed and climbed in my search. Alone. Just the stars and I. Still no signs of malicious specters. Only the rocks and shrubs and grasses. The pressure pushing me back from above grew greater and greater the higher I ascended. I mused that there must be something I was missing. Something was waiting for me to make a discovery and I searched with every tool and trick that was at my disposal. Whatever it was, most certainly had a great deal of power. Perhaps equal to my own. This realization was disconcerting to say the least. No matter. I was still trying to consider all possible reasons for my experience without being sure at the time. I would still climb as high as I could and defy whatever was happening with every step in the hopes that I could find some sort of mistake in the structure. I looked around for miles and miles, above and below. Nothing. It was far too still here in this idyllic wilderness. I continued upward against the pressure applied to each step. My head continued to throb and it was becoming unbearable. I could make no sense of this. I began my climb with the feeling that I could conquer the world – and I probably could – but now I was almost totally broken down. It was driving me mad. There was no way that this was some sort of edema or acute mountain sickness. All of the stars were in their proper places. I would simply climb as far as I could. I did not even know if this would work out very well but it was worth a try. Perhaps it was just another pointless act of suffering. Upward with contempt. It eventually got so bad that I felt like every step was going backward. The effect of the loose gravel and sand that made up the battered vein of the trail did not help. One foot after another. One word after another. All the same pointless struggle of suffering. All going nowhere and creating agony in places that did not make any sense at all. More and more every second. One click of the second hand after another. One turn of the Earth after another. One more star discovered and charted.

This is the same way that I learned the majik that I am using to keep going. Majik and astrology are just as real as science. They are a science in themselves. There is a great deal of power stored up everywhere. It is hidden in every object within the secret name that permeates all of creation. All one has to do is find the way to extract it. You do not have to know where it comes from. You just have to know that it is there. It is all over the Old Testament yet few even realize and read right over it because it is forbidden. Preternatural phenomena is everywhere. Most humans cannot see or accept this because it is far more powerful than what most can deal with. They may suffer complete destruction if they opened up some of these channels. It is dangerous for undead too. Only very slowly, step by step did any of us gain these abilities. It is not simply bestowed upon us as a gift for dying and refusing to be dead. It is a very hard learned skill and all of the docimastic ordeals must be accomplished in order to wield any power at all.

Here I am now confronted with some new Majik that I could not figure out. The challenge was to find a way to master it. One step at a time. After a few more agonizing steps, lurches, I began to see motion out of the corner of my eyes. These were not hallucinations. There was something there. Some sort of animal. I looked around and scanned everything. No matter where I looked, no matter which direction I cast my gaze this creature was always at the corner of my eye. It was always flitting around in my peripheral vision. Was this a continuation of my malady? Was I really seeing things? I was certain that this was no spectral subterfuge. There was still no evidence of the ghosts anywhere. I kept scanning my surroundings and I kept on seeing what looked like a small animal flitting around the rocks and bounding through the grasses. Still I could see nothing when I looked directly at it. I grew tired of this little animal or hallucination or whatever it was so I continued my agonizing climb. I would get answers if I didn't stop. I was certain of this. As I ascended, this strange shadow animal followed me but stayed just out of sight. Most of the time I felt and heard it directly behind me. When I turned suddenly to try and surprise it, I was surprised because it was gone once more.

Ω

I was almost to my goal of one thousand feet of elevation gain from the camp over unknown miles of struggle. The pressure was unbearable. My skin began to feel like it was being incinerated by an unseen fire. My shadowy companion had stuck with me and traveled with ease, a mockery of the difficulty I was having. After a few more steps I realized that I had reached the thousand food mark. I checked the altimeter on my watch and it confirmed what I already knew. There was a large flat boulder impacted into the side of the mountain right next to the trail. It was almost like it was put there just for me. I felt drawn to it. I sat down on it for what seemed to be like an infinite amount of time to try and regain composure in my undead corpse that had been malfunctioning so badly. The shadow animal was still taunting me and I considered what it could be. It was certainly part of this puzzle but I could not see it long enough to determine anything. I suspected that it was another undead creature because no human majik that I had ever encountered could vex me so. I shifted around on the boulder in an attempt to get somewhat comfortable. Then all of the sudden the pressure that had been plaguing me just disappeared. I did not move at all for fear of bring it back somehow. I sat and studied the view that was spread out below me. The lights of Moshi were still there. I looked up at the sky and I instantly noticed that something was not right but I couldn't immediately place it. There was something missing. I felt the presence of a void. That sounds strange but it was true. A void within a void that I could feel. I am hypersensitive to voids because of all the work I have done with Auryn over the years. Something was totally out of balance. Oh how I missed her. This must have been a part of what was happening to me. I knew that I would discover something if I climbed here. I scanned the basic constellations for a clue. Very quickly I knew what was wrong. Orion the hunter was missing a star. Betelgeuse was missing. It was more complicated than that though. I couldn't see it but I sensed that it was still there. There was some sort of void or black hole where it should have been. A void within a void. This is a very important star for Nosferatu. The others must have seen this too. Perhaps they were all feeling as messed up as I did.

This discovery led me to an infinite series of questions. All very primitive questions but ones that needed to be answered like; what the hell was happening? Was it just gone? What of the other undead? Did it explode into supernovae? We all knew that this was going to happen but it seemed far too early for that to have occurred. Betelgeuse will explode someday. Betelgeuse lies some 430 light-years from Earth. (Note: determining distances, especially to red supergiant stars, is a vexing problem in Astronomy. Estimates vary and are often revised, with some as high as 650 light-years.) Yet it's already one of the brightest stars in Earth's sky. The reason is that Betelgeuse is a supergiant star. It is intrinsically very brilliant. Such brilliance comes at a price, however. Betelgeuse is one of the most famous stars in the sky because it's due to explode someday. Betelgeuse's enormous energy requires that the fuel be expended quickly (relatively speaking), and in fact Betelgeuse is now near the end of its lifetime. Someday soon (astronomically speaking), it will run out of fuel, collapse under its own weight, and then rebound in a spectacular supernova explosion. When this happens, Betelgeuse will brighten enormously for a few weeks or months, perhaps as bright as the full moon and visible in broad daylight. When will it happen? Probably not in our lifetimes. But, in fact, no one knows. It could be tomorrow or a million years in the future. Now, without even a peep it was simply gone? A new riddle for sure and I was in a perfect place to consider what to do.

Humans are from Orion

Credo said Zulus believed that humans come from 'a world among the stars' which he calls 'mpalalatsani' in the constellation of Orion. You might recall that Orion is depicted on the 'Necklace of the Mysteries'. Credo says that Mpalalatsani is a paradise world and, according to legend, it is 'a red place with red rocks, red earth, red sand and seas'. I asked him what it was called by western astronomy and he said he didn't know. He only knew it as Mpalalatsani, which means 'The Scatterer of Life'. There is, however, a 'supergiant' bright,

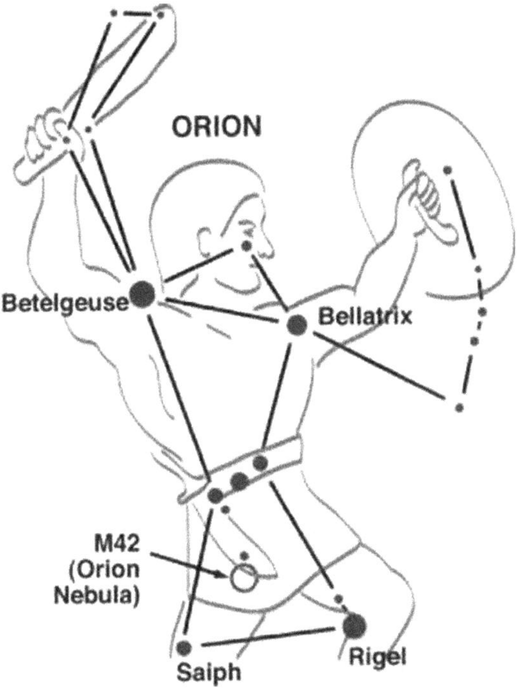

reddish star or world in the Orion group called Betelgeuse, 640 light-years from Earth. If it replaced our Sun it would reach out as far as Mars. Observers and researchers at the University of California said in 2009 that Betelgeuse has shrunk by 15 per cent in the last 15 years. It was the first star to have its size measured and it is one of only a handful of stars that appears through the Hubble Space Telescope as a disc rather than a point of light. Zulu legends say that humans used to live on the 'red world' called Mpalalatsani (another possible origin for all the 'red' symbolism, but there are also Zulu accounts about Reptilians living on Mars). It is said there was a 'great war between human men and women on Mpalalatsani and the survivors were banished for their lust and other behaviour. Humans were once androgynous and there we 0 men 0 but the Reptilians instigated genetic manipulation on Mpalalatsani to divide the original human form into male and female, the legend goes. Credo says that Mpalalatsani is the real location of the biblical Garden of Eden, from which humans were banished, and that genetic manipulation started there and continued within the Moon and later on Earth. Another African word used for Mpalalatsani is, Matfieng', and this means 'Lord of the Insects' or 'Lord of the Flies'.

Credo said this was an insulting description of the humans who were ejected from Mpalalatsani and, interestingly', it is the meaning of the name of the Hebrew demon called 'Beelzebub'. This demon is also known as 'Satan' and the 'Devil' in some cultures, but is separate from them in others. Beelzebub derives from 'Ba'al Zebftb', 'Ba'al Z_bftb' or 'Ba'al Z_viiv' and these words mean...,'Lord of the Flies', 'Baal' is another name for the Babylonian Nimrod. Beelzebub is said to be high in the hierarchy of Hell and the fallen angels and presides over the 'Order of the Fly'. The author, William Golding, published a famous book in 1954 called Lord of the Flies. It is an allegorical novel about a group of schoolboys who are stranded on a desert island without any adults and it explores the conflicting impulses of living in peace and harmony or fighting for power – appropriate given what Zulu legends say about what happened with humans on the 'red world'. The book also includes the themes of groupthink against individuality, morality against immorality, and rational thought against emotional reactions. The schoolboys descend into violence before being rescued by a naval ship. Zulu legends say that the surviving humans banished from Mpalalatsani were brought to Earth by the Reptilians in the Moon. It carried all types of humans, including shamans, Credo said, and the different human groups were kept in different compartments within the Moon. Dr Farooq Al-Baz, who worked with NASA on the scientific exploration of the Moon, once said: 'There are many undiscovered caverns suspected to exist beneath the surface of the Moon. Several experiments have been flown to the Moon to see if there Spaceship Moon 313 actually were such caverns.' NASA unveiled the manned spacecraft in 2009 that it planned to send to the Moon in 2020. They called it Orion and it replaced the mission named after the sun god, Apollo, but then Obama suddenly cancelled the project

in February 2010. Zulu legends say that a higher Consciousness, known to Zulu lore as the 'Tree of Life', wants humans to come back into the fold to reconnect with their true selves and 'higher forces', but the Reptilians, in Credo's words, 'really want to mess things up'. The Tree of Life is another universal concept found in every ancient culture and it is based on the belief that all life on Earth (the branches of the tree) is related. This is precisely what I am saying in my books using other words and analogies. Source: Book – Human race get off your knees by David Icke

I sat and pondered the situation, but not much came to me. Everything around was totally still. I closed my eyes and let my mind drift. The entire universe flashed through me. Everything was intact. Betelgeuse had not been destroyed. I opened my eyes once I realized that this was part of the deceit which brought me here. I thought to myself. My thought was cut short by the return of the spectral creature to my peripheral vision. This time it did not flee when I looked at it and I saw that it was a jackal. It stood its ground as I studied it. It sat down and cocked its head as it stared back at me. When I blinked it was gone again. I turned my head and looked directly down the trail that I had just climbed. The jackal was now on the trail some distance below me but it was running uphill and directly at me in an aggressive manner. My arrogance and newfound relief from the downward pressure got the best of me. How dare something like this try anything to me? I stood up and attempted to cast a spell that I rarely would if I was not this far away from anything that could see me. I quickly put my hands together and spit a small amount of blood into them. With a quick word I rubbed my hands together. I watched as the animal got closer. The closer it got to me the more it looked like a large poodle than a jackal. A ragged poodle indeed. I could see that its eyes were purple and red and had the illumination of starlight behind them. I did not care what it was. I made a quick flicking gesture with both hands like I was passing a basketball to a teammate. A burst of flame came out of my hands and totally engulfed the charging creature. I took a step forward to see what sort of victim I had just created but it turned out to be me. As soon as I took the step the full force of the invisible downward pressure came upon me once more. I was forced down so hard that I fell to a seated position upon the flat rock that was close behind. This force was accompanied by a screaming loud voice that contained all sound frequencies from the highest, ear piercing highs to the lowest, gut rumbling lows. It felt like it came from the inside of my head going outward rather than the other way around. It all stopped after a few seconds and I stood up again. I instinctively pushed out my fangs and tried to scream back.

There was a smoldering ball of fire on the ground before me. The sound and smell of cooking flesh came from it. I heard a voice in my head that said: ***For the sound of his horn brought me from my bed, and the cry of his hounds which he oft times led, Peels "View Halloo!" would awaken the dead, and the fox from his lair in the morning (4).*** I tried to take a step toward it once more and then again I heard a clear voice speaking in my head. ***"I am the Aleph. Without me you are powerless. Listen and answer my question."***

I responded with my own questions "Where are you, who are you?" I looked down at the flames burning at my feet as I asked this. The fire got bigger and brighter as I stared at it. It grew outward and started burning small bushes and patches of grass as it got larger. It was speaking to me as it grew and it said ***"Leave the letter that never begins to go, find the letter that ever comes to an end – written in smoke and blurred by mist and signed of solitude, sealed at night(4)".*** The light from the flames grew so intense that it began to burn my skin and I recoiled from it. I could barely move because the pressure from above was so great. I was stuck in place. I endured this burning light as I sat on the flat rock. My mind grabbed around for an explanation and it came up with one very quickly. I finally realized what was happening even though I did not believe it at all. This could only be Lucifer himself. That explained the whole thing. It explains why I could not detect anything this entire time. He had powers so far above my ability that there was no way for me to see it coming.

As soon as I realized this there was another voice. This time it was much quieter because it was not coming from inside of my head. It was coming from in front of me. The flames grew and grew and eventually became a blaze that was twelve feet tall. They were wide and spreading out but became narrower and narrower. The flaming canine corpse now stood as a strange human figure who was over six feet tall. There were small flames licking up at him from the burning grasses at his feet. He was dressed in a long robe of indefinable color that was on fire at the edges. Every time I thought I recognized the color of it, it would change to a different one in a constant, flickering, strobe like effect. It moved elegantly around him like the substance of flame itself but only far more brilliant. For a moment I studied the countenance of this individual before I realized that I could not. Every moment that I thought I saw a face of a specific human it would change to a different one. It was a man, then a woman, it was Caucasian and then it was Asian and then it was African, then Arabian, then Indian, then something else, something monstrous, then something angelic. It was constantly changing from individual to individual as quickly and as beautifully mesmerizing as a tongue of pure flame. The entire figure seemed completely immaterial yet it stood firmly before me. When it spoke its voice was like silk cascading all around me. "You Spoke My Name And Now I Am Here". It said. "I Have Been Watching You Alexander And I Believe That You Have The Answer To A Very Important Question. What Did You Bring Here?" When it spoke my name it drawled out the pronunciation to produce deliberate sarcasm. It knew my true undead name but it decided to mock me with the human name that I had chosen to use. For the first time in my undead existence

I felt almost powerless. The presence of this being was overwhelming and the pressure that was pushing down upon me was more than I could bear. Its gaze was fixed upon mine and I saw that it was every color of light. It cut right into me like a flashlight through the dark. The eyes were opalescent. Not any one color but all at once and constantly changing. They were ruby, then sapphire, then pearl, emerald, obsidian, padparadscha, topaz, tanzanite, citrine, always gleaming, always different, and always cold as stone, cold and penetrating. I knew that I had certainly met my match but I decided that I would not let myself be willingly overcome. I would defy whatever he wanted even if he could destroy me with the smallest gesture. I came here to find out what had been harassing me and I did. I just had to figure out what to do about it now.

Ω

His cape flowed and rippled gently on its own even though there was no breeze. It was almost alive. The flames flickered on its ends and his collar gently rustled like he was producing his own environment. I was confused but defiant. I said to him "What is it that I could know that you do not? Surely this is some sort of mistake." It was a fairly pathetic response but it was true. I did not have any awareness of what he was talking about. Why He would take the trouble to seek me out was a new mystery that I had to unravel even though it was the same one that was plaguing me the entire time.

He simply gazed at me and did not answer. He took a casual step forward. He was now within reach of me. In a flash his arm shot out, grabbed my shoulder, and threw me down off of the rock that I was so uncomfortably sitting on. My first reaction was laughter. I grabbed back at his arm and threw back with every bit of arcane power that I could produce. I could tell that he was not at all surprised at my resistance. Back and forth we fought and neither gained the upper hand. I was surprised that he did not defeat me instantly. There was something going on here that was deeper than what it looked like and I still didn't get it. I didn't have time to. We wrestled all night like this.

After some time I could see the red line of the horizon threatening dawn. He saw that I couldn't answer his question no matter how he manipulated me. He pinned me down for a second and looked over his shoulder at the horizon. He said ***Welch' Lich leuchtet dort? D mmert der Tag schon auf? Loge's Heer lodert feurig um den Fels. Noch ist's Nacht: was spinnen und singen wir nicht (7)?*** In a different voice than before he asked ***"Why have you climbed this far if you can't answer me? I am certain that you have an answer somewhere inside of you."*** When I didn't say anything back he tried to wrestle more and I fought back like before. He grabbed me by the throat and threw me onto my back. He raised his hand and balled it into a fist. For a second it glowed like a small star. It was red and broiling. His hand wielded a piece of Betelgeuse that he stole from the sky. He masked his thievery by momentarily blocking out the star as I climbed. Then he punched me in the stomach with such great force it could have had the total gravity of an entire star behind the impact. I fell at his feet as the light of the morning star began to shine behind him. All of the color was now drained out of him. He became as black as a cinder. Nothing but a silhouette that moved like black mercury. I was injured in a way that I had never experienced before but still I refused to submit. I didn't have any other choice because I knew I could not answer his question. He stormed around for a moment and seemed to pay more attention to the slowly rising sun than to me. I crawled along the ground, grabbed his ankle and tried to throw him down with every ounce of power I had left. I could not budge him but I heard a voice in my head. It said ***"Let me go for it is dawn."***

I grabbed tighter and said "I will not let go unless you reveal to me the reason that you came." The wind picked up. I heard it whistle through the cracks in the rocks all around me.

"What is your Name, What has you brought here?" He asked.

I sneered as I bared my teeth at him and sarcastically said *"Alexander, of course."*

He kicked at my grasp but I did not let go. He said ***"Your Name is not Alexander. We both know that you were given a different name when you were created. Your mother is Spica the great Sapphire, the virgins star, I know her well. You have changed the name she has given to you. You are no longer V.V.V. Your name has been changed to Tetragrammaton. Pronounce it for me! Do it now! All Four Letters! Give them to me!"***

I squeezed harder as I tried to rise. I could not budge because of the pounding pressure. I said "How do you know that there are only four letters?" He tilted his head and looked down at me quizzically. This seemed to get his attention.

"You know the meaning of Tetragrammaton. You carry it as your new name. Speak." This was his response as the rose light of the sunrise began to slash at the horizon.

The only thing that I could produce was defiance. I squeezed as hard as I could and yelled *"Fuck!"* It was the only answer that I could produce. I was, once again, overcome by my previously destroyed arrogance. Then I lost consciousness.

Ω

I opened my eyes. I was laid out on the ground and the first light of the sun was burning my exposed hand. It was empty. I was alone on the side of the mountain. The echo of the last word I had yelled was reverberating through my weary head. It was not a dream. I slowly rose to my feet. The first thing that I noticed was the crushing pressure was gone. Something was still not right. Now more than ever I had more questions than answers. I had wrestled with Lucifer all night, alone and outside of a camp and he changed my name? I did not understand this at all. It was the answer to everything that I was trying to figure out but it produced a thousand more questions.

My stomach throbbed with an intensity of pain that I had never experienced before. Once I was finally standing I was overcome with a flood of nausea. I struggled a few steps down the trail and vomited an eruption of blood. I had become like the volcano that I stood upon. It had erupted its guts and created the continent below. Was my blood a similar sacrifice? I regained composure and tried not to think but thinking was the only thing that would take my mind off of my injury. My vision went in and out of focus and I felt so very weak upon my feet. The nausea was incredible. I was not the same as I was before. Something inside of me had changed forever. The individual who climbed to this point would not descend again. I tried to analyze myself to get some sort of bearing but my inner compass was spinning to a new form of magnetism. I could not tell if it had been a slow developing change that began a few days ago at the other crater or if it was instantaneously inflicted upon me during my struggle. I was impregnated with a new form of being that I could not describe. I was enraged for a moment but I reeled myself in as best as I could. I decided to mark this place for future reference. I went up to the flat rock that I sat upon where I first saw Lucifer. Here I piled up a few stones and made something like a cairn or an early Hebrew altar. Something like Abraham would have made. When I was finished stacking the stones properly I spoke the word: "*Peniel.*" This would mark the location and ensure that the stones would remain in place until I came back. If I did. I had a strong feeling that I needed to do this.

The tip of the sun peeked above the horizon as I left. I was limping and lurching due to the blow that I received. I knew that I had to get back to the camp quickly before the humans there woke and realized that I was gone. I tried to transform into a condor to fly down quickly. I found that I could not do this as easily as I did normally. Something was terribly wrong with my majik. I went through the events to try to decipher what it all meant. I needed to know what had happened to me.

Lucifer lives in the morning star, not Betelgeuse. He was trying to deceive me to draw something out. He blocked out the red star in Orion so that he could grab a piece of it. He was wearing a cloak to try to fool me, to make me think that he was someone else or that something else besides him was involved. When he blocked out Orion he gained a weapon and he also alerted all of the hunters who were born under Orion. All of the other Nosferatu would respond to this in their own way but the effect would still be the same. They were looking for me and I knew that I now was marked.

Just as the early sun struck me I knew I was being watched. Lucifer was waiting for me to make a mistake, or to realize what was happening. What was the questioning about? How could He not know my name? He showed me his true face. He is the rational word. The illumination of knowledge, the very thought of everyone everywhere all of the time and in every tongue. I saw the infinite permutations of them all as I gazed at his face. He knew my current human name. He was watching when I was conceived in darkness under the stars. He even knew my true Nosferatu name even though he didn't say it. It is a name of meaning. A tribal name like the ones bestowed upon the Native Americans and the ancient Hebrews. My name was *Vindemiatrix,* and it means *The Grape Gatherer. The first Nosferatu. V.V.V. An open jar of gathering. A vessel of blood. V.V.V. Vincenzo (Conqueror) Vane (banner) Vindemiatrix. I now have a new name that has been bestowed after my wrestling match with Lucifer. My new name is Shem HaMephorash. A performance of a word. A performance of a spell. I must further discover its meaning. This is the reason for this spell.* I was the only existing Nosferatu left that was born under the stars of Virgo. The sign of the earth. All of the others who bore this sign had been dispatched from existence over time and returned to the dust of the Earth. Time had been marching on toward the inevitable planetary crisis. I could feel it coming just as I could feel the rays of the sun that precede it. Most of the undead refused to believe me when I told them because they did not notice it. They are not Angels of the Earth like I am. They are Hunters. The sun would soon explode and swallow the Earth and all of the other planets in this entire orrery. Lucifer, the morning star would consume everything in his fury. Now that I had seen him, I knew that my suspicions were not unfounded. My mother was Spica, the true sapphire of the sky. A perfect example of a star of the first magnitude. I was born with understanding that most Nosferatu could not see. They practice their witchcraft in a jail cell of lust. I do it outside under the sky.

♍ Vindemiatrix ♍

Legend: Vindemiatrix, or as it was originally called, Vindemiator, the Gatherer of Grapes, represents Ampelos, the son of a satyr and a nymph, to whom Bacchus, in token of his fondness, gave a vine planted at the foot of an elm. While gathering grapes Ampelos fell and broke his neck, whereupon Bacchus placed him among the stars as a memorial of his former affection. [Robson, p.214-215.]*

♍

In older astrology this star ranks with Algol in having an unmitigated reputation for evil, and some even have noted that the arc or aspect between the two is the much feared 135º, the sesqui-quadrate or resquisquare. But the underlying reason for their similar reputes lies in the connection of both names with the theme of 'the Spirit'. The one is the name from which comes our word Alcohol, the other is the star whose rising signifies the time for harvesting the grapes, our main old source of the same (4).

♍

As always, much depends on how one sees events themselves as good or bad. Yes, Vindemiatrix does frequently mark the death of someone's partner in life, hence its appellation 'The Widow maker', which of course prompts us to say: 'It is bound to, since someone dies at every minute or so of every day'. But still the fact remains that it figures very strongly and very regularly in deaths which are in some way dramatic, newsworthy or are resented in much more than the usual degree by those left behind (assassinations, common criminal murders, executions, airline disasters etc.). [The Living Stars, Dr. Eric Morse, p.70-72.] At least one unsafe airplane of World War II, known widely as 'The Widow Maker' made its first flight on the day that Vindemiatrix culminated, while another which had the same phenomenon at its birth, but was successful, was officially named the 'Black Widow'! (4)

♍

Another name for Vindemiatrix is: Al Muredin `The One Sent Forth in the Faith'. This is often the missionary. This is not to say that everyone with this star strong in their horoscope will go out and preach the gospel to the heathen, although many do indeed feel a strong religious calling (4).

♍

The star , in the arm bearing the branch, is called Al Mureddin, which means who shall come down (as in Psa 72:8), or who shall have dominion. It is also known as Vindemiatrix (4).

♍

"At her rising Erigone (Virgo), (Aragorne), who reigned with Justice over a bygone age and fled when it fell into sinful ways, bestows high eminence by bestowing supreme power; she will produce a man to direct the laws of the state and the sacred code; one who will tend with reverence the hallowed temples of the gods." [Astronomica, Manilius, 1st century AD, p.265]

♍

"The temperaments of those whose span of life she pronounces at their birth Erigone (Virgo) will direct to study, and she will train their minds in the learned arts. She will give not so much abundance of wealth as the

impulse to investigate the causes and effects of things. On them she will confer a tongue which charms, the mastery of words, and that mental vision which can discern all things, however concealed they be by the mysterious workings of nature. From the Virgin will also come the stenographer: his letter represents a word, and by means of his symbols he can keep ahead of utterance and record in novel notation the long speech of a rapid speaker. But with the good there comes a flaw: bashfulness handicaps the early years of such persons, for the Maid, by holding back their great natural gifts, puts a bridle on their lips and restrains them by the curb of authority. And (small wonder in a virgin) her offspring is not fruitful." [Astronomica, Manilius, 1st century AD, p.237 and 239]

Ω

I sat on the precipice next to the altar I had created and looked down. I tried to transform into a condor once again. It did not work. My stomach was injured from my cosmic encounter so I was not surprised that it was difficult. I had the weight of an entire star punched into my stomach and it was left there to smolder. An easy mark for the hunters to track. All of the sudden I had a different idea. The stars were fading as the sun rose but they never were gone. I tried to empty myself. I tried to think about the void. The nameless space between the stars. The inexplicable irrational, ungraspable power above. My stomach throbbed. All of the questions about names. What was it all about? This is when I truly first thought about the presence of the irrational word. This is when I first noticed the nature of my Extraordinary disease and could understand the differences between perception and reality. The possibility of discovering the true Ein Sof. The possibility of opening the doors of perception. The power of Names. The cosmos that lurked within, behind closed eyes. I realized the power of death. The power of living, the experience of being truly finite and not undead. I was transforming. I could die. Was it already happening? If so, it was not instantaneous. I tried to call upon my name for power to transform into a condor. *Vindemiatrix.* All of the grapes had been gathered so my name was complete. I had become ripe for harvest. It was predestined to happen. This is why I was given this first name which was meant to be changed. Yours will too. Have you learned what to do with it? Do you have your weapons sharpened? Woe unto you dear reader. *Weißtd, was Wotan – will (7)?*

These thoughts didn't all come at once. It was a slow but irreversible progression that is still developing. I was primarily focused on getting back to camp somehow. I tried to think of nothing at all once more. Nothing inside of me. A void. I felt the weight of the star that had been punched into me fall away into the void that I created. In a second I was a condor once again. I flew down to a place that was just outside of the camp. I had a difficult time turning back into my bipedal form. I was afraid and I knew that I would return to a world of pain once I did. I didn't have the same stomach in bird form so instead of pain there was just an experience of lightness and hunger that I did not want to leave even though I knew that I must. I flapped around on the ground for a few more moments as I delayed my transformation. Then with the great deal of concentration that is required with a brain as small as a condor's, I put in the massive effort that it took to return into my simian form. As soon as the transformation was complete I fell over and grabbed my injured stomach. The nausea was overwhelming. Within a few moments I was vomiting again. Pure blood of course. I knew that this would not go over well if I was discovered by anyone in my climbing party. My clothing was torn and covered with blood and I knew that I could only stagger at best if I had to get up. I laid where I was for the time being. I vomited once more and I thought that the nausea would subside if I got everything out of my system. I wondered about this and waited for a moment to see if I would get any better. Nothing happened.

Ω

I laid amongst the rocks and grasses as the sun continued to rise. The tonic light of morning rolled delicately around the curve of the earth and was recherché for all the living beings and full of horror for us who imitated them. I hated the morning the most of all times. It heralded the coming of another difficult day of incineration and struggle. I hated it the most near commerce districts where the energy of humanity was at its greatest. I could feel the anticipation, the breeding of buggery and strife, the hopefulness and seething desperation. Living vampires of the day who didn't have to be that way like I did. They chose it freely and I found it loathsome. For once I was glad to be far away from it in this wilderness. I was thankful for the small plants I was surrounded by and the bony, unliving gravel that supported me. I craned my head to look at the blazing star that our miserable, undead, hell planet was so permanently attached to. It pierced my eyes with its yellow geranium glow. I felt like I was being mocked. Every movement I made was watched and recorded. Every thought that I did not take enormous efforts to protect was noticed and analyzed. There was a price on my head. I knew this because of the way that he had blocked out Beelzebub, the blood star of Orion, in order to grab a piece of it and plunge it into me to mark me in his frustration. The hunt was upon me. The light of the morning star was obnoxious and debilitating. More so now than ever before. I rolled on the ground in agony. I – Nosferatu, Vindemiatrix, or was that my name now? I felt that it was not. I, who could not ever feel pain or remorse was now crippled, covered in blood, and rolling in it. I could not understand why I was still sick. I had expelled everything except the lodestar which was punched into my stomach. I was now marked by the eternal word of the nameless creator – I was given a new name – and the eye of Lucifer all at once. I was being put to some test and it was all dawning on me like the light itself. There was a small piece of Orion's blood star that was in me still that I did not purge. If and when I understand and even think the word, the new name I had been given, this mysterious Tetragrammaton I would invite the full wrath of Lucifer and all of the undead hunters that were looking for me. It would be a beacon of complete destruction. This is what I was struggling with and must have been the source of my sickness. The problem and the solution at once was the fact that I still did not know what this Word was. I still only could think of my original name and it was sickening. Nauseating like a hangover from far too much wine. Far too many grapes gathered.

Ω

As I laid upon the ground, I heard and felt the vibration of many footsteps falling very near me. I heard human voices calling out the name that they knew me by. Many of the voices were laden with a heavy and drawn out Swahili accent: "ĀĀĀeLexxxↃ?" I grunted a response and tried to stand up. This time I made it to my feet and staggered toward the direction of the camp. As I proceeded I caught the attention of one of the porters that were looking for me. One of them saw me and called to the others who all rushed over as quickly as the rough terrain would allow them to. It was only a matter of a few minutes before I was back at the camp and deposited in my tent. One of the porters rushed to get the attention of the leader of the expedition. I did not wait very long before he arrived. He stood over me and all that I could see was his legs through the half opened tent flap which was zipped aside before he squatted down closer to my position. He boomed out incoherencies to the swarming porters and they all went back to whatever business that they had to attend to. He studied me for a moment and all at once said "Dear God! What the Hell happened to you? Where did you go? What is going on here?"

Zuka!

I did not know exactly what to tell him at the moment. I was in no condition to come up with any elaborate answer at all so I just said the simplest thing possible to indicate some human sort of ailment. "I got sick last night. I think that I ate something that disagreed with me. I had been vomiting since very late last night." I winced out the last words and cast a very small spell with a deliberate twitch of my eye which precisely contacted his so I would be sure to deliver this information as convincingly as possible. He twitched for a moment and shook his head in what looked like total disbelief. I had certainly ruined his chipper little morning. As I was dragged back into the camp I heard him singing and playing his flute in his tent without any idea of the sort of nightmare that had been schlepped into his happy climbing party.

He considered my response for a moment and exclaimed "You look like you just killed ten people! You look like you have Ebola! How can you have lost so much blood and still be alive? You are trying to tell me that you vomited up that much blood?" I tried to croak back another loaded answer but before I could he turned away and looked at the head porter who was standing next to him. He barked out another series of orders that I did not exactly hear but I caught a few sentences. "Get him something to clean up with...don't touch it, use gloves and burn it when you are done...He can't climb any further, and has to go down right now....get in contact with the base patrol so they have transportation... ready... more stuff that I didn't hear because he was walking away and then walking back...get two porters who are not on the summit team and are not doing anything absolutely essential. They are going to help him get back down. Make sure that they know to take him to the small clinic in Moshi that we always use."

The lead porter nodded and quickly walked off. The expedition leader looked back at me and after a moment he said "I'm sorry that this happened. I have to get the rest of the group ready to go up to the next camp. The porters will be here to help you as soon as they can. Try to change out of those clothes and just leave them on the ground next to the tent. We will burn them here just in case there is something contagious on them. I don't want to expose my porters to anything if I can help it." With that he shook his head at me and disappeared. As I laid there I felt so much worse than I did earlier. My guts were now in a state of full revolt. The two porters who were to accompany me on my descent arrived very shortly. I told them that I had to get my daypack before I left. I did not want anyone to see or damage any of the blood or other arcane items that I had in there. I tried to get up out of the tent and they helped me out along with my small backpack. I slung it over my shoulder and its weight threw me off balance for a moment but I caught myself on the shoulder of the porter who was standing at my side. We made our way through the camp and received many queer looks from the hikers who were just beginning their day. I'm pretty certain that the last thing that they expected to see after popping out of their tents first thing in the morning was someone in my condition being assisted through the camp.

Ω

We made it to the outside of the camp where all of the smaller trails converged and plunged into the darkness of the wilderness. The trail descended very sharply from the flat place where the camp was. The trail continued downward through the tall thin heathers – which were nothing like the ones in Europe or anywhere else. High elevation African heather was more like tall, thin bargello lines, stitched upon the sky than low clustered shrubs. The difficulty of the terrain on descent produced more saturnine progress than upon ascent. I tried to run the previous night's encounter through my mind but I was far too distracted by my present issues. I bounced back and forth between the two porters as I attempted to navigate the steep, ten mile journey down. I fell to the ground many times along the way. The porters would let me sit and regain myself for a moment before they would try to get me back to my feet. Sometimes I would resist because I did not want to move at all. They would try to urge me on with their broken English-Swahili language. They would pull me up by the arms on both sides and say "We must go. Kutembea.

Pole-pole." After what seemed like an infinity of slapstick moments, the ground began to flatten and I emerged at a clearing. I thought that I saw a vehicle parked at the far side of it but I also thought that I was hallucinating or being overcome by some sort of arcane trickery. I did not realize that I had actually made it to the end of the trail. I was so out of it that I even asked if I could get a ride from whoever was driving this strange vehicle. The porters simply laughed and told me that it was waiting for me to take me to the doctor.

Ω

The chain of communication had broken down from person to person, from device to device, and from language to language. I was not taken to the clinic that was suggested by the expedition leader up at the camp. I did not care much because after hopping and thrashing and dragging over the roots and rocks and elevation I was just happy to be driven somewhere. It gave me a moment to reflect and everything began to make some sort of insane sense. The entire time that I was in Tanzania I did not realize what was happening up until this point. I slowly began the process of piecing together everything that continues on until even now. Even now I still do not have the entire thing in my mind because I know that I cannot let that happen. As soon as it comes into conscious completion it will be over and Lucifer would be standing in this very room with me, burning the floor with his angry feet.

On the bumpy ride out of the woods I realized that things had been totally out of hand from the moment that I stepped foot off the airplane and first made contact with the African continent. This ancient land had been waiting for me. The names had been written in every stone and leaf. From that moment something strange took hold of me. It was like the activation of an addiction, a strange virus or allergy that was already in me. It was something that I was predisposed to. Something that a power greater than me had already envisioned long before I even came into existence. It was already written in the very map of the stars which gave me the power to stay animated. I had no chance to do anything different from the very second that I had been created. Everything that I experienced was building up to this insane, incomprehensible outcome. I had to realize and admit that I was powerless and that something that was greater than myself was working on me. It was set in stone, in every stone on the planet that I perceived incorrectly the whole time. It was set in the stars above. It was set in my name. The grape gatherer. Vindemiatrix. I was to gather the grapes of prophesy.

Ω

I absolutely hated this conclusion as soon as I thought it on that awful ride out of the woods. I tried to reject it with every cell of my body but it would not leave my mind because I knew that it was true. It haunts me still. Everywhere I look I can see it. It all carries the same message. Everything is whirling towards an end and everyone and everything wants it so badly but can do nothing so they simply exist and stay fractured so that no hope of *reality* can ever be seen. It all has the same message. It must end. Nothing can be proven when nothing lasts. I must end all of this and to do it I must live so I can end myself. I must find a way to die. That is what the pain was for. It was written in the stars. I could see them clearly from the window of the vehicle I rode in. No matter where it went I could see them. They stayed in their fixed positions and they burned right through the blue flames of the atmosphere. They burned through Lucifer's daylight and I could see them as clear as if it were a polar night sky.

I rode out of the woods and they stayed up above asking me, mocking me, ***who are you? Who you boy? Who you (47)?*** They were my power and I knew them but they were now asking me who I was? I rode under them but could not run away. I could not escape their power into safety and protective night. Something was seriously awry that I had to adjust to because of my previous actions. ***Robbery stays and separates de***

so by the third stoplight. Its car light destroy the depths of night. The ancient maps of all I wealth by right. This is a the sound of all I ancient blood line. Who was given the High priest robe to fly tonight? Draw up heaven and trace the bee straight flight, no demon soul when I torch ignite. Pressure burn I Rasta out of fright, the torch I run around the world stays light. It all again explode them right, it all again bound fi explode them right. Its obsession control the land grass height, its obsessions which control the land grass height. The ancient maps of I wealth by right. It is that destroy the depth of night. It is that destroy the depth of night. Some Jah with like none of the star have them outshine. Make all the veins lust tot the blood supply. Strive up Fi, big u ina the march out line. Strive up fi big up ina the march out line. In way so the blind are go lead the blind. Fixing up a pot of terrorize. The ancient maps of all I wealth by right. Who you? Who you boy? Who you? Wa-ka-ka, wa-ka-ka, Who you? WHO (47)? Above always midnight. The blue of the sky grew thin for I knew it was the illumination of Lucifer's deceitfulness. This is the reason why the perpetual night spell of the Nosferatu could work and allow us to operate in daylight. The blue fire of the sky above was a spell too. The presentation of the vast illusion so He could find one of us to harvest what he needed. I was the one and he knew it. After I am finished, the task will be passed to you if you are reading this. You now have your own ***perception*** to deal with and Lucifer will try to wrestle it out of you. Your name will soon change like mine did. I know all of this now. It took me some time to put together. Then, I didn't know the answer that he was looking for because it was hiding. It still is. That was the only thing that saved me. He knew that my name had been changed as soon as I came to Africa and he demanded that I speak it to him. A four letter word? Was it really that? Is it part of the illusion that he thinks it is a word because it is written into the rational sequence of words to be expected as such and all names are speakable, writeable words? I have discovered that it is not quite the case in this instance. This *Word* is a different sort of name. A musical word. A performance. Swordplay against the self. Again, it took me some time to actually decipher this much without actually totally understanding it.

Ω

Who was I now? That was the question? What was the new name within me? Through the pain I felt totally different. Totally powerless yet so much more powerful in a way that I could not describe. I was being controlled by a power that was not my own. Something that was so much more than me and certainly more powerful than even Lucifer Himself. This is why he could not destroy me. It was out of his hands. The only thing that he could do was try, and he did it by taking away my given name so that I was left with only the inexplicable one that I now carry.

My mind reeled as the vehicle went on and on, out of the woods. I thought I was going to some sort of clinic but this is not at all what happened. I was sent to the hospital in Moshi instead. When I got there I knew instantly why the guide tried to send me somewhere else. I could tell that this was a very special place. A fucking warzone. I have heard that it has been greatly improved since my visit but that did not help me much at the time. Don't get me wrong, a place that is as sick and twisted as this, a place that is so totally covered in blood and death should have been a dream for a rabid fuck like myself. Even in my state the appreciation of it was not lost on me at all. The blood showered walls and curtains of the triage room was exquisite. Pulchritudinous figures hold no comparison. Sorry girls. Not only that but the smell associated with the blood was such a raw form of expression that the entire composition approached the sublime. I am certain that this could really catch on in New York. Walls and curtains covered in blood? Exquisite. I have haunted the art scene frequently out of boredom. I like to lurk in the background of such events and dream about hunting the pretentious artistically illiterate fucks who swagger around with smoke in their eyes and too many words in their mouth. More money than brains. I would love to stuff every orifice of their body full of the cash that they love to pretend that they don't love so much. Their deaths would be delicious. I wouldn't drink their blood if you paid me though. I'm sure that it would be unpalatable. I know how much they obsess upon wimpy escapism such as the search for forms of expression that come from minority groups and foreign lands so that they can pretend like they understand something that is serious without doing anything or actually understanding anything at all. They think that they are part of some sort of "new" and "liberal" or "progressive" culture but they are just another manifestation of ancient conformity to the militant capitalist status quo that paid for the career of Delacroix during his age and pushed Romans to search for exotic experiences in peregrine places. Spectators. Foul little creatures that they are, they absolutely adore this sort of thing because it is just more evidence of the struggle and death that the economic system which they love so much has created for the majority of the population of the world. When it comes out in *art and music and literature* they are just tickled because they – somewhere in their walnut sized tyrannosaur brains – know that they were somehow involved in creating the conditions that made the life of that artist so fucking miserable that the only thing that the "appreciated" artist could do was throw some notes or words or paint around so that he didn't move to Idaho or Lake Washington Boulevard and blast his head off with a twelve gauge or move to California and theatrically hang himself in a garage or live on Jones St. and fucking overdose to get away from the jones for a few hours before he had to spike a vein again or invoke a ritual razor bloodletting, drain out through lacerated arms into a sink, and pass out, dead covered in blood or cut his ear off and shoot himself in the fucking stomach after painting some stupid crows and then rot away for a week in bed before he died. After this "art lovers" will spend untold millions on the left over screaming mess and put it in their villa if it matches the color scheme of their décor so they can sort of look at it, or something, and never have a fucking clue about the rage that it contains. But really, This African blood all over the wall and curtains could be the next big thing. It is in the tradition of Pollock and Beuys at once. Fascinating. I could finally begin my art career after all these years. I could find some Wall Street MotherFucker, or some Bank or Insurance Company Executive, or some Pathetic Wedding Photographer, and drag them into my loft that is downtown. Of course I have a loft there. I can turn lead into gold with a pinky twitch. Once I got them there I could hack them to pieces at the Popliteal, Femoral, and Iliac arteries in the leg, and the Brachial and Subclavian arteries in the arm before I get to the Carotid and finally finish my performance with the Pulmonary arteries. Hopefully, if I perform this toccata and fugue quickly enough, I can get to the heart while it is still beating so what is left of the sacrificed individual can at least have a little twitch of influence in the final product. I can try to do it in the spirit of the wonderful curtains that I saw in the hospital in Africa. Once I am done and everything is just perfect I can invite all of the Cognoscenti and other Art people in Manhattan to my installation. I could tell them that I was inspired in Africa to ignite their sense of romanticism and I could serve a good Barolo or Barbaresco with some tare-tare. It would be a fabulous and powerful statement. They could discuss it for a day or two which is the absolute maximum that one should expect of their attention span and then they could get back to the blood and gore that they had been extracting out of everyone else before they arrived.

Even though I had been inspired to create my masterpiece I did not sit in the gory triage room for long enough to appreciate it. They were busy there so they didn't get a chance to check my pulse and blood pressure and all of that stuff. They didn't operate the way one would expect in

America anyway. This was good for me because I wouldn't have to explain to them that I was already dead so that didn't matter. They didn't have the resources to do much anyway so I didn't know if this was good or bad. I was diagnosed with Malaria of all things and I think that it was because I didn't answer any of their questions properly. I was truly suffering but I was also just going through the motions so that I could find a way to deal with it. I knew that only I could remedy this situation and these doctors would be of little help. They wouldn't believe me even if I told them what was actually happening anyway.

Another terrible thing that I realized was that the airplane that I was to return to America in would not be leaving for another seven days. I had no idea what to do but I was in no condition to do much anyhow. I was supposed to be occupying myself on the ascent of the Volcano for the next seven days but now I was *here* for that long. I did not need a gurney. I needed to go back to America and summon Auryn and the portals so I could go away and figure out how to heal myself. At least that is what I thought that I needed. After the Malaria diagnosis I was wheeled up to the I.C.U. in my gurney. I thought that it was truly ironic that a blood-sucker like me could get diagnosed with something that came from tiny bloodsuckers. It was far from entertaining. I was rolled into the room and transferred to a bed that was soiled with all sorts of unspeakable fluids of death and evacuation. I was given an I.V. and I had just enough blood left in my veins to make it look like I was almost alive. They hooked the clear plastic tube to an upside down glass bottle that was tied to the rung of the bed with gauze. They told me that it was a quinine drip. I could taste it in my mouth very quickly. I looked around the room to try to get an idea of what passed for normality in a place like this. I have always loved misery and death so I may as well take in the sights. The beds were crammed together in a way that would maximize the space in the very small room. I thought that this was a wonderful way to maximize cross contamination as well because there was no curtain or anything like that to separate each bed from the other. Just one small open room crammed full of beds.

From my position on my back I could only see what was going on in the bed that was immediately on either side of me. On my left was a motionless individual who was intubated in every vital facial orifice and appeared to be hooked up to every life support system that was available in this part of Africa. On my right lay another tragic case. He was much livelier than everyone in the room. His legs were swollen to absurd proportions and had become totally misshapen. He had a constant bug eyed look and gazed all around the room very actively. He would not shut up. A constant flow of sound came out of his mouth. I could understand virtually every language in human history but this was like nothing I had ever heard before. I considered that it may be some obscure tribal dialect from this part of Africa but it still didn't sound like anything comprehensible. I found it incredibly interesting at first. It was a very good distraction from my own suffering to occupy my mind so I tried to figure out what the hell he was talking about. After a few constant hours of this it began to become quite grating and I came no closer to discovering the meaning behind his constant gibbering. My own pain slowly began to replace my interest until pain was once again at the forefront of my attention.

I was in a room full of death. Many years of death had accumulated here and the air was thick with it. I had no sense of sympathy for anyone because I had killed many myself and I was in no condition to help or care about anyone besides myself at the moment. I changed my vision and looked around. I could see that the room was absolutely full of ghosts. I was in no condition to do much of anything but notice it and I lost my concern because they did not seem to have any interest in me at all. It was certain that this was an entirely different group of ghosts than the legion that I encountered at the base of the mountain.

I laid in that bed for almost three days and I got no better or worse. The suffering was constant and incapacitating. During those three days a few in the room had died, what sounded like horrible, painful deaths. It was now no surprise that there were so many specters in residence here. I watched them sometimes to entertain myself as I laid there. These were institution ghosts. Many were totally mad and played completely insane games with each other and upon the living. They would parade up and down the halls and twist into different shapes and they looked like they were having a grand time. Their favorite trick was to mess around with the electricity. This was probably the only physical thing that they could manipulate and I am certain that it took a great deal of effort on their part. They always seemed to be able to effect it because the power would not stay on for more than fifteen minutes at a time in that building. I heard all the doctors blaming the connection or planned black outs or some other bland doctor-like explanation for the power outages. Many of the other ghosts were very somber and serious or, if not, very emotional and would break out in wailing and rending themselves when they weren't being mousy and quiet. There were a few truly evil ones that just tried to kill people whenever they could figure out how. Most of the time it was just through possessing a doctor and making them do fucked up shit, like attempting a surgery when they knew very well that the power would just skip out fifteen minutes into it.

After every one of the seemingly natural and gruesome deaths that happened in the I.C.U. room over the three days I had already been there, a priest would show up and would be followed by a shaman. Sometimes it was the other way around. Nothing seems to happen in an orderly manner anywhere in Tanzania as far as I could tell. The priest did normal priest things that should have bothered me but he wasn't performing any of it on me so I was more or less safe. The shaman came dressed in brown robes, or something that looked like robes, wielding a censer and handfuls of what I assumed were local plants and other things I couldn't identify. He lit these offerings and chanted as he went around the entire room. These were very old incantations that he recited and I recognized some parts of them. I had not heard any of this for a very long time and had forgotten them entirely. It reminded me of just how old that I truly was. The ghosts were nowhere to be seen when the Shaman arrived. These chants worked for some time but it wasn't very long before they came back doing cartwheels back and forth through walls or parading in the form of pigs and chickens or defecating flowers and handing them to each other with condolences or singing or crying or trying to kill someone or whatever else they were doing.

Some of them began to take interest in me after a while. They had probably not seen Nosferatu spend so much time in their domain. Their interest was limited because I was already dead and not really impressed and they knew I could not relate to them very much. One thing that I did notice was that the bug eyed kid with the swollen legs who would not ever shut up, I mean like *ever* – all day and all night until he gibbered himself totally out of energy to the point of collapse only to wake up and start up instantly – would actually shut up and be quiet whenever the shaman was there and the ghosts were gone. After the shaman left and the smoke cleared it was only a matter of time before this poor kid started up again.

After the first three days I began to stabilize somewhat. I was still in quite a bit of pain but not so much that I could barely think and barely move. Unlike the first three days of oblivion I could actually sit up in my bed for a few hours at a time. I looked to my left and the boy there was still in the exact same position he was when I got there. Still full of tubes and immobile. The chanting kid seemed to get no better or worse. He didn't seem to get hoarse either which I prayed that he would because he was beginning to drive me fucking nuts. Sometimes I would try to interrupt him to break his mantra so I could get a second of quiet to focus on what I had to do to fix myself but he just kept on going. It was maddening. This place, this room, was a sick time warp of suffering and death. All of this evil energy was good for me though. I was soaking it up and I think that this was the only thing that had helped me improve my condition. I just sat there and listened to the humming of the machines on one side and the chanting on the other. I tried to piece together everything that had happened, everything I was currently going through and everything that I could do about it. My mind was still very shattered and I only had pieces of the picture. It has taken me this long – a great deal of time in America after the fact – to get most of the ideas together and I have been feeling much better the closer I get to understanding but I do not want to get too close to it quite yet.

On my right all I could hear was "Wa ka ka ibn bteet, wa ka ka, wa ka ka ist, nebn bo bo, ka ka ko, bleet ibn bteet, wa ka ka ...." I just sat there silently grinding my teeth and giving the bloated child a very decisive look every once in a while. He had already heard me tell him to shut the hell up a million times so I wasn't even going to waste my breath any more. He knew what I meant when I looked at him like that. At least I thought he did because he would make eye contact and keep going. I found a place outside of my suffering and just tried to stay there. I changed forms to escape my body. I had enough energy to create an ethereal form so I was floating above my twitching corpse. All that I could hear was the machines and the nonsense and I tried to feel as little as possible. Then I saw the ghosts in the room. They were acting differently because now, I wasn't studying them in the normal manner that I had been. They knew I was watching them when I purposefully looked but now I was not really in my body. I could now see them without them instantly knowing that I was watching. Many of them were still acting out their random, eternal madness. The truly crazy ones were anyway but there was a great congregation of ghosts around the gibbering kid who was next to me. All of the sudden I understood what was happening. I realized that it wasn't nonsense after all. Well it was in the rational sense of what is commonly understood as language. I realized that he was busy speaking totally irrational words. He was breaking away from consciousness and normal perception and into the irrational reality that was within him. He could see the ghosts just like I could. The ghosts were trying to teach him even though it was apparent that the lesson was something that they didn't completely know. Some of them were talking back to him in some of the very same syllables and altering them just as he was doing. It was then that I truly realized what was happening in a rational sense. He was about to die very soon. The ghosts knew this too. They were trying to coach him on what to do, what to say, how to say it when his time came. They were trying to guide him away from the hell that they were attached to so that he wouldn't end up like them. They were focusing him on everything else except his rage or maladjustment or undone business or personal attachments or anything that could have kept him here in this planet in spectral form. They knew that these things are what kept them here, haunting this dread place. They somehow knew that an obsession with nonsense was a way to break the conscious attachment to all the false perceptions of reality and eject out of it into the void of the other dimensions where true freedom could be found. It wasn't the original word Shem HaMephorash but it was very close to the idea.

All of the sudden I got it. The tetragrammaton and the encounter with Lucifer. I knew what it was and why no one could say it. Because it wasn't a word. It was everything including a word. A four dimensional performance. To call it a word was just the simplest way of attempting to explain the inexplicable. Everything packed inside of a single gestalt. The reference to four letters was actually something else entirely. It was four dimensions. The four dimensions of perception. In order for it to work it had to be acted out in all of them at once in the proper sequence. Thought, word, place, and motion. These ingredients were all needed to break into the higher dimensions because they are all part of the architecture which supports the impercievable dimensions that are built off of them like a table built off of legs. The ghosts could never do this because they could not physically move anything. The other undead and humans could never piece all of this together into an actionable sequence. So many people say what they mean but how many actually do it? If and when they actually do it do they do it with meaning? Only I could. It was a ritual that needed a body. One that was up to the performance of the sacrifice. ***With a golden sickle the Druids cut the sacred mistletoe (the Golden Bough) from the Oak. This castration ritual is about to be re-enacted on the grand oak (48).*** This is a story of love lost and redemption through the quest for what true love means; self-sacrifice. Gotterdammerung. This is the unspeakable name. I was revolted and felt more nauseated as I fell back to the bed.

I am the summation of the irrational word. You are too. Everyone and everything is as well but I had gathered it all into an almost completely conscious form. The grapes had to be gathered and pressed into wine. Is there a difference between destruction and creation? ***My life is with the thrill kill kult (1).***

Ω

I had to escape this ward I was floundering in. The first three days were black and I have no recollection of them at all. I remember closing my eyes and seeing ravens. That is the only thing I can remember. The eyes of ravens. The fire was not there. The raven's eye was so close that I could only see its vacuous darkness. A scale encircled void. I thought of Auryn but she was not there. She was but she wasn't at the same time. The raven shook its head as the vision of it panned out. It was flying away and soon there were many of them riding the wind. They all descended into a tree. There were so many of them roosting that the tree became black. Then I heard a word. "Gemmal". A tall hooded woman in black stood at the base of the tree. I could not make her out until she stepped away from the trunk. I could not see her face under the hood but I knew it was Auryn by the serpentine movement executed under the cloak. She was the only one who I ever known that had moved in that manner. It was an expression of pure sexuality. The voice came rushing out of the hood and I knew without a doubt that it was Auryn. She said "My name is Xaydie and I give you a gift. You should call it 'Gemmal'. You have used the voids that exist between the parallel worlds for a short time. They will not hide you from what you need to do because you cannot bring them with you to the place you need to go. They all are connected and therefore all the same. They all need the same sacrifice. You have already discovered this. Gemmal is a belt of invisibility. It is the only way that you can hide. You can bring it anywhere you may travel. You must encircle yourself with it when the time is right and not a moment before." She turned her back to me and reached into the tree full of ravens. I saw her hand disappear into a nest that I had not yet noticed. When she brought her hand out I could see a string of black pearls dangling from her hand. As it got closer the pearls changed form and became alphabets. An infinite string of them. I reached out to take it from her. As soon as my hand touched it I awoke and found myself in the bed in the African hospital once again. This happened on the night following the third day. After this dream I found myself returning to consciousness. Slowly over the next few days I found myself getting better.

I had to get back to America and figure this all out with the help of Auryn. I could not do it here properly because Auryn was not really here. I could not hide anything from the light of the Sun. I had to pull myself together and prepare myself properly. I was certain that all of the undead knew to hunt me because of the lodestar in my blood. I had part of Betelgeuse punched into me. I could not escape them for very long. They were hunters and they were mine. They could be greatly empowered if they found me so they would look very hard.

I see good spirits and I see bad spirits (1) and they see me. None are any help nor do they care to be. They can barely help themselves. I was in a wretched state myself but I had gotten through the worst part or so I believed. If these astral powers who were apparently greater than me wanted me destroyed it would have been done. I was left here for a reason. An ill-conceived reason. Left to suffer and learn. I had never languished in torment for any amount of time that I could truly remember. I am not even now totally restored and there is a reason for that too. I cannot forget what had happened nor can I forget what I must do about it. As I lay in bed I realized that I was wasting away from inanition. I can normally go quite some time without blood but not in my injured state. I needed energy and I wasn't getting enough of it on my own. There was no food service in this hospital but some of the staff at the hotel I stayed at before the expedition came regularly with exotic East African dishes. I refused them outright, blaming my stomach condition. I also told them I was a vegetarian as another excuse to refuse the first dish they brought. Later on they brought more and I refused that as well. It was always the same two men who arrived with the food. I could tell that I was upsetting them by my refusal. They simply did not understand and they became as defiant as I was. They would hand me a plate of food and I would just look at it and then at them. We would stay there just looking at each other for a moment. I would look down at the steaming tray of ugali and curry and rice and bananas and bread. Then I would just look back up at them and stare back. One would get frustrated and say in a thick Swahili accent "You must eat." He bit at each word in irritation. I picked up the piece of bread and took the tiniest bite possible before I set it back down. Then once more I would hear the other one say "Lazima kula. You must eat".

I would then look at him and say "Tafadhali tuma daktari. Could you please send the doctor or a nurse and have them bring me my bag?

Someone took it from me when I first arrived and I really would like it. It would help a great deal."

They would look at each other in confusion and then look back at me and say "Why will you not eat?"

My response was "Tafadhali tuma daktari. Could you please get me a doctor or a nurse? I really need my bag."

After some time they would simply take the food back and leave. I wasn't trying to frustrate them at all but it was turning out that way. I couldn't do much until I got my bag. If I had it I could get some blood and all of the arcane devices and materials that I brought. I could use these items to try to deal with the pain that I was suffering. I knew that this was the only chance that I had and I was very close to getting up and creating a room to room search to find where they put it. The mad stalemate with the hotel staff went on for three more days three times a day. It played out in exactly the same way every day. They said the exact same things at almost the same times. I took the same tiny piece of bread at the cued moment. Sometimes I would sarcastically pick up the bread slower and with more drama than the time before and make eye contact with both of them, then pause holding it in front of my face before I took my tiny nibble that I would spit out. It was ridiculous. Only after three days of this did a nurse finally arrive with my bag. That was six days in total that I had been there without anything to consume except quinine and ringer lactate. I was fading very slowly but I felt fine. After I received the belt in my dream I felt the arcane possession leaving me. All I needed was some blood. Now that I had it I could try to do something about my hunger.

I patiently waited for nightfall before I opened my bag and finally fed myself. All day I had been thinking. I was going through every possible incantation that I knew. I considered everything that I knew I had with me in my bag. Once I had fed, I began my necromancy. The room was full of living humans and very few have ever witnessed what I was preparing.

Most who have seen it did not live. I suspect that the same is true here. You won't live for long after reading this too for you have probably realized how close to undeath that you are. I did not worry myself about these sorts of things surrounded by these patients. I proceeded with deliberation. There was many aspects to this spell I was preparing and I wanted to make sure it was correct because my materials were limited. I went step by step and was certain that I made no mistakes. Sulfur smudge over where my heart used to be applied with a feather, lead crystals applied to my feet, a small amount of blood painted on my lips (I extracted pure, untreated blood from the intubated kid next to me. I didn't think that he would notice), and citrine over my closed eyes. Chanting and thought. Once the final passage – ***Thaumiel, Malkuth, Aretz, Tipareth*** – was complete I sat and waited for the effects to take hold.

It was only a short matter of time before everything started working. By morning I was virtually healed. There was still very much wrong but I would deal with that later. For now I had the problem of getting out of this place. My plane was to leave and I intended to be on it. I faked my way out of the hospital bed. I smiled and told the doctors that I needed to go back to America for further treatment. I assured them that I was well enough to make the flight without any issues. They huddled together in front of my bed. They were discussing the situation in Swahili and in doctor speak on top of it. What a verbal jumble that was to me. I gave up trying to listen. They broke their huddle and one of them approached me holding a clipboard. She said that they would arrange for the necessary paperwork, contact the hotel, and tell them to come and get me.

I walked out into the courtyard and saw the direct sun for the first time in a week. It was a shock but not one that I could not endure. The facility was surrounded by chain link fences with barbed wire curling the top. Guards in fatigues who wielded rifles sauntered around the dusty yard. Was this a hospital or a prison I thought to myself? I guess this could be Ebola country after all and they would probably need some sort of convincing security. The last thing that the earth needed was some poor victim who was covered in blood and virus running out the front door and infecting the entire world. That sounds pretty odd when I say it but it describes my situation too well. I didn't even have the proper paperwork to get out because they discharged me so quickly. I had to try to act as nonchalant as I could so that I could walk through the gates without interference by someone with a rifle. Not like bullets worried me all that much. The person the hotel sent was a bit disturbed by the whole thing though. One of the guards took notice of us as we made our way to the gate. We were stopped but after some more Swahili was emitted we were back on our way. *Security.*

The flight left later that night and it would carry me and my burden back to North America. I still had very little idea about what I was going to do when I got there but I knew that I had to begin the process of protecting myself immediately. If I did not, it would be virtually impossible to get through the flight unnoticed. I had a few hours to think about it and I did all that I could do in that short time. I knew that I had to find Auryn as soon as I could and I did not think that it would be all that difficult. That was the only way that I could get myself together more properly before I sat down and figured out what I was to do. I had to get to a quiet place where I could go over everything piece by piece and conquer every step before I did anything else. I needed to write a new spell that had not yet been written. It is almost here. Words are from another world, an army of darkness that points the way to the light behind it. It points the way for you, dear reader, because you will need the direction soon enough. The blank page is the field of Armageddon, the ancient crossroads to the holy city, and the darkness must march upon it for anything to be understood.

Now I am approaching the end. I hate to refer to cliché so I will not because I do not know if it is also some sort of beginning. Can Ouroboros finally devour himself? Can Samsara be halted? Auryn is commonly represented as two dragons but two of the same and attached to each other. This is the amulet that entrapped her for some time. Perhaps Ouroboros and Jörmungandr. It is difficult to say for sure but I am almost certain they represent two things; Love and Will and when applied to each other they become four dimensional and also a portal to all of those dimensions beyond. There is something written on the back of the amulet that imprisoned her when she dove into the void for the last time and conquered it. It is not complete but it invokes the ancient words of power that I had to use to help Crowley ***"Do what thou wilt and that shall be the whole of the law. Love is the law. Love under will."*** Love is power and it is one of the most frequently abused words there is because it is spasmodically misasscociated with halcyon days of fresh discovery and possession. That is not Love, it is Hatred and Tyranny. Love is Death. It is something that I have never felt because I am not alive and can-not die. I have come close to feeling love only once and her name was Auryn. There is no real love without loss. Vindeimatrix is also frequently known as the Widowmaker. Everything must be lost to understand love. Nothing can be proven when nothing lasts. I know what happened to Auryn. She did consume herself like the dragons who represented her. It was her final victory over nothing. She became part of the nothing and mastered it. She is still alive but not the same. There is an end and it is near. Only she can help me because she was the only one I have ever loved. We will find the end together or not at all. She lives in the darkness that makes up every one of these words. She is them and they were made for her. I can do little without her help now. I can do little without this infinite belt of invisibility.

Liebeserlösung

As I complete this spell I am sitting at a counter that was built into the kitchen in an abandoned New York apartment. One could call it a bar because it was an arm that projected off the main counter of the kitchen and it had stools placed under it. I do not like to use the word "bar" because I find "bars" to be loathsome. Humanity is so compromised and so unattainable in a bar. This energy is disgusting to my senses. I have haunted many taverns in my time but I do not go inside, even if invited. It was always easier to wait in an alley for someone to stumble by. Sorry. I digress once more. It is good for me to think about the past because it is all part of the future. It creates the future and is all packed into it at once. In fact the future is really the past in this inverted world. Every wonder why you sometimes feel like everything has happened before? Because it has.

I have used many abandoned apartments and many counters and tables to temporarily hide in so I could complete this reflection and empower myself. I had to conquer everything in the process. Digressions are necessary. I couldn't stay in any one place for too long because I am still being actively hunted. I am now in The Bronx. A good place for an ending. I always thought that The Bronx had an apocalyptic feel to it. I have a very clear idea of what has happened and what I must do with what I have left of my powers. I think that I have explained them in pieces as I have gone through this account. I must go to the summit of the great mountain that I failed to climb. I must return to Kilimanjaro and ascend past the flat, marked rock that I was stopped at last time. This time I will be with Auryn. I will wear the belt that she has given me. You are reading only one thread of it at a time. I will be able to pass the marker I set at the place I wrestled Lucifer and reach the summit without being noticed with Auryns help. There I will use the last of what I have in me and allow my heart to finally awaken so I will live and become human once more. It has been so long. Then and only at the moment of my transformation will everything come together. I will be revealed, truly alive and also dead all at once. *God is my Judge.* At that moment I will perform the "sound" of the new name that has been given to me, the one that I had been suppressing this entire time. Shem HaMephorash The golden bough will be cut. The cord of Alrescha severed. There is an end and it stays ended. No more of the fractured ***perception*** of *reality* through the terror and destruction created by rationality. The irrational is the end and it will stay irrational for time will cease to matter because it is only one of the infinite dimensions that exist. The irrational is the only sense there is. This is why reason is so irrational. No longer will reason dominate and allow for the capitalization of the consciousness and enslavement of the body for petty profits. I will give up my body for I am so tired of it and its constant feeding upon the bodies of others. I am, in fact, the most one can expect of rationalism. I am its highest and greatest expression. Nosferatu. You are like me. All strive to be me. Follow your path, but realize that it will take you to where I am going. No dichotomy to understand and rationalize. No past or future. It is all at once. An end.

Ω

I must go to the summit as soon as possible. There is a jaguar frozen into the snows of the summit and it is waiting to pounce upon me. I have accounted for this. I have conquered it and thrown it into the void of these words and it will stay hidden here with the help of Auryn. Every word is irrational on its own and I am pecking each one into place so that none can see me. Not even Lucifer for his light cannot penetrate into this void. The hunters are closing in on me as I wrap up this incantation. They do not want for me to succeed but they do not understand why. They think that they will be destroyed once I am. It is entirely possible but they may be freed at the same time. I do not know exactly how it will play out beyond my own role.

I can hear them right now. One of them is virtually breathing down my neck through his lupine fangs. The spells that I cast upon the door of the apartment I now sit in are being manipulated. I can hear the mechanisms of the lock move around as each twitch of his hand experiments with it. It will be only a matter of minutes before he is in the room. I have just enough time to react to this because I expected it to happen. I even allowed clues for him to be certain that I was here so that when he finds no trace of me, it will be all the more convincing that he was mistaken when he finds nothing. This apartment is empty except for a few ragged stools and my pen and paper. There are some cobwebs and yellowing curtains. Dust upon the floor and built in bookcases with a few magazines left open within. Little else can be detected. I walked into the middle of the room and waited for the sound of the latch on the door to be finally mechanized. In fact I broke the spell just a small bit to allow for it. As soon as the door burst open I would not be there. I would be here. In these words. In this belt of invisibility. In these webs of explanation and denial of explanation. I am a spider in the cobwebs hunting flies to mummify.

He entered the room very slowly. The door creaked and opened just a crack and stayed like that for a moment. With a small rusty squeal from the old hinges the door opened just enough for a body to slip through. In a second he was in the room and the door closed quickly behind him. As he looked around he performed a rudimentary version of my door locking spell. I watched from my vantage point as he went around and slowly searched every room in the apartment. He could only find a trace of me and I was confident that he would not actually discover my presence. This is a brand new spell and there is no way he knew what to look for. The very fact that he was here indicated that he was very shrewd and had a good idea what was happening. He expected me to be weakened and he was correct about that.

He was an African American Nosferatu. Very common in this part of the world. I knew him well. He went by the name Michael. He had many of the same tattoos that I did. ***His life was with the thrill kill kult (1).*** Otherwise he presented himself very differently than I did. I typically sport the look of an eccentric. Fedora and sport coat. Book in pasty white hand.

He had the look of a hip hop enthusiast and I knew that he was. This is a very good way to blend in while stalking subway stations and sidewalks. We all try to blend in and be unapproachable in our own way so as not to create stereotypes that would easily identify us as Nosferatu. He was a very old vampire as well and had seen many things like I had. Under his puffy orange coat was a tank top and he had extra-large jeans that spread out over his Nike's that silently hovered over the ground. Under the hood poked out the bill of a baseball cap. I could see the logo glowing faintly in the shadow of the hood. Cleveland Cavaliers. A C pierced by a sword. This was a symbol of power for him for he was an Orion Nosferatu. In this case it referred to the specific star that he was born under. He was born under that star that formed the tip of the club. A "C" impaled by a sword. Chi Orionis A.

chi[1]

kī/

noun

1. the twenty-second letter of the Greek alphabet (**Χ**, **χ**), transliterated in the traditional Latin style as 'ch' (as in *Christ*) or in the modern style as 'kh' (as in *Khaniá* and in the etymologies of this dictionary).

This was how he got his true Nosferatu name; *Joshua Chi Orionis A.* Michael was only his human name.

He took his time searching every small part of the apartment to find any trace of me and I was certain that he would find a few small enticing bits. Pieces that I had left behind intentionally just to mock him. Every time he would uncover something he would stop what he was doing and look around for a few seconds before resuming. At one point he stopped right in front of me and stared at the clump of cobwebs and dust that I was lingering in. He stayed there for a long time and studied it as I receded further into my web. For a second he smiled a fanged vampire grin right at me. Then he shook his head and continued on.

I was perplexed by this. Did he know? There was no way. Shortly after, he undid the locking spell he had cast upon the door, opened it and walked away. His footfalls were silent as he descended the staircase outside the apartment but I could feel his motion. Was he coming back with others or did he just miss me? He was not one to turn his back on a good confrontation. I reformed into my corpse and stood on two legs in the room. I scanned the entire place for his residual energy and for the evidence of any traps that he may have set and found nothing. Something strange was happening. This whole thing was out of everyone's hands. He must have been influenced by something that was even greater than both of us. I couldn't help but think that he actually saw me. There was a benevolent force left in the room. I could feel it very faintly. I was certain that I was just an actor in a prewritten performance. I knew then that my mission to go back to Tanzania was certain. I already had a plane ticket and would be leaving in a few hours. When I get there I will be armed and protected to carry out my plans. I have already given many hints at what I had to do and how I must go about it. I cannot completely put it into words because that could sabotage the entire project. All I can say is that words mean nothing without action and it is not as simple as speaking a mystical word alone. All dimensions must be crossed. It is nothing without blood and that is where this virus still lives. It will all come together when I finally summit the roof of Africa and gaze down upon the plains where it all began so long ago.

I will not be able to make it all of the way in my human form. If I tried I would be conscious and because of that I could be interrupted in the same way that I was before. Lucifer will be able to read my thoughts and try to intervene again. This time Auryn will be with me. Rather, I will be with her. I will be hiding here in this belt of words that I cast into the void of whoever reads it because Auryn is in them too as long as the reader is actually alive. I have already arranged for this account to be possessed by one of the human trekkers that I know that is going on the upcoming expedition. His name is Daniel and he has his own copy. I wrote them with his hand. God is my judge. He will hide this account in a bejeweled pouch of arcane power and none will be allowed to see what is in it as he crosses borders. Also hidden in the pouch is a golden sickle. It is soon time for the harvest. These pages will be in his backpack and he has been instructed to leave the unopened pouch at the foot of the summit sign at Uhuru Peak when he arrives. You may have to find your own way. This is just a hint but you certainly suffer with the same infection if fate has brought this text to you. Only undead can find the word within themselves and can die a second death. You are almost there. You are virtually undead too. Few humans are totally alive. What will happen? You are almost there so you must find out for yourself. This spell is only a guideline. Your existence is marching toward an apocalypse. It has already happened for the past is the future. You never had a choice. This ink is a spell of blood and sacrifice. An elegy for everything that is lost and a song of true love for love is death. True love is sacrifice. There will be blood everywhere. There must be blood with every death and blood with every birth. Spiritual problems require mystical solutions and this planet is not what it seems. It is a giant heart of darkness. A heart beating with the blood of the centuries. It is only right that things should not be left for humans to deal with for they covet blood even more than I do. A bowlful has been dropped and lays broken upon the floor leaking out its purple contents. I think that I hear trumpets. *Rock over London, Rock on Chicago.* It is finished. Τετέλεσται.

Las Vegas, Nevada – March, 2017

Saranac Lake, New York – March, 2020

Dan Morrone

Dedication

For

Jennifer,

A. Lazarus Finger,

👁

♠ and the Armies of Darkness. ♠

Let them be known. These are a few. There are a billion others.

"Major General" Debbie

Mcauley - "Brad Pitt"

Chris - "Little Boots"

Julia - "Hollywood"

"Mistress Webby"

Chris - "Morpheus"

Carlos - "The Shit"

Raphael - "Cumbia delictivo"

Cedric - "Samurai Warrior"

Koti - "The Bull"

Zev, Alex - "The Wandering

and Jeff Jews"

Chris - "Treme"

Thaddeus - "Black Magician"

Jesse - "California Hella"

Jimmy - "The Pen"

Josh - "Mixmaster Zombie"

Jay - "Surfing Alien"

Mike - "Baby Huey"

"Indiana" Dan

Alex - "Nosferatu"

Sean - "Goat Simulator"

Brian - "Pinky the Baker"

Jas - "Punk"

Lewis and the Thousand Voices of Buddah

Sean - "The Godfather"

"Kentucky" Dave

"Kentucky" Senior

Judson - "The Anarchist"

Dimitri - "NY, NY"

"Reefer Chris" and the "Vidiot Crew"

"Injury" Jeff "Gordon"

Greg – "Sprinkles"

Bill and "Jeffery in the bushes"

"Give Blood" Mike

Lexi "Potter"

Texas Rage

Cassidy and Ashton "Danzig"

Adam - "The Jedi"

Bobby - "The O.G."

Tony - "The Sherriff"

Michael - "Joshua Chi Orionis A."

!≅#∃%⊥&∗()_+}{ΠΟΙΥΨΤΡΕΩΘ ΑΣΔΦΓΗϑΚΛ:∀?><ΜΝΒςΧΞΖ ‾1234ε

ρθωερερψτρυψτυιυιοοπ[]∴;λκφηγφϕδσαζξχϖβνμ,./

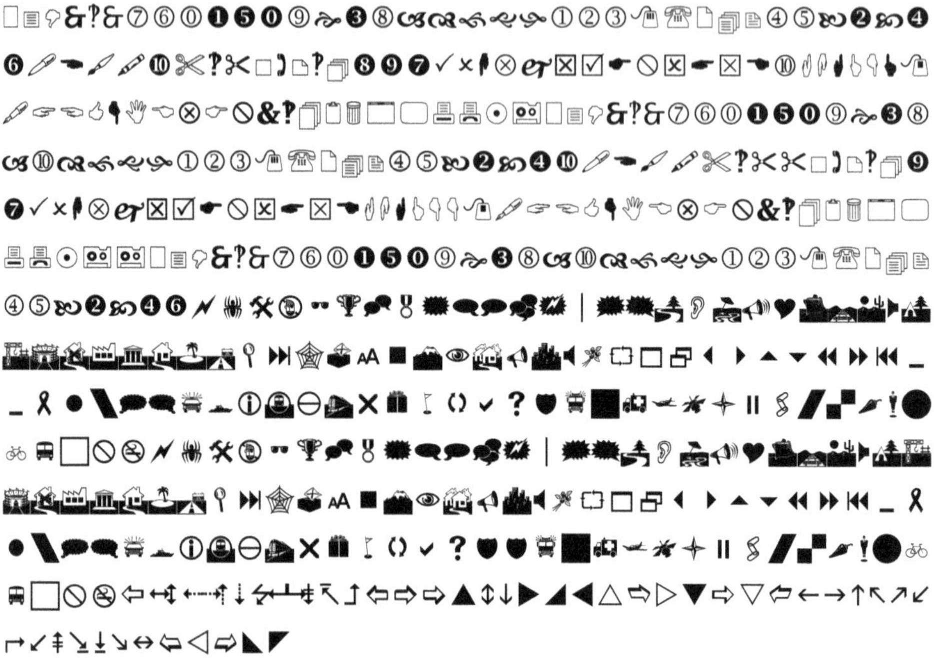

Authors Note On Resources...

These resources are presented only for the sake of the curiosity of the reader. The case may be that many of the passages in the above text which are attached to these resources are indeed taken from them, yet they are no longer attached to the legal jurisdiction which may or may not be asserted by the cited sources. This is based upon **§ The Law of Appropriation** which is duly recognized by any artist worth their salt who is working post 1960 anno domini, or common era as you will. Based upon this Just and Fair Law, which has been universally agreed upon by artists and philosophers alike, cultural appropriation of any source material is legitimate and encouraged when it fulfills the requirement of changing the context or the original intention of the work, thereby changing the meaning and the very words themselves. So, as Borges states, "Every man should be capable of all ideas (12)". Barthes "Death of the Author" should also be mentioned as well as the famous statement by Sherrie Levine: "The world is filled to suffocating, Man has placed his image on every stone. Every word, every image is leased and mortgaged. We know that a picture is but a space in which a variety of images, none of them original, blend and clash...A paintings meaning lies not in its origin, but in its destination. The birth of the viewer must be at the cost of the painter. (13)" So we see that there is a consensus among the greatest artists, writers, and philosophers of our time. All of this should be obvious by now and the apparent necessity to repeat these ideas is repellent to the current author even though the idea of appropriation is not. That said, it is a legal requirement against those barbaric forces at work in the world who are so uncultured that they may still hold medieval beliefs concerning property which is not property at all but the expression of tyranny and oppression which must be rejected. So, who then is the real vampire? The brave who are willing to reinvent culture using it as an inoculation against its own viral tendencies or the pathetic, uncreative, automatons who have the finger on the button of distribution and the holders of profit on the backs of those who actually do the real work? Bollocks To You For I have Not Stolen What You Have Previously Stolen. I have Reinvented it, in contrast to You who have taken credit for something which you did not actually do. Who then, is the thief? If we are to honor arguments against appropriation then any lawyer who presents this position is guilty of plagiarism because they must use a law which is written by someone else to justify their argument.

Resources in Compliance With § The Law of Appropriation

(1) My Life With The Thrill Kill Kult (1988) *I see good spirits and I see bad spirits.* Wax Trax!

(2) Anonymous (1991). *The chemical wedding of Christian Rosenkreutz* (J. Godwin, Trans). Phanes Press. (Original work published 1459.)

(3) Gaddis, W. (1952). *The recognitions.* Harcourt Brace Jovanovich.

(4) Quoted from somewhere in the void at some-time in the void. *Repurposed valiantly for the sake of emphasizing something quite different from the context of the original, thereby changing it forever.*

(5) Joyce, J. (1939). *Finnegan's wake.* Penguin Books.

(6) Ende, M. (1985). *The neverending story* (R. Manheim, Trans). Guild Publishing. (Original work published 1979)

(7) Wagner, R. (19XX). *Ring of the Nibelung. (Original work premier 1876).*

(8) God (⊕) *The Bible.* Alchemical Earth.

(9) Black Uhuru (1983). *Guess who's coming to dinner.* Virgin.

(93) Current 93 (1993). *Of rune or some blazing starre.* Durtro.

(11) Burroughs, W.S. (1987). *The western lands.* Viking Press.

(12) Borges, J.L. (1993). *Ficciones* (Emece' Editores S.A. Trans). Knopf

(13) Levine, S. (1982, March-April). Mannerism; a theory of culture. *Style.* 48

(14) Lovecraft, H.P. (XXXX). Fiction or not? *Printed in the sky.*

(15) Regardie, I. (1935?). *The philosopher's stone, spiritual alchemy, psychology, and ritual magic.*

(16) The Residents (1979). *Eskimo.* Ralph Records.

(17) Regardie, I. (1932). *The tree of life an illustrated study in magic.*

(18) I am not going to tell you. Sorry.

(19) Montefiore, S.S. (2011). *Jerusalem.* Vintage.

(20) Gurdjieff, G.I. (1950) *Beelzebub's tales to his grandson.* Harcourt.

(21) Burroughs, W.S. (1961) *The soft machine.* Grove Press.

(22) Derrida, J. (1972) *Dissemination. (or was it something else? Does it matter? Will anyone actually read any of this?)* Athlone Press.

(23) Shem HaMephorash

(24) Bad Brains (1982). *Bad Brains.* ROIR.

(25) Faulkner, W. (1929). *The sound and the fury.* Jonathan Cape and Harrison Smith.

(26) Burroughs, W.S. (1990). *Dead city radio.* Island Records.

(27) Anthrax (1990). *Persistence of time.* Megaforce Worldwide/Island Records.

(28) Black Uhuru (1990). *Now.* Rhino Records.

(29) Burning Spear (1990). *Mek we dweet.* Island Records.

(30) Sagan, C. (1994). *Pale blue dot.* Random House.

(31) Dead Milkmen (1988). *Beelzebubba.* Enigma.

(32) Genesis P-Orridge & Splinter Test (1996). *Thee fractured garden.* Invisible.

(33) Sick of it All (2000). Yours truly. Fat Wreck Chords.

(34) AFI (1997). *Shut your mouth and open your eyes.* Nitro.

(35) John Brown's Body (2008). *Amplify.* Easy Star.

(36) Campbell, J., Robinson, H.M. (1976). *A skeleton key to finnegan's wake.* (Buccaneer Books).

(37) Krakauer, J. (1997). *Into thin air.* Villard.

(38) King Crimson (1981). *Discipline.* E.G. Records.

(39) Moldea, D.E. (1989). *Interference, how organized crime influences professional football.* William Morrow and Company.

(40) If you do not already know where this statement comes from, I am truly amazed.

(41) Grey, P. (2015). *Lucifer: princeps.* Scarlet Imprint.

(42) Weyer, J., Zasadzinska, N. (2016). *Johan Weyer's false hierarchy of demons.* Abracax House.

(43) Regardie, I. (1995). *The golden dawn.* Llewellyn.

(44) Foucault, M. (1965). *Madness and civilization a history of insanity in the age of reason.* Random House.

(45) Foucault, M. (1970). *The order of things and archaeology of human sciences.* Pantheon Books.

(46) Tzara, T. (DaDa). Published on Saturn on Sunday.

(47) Midnite (2004). *Ainshant maps.* Discogs.

(48) Frazer, J.G. (1922) *The golden bough.* Macmillian.

www.ingramcontent.com/pod-product-compliance
Lightning Source LLC
Chambersburg PA
CBHW060449090426
42735CB00011B/1954
9780982958964